THE SUPERVISED LEARNING WORKSHOP

SECOND EDITION

Predict outcomes from data by building your own powerful predictive models with machine learning in Python

Blaine Bateman, Ashish Ranjan Jha, Benjamin Johnston, and Ishita Mathur

THE SUPERVISED LEARNING WORKSHOP
SECOND EDITION

Authors: Blaine Bateman, Ashish Ranjan Jha, Benjamin Johnston, and Ishita Mathur

Reviewers: Tiffany Ford, Sukanya Mandal, Ashish Pratik Patil, and Ratan Singh

Managing Editor: Snehal Tambe

Acquisitions Editors: Manuraj Nair, Sneha Shinde, and Anindya Sil

Production Editor: Salma Patel

Editorial Board: Megan Carlisle, Samuel Christa, Mahesh Dhyani, Heather Gopsill, Manasa Kumar, Alex Mazonowicz, Monesh Mirpuri, Bridget Neale, Dominic Pereira, Shiny Poojary, Abhishek Rane, Brendan Rodrigues, Erol Staveley, Ankita Thakur, Nitesh Thakur, and Jonathan Wray

First published: April 2019

Second edition: February 2020

Production reference: 3230221

ISBN: 978-1-80020-904-6

Published by Packt Publishing Ltd.

Livery Place, 35 Livery Street

Birmingham B3 2PB, UK

WHY LEARN WITH A PACKT WORKSHOP?

LEARN BY DOING

Packt Workshops are built around the idea that the best way to learn something new is by getting hands-on experience. We know that learning a language or technology isn't just an academic pursuit. It's a journey towards the effective use of a new tool—whether that's to kickstart your career, automate repetitive tasks, or just build some cool stuff.

That's why Workshops are designed to get you writing code from the very beginning. You'll start fairly small—learning how to implement some basic functionality—but once you've completed that, you'll have the confidence and understanding to move onto something slightly more advanced.

As you work through each chapter, you'll build your understanding in a coherent, logical way, adding new skills to your toolkit and working on increasingly complex and challenging problems.

CONTEXT IS KEY

All new concepts are introduced in the context of realistic use-cases, and then demonstrated practically with guided exercises. At the end of each chapter, you'll find an activity that challenges you to draw together what you've learned and apply your new skills to solve a problem or build something new.

We believe this is the most effective way of building your understanding and confidence. Experiencing real applications of the code will help you get used to the syntax and see how the tools and techniques are applied in real projects.

BUILD REAL-WORLD UNDERSTANDING

Of course, you do need some theory. But unlike many tutorials, which force you to wade through pages and pages of dry technical explanations and assume too much prior knowledge, Workshops only tell you what you actually need to know to be able to get started making things. Explanations are clear, simple, and to-the-point. So you don't need to worry about how everything works under the hood; you can just get on and use it.

Written by industry professionals, you'll see how concepts are relevant to real-world work, helping to get you beyond "Hello, world!" and build relevant, productive skills. Whether you're studying web development, data science, or a core programming language, you'll start to think like a problem solver and build your understanding and confidence through contextual, targeted practice.

ENJOY THE JOURNEY

Learning something new is a journey from where you are now to where you want to be, and this Workshop is just a vehicle to get you there. We hope that you find it to be a productive and enjoyable learning experience.

Packt has a wide range of different Workshops available, covering the following topic areas:

- Programming languages
- Web development
- Data science, machine learning, and artificial intelligence
- Containers

Once you've worked your way through this Workshop, why not continue your journey with another? You can find the full range online at http://packt.live/2MNkuyl.

If you could leave us a review while you're there, that would be great. We value all feedback. It helps us to continually improve and make better books for our readers, and also helps prospective customers make an informed decision about their purchase.

Thank you,
The Packt Workshop Team

Table of Contents

Chapter 2: Exploratory Data Analysis and Visualization   43

Chapter 5: Classification Techniques 239

Chapter 6: Ensemble Modeling 317

PREFACE

ABOUT THE BOOK

Would you like to understand how and why machine learning techniques and data analytics are spearheading enterprises globally? From analyzing bioinformatics to predicting climate change, machine learning plays an increasingly pivotal role in our society.

Although the real-world applications may seem complex, this book simplifies supervised learning for beginners with a step-by-step interactive approach. Working with real-time datasets, you'll learn how supervised learning, when used with Python, can produce efficient predictive models.

Starting with the fundamentals of supervised learning, you'll quickly move to understand how to automate manual tasks and the process of assessing data using Jupyter and Python libraries like pandas. Next, you'll use data exploration and visualization techniques to develop powerful supervised learning models, before understanding how to distinguish variables and represent their relationships using scatter plots, heatmaps, and box plots. After using regression and classification models on real-time datasets to predict future outcomes, you'll grasp advanced ensemble techniques such as boosting and random forests. Finally, you'll learn the importance of model evaluation in supervised learning and study metrics to evaluate regression and classification tasks.

By the end of this book, you'll have the skills you need to work on your own real-life supervised learning Python projects.

AUDIENCE

If you are a beginner or a data scientist who is just getting started and looking to learn how to implement machine learning algorithms to build predicting models, then this book is for you. To expedite the learning process, a solid understanding of Python programming is recommended as you'll be editing the classes or functions instead of creating from scratch.

ABOUT THE CHAPTERS

Chapter 1, Fundamentals, introduces you to supervised learning, Jupyter notebooks, and some of the most common pandas data methods.

Chapter 2, Exploratory Data Analysis and Visualization, teaches you how to perform exploration and analysis on a new dataset.

Chapter 3, Linear Regression, teaches you how to tackle regression problems and analysis, introducing you to linear regression as well as multiple linear regression and gradient descent.

Chapter 4, Autoregression, teaches you how to implement autoregression as a method to forecast values that depend on past values.

Chapter 5, Classification Techniques, introduces classification problems, classification using linear and logistic regression, k-nearest neighbors, and decision trees.

Chapter 6, Ensemble Modeling, teaches you how to examine the different ways of ensemble modeling, including their benefits and limitations.

Chapter 7, Model Evaluation, demonstrates how you can improve a model's performance by using hyperparameters and model evaluation metrics.

CONVENTIONS

Code words in text, database table names, folder names, filenames, file extensions, pathnames, dummy URLs, user input, and Twitter handles are shown as follows: "Use the pandas **read_csv** function to load the CSV file containing the **synth_temp. csv** dataset, and then display the first five lines of data."

Words that you see on screen, for example, in menus or dialog boxes, also appear in the text like this: "Open the **titanic.csv** file by clicking on it on the Jupyter notebook home page."

A block of code is set as follows:

```
print(data[pd.isnull(data.damage_millions_dollars)].shape[0])
print(data[pd.isnull(data.damage_millions_dollars) &
          (data.damage_description != 'NA')].shape[0])
```

New terms and important words are shown like this: "**Supervised** means that the labels for the data are provided within the training, allowing the model to learn from these labels."

CODE PRESENTATION

Lines of code that span multiple lines are split using a backslash (\ ). When the code is executed, Python will ignore the backslash, and treat the code on the next line as a direct continuation of the current line.

For example:

```
history = model.fit(X, y, epochs=100, batch_size=5, verbose=1, \
                    validation_split=0.2, shuffle=False)
```

Comments are added into code to help explain specific bits of logic. Single-line comments are denoted using the # symbol, as follows:

```
# Print the sizes of the dataset
print("Number of Examples in the Dataset = ", X.shape[0])
print("Number of Features for each example = ", X.shape[1])
```

Multi-line comments are enclosed by triple quotes, as shown below:

```
"""
Define a seed for the random number generator to ensure the
result will be reproducible
"""
seed = 1
np.random.seed(seed)
random.set_seed(seed)
```

SETTING UP YOUR ENVIRONMENT

Before we explore the book in detail, we need to set up specific software and tools. In the following section, we shall see how to do that.

INSTALLATION AND SETUP

All code in this book is executed using Jupyter Notebooks and Python 3.7. Jupyter Notebooks and Python 3.7 are available once you install Anaconda on your system. The following sections lists the instructions for installing Anaconda on Windows, macOS, and Linux systems.

INSTALLING ANACONDA ON WINDOWS

Here are the steps that you need to follow to complete the installation:

1. Visit https://www.anaconda.com/products/individual and click on the **Download** button.

2. Under the **Anaconda Installer/Windows** section, select the Python 3.7 version of the installer.

3. Ensure that you install a version relevant to the architecture of your computer (either 32-bit or 64-bit). You can find out this information in the **System Properties** window of your OS.

4. Once the installer has been downloaded, double-click on the file, and follow the on-screen instructions to complete the installation.

These installations will be executed in the 'C' drive of your system. However, you can choose to change the destination.

INSTALLING ANACONDA ON MACOS

1. Visit https://www.anaconda.com/products/individual and click on the **Download** button.

2. Under the **Anaconda Installer/MacOS** section, select the (Python 3.7) **64-Bit Graphical Installer**.

3. Once the installer has been downloaded, double-click on the file, and follow the on-screen instructions to complete the installation.

INSTALLING ANACONDA ON LINUX

1. Visit https://www.anaconda.com/products/individual and click on the **Download** button.

2. Under the **Anaconda Installer/Linux** section, select the (Python 3.7) **64-Bit (x86)** installer.

3. Once the installer has been downloaded, run the following command in your terminal: `bash ~/Downloads/Anaconda-2020.02-Linux-x86_64.sh`

4. Follow the instructions that appear on your terminal to complete the installation.

You can find more details regarding the installation for various systems by visiting this site: https://docs.anaconda.com/anaconda/install/.

INSTALLING LIBRARIES

`pip` comes pre-installed with Anaconda. Once Anaconda is installed on your machine, all the required libraries can be installed using `pip`, for example, `pip install numpy`. Alternatively, you can install all the required libraries using `pip install -r requirements.txt`. You can find the `requirements.txt` file at https://packt.live/3hSJgYy.

The exercises and activities will be executed in Jupyter Notebooks. Jupyter is a Python library and can be installed in the same way as the other Python libraries – that is, with `pip install jupyter`, but fortunately, it comes pre-installed with Anaconda. To open a notebook, simply run the command `jupyter notebook` in the Terminal or Command Prompt.

ACCESSING THE CODE FILES

You can find the complete code files of this book at https://packt.live/2TlcKDf. You can also run many activities and exercises directly in your web browser by using the interactive lab environment at https://packt.live/37QVpsD.

We've tried to support interactive versions of all activities and exercises, but we recommend a local installation as well for instances where this support isn't available.

If you have any issues or questions about installation, please email us at workshops@packt.com.

1

FUNDAMENTALS

OVERVIEW

This chapter introduces you to supervised learning, using Anaconda to manage coding environments, and using Jupyter notebooks to create, manage, and run code. It also covers some of the most common Python packages used in supervised learning: pandas, NumPy, Matplotlib, and seaborn. By the end of this chapter, you will be able to install and load Python libraries into your development environment for use in analysis and machine learning problems. You will also be able to load an external data source using pandas, and use a variety of methods to search, filter, and compute descriptive statistics of the data. This chapter will enable you to gauge the potential impact of various issues such as missing data, class imbalance, and low sample size within the data source.

INTRODUCTION

The study and application of machine learning and artificial intelligence has recently been the source of much interest and research in the technology and business communities. Advanced data analytics and machine learning techniques have shown great promise in advancing many sectors, such as personalized healthcare and self-driving cars, as well as in solving some of the world's greatest challenges, such as combating climate change (see *Tackling Climate Change with Machine Learning*: https://arxiv.org/pdf/1906.05433.pdf).

This book has been designed to help you to take advantage of the unique confluence of events in the field of data science and machine learning today. Across the globe, private enterprises and governments are realizing the value and efficiency of data-driven products and services. At the same time, reduced hardware costs and open source software solutions are significantly reducing the barriers to entry of learning and applying machine learning techniques.

Here, we will focus on supervised machine learning (or, supervised learning for short). We'll explain the different types of machine learning shortly, but let's begin with some quick information. The now-classic example of supervised learning is developing an algorithm to distinguish between pictures of cats and dogs. The supervised part arises from two aspects; first, we have a set of pictures where we know the correct answers. We call such data labeled data. Second, we carry out a process where we iteratively test our algorithm's ability to predict "cat" or "dog" given pictures, and we make corrections to the algorithm when the predictions are incorrect. This process, at a high level, is similar to teaching children. However, it generally takes a lot more data to train an algorithm than to teach a child to recognize cats and dogs! Fortunately, there are rapidly growing sources of data at our disposal. Note the use of the words learning and train in the context of developing our algorithm. These might seem to be giving human qualities to our machines and computer programs, but they are already deeply ingrained in the machine learning (and artificial intelligence) literature, so let's use them and understand them. Training in our context here always refers to the process of providing labeled data to an algorithm and making adjustments to the algorithm to best predict the labels given the data. Supervised means that the labels for the data are provided within the training, allowing the model to learn from these labels.

Let's now understand the distinction between supervised learning and other forms of machine learning.

WHEN TO USE SUPERVISED LEARNING

Generally, if you are trying to automate or replicate an existing process, the problem is a supervised learning problem. As an example, let's say you are the publisher of a magazine that reviews and ranks hairstyles from various time periods. Your readers frequently send you far more images of their favorite hairstyles for review than you can manually process. To save some time, you would like to automate the sorting of the hairstyle images you receive based on time periods, starting with hairstyles from the 1960s and 1980s, as you can see in the following figure:

Figure 1.1: Images of hairstyles from different time periods

To create your hairstyles-sorting algorithm, you start by collecting a large sample of hairstyle images and manually labeling each one with its corresponding time period. Such a dataset (known as a labeled dataset) is the input data (hairstyle images) for which the desired output information (time period) is known and recorded. This type of problem is a classic supervised learning problem; we are trying to develop an algorithm that takes a set of inputs and learns to return the answers that we have told it are correct.

PYTHON PACKAGES AND MODULES

Python is one of the most popular programming languages used for machine learning, and is the language used here.

While the standard features that are included in Python are certainly feature-rich, the true power of Python lies in the additional libraries (also known as packages), which, thanks to open source licensing, can be easily downloaded and installed through a few simple commands. In this book, we generally assume your system has been configured using Anaconda, which is an open source environment manager for Python. Depending on your system, you can configure multiple virtual environments using Anaconda, each one configured with specific packages and even different versions of Python. Using Anaconda takes care of many of the requirements to get ready to perform machine learning, as many of the most common packages come pre-built within Anaconda. Refer to the preface for Anaconda installation instructions.

In this book, we will be using the following additional Python packages:

- NumPy (pronounced *Num Pie* and available at https://www.numpy.org/): NumPy (short for numerical Python) is one of the core components of scientific computing in Python. NumPy provides the foundational data types from which a number of other data structures derive, including linear algebra, vectors and matrices, and key random number functionality.

- SciPy (pronounced *Sigh Pie* and available at https://www.scipy.org): SciPy, along with NumPy, is a core scientific computing package. SciPy provides a number of statistical tools, signal processing tools, and other functionality, such as Fourier transforms.

- pandas (available at https://pandas.pydata.org/): pandas is a high-performance library for loading, cleaning, analyzing, and manipulating data structures.

- Matplotlib (available at https://matplotlib.org/): Matplotlib is the foundational Python library for creating graphs and plots of datasets and is also the base package from which other Python plotting libraries derive. The Matplotlib API has been designed in alignment with the Matlab plotting library to facilitate an easy transition to Python.

- Seaborn (available at https://seaborn.pydata.org/): Seaborn is a plotting library built on top of Matplotlib, providing attractive color and line styles as well as a number of common plotting templates.

- Scikit-learn (available at https://scikit-learn.org/stable/): Scikit-learn is a Python machine learning library that provides a number of data mining, modeling, and analysis techniques in a simple API. Scikit-learn includes a number of machine learning algorithms out of the box, including classification, regression, and clustering techniques.

These packages form the foundation of a versatile machine learning development environment, with each package contributing a key set of functionalities. As discussed, by using Anaconda, you will already have all of the required packages installed and ready for use. If you require a package that is not included in the Anaconda installation, it can be installed by simply entering and executing the following code in a Jupyter notebook cell:

```
!conda install <package name>
```

As an example, if we wanted to install Seaborn, we'd run the following command:

```
!conda install seaborn
```

To use one of these packages in a notebook, all we need to do is import it:

```
import matplotlib
```

LOADING DATA IN PANDAS

pandas has the ability to read and write a number of different file formats and data structures, including CSV, JSON, and HDF5 files, as well as SQL and Python Pickle formats. The pandas input/output documentation can be found at https://pandas. pydata.org/pandas-docs/stable/user_guide/io.html. We will continue to look into the **pandas** functionality by loading data via a CSV file.

> **NOTE**
>
> The dataset used in this chapter is available on our GitHub repository via the following link: https://packt.live/2vjyPK9. Once you download the entire repository on your system, you can find the dataset in the **Datasets** folder. Furthermore, this dataset is the *Titanic: Machine Learning from Disaster* dataset, which was originally made available at https://www.kaggle. com/c/Titanic/data.

The dataset contains a roll of the guests on board the famous ship Titanic, as well as their age, survival status, and number of siblings/parents. Before we get started with loading the data into Python, it is critical that we spend some time looking over the information provided for the dataset so that we can have a thorough understanding of what it contains. Download the dataset and place it in the directory you're working in.

Looking at the description for the data, we can see that we have the following fields available:

- **survival**: This tells us whether a given person survived (**0** = No, **1** = Yes).

- **pclass**: This is a proxy for socio-economic status, where first class is upper, second class is middle, and third class is lower status.

- **sex**: This tells us whether a given person is male or female.

- **age**: This is a fractional value if less than 1; for example, *0.25* is 3 months. If the age is estimated, it is in the form of *xx.5*.

- **sibsp**: A sibling is defined as a brother, sister, stepbrother, or stepsister, and a spouse is a husband or wife.

- **parch**: A parent is a mother or father, while a child is a daughter, son, stepdaughter, or stepson. Children that traveled only with a nanny did not travel with a parent. Thus, *0* was assigned for this field.

- **ticket**: This gives the person's ticket number.

- **fare**: This is the passenger's fare.

- **cabin**: This tells us the passenger's cabin number.

- **embarked**: The point of embarkation is the location where the passenger boarded the ship.

Note that the information provided with the dataset does not give any context as to how the data was collected. The **survival**, **pclass**, and **embarked** fields are known as categorical variables as they are assigned to one of a fixed number of labels or categories to indicate some other information. For example, in **embarked**, the C label indicates that the passenger boarded the ship at Cherbourg, and the value of **1** in **survival** indicates they survived the sinking.

EXERCISE 1.01: LOADING AND SUMMARIZING THE TITANIC DATASET

In this exercise, we will read our Titanic dataset into Python and perform a few basic summary operations on it:

1. Open a new Jupyter notebook.

2. Import the **pandas** and **numpy** packages using shorthand notation:

```
import pandas as pd
import numpy as np
```

3. Open the **titanic.csv** file by clicking on it in the Jupyter notebook home page as shown in the following figure:

Figure 1.2: Opening the CSV file

The file is a CSV file, which can be thought of as a table, where each line is a row in the table and each comma separates columns in the table. Thankfully, we don't need to work with these tables in raw text form and can load them using **pandas**:

Figure 1.3: Contents of the CSV file

> **NOTE**
>
> Take a moment to look up the pandas documentation for the **read_csv** function at https://pandas.pydata.org/pandas-docs/stable/reference/api/pandas.read_csv.html. Note the number of different options available for loading CSV data into a pandas DataFrame.

4. In an executable Jupyter notebook cell, execute the following code to load the data from the file:

```
df = pd.read_csv(r'..\Datasets\titanic.csv')
```

The pandas DataFrame class provides a comprehensive set of attributes and methods that can be executed on its own contents, ranging from sorting, filtering, and grouping methods to descriptive statistics, as well as plotting and conversion.

> **NOTE**
>
> Open and read the documentation for pandas DataFrame objects at https://pandas.pydata.org/pandas-docs/stable/reference/frame.html.

5. Read the first ten rows of data using the **head()** method of the DataFrame:

> **NOTE**
>
> The **#** symbol in the code snippet below denotes a code comment.
> Comments are added into code to help explain specific bits of logic.

```
df.head(10)  # Examine the first 10 samples
```

The output will be as follows:

	Unnamed: 0	Cabin	Embarked	Fare	Pclass	Ticket	Age	Name	Parch	Sex	SibSp	Survived
0	0	NaN	S	7.2500	3	A/5 21171	22.0	Braund, Mr. Owen Harris	0	male	1	0.0
1	1	C85	C	71.2833	1	PC 17599	38.0	Cumings, Mrs. John Bradley (Florence Briggs Th...	0	female	1	1.0
2	2	NaN	S	7.9250	3	STON/O2. 3101282	26.0	Heikkinen, Miss. Laina	0	female	0	1.0
3	3	C123	S	53.1000	1	113803	35.0	Futrelle, Mrs. Jacques Heath (Lily May Peel)	0	female	1	1.0
4	4	NaN	S	8.0500	3	373450	35.0	Allen, Mr. William Henry	0	male	0	0.0
5	5	NaN	Q	8.4583	3	330877	NaN	Moran, Mr. James	0	male	0	0.0
6	6	E46	S	51.8625	1	17463	54.0	McCarthy, Mr. Timothy J	0	male	0	0.0
7	7	NaN	S	21.0750	3	349909	2.0	Palsson, Master. Gosta Leonard	1	male	3	0.0
8	8	NaN	S	11.1333	3	347742	27.0	Johnson, Mrs. Oscar W (Elisabeth Vilhelmina Berg)	2	female	0	1.0
9	9	NaN	C	30.0708	2	237736	14.0	Nasser, Mrs. Nicholas (Adele Achem)	0	female	1	1.0

Figure 1.4: Reading the first 10 rows

> **NOTE**
>
> To access the source code for this specific section, please refer to
> https://packt.live/2Ynb7sf.
>
> You can also run this example online at https://packt.live/2BvTRrG.
> You must execute the entire Notebook in order to get the desired result.

In this sample, we have a visual representation of the information in the DataFrame. We can see that the data is organized in a tabular, almost spreadsheet-like structure. The different types of data are organized into columns, while each sample is organized into rows. Each row is assigned an index value and is shown as the numbers **0** to **9** in bold on the left-hand side of the DataFrame. Each column is assigned to a label or name, as shown in bold at the top of the DataFrame.

The idea of a DataFrame as a kind of spreadsheet is a reasonable analogy. As we will see in this chapter, we can sort, filter, and perform computations on the data just as you would in a spreadsheet program. While it's not covered in this chapter, it is interesting to note that DataFrames also contain pivot table functionality, just like a spreadsheet (https://pandas.pydata.org/pandas-docs/stable/reference/api/pandas.pivot_table.html).

EXERCISE 1.02: INDEXING AND SELECTING DATA

Now that we have loaded some data, let's use the selection and indexing methods of the DataFrame to access some data of interest. This exercise is a continuation of *Exercise 1.01, Loading and Summarizing the Titanic Dataset*:

1. Select individual columns in a similar way to a regular dictionary by using the labels of the columns, as shown here:

```
df['Age']
```

The output will be as follows:

```
0          22.0
1          38.0
2          26.0
3          35.0
4          35.0
           ...
1304        NaN
1305       39.0
1306       38.5
1307        NaN
1308        NaN
Name: Age, Length: 1309, dtype: float64
```

If there are no spaces in the column name, we can also use the dot operator. If there are spaces in the column names, we will need to use the bracket notation:

```
df.Age
```

The output will be as follows:

```
0          22.0
1          38.0
2          26.0
3          35.0
```

```
4        35.0
         ...
1304     NaN
1305     39.0
1306     38.5
1307     NaN
1308     NaN
Name: Age, Length: 1309, dtype: float64
```

2. Select multiple columns at once using bracket notation, as shown here:

```
df[['Name', 'Parch', 'Sex']]
```

The output will be as follows:

	Name	Parch	Sex
0	Braund, Mr. Owen Harris	0	male
1	Cumings, Mrs. John Bradley (Florence Briggs Th...	0	female
2	Heikkinen, Miss. Laina	0	female
3	Futrelle, Mrs. Jacques Heath (Lily May Peel)	0	female
4	Allen, Mr. William Henry	0	male
...	...	...	...
1304	Spector, Mr. Woolf	0	male
1305	Oliva y Ocana, Dona. Fermina	0	female
1306	Saether, Mr. Simon Sivertsen	0	male
1307	Ware, Mr. Frederick	0	male
1308	Peter, Master. Michael J	1	male

1309 rows × 3 columns

Figure 1.5: Selecting multiple columns

NOTE

The output has been truncated for presentation purposes.

3. Select the first row using `iloc`:

```
df.iloc[0]
```

The output will be as follows:

```
Unnamed: 0                              0
Cabin                                 NaN
Embarked                                S
Fare                                 7.25
Pclass                                  3
Ticket                          A/5 21171
Age                                    22
Name              Braund, Mr. Owen Harris
Parch                                   0
Sex                                  male
SibSp                                   1
Survived                                0
Name: 0, dtype: object
```

Figure 1.6: Selecting the first row

4. Select the first three rows using `iloc`:

```
df.iloc[[0,1,2]]
```

The output will be as follows:

	Unnamed: 0	Cabin	Embarked	Fare	Pclass	Ticket	Age	Name	Parch	Sex	SibSp	Survived
0	0	NaN	S	7.2500	3	A/5 21171	22.0	Braund, Mr. Owen Harris	0	male	1	0.0
1	1	C85	C	71.2833	1	PC 17599	38.0	Cumings, Mrs. John Bradley (Florence Briggs Th...	0	female	1	1.0
2	2	NaN	S	7.9250	3	STON/O2. 3101282	26.0	Heikkinen, Miss. Laina	0	female	0	1.0

Figure 1.7: Selecting the first three rows

5. Next, get a list of all of the available columns:

```
columns = df.columns # Extract the list of columns
print(columns)
```

The output will be as follows:

```
Index(['Unnamed: 0', 'Cabin', 'Embarked', 'Fare', 'Pclass', 'Ticket', 'Age',
       'Name', 'Parch', 'Sex', 'SibSp', 'Survived'],
     dtype='object')
```

Figure 1.8: Getting all the columns

6. Use this list of columns and the standard Python slicing syntax to get columns 2, 3, and 4, and their corresponding values:

```
df[columns[1:4]] # Columns 2, 3, 4
```

The output will be as follows:

	Cabin	Embarked	Fare
0	NaN	S	7.2500
1	C85	C	71.2833
2	NaN	S	7.9250
3	C123	S	53.1000
4	NaN	S	8.0500
...	...	...	...
1304	NaN	S	8.0500
1305	C105	C	108.9000
1306	NaN	S	7.2500
1307	NaN	S	8.0500
1308	NaN	C	22.3583

1309 rows × 3 columns

Figure 1.9: Getting the second, third, and fourth columns

7. Use the **len** operator to get the number of rows in the DataFrame:

```
len(df)
```

The output will be as follows:

```
1309
```

8. Get the value for the **Fare** column in row 2 using the row-centric method:

```
df.iloc[2]['Fare']  # Row centric
```

The output will be as follows:

```
7.925
```

9. Use the dot operator for the column, as follows:

```
df.iloc[2].Fare  # Row centric
```

The output will be as follows:

```
7.925
```

10. Use the column-centric method, as follows:

```
df['Fare'][2]  # Column centric
```

The output will be as follows:

```
7.925
```

11. Use the column-centric method with the dot operator, as follows:

```
df.Fare[2]  # Column centric
```

The output will be as follows:

```
7.925
```

> **NOTE**
>
> To access the source code for this specific section, please refer to https://packt.live/2YmA7jb.
>
> You can also run this example online at https://packt.live/3dmk0qf.
> You must execute the entire Notebook in order to get the desired result.

In this exercise, we have seen how to use pandas' **read_csv()** function to load data into Python within a Jupyter notebook. We then explored a number of ways that pandas, by presenting the data in a DataFrame, facilitates selecting specific items in a DataFrame and viewing the contents. With these basics understood, let's look at some more advanced ways to index and select data.

EXERCISE 1.03: ADVANCED INDEXING AND SELECTION

With the basics of indexing and selection under our belt, we can turn our attention to more advanced indexing and selection. In this exercise, we will look at a few important methods for performing advanced indexing and selecting data. This exercise is a continuation of *Exercise 1.01, Loading and Summarizing the Titanic Dataset*:

1. Create a list of the passengers' names and ages for those passengers under the age of 21, as shown here:

```
child_passengers = df[df.Age  < 21][['Name', 'Age']]
child_passengers.head()
```

The output will be as follows:

	Name	Age
7	Palsson, Master. Gosta Leonard	2.0
9	Nasser, Mrs. Nicholas (Adele Achem)	14.0
10	Sandstrom, Miss. Marguerite Rut	4.0
12	Saundercock, Mr. William Henry	20.0
14	Vestrom, Miss. Hulda Amanda Adolfina	14.0

Figure 1.10: List of passengers' names and ages for those passengers under the age of 21

2. Count how many child passengers there were, as shown here:

```
print(len(child_passengers))
```

The output will be as follows:

```
249
```

3. Count how many passengers were between the ages of 21 and 30. Do not use Python's **and** logical operator for this step, but rather the ampersand symbol (**&**). Do this as follows:

> **NOTE**
>
> The code snippet shown here uses a backslash (****) to split the logic across multiple lines. When the code is executed, Python will ignore the backslash, and treat the code on the next line as a direct continuation of the current line.

```
young_adult_passengers = df.loc[(df.Age > 21) \
                        & (df.Age < 30)]
len(young_adult_passengers)
```

The output will be as follows:

```
279
```

4. Find the passengers who were either first- or third-class ticket holders. Again, we will not use the Python logical **or** operator but the pipe symbol (**|**) instead. Do this as follows:

```
df.loc[(df.Pclass == 3) | (df.Pclass ==1)]
```

The output will be as follows:

	Unnamed: 0	Cabin	Embarked	Fare	Pclass	Ticket	Age	Name	Parch	Sex	SibSp	Survived
0	0	NaN	S	7.2500	3	A/5 21171	22.0	Braund, Mr. Owen Harris	0	male	1	0.0
1	1	C85	C	71.2833	1	PC 17599	38.0	Cumings, Mrs. John Bradley (Florence Briggs Th...	0	female	1	1.0
2	2	NaN	S	7.9250	3	STON/O2. 3101282	26.0	Heikkinen, Miss. Laina	0	female	0	1.0
3	3	C123	S	53.1000	1	113803	35.0	Futrelle, Mrs. Jacques Heath (Lily May Peel)	0	female	1	1.0
4	4	NaN	S	8.0500	3	373450	35.0	Allen, Mr. William Henry	0	male	0	0.0
...	...	...	...	...	...	...	...	...	...	...	...	...
1304	1304	NaN	S	8.0500	3	A.5. 3236	NaN	Spector, Mr. Woolf	0	male	0	NaN
1305	1305	C105	C	108.9000	1	PC 17758	39.0	Oliva y Ocana, Dona. Fermina	0	female	0	NaN
1306	1306	NaN	S	7.2500	3	SOTON/O.Q. 3101262	38.5	Saether, Mr. Simon Sivertsen	0	male	0	NaN
1307	1307	NaN	S	8.0500	3	359309	NaN	Ware, Mr. Frederick	0	male	0	NaN
1308	1308	NaN	C	22.3583	3	2668	NaN	Peter, Master. Michael J	1	male	1	NaN

Figure 1.11: The number of passengers who were either first- or third-class ticket holders

5. Find the passengers who were not holders of either first- or third-class tickets. Do not simply select those second-class ticket holders, but use the ~ symbol for the **not** logical operator instead. Do this as follows:

```
df.loc[~((df.Pclass == 3) | (df.Pclass == 1))]
```

The output will be as follows:

	Unnamed: 0	Cabin	Embarked	Fare	Pclass	Ticket	Age	Name	Parch	Sex	SibSp	Survived
9	9	NaN	C	30.0708	2	237736	14.0	Nasser, Mrs. Nicholas (Adele Achem)	0	female	1	1.0
15	15	NaN	S	16.0000	2	248706	55.0	Hewlett, Mrs. (Mary D Kingcome)	0	female	0	1.0
17	17	NaN	S	13.0000	2	244373	NaN	Williams, Mr. Charles Eugene	0	male	0	1.0
20	20	NaN	S	26.0000	2	239865	35.0	Fynney, Mr. Joseph J	0	male	0	0.0
21	21	D56	S	13.0000	2	248698	34.0	Beesley, Mr. Lawrence	0	male	0	1.0
...	...	...	...	...	...	...	...	...	...	...	...	...
1278	1278	NaN	S	13.0000	2	244346	57.0	Ashby, Mr. John	0	male	0	NaN
1284	1284	NaN	S	10.5000	2	C.A. 30769	47.0	Gilbert, Mr. William	0	male	0	NaN
1292	1292	NaN	S	21.0000	2	28664	38.0	Gale, Mr. Harry	0	male	1	NaN
1296	1296	D38	C	13.8625	2	SC/PARIS 2166	20.0	Nourney, Mr. Alfred (Baron von Drachstedt")"	0	male	0	NaN
1297	1297	NaN	S	10.5000	2	28666	23.0	Ware, Mr. William Jeffery	0	male	1	NaN

Figure 1.12: Count of passengers who were not holders of either first- or third-class tickets

6. We no longer need the **Unnamed: 0** column, so delete it using the **del** operator:

```
del df['Unnamed: 0']
df.head()
```

The output will be as follows:

	Cabin	Embarked	Fare	Pclass	Ticket	Age	Name	Parch	Sex	SibSp	Survived
0	NaN	S	7.2500	3	A/5 21171	22.0	Braund, Mr. Owen Harris	0	male	1	0.0
1	C85	C	71.2833	1	PC 17599	38.0	Cumings, Mrs. John Bradley (Florence Briggs Th...	0	female	1	1.0
2	NaN	S	7.9250	3	STON/O2. 3101282	26.0	Heikkinen, Miss. Laina	0	female	0	1.0
3	C123	S	53.1000	1	113803	35.0	Futrelle, Mrs. Jacques Heath (Lily May Peel)	0	female	1	1.0
4	NaN	S	8.0500	3	373450	35.0	Allen, Mr. William Henry	0	male	0	0.0

Figure 1.13: The del operator

> **NOTE**
>
> To access the source code for this specific section, please refer to https://packt.live/3empSRO.
>
> You can also run this example online at https://packt.live/3fEsPgK. You must execute the entire Notebook in order to get the desired result.

In this exercise, we have seen how to select data from a **DataFrame** using conditional operators that inspect the data and return the subsets we want. We also saw how to remove a column we didn't need (in this case, the **Unnamed** column simply contained row numbers that are not relevant to analysis). Now, we'll dig deeper into some of the power of pandas.

PANDAS METHODS

Now that we are confident with some **pandas** basics, as well as some more advanced indexing and selecting tools, let's look at some other **DataFrame** methods. For a complete list of all methods available in a DataFrame, we can refer to the class documentation.

> **NOTE**
>
> The pandas documentation is available at https://pandas.pydata.org/pandas-docs/stable/reference/frame.html.

You should now know how many methods are available within a **DataFrame**. There are far too many to cover in detail in this chapter, so we will select a few that will give you a great start in supervised machine learning.

We have already seen the use of one method, **head()**, which provides the first five lines of the DataFrame. We can select more or fewer lines if we wish by providing the number of lines as an argument, as shown here:

```
df.head(n=20)  # 20 lines
df.head(n=32)  # 32 lines
```

Alternatively, you can use the **tail()** function to see a specified number of lines at the end of the DataFrame.

Another useful method is **describe**, which is a super-quick way of getting the descriptive statistics of the data within a DataFrame. We can see next that the sample size (count), mean, minimum, maximum, standard deviation, and the 25th, 50th, and 75th percentiles are returned for all columns of numerical data in the DataFrame (note that text columns have been omitted):

```
df.describe()
```

The output will be as follows:

	Unnamed: 0	Fare	Pclass	Age	Parch	SibSp	Survived
count	1309.000000	1308.000000	1309.000000	1046.000000	1309.000000	1309.000000	891.000000
mean	654.000000	33.295479	2.294882	29.881138	0.385027	0.498854	0.383838
std	378.020061	51.758668	0.837836	14.413493	0.865560	1.041658	0.486592
min	0.000000	0.000000	1.000000	0.170000	0.000000	0.000000	0.000000
25%	327.000000	7.895800	2.000000	21.000000	0.000000	0.000000	0.000000
50%	654.000000	14.454200	3.000000	28.000000	0.000000	0.000000	0.000000
75%	981.000000	31.275000	3.000000	39.000000	0.000000	1.000000	1.000000
max	1308.000000	512.329200	3.000000	80.000000	9.000000	8.000000	1.000000

Figure 1.14: The describe method

Note that only columns of numerical data have been included within the summary. This simple command provides us with a lot of useful information; looking at the values for **count** (which counts the number of valid samples), we can see that there are 1,046 valid samples in the **Age** category, but 1,308 in **Fare**, and only 891 in **Survived**. We can see that the youngest person was 0.17 years, the average age is 29.898, and the eldest passenger was 80. The minimum fare was £0, with £33.30 the average and £512.33 the most expensive. If we look at the **Survived** column, we have 891 valid samples, with a mean of 0.38, which means about 38% survived.

We can also get these values separately for each of the columns by calling the respective methods of the DataFrame, as shown here:

```
df.count()
```

The output will be as follows:

```
Cabin        295
Embarked    1307
Fare        1308
Pclass      1309
Ticket      1309
Age         1046
Name        1309
Parch       1309
Sex         1309
SibSp       1309
Survived     891
dtype: int64
```

But we have some columns that contain text data, such as **Embarked, Ticket, Name**, and **Sex**. So what about these? How can we get some descriptive information for these columns? We can still use **describe**; we just need to pass it some more information. By default, **describe** will only include numerical columns and will compute the 25th, 50th, and 75th percentiles, but we can configure this to include text-based columns by passing the **include = 'all'** argument, as shown here:

```
df.describe(include='all')
```

The output will be as follows:

	Unnamed: 0	Cabin	Embarked	Fare	Pclass	Ticket	Age	Name	Parch	Sex	SibSp	Survived
count	1309.000000	295	1307	1308.000000	1309.000000	1309	1046.000000	1309	1309.000000	1309	1309.000000	891.000000
unique	NaN	186	3	NaN	NaN	929	NaN	1307	NaN	2	NaN	NaN
top	NaN	C23 C25 C27	S	NaN	NaN	CA. 2343	NaN	Connolly, Miss. Kate	NaN	male	NaN	NaN
freq	NaN	6	914	NaN	NaN	11	NaN	2	NaN	843	NaN	NaN
mean	654.000000	NaN	NaN	33.295479	2.294882	NaN	29.881138	NaN	0.385027	NaN	0.498854	0.383838
std	378.020061	NaN	NaN	51.758668	0.837836	NaN	14.413493	NaN	0.865560	NaN	1.041658	0.486592
min	0.000000	NaN	NaN	0.000000	1.000000	NaN	0.170000	NaN	0.000000	NaN	0.000000	0.000000
25%	327.000000	NaN	NaN	7.895800	2.000000	NaN	21.000000	NaN	0.000000	NaN	0.000000	0.000000
50%	654.000000	NaN	NaN	14.454200	3.000000	NaN	28.000000	NaN	0.000000	NaN	0.000000	0.000000
75%	981.000000	NaN	NaN	31.275000	3.000000	NaN	39.000000	NaN	0.000000	NaN	1.000000	1.000000
max	1308.000000	NaN	NaN	512.329200	3.000000	NaN	80.000000	NaN	9.000000	NaN	8.000000	1.000000

Figure 1.15: The describe method with text-based columns

That's better—now we have much more information. Looking at the **Cabin** column, we can see that there are 295 entries, with 186 unique values. The most common values are **C32**, **C25**, and **C27**, and they occur 6 times (from the **freq** value). Similarly, if we look at the **Embarked** column, we see that there are 1,307 entries, 3 unique values, and that the most commonly occurring value is **S**, with 914 entries.

Notice the occurrence of **NaN** values in our **describe** output table. **NaN**, or **Not a Number**, values are very important within DataFrames as they represent missing or not available data. The ability of the pandas library to read from data sources that contain missing or incomplete information is both a blessing and a curse. Many other libraries would simply fail to import or read the data file in the event of missing information, while the fact that it can be read also means that the missing data must be handled appropriately.

When looking at the output of the **describe** method, you should notice that the Jupyter notebook renders it in the same way as the original DataFrame that we read in using **read_csv**. There is a very good reason for this, as the results returned by the **describe** method are themselves a pandas DataFrame and thus possess the same methods and characteristics as the data read in from the CSV file. This can be easily verified using Python's built-in **type** function, as in the following code:

```
type(df.describe(include='all'))
```

The output will be as follows:

```
pandas.core.frame.DataFrame
```

Now that we have a summary of the dataset, let's dive in with a little more detail to get a better understanding of the available data.

> **NOTE**
>
> A comprehensive understanding of the available data is critical in any supervised learning problem. The source and type of the data, the means by which it is collected, and any errors potentially resulting from the collection process all have an effect on the performance of the final model.

Hopefully, by now, you are comfortable with using pandas to provide a high-level overview of the data. We will now spend some time looking into the data in greater detail.

EXERCISE 1.04: USING THE AGGREGATE METHOD

We have already seen how we can index or select rows or columns from a DataFrame and use advanced indexing techniques to filter the available data based on specific criteria. Another handy method that allows for such selection is the **groupby** method, which provides a quick method for selecting groups of data at a time and provides additional functionality through the **DataFrameGroupBy** object. This exercise is a continuation of *Exercise 1.01, Loading and Summarizing the Titanic Dataset*:

1. Use the **groupby** method to group the data under the **Embarked** column to find out how many different values for **Embarked** there are:

```
embarked_grouped = df.groupby('Embarked')
print(f'There are {len(embarked_grouped)} Embarked groups')
```

The output will be as follows:

```
There are 3 Embarked groups
```

2. Display the output of **embarked_grouped.groups** to find what the **groupby** method actually does:

```
embarked_grouped.groups
```

The output will be as follows:

```
{'C': Int64Index([    1,     9,    19,    26,    30,    31,    34,    36,    39,    42,
            ...
            1260, 1262, 1266, 1288, 1293, 1295, 1296, 1298, 1305, 1308],
           dtype='int64', length=270),
 'Q': Int64Index([    5,    16,    22,    28,    32,    44,    46,    47,    82,   109,
            ...
            1206, 1249, 1271, 1272, 1279, 1287, 1290, 1299, 1301, 1302],
           dtype='int64', length=123),
 'S': Int64Index([    0,     2,     3,     4,     6,     7,     8,    10,    11,    12,
            ...
            1289, 1291, 1292, 1294, 1297, 1300, 1303, 1304, 1306, 1307],
           dtype='int64', length=914)}
```

Figure 1.16: Output of embarked_grouped.groups

We can see here that the three groups are **C**, **Q**, and **S**, and that **embarked_grouped.groups** is actually a dictionary where the keys are the groups. The values are the rows or indexes of the entries that belong to that group.

3. Use the **iloc** method to inspect row **1** and confirm that it belongs to embarked group **C**:

```
df.iloc[1]
```

The output will be as follows:

```
Cabin                                                   C85
Embarked                                                  C
Fare                                                71.2833
Pclass                                                    1
Ticket                                            PC 17599
Age                                                      38
Name        Cumings, Mrs. John Bradley (Florence Briggs Th...
Parch                                                     0
Sex                                                  female
SibSp                                                     1
Survived                                                  1
Name: 1, dtype: object
```

Figure 1.17: Inspecting row 1

4. As the groups are a dictionary, we can iterate through them and execute computations on the individual groups. Compute the mean age for each group, as shown here:

```
for name, group in embarked_grouped:
    print(name, group.Age.mean())
```

The output will be as follows:

```
C 32.33216981132075
Q 28.63
S 29.245204603580564
```

5. Another option is to use the **aggregate** method, or **agg** for short, and provide it with the function to apply across the columns. Use the **agg** method to determine the mean of each group:

```
embarked_grouped.agg(np.mean)
```

The output will be as follows:

Embarked	Fare	Pclass	Age	Parch	SibSp	Survived
C	62.336267	1.851852	32.332170	0.370370	0.400000	0.553571
Q	12.409012	2.894309	28.630000	0.113821	0.341463	0.389610
S	27.418824	2.347921	29.245205	0.426696	0.550328	0.336957

Figure 1.18: Using the agg method

So, how exactly does **agg** work and what type of functions can we pass it? Before we can answer these questions, we need to first consider the data type of each column in the DataFrame, as each column is passed through this function to produce the result we see here. Each DataFrame comprises a collection of columns of pandas series data, which, in many ways, operates just like a list. As such, any function that can take a list or a similar iterable and compute a single value as a result can be used with **agg**.

6. Define a simple function that returns the first value in the column and then pass that function through to **agg**, as an example:

```
def first_val(x):
    return x.values[0]


embarked_grouped.agg(first_val)
```

The output will be as follows:

	Cabin	Fare	Pclass	Ticket	Age	Name	Parch	Sex	SibSp	Survived
Embarked										
C	C85	71.2833	1	PC 17599	38.0	Cumings, Mrs. John Bradley (Florence Briggs Th...	0	female	1	1.0
Q	NaN	8.4583	3	330877	NaN	Moran, Mr. James	0	male	0	0.0
S	NaN	7.2500	3	A/5 21171	22.0	Braund, Mr. Owen Harris	0	male	1	0.0

Figure 1.19: Using the .agg method with a function

> **NOTE**
>
> To access the source code for this specific section, please refer to https://packt.live/2NlEkgM.
>
> You can also run this example online at https://packt.live/2AZnq51. You must execute the entire Notebook in order to get the desired result.

In this exercise, we have seen how to group data within a DataFrame, which then allows additional functions to be applied using `.agg()`, such as to calculate group means. These sorts of operations are extremely common in analyzing and preparing data for analysis.

QUANTILES

The previous exercise demonstrated how to find the mean. In statistical data analysis, we are also often interested in knowing the value in a dataset below or above which a certain fraction of the points lie. Such points are called quantiles. For example, if we had a sequence of numbers from 1 to 10,001, the quantile for 25% is the value 2,501. That is, at the value 2,501, 25% of our data lies below that cutoff. Quantiles are often used in data visualizations because they convey a sense of the distribution of the data. In particular, the standard boxplot in Matplotlib draws a box bounded by the first and third of 4 quantiles.

For example, let's establish the 25% quantile of the following dataframe:

```
import pandas as pd
df = pd.DataFrame({"A":[1, 6, 9, 9]})

#calculate the 25% quantile over the dataframe
df.quantile(0.25, axis = 0)
```

The output will be as follows:

```
A     4.75
Name: 0.25, dtype: float64
```

As you can see from the preceding output, **4.75** is the **25%** quantile value for the DataFrame.

> **NOTE**
>
> For more information on quantile methods, refer to
> https://pandas.pydata.org/pandas-docs/stable/reference/frame.html.

Later in this book, we'll use the idea of quantiles as we explore the data.

LAMBDA FUNCTIONS

One common and useful way of implementing **agg** is through the use of Lambda functions.

Lambda, or anonymous, functions (also known as inline functions in other languages) are small, single-expression functions that can be declared and used without the need for a formal function definition via the use of the **def** keyword. Lambda functions are essentially provided for convenience and aren't intended to be used for extensive periods. The main benefit of Lambda functions is that they can be used in places where a function might not be appropriate or convenient, such as inside other expressions or function calls. The standard syntax for a Lambda function is as follows (always starting with the **lambda** keyword):

```
lambda <input values>: <computation for values to be returned>
```

Let's now do an exercise and create some interesting Lambda functions.

EXERCISE 1.05: CREATING LAMBDA FUNCTIONS

In this exercise, we will create a Lambda function that returns the first value in a column and use it with **agg**. This exercise is a continuation of *Exercise 1.01, Loading and Summarizing the Titanic Dataset*:

1. Write the **first_val** function as a Lambda function, passed to **agg**:

```
embarked_grouped = df.groupby('Embarked')
embarked_grouped.agg(lambda x: x.values[0])
```

The output will be as follows:

	Cabin	Fare	Pclass	Ticket	Age	Name	Parch	Sex	SibSp	Survived
Embarked										
C	C85	71.2833	1	PC 17599	38.0	Cumings, Mrs. John Bradley (Florence Briggs Th...	0	female	1	1.0
Q	NaN	8.4583	3	330877	NaN	Moran, Mr. James	0	male	0	0.0
S	NaN	7.2500	3	A/5 21171	22.0	Braund, Mr. Owen Harris	0	male	1	0.0

Figure 1.20: Using the agg method with a Lambda function

Obviously, we get the same result, but notice how much more convenient the Lambda function was to use, especially given the fact that it is only intended to be used briefly.

2. We can also pass multiple functions to **agg** via a list to apply the functions across the dataset. Pass the Lambda function as well as the NumPy mean and standard deviation functions, like this:

```
embarked_grouped.agg([lambda x: x.values[0], np.mean, np.std])
```

The output will be as follows:

	Fare			Pclass			Age			Parch
	<lambda_0>	mean	std	<lambda_0>	mean	std	<lambda_0>	mean	std	<lambda_0>
Embarked										
C	71.2833	62.336267	84.185996	1	1.851852	0.936802	38.0	32.332170	15.258092	0
Q	8.4583	12.409012	13.616133	3	2.894309	0.380099	NaN	28.630000	15.045784	0
S	7.2500	27.418824	37.096402	3	2.347921	0.784126	22.0	29.245205	14.047507	0

Figure 1.21: Using the agg method with multiple Lambda functions

3. Apply **numpy.sum** to the **Fare** column and the Lambda function to the **Age** column by passing **agg** a dictionary where the keys are the columns to apply the function to, and the values are the functions themselves to be able to apply different functions to different columns in the DataFrame:

```
embarked_grouped.agg({'Fare': np.sum, \
                      'Age': lambda x: x.values[0]})
```

The output will be as follows:

	Fare	Age
Embarked		
C	16830.7922	38.0
Q	1526.3085	NaN
S	25033.3862	22.0

Figure 1.22: Using the agg method with a dictionary of different columns

4. Finally, execute the **groupby** method using more than one column. Provide the method with a list of the columns (**Sex** and **Embarked**) to **groupby**, like this:

```
age_embarked_grouped = df.groupby(['Sex', 'Embarked'])
age_embarked_grouped.groups
```

The output will be as follows:

```
{('male',
  'S'): Int64Index([    0,     4,     6,     7,    12,    13,    17,    20,    21,    23,
              ...
              1283, 1284, 1285, 1289, 1292, 1294, 1297, 1304, 1306, 1307],
             dtype='int64', length=623),
 ('female',
  'C'): Int64Index([    1,     9,    19,    31,    39,    43,    52,   111,   114,   128,
              ...
              1238, 1241, 1252, 1255, 1259, 1262, 1266, 1288, 1293, 1305],
             dtype='int64', length=113),
 ('female',
  'S'): Int64Index([    2,     3,     8,    10,    11,    14,    15,    18,    24,    25,
              ...
              1265, 1267, 1273, 1274, 1276, 1282, 1286, 1291, 1300, 1303],
             dtype='int64', length=291),
 ('male',
  'Q'): Int64Index([    5,    16,    46,   116,   126,   143,   171,   188,   196,   214,   245
               260,   278,   280,   301,   364,   388,   411,   421,   428,   459,   468,
               510,   517,   525,   552,   560,   613,   626,   629,   703,   718,   749,
               768,   776,   778,   787,   790,   825,   828,   890,   891,   893,   907,
               938,   946,   975,   993,   997,   998,  1012, 1015, 1074, 1084, 1124,
              1147, 1162, 1249, 1271, 1272, 1279, 1287, 1290],
             dtype='int64'),
 ('female',
  'Q'): Int64Index([   22,    28,    32,    44,    47,    82,   109,   156,   186,   198,   208
               241,   264,   274,   289,   300,   303,   322,   330,   358,   359,   368,
               412,   501,   502,   573,   593,   612,   653,   654,   657,   680,   697,
               727,   767,   885,   897,   954,   957,   961,   970,   977,   979, 1002,
              1004, 1018, 1051, 1091, 1097, 1107, 1118, 1164, 1173, 1182, 1195,
              1204, 1206, 1299, 1301, 1302],
             dtype='int64'),
 ('male',
  'C'): Int64Index([   26,    30,    34,    36,    42,    48,    54,    57,    60,    64,
              ...
              1222, 1223, 1228, 1230, 1257, 1260, 1295, 1296, 1298, 1308],
             dtype='int64', length=157),
 ('female', nan): Int64Index([61, 829], dtype='int64')}
```

Figure 1.23: Using the groupby method with more than one column

Similar to when the groupings were computed by just the **Embarked** column, we can see here that a dictionary is returned where the keys are the combination of the **Sex** and **Embarked** columns returned as a tuple. The first key-value pair in the dictionary is a tuple, **('Male', 'S')**, and the values correspond to the indices of rows with that specific combination. There will be a key-value pair for each combination of unique values in the **Sex** and **Embarked** columns.

> ### NOTE
>
> To access the source code for this specific section, please refer to
> https://packt.live/2B1jAZl.
>
> You can also run this example online at https://packt.live/3emqwPe.
> You must execute the entire Notebook in order to get the desired result.

This concludes our brief exploration of data inspection and manipulation. We now move on to one of the most important topics in data science, data quality.

DATA QUALITY CONSIDERATIONS

The quality of data used in any machine learning problem, supervised or unsupervised, is critical to the performance of the final model, and should be at the forefront when planning any machine learning project. As a simple rule of thumb, if you have clean data, in sufficient quantity, with a good correlation between the input data type and the desired output, then the specifics regarding the type and details of the selected supervised learning model become significantly less important in achieving a good result.

In reality, however, this is rarely the case. There are usually some issues regarding the quantity of available data, the quality or signal-to-noise ratio in the data, the correlation between the input and output, or some combination of all three factors. As such, we will use this last section of this chapter to consider some of the data quality problems that may occur and some mechanisms for addressing them. Previously, we mentioned that in any machine learning problem, having a thorough understanding of the dataset is critical if we are to construct a high-performing model.

This is particularly the case when looking into data quality and attempting to address some of the issues present within the data. Without a comprehensive understanding of the dataset, additional noise or other unintended issues may be introduced during the data cleaning process, leading to further degradation of performance.

> **NOTE**
>
> A detailed description of the Titanic dataset and the type of data included is contained in the *Loading Data in pandas* section. If you need a quick refresher, go back and review that section now.

MANAGING MISSING DATA

As we discussed earlier, the ability of pandas to read data with missing values is both a blessing and a curse and, arguably, is the most common issue that needs to be managed before we can continue with developing our supervised learning model. The simplest, but not necessarily the most effective, method is to just remove or ignore those entries that are missing data. We can easily do this in pandas using the **dropna** method on the DataFrame:

```
complete_data = df.dropna()
```

There is one very significant consequence of simply dropping rows with missing data and that is we may be throwing away a lot of important information. This is highlighted very clearly in the Titanic dataset as a lot of rows contain missing data. If we were to simply ignore these rows, we would start with a sample size of 1,309 and end with a sample of 183 entries. Developing a reasonable supervised learning model with a little over 10% of the data would be very difficult indeed. The following code displays the use of the **dropna()** method to handle the missing entries:

```
len(df)
```

The preceding input produces the following output:

```
1309
```

The **dropna()** method is implemented as follows:

```
len(df.dropna())
```

The preceding input produces the following output:

```
183
```

So, with the exception of the early, explorative phase, it is rarely acceptable to simply discard all rows with invalid information. We can identify which rows are actually missing information and whether the missing information is a problem unique to certain columns or is consistent throughout all columns of the dataset. We can use **aggregate** to help us here as well:

```
df.aggregate(lambda x: x.isna().sum())
```

The output will be as follows:

```
Cabin        1014
Embarked        2
Fare            1
Pclass          0
Ticket          0
Age           263
Name            0
Parch           0
Sex             0
SibSp           0
Survived      418
dtype: int64
```

Now, this is useful! We can see that the vast majority of missing information is in the **Cabin** column, some in **Age**, and a little more in **Survived**. This is one of the first times in the data cleaning process that we may need to make an educated judgment call.

What do we want to do with the **Cabin** column? There is so much missing information here that, in fact, it may not be possible to use it in any reasonable way. We could attempt to recover the information by looking at the names, ages, and number of parents/siblings and see whether we can match some families together to provide information, but there would be a lot of uncertainty in this process. We could also simplify the column by using the level of the cabin on the ship rather than the exact cabin number, which may then correlate better with name, age, and social status. This is unfortunate as there could be a good correlation between **Cabin** and **Survived**, as perhaps those passengers in the lower decks of the ship may have had a harder time evacuating. We could examine only the rows with valid **Cabin** values to see whether there is any predictive power in the **Cabin** entry; but, for now, we will simply disregard **Cabin** as a reasonable input (or feature).

We can see that the **Embarked** and **Fare** columns only have three missing samples between them. If we decided that we needed the **Embarked** and **Fare** columns for our model, it would be a reasonable argument to simply drop these rows. We can do this using our indexing techniques, where ~ represents the **not** operation, or flipping the result (that is, where **df.Embarked** is not **NaN** and **df.Fare** is not **NaN**):

```
df_valid = df.loc[(~df.Embarked.isna()) & (~df.Fare.isna())]
```

The missing age values are a little more interesting, as there are too many rows with missing age values to just discard them. But we also have a few more options here, as we can have a little more confidence in some plausible values to fill in. The simplest option would be to simply fill in the missing age values with the mean age for the dataset:

```
df_valid[['Age']] = df_valid[['Age']]\
                    .fillna(df_valid.Age.mean())
```

This is okay, but there are probably better ways of filling in the data rather than just giving all 263 people the same value. Remember, we are trying to clean up the data with the goal of maximizing the predictive power of the input features and the survival rate. Giving everyone the same value, while simple, doesn't seem too reasonable. What if we were to look at the average ages of the members of each of the classes (**Pclass**)? This may give a better estimate, as the average age reduces from class 1 through 3, as you can see in the following code:

```
df_valid.loc[df.Pclass == 1, 'Age'].mean()
```

The preceding input produces the following output:

```
37.956806510096975
```

Average age for class 2 is as follows:

```
df_valid.loc[df.Pclass == 2, 'Age'].mean()
```

The preceding input produces the following output:

```
29.52440879717283
```

Average age for class 3 is as follows:

```
df_valid.loc[df.Pclass == 3, 'Age'].mean()
```

The preceding input produces the following output:

```
26.23396338788047
```

What if we were to consider the sex of the person as well as ticket class (social status)? Do the average ages differ here too? Let's find out:

```
for name, grp in df_valid.groupby(['Pclass', 'Sex']):
    print('%i' % name[0], name[1], '%0.2f' % grp['Age'].mean())
```

The output will be as follows:

```
1 female 36.84
1 male 41.03
2 female 27.50
2 male 30.82
3 female 22.19
3 male 25.86
```

We can see here that males in all ticket classes are typically older. This combination of sex and ticket class provides much more resolution than simply filling in all missing fields with the mean age. To do this, we will use the **transform** method, which applies a function to the contents of a series or DataFrame and returns another series or DataFrame with the transformed values. This is particularly powerful when combined with the **groupby** method:

```
mean_ages = df_valid.groupby(['Pclass', 'Sex'])['Age'].\
                        transform(lambda x: \
                        x.fillna(x.mean()))
df_valid.loc[:, 'Age'] = mean_ages
```

There is a lot in these two lines of code, so let's break them down into components. Let's look at the first line:

```
mean_ages = df_valid.groupby(['Pclass', 'Sex'])['Age'].\
                        transform(lambda x: \
                        x.fillna(x.mean()))
```

We are already familiar with **df_valid.groupby(['Pclass', 'Sex']) ['Age']**, which groups the data by ticket class and sex and returns only the **Age** column. The **lambda x: x.fillna(x.mean())** Lambda function takes the input pandas series and fills the **NaN** values with the mean value of the series.

The second line assigns the filled values within **mean_ages** to the **Age** column. Note the use of the **loc[:, 'Age']** indexing method, which indicates that all rows within the **Age** column are to be assigned the values contained within **mean_ages**:

```
df_valid.loc[:, 'Age'] = mean_ages
```

We have described a few different ways of filling in the missing values within the **Age** column, but by no means has this been an exhaustive discussion. There are many more methods that we could use to fill the missing data: we could apply random values within one standard deviation of the mean for the grouped data, and we could also look at grouping the data by sex and the number of parents/children (**Parch**) or by the number of siblings, or by ticket class, sex, and the number of parents/children. What is most important about the decisions made during this process is the end result of the prediction accuracy. We may need to try different options, rerun our models, and consider the effect on the accuracy of final predictions. Thus, selecting the features or components that provide the model with the most predictive power. You will find that, during this process, you will try a few different features, run the model, look at the end result, and repeat this process until you are happy with the performance.

The ultimate goal of this supervised learning problem is to predict the survival of passengers on the Titanic given the information we have available. So, that means that the **Survived** column provides our labels for training. What are we going to do if we are missing 418 of the labels? If this was a project where we had control over the collection of the data and access to its origins, we would obviously correct this by recollecting or asking for the labels to be clarified. With the Titanic dataset, we do not have this ability so we must make another educated judgment call. One approach would be to drop those rows from the training data, and later use a model trained on the (smaller) training set to predict the outcome for the others (this is, in fact, the task given in the Kaggle Titanic competition). In some business problems, we may not have the option of simply ignoring these rows; we might be trying to predict future outcomes of a very critical process and this data is all we have. We could try some unsupervised learning techniques to see whether there are some patterns in the survival information that we could use. However, by estimating the ground truth labels by means of unsupervised techniques, we may introduce significant noise into the dataset, reducing our ability to accurately predict survival.

CLASS IMBALANCE

Missing data is not the only problem that may be present within a dataset. Class imbalance – that is, having more of one class or classes compared to another – can be a significant problem, particularly in the case of classification problems (we'll see more on classification in *Chapter 5, Classification Techniques*), where we are trying to predict which class (or classes) a sample is from. Looking at our **Survived** column, we can see that there are far more people who perished (**Survived** equals **0**) than survived (**Survived** equals **1**) in the dataset, as you can see in the following code:

```
len(df.loc[df.Survived ==1])
```

The output is as follows:

```
342
```

The number of people who perished are:

```
len(df.loc[df.Survived ==0])
```

The output is as follows:

```
549
```

If we don't take this class imbalance into account, the predictive power of our model could be significantly reduced as, during training, the model would simply need to guess that the person did not survive to be correct 61% (*549 / (549 + 342)*) of the time. If, in reality, the actual survival rate was, say, 50%, then when being applied to unseen data, our model would predict *did not survive* too often.

There are a few options available for managing class imbalance, one of which, similar to the missing data scenario, is to randomly remove samples from the over-represented class until balance has been achieved. Again, this option is not ideal, or perhaps even appropriate, as it involves ignoring available data. A more constructive example may be to oversample the under-represented class by randomly copying samples from the under-represented class in the dataset to boost the number of samples. While removing data can lead to accuracy issues due to discarding useful information, oversampling the under-represented class can lead to being unable to predict the label of unseen data, also known as overfitting (which we will cover in *Chapter 6, Ensemble Modeling*).

Adding some random noise to the input features for oversampled data may prevent some degree of overfitting, but this is highly dependent on the dataset itself. As with missing data, it is important to check the effect of any class imbalance corrections on the overall model performance. It is relatively straightforward to copy more data into a DataFrame using the **append** method, which works in a very similar fashion to lists. If we wanted to copy the first row to the end of the DataFrame, we would do this:

```
df_oversample = df.append(df.iloc[0])
```

LOW SAMPLE SIZE

The field of machine learning can be considered a branch of the larger field of statistics. As such, the principles of confidence and sample size can also be applied to understand the issues with a small dataset. Recall that if we were to take measurements from a data source with high variance, then the degree of uncertainty in the measurements would also be high and more samples would be required to achieve a specified confidence in the value of the mean. The sample principles can be applied to machine learning datasets. Those datasets with a variance in the features with the most predictive power generally require more samples for reasonable performance as more confidence is also required.

There are a few techniques that can be used to compensate for a reduced sample size, such as transfer learning. However, these lie outside the scope of this book. Ultimately, though, there is only so much that can be done with a small dataset, and significant performance increases may only occur once the sample size is increased.

ACTIVITY 1.01: IMPLEMENTING PANDAS FUNCTIONS

In this activity, we will test ourselves on the various pandas functions we have learned about in this chapter. We will use the same Titanic dataset for this.

The steps to be performed are as follows:

1. Open a new Jupyter notebook.

2. Use pandas to load the Titanic dataset and use the **head** function on the dataset to display the top rows of the dataset. Describe the summary data for all columns.

3. We don't need the **Unnamed: 0** column. In *Exercise 1.03: Advanced Indexing and Selection*, we demonstrated how to remove the column using the **del** command. How else could we remove this column? Remove this column without using **del**.

4. Compute the mean, standard deviation, minimum, and maximum values for the columns of the DataFrame without using **describe**. Note that you can find the minimum and maximum values using the **df.min()** and **df.max()** functions.

5. Use the **quantile** method to get values for the 33, 66, and 99% quantiles.

6. Find how many passengers were from each class using the **groupby** method.

7. Find how many passengers were from each class answer by using selecting/ indexing methods to count the members of each class. You can use the **unique()** method to find out the unique values of each class.

   Confirm that the answers to *Step 6* and *Step 7* match.

8. Determine who the eldest passenger in third class was.

9. For a number of machine learning problems, it is very common to scale the numerical values between 0 and 1. Use the **agg** method with Lambda functions to scale the **Fare** and **Age** columns between 0 and 1.

10. There is one individual in the dataset without a listed **Fare** value, which can be established as follows:

```
df_nan_fare = df.loc[(df.Fare.isna())]
df_nan_fare
```

The output will be as follows:

	Embarked	Fare	Pclass	Ticket	Age	Name	Parch	Sex	SibSp	Survived
1043	S	NaN	3	3701	60.5	Storey, Mr. Thomas	0	male	0	NaN

Figure 1.24: Individual without a listed fare value

11. Replace the **NaN** value of this row in the main DataFrame with the mean **Fare** value for those corresponding to the same class and **Embarked** location using the **groupby** method.

The output will be as follows:

```
Embarked                         S
Fare                       14.4354
Pclass                           3
Ticket                        3701
Age                           60.5
Name          Storey, Mr. Thomas
Parch                            0
Sex                           male
SibSp                            0
Survived                       NaN
Name: 1043, dtype: object
```

Figure 1.25: Output for the individual without listed fare details

NOTE

The solution to this activity can be found on page 398.

With this activity, we have reviewed all the basic data loading, inspection, and manipulation methods, as well as some basic summary statistics methods.

SUMMARY

In this chapter, we introduced the concept of supervised machine learning, along with a number of use cases, including the automation of manual tasks such as identifying hairstyles from the 1960s and 1980s. In this introduction, we encountered the concept of labeled datasets and the process of mapping one information set (the input data or features) to the corresponding labels. We took a practical approach to the process of loading and cleaning data using Jupyter notebooks and the extremely powerful pandas library. Note that this chapter has only covered a small fraction of the functionality within pandas, and that an entire book could be dedicated to the library itself. It is recommended that you become familiar with reading the pandas documentation and continue to develop your pandas skills through practice. The final section of this chapter covered a number of data quality issues that need to be considered to develop a high-performing supervised learning model, including missing data, class imbalance, and low sample sizes. We discussed a number of options for managing such issues and emphasized the importance of checking these mitigations against the performance of the model. In the next chapter, we will extend the data cleaning process that we covered and investigate the data exploration and visualization process. Data exploration is a critical aspect of any machine learning solution since without a comprehensive knowledge of the dataset, it would be almost impossible to model the information provided.

2

EXPLORATORY DATA ANALYSIS
AND VISUALIZATION

OVERVIEW

This chapter takes us through how to perform exploration and analysis on a new dataset. By the end of this chapter, you will be able to explain the importance of data exploration and communicate the summary statistics of a dataset. You will visualize patterns in missing values in data and be able to replace null values appropriately. You will be equipped to identify continuous features, categorical features and visualize distributions of values across individual variables. You will also be able to describe and analyze relationships between different types of variables using correlation and visualizations.

INTRODUCTION

Say we have a problem statement that involves predicting whether a particular earthquake caused a tsunami. How do we decide what model to use? What do we know about the data we have? Nothing! But if we don't know and understand our data, chances are we'll end up building a model that's not very interpretable or reliable. When it comes to data science, it's important to have a thorough understanding of the data we're dealing with, in order to generate features that are highly informative and, consequently, to build accurate and powerful models. To acquire this understanding, we perform an exploratory analysis of the data to see what the data can tell us about the relationships between the features and the target variable (the value that you are trying to predict using the other variables). Getting to know our data will even help us interpret the model we build and identify ways we can improve its accuracy. The approach we take to achieve this is to allow the data to reveal its structure or model, which helps us gain some new, often unsuspected, insight into the data.

We will first begin with a brief introduction to exploratory data analysis and then progress to explaining summary statistics and central values. This chapter also teaches you how to find and visualize missing values and then describes the various imputation strategies for addressing the problem of missing values. The remainder of the chapter then focuses on visualizations. Specifically, the chapter teaches you how to create various plots such as scatter plot, histograms, pie charts, heatmaps, pairplots and more. Let us begin with exploratory data analysis.

EXPLORATORY DATA ANALYSIS (EDA)

Exploratory data analysis (**EDA**) is defined as a method to analyze datasets and sum up their main characteristics to derive useful conclusions, often with visual methods.

The purpose of EDA is to:

- Discover patterns within a dataset

- Spot anomalies

- Form hypotheses regarding the behavior of data

- Validate assumptions

Everything from basic summary statistics to complex visualizations helps us gain an intuitive understanding of the data itself, which is highly important when it comes to forming new hypotheses about the data and uncovering what parameters affect the target variable. Often, discovering how the target variable varies across a single feature gives us an indication of how important a feature might be, and a variation across a combination of several features helps us to come up with ideas for new informative features to engineer.

Most explorations and visualizations are intended to understand the relationship between the features and the target variable. This is because we want to find out what relationships exist (or don't exist) between the data we have and the values we want to predict.

EDA can tell us about:

- Features that are unclean, have missing values, or have outliers
- Features that are informative and are a good indicator of the target
- The kind of relationships features have with the target
- Further features that the data might need that we don't already have
- Edge cases you might need to account for separately
- Filters you might need to apply to the dataset
- The presence of incorrect or fake data points

Now that we've looked at why EDA is important and what it can tell us, let's talk about what exactly EDA involves. EDA can involve anything from looking at basic summary statistics to visualizing complex trends over multiple variables. However, even simple statistics and plots can be powerful tools, as they may reveal important facts about the data that could change our modeling perspective. When we see plots representing data, we are able to easily detect trends and patterns, compared to just raw data and numbers. These visualizations further allow us to ask questions such as "How?" and "Why?", and form hypotheses about the dataset that can be validated by further visualizations. This is a continuous process that leads to a deeper understanding of the data.

The dataset that we will use for our exploratory analysis and visualizations has been taken from the *Significant Earthquake Database* from NOAA, available as a public dataset on Google BigQuery (**table ID: 'bigquery-public-data. noaa_significant_earthquakes.earthquakes'**). We will be using a subset of the columns available, the metadata for which is available at https://console. cloud.google.com/bigquery?project=packt-data&folder&organizationId&p=bigquery-public-data&d=noaa_significant_earthquakes&t=earthquakes&page=table, and will load it into a pandas DataFrame to perform the exploration. We'll primarily be using Matplotlib for most of our visualizations, along with the Seaborn and Missingno libraries for some. It is to be noted, however, that Seaborn merely provides a wrapper over Matplotlib's functionalities, so anything that is plotted using Seaborn can also be plotted using Matplotlib. We'll try to keep things interesting by using visualizations from both libraries.

The exploration and analysis will be conducted keeping in mind a sample problem statement: *Given the data we have, we want to predict whether an earthquake caused a tsunami*. This will be a classification problem (more on this in *Chapter 5, Classification Techniques*) where the target variable is the **flag_tsunami** column.

Before we begin, let's first import the required libraries, which we will be using for most of our data manipulations and visualizations.

In a Jupyter notebook, import the following libraries:

```
import json
import pandas as pd
import numpy as np
import missingno as msno
from sklearn.impute import SimpleImputer
import matplotlib.pyplot as plt
import seaborn as sns
```

We can also read in the metadata containing the data types for each column, which are stored in the form of a JSON file. Do this using the following command. This command opens the file in a readable format and uses the **json** library to read the file into a dictionary:

```
with open('..\dtypes.json', 'r') as jsonfile:
    dtyp = json.load(jsonfile)
```

> **NOTE**
>
> The output of the preceding command can be found here:
> https://packt.live/3a4Zjhm

SUMMARY STATISTICS AND CENTRAL VALUES

In order to find out what our data really looks like, we use a technique known as **data profiling**. This is defined as the process of examining the data available from an existing information source (for example, a database or a file) and collecting statistics or informative summaries about that data. The goal is to make sure that you understand your data well and are able to identify any challenges that the data may pose early on in the project, which is done by summarizing the dataset and assessing its structure, content, and quality.

Data profiling includes collecting descriptive statistics and data types. Common data profile commands include those you have seen previously, including **data. describe()**, **data.head()**, and **data.tail()**. You can also use **data. info()**, which tells you how many non-null values there are in each column, along with the data type of the values (non-numeric types are represented as **object** types).

EXERCISE 2.01: SUMMARIZING THE STATISTICS OF OUR DATASET

In this exercise, we will use the summary statistics functions we read about previously to get a basic idea of our dataset:

> **NOTE**
>
> The dataset can be found on our GitHub repository here:
> https://packt.live/2TjU9aj

1. Read the earthquakes data into a **data** pandas DataFrame and use the **dtyp** dictionary we read using the **json** library in the previous section, to specify the data types of each column in the CSV. Begin by loading the requisite libraries and the JSON file we have prepared with the data types. You can inspect the data types before reading the data:

```
import json
import pandas as pd
import numpy as np
import missingno as msno
from sklearn.impute import SimpleImputer
import matplotlib.pyplot as plt
import seaborn as sns
with open('../dtypes.json', 'r') as jsonfile:
    dtyp = json.load(jsonfile)
dtyp
```

The output will be as follows:

```
{'id': 'float',
 'flag_tsunami': 'str',
 'year': 'float',
 'month': 'float',
 'day': 'float',
 'hour': 'float',
 'minute': 'float',
 'second': 'float',
 'focal_depth': 'float',
 'eq_primary': 'float',
 'eq_mag_mw': 'float',
 'eq_mag_ms': 'float',
 'eq_mag_mb': 'float',
 'intensity': 'float',
 'country': 'str',
 'state': 'str',
 'location_name': 'str',
 'latitude': 'float',
 'longitude': 'float',
 'region_code': 'str',
 'injuries': 'float',
 'injuries_description': 'str',
 'damage_millions_dollars': 'float',
 'damage_description': 'str',
 'total_injuries': 'float',
 'total_injuries_description': 'str',
 'total_damage_millions_dollars': 'float',
 'total_damage_description': 'str'}
```

Figure 2.1: Inspecting data types

2. Use the **data.info()** function to get an overview of the dataset:

```
data = pd.read_csv('../Datasets/earthquake_data.csv', dtype = dtyp)
data.info()
```

The output will be as follows:

```
<class 'pandas.core.frame.DataFrame'>
RangeIndex: 6072 entries, 0 to 6071
Data columns (total 28 columns):
id                              6072 non-null float64
flag_tsunami                    6072 non-null object
year                            6072 non-null float64
month                           5667 non-null float64
day                             5515 non-null float64
hour                            4044 non-null float64
minute                          3838 non-null float64
second                          2721 non-null float64
focal_depth                     3120 non-null float64
eq_primary                      4286 non-null float64
eq_mag_mw                       1216 non-null float64
eq_mag_ms                       2916 non-null float64
eq_mag_mb                       1786 non-null float64
intensity                       2748 non-null float64
country                         6072 non-null object
state                           308 non-null object
location_name                   6071 non-null object
latitude                        6018 non-null float64
longitude                       6022 non-null float64
region_code                     6072 non-null object
injuries                        1169 non-null float64
injuries_description            1349 non-null object
damage_millions_dollars         478 non-null float64
damage_description              4327 non-null object
total_injuries                  1184 non-null float64
total_injuries_description      1357 non-null object
total_damage_millions_dollars   418 non-null float64
total_damage_description        3148 non-null object
dtypes: float64(19), object(9)
memory usage: 1.3+ MB
```

Figure 2.2: Overview of the dataset

3. Print the first five and the last five rows of the dataset. The first five rows are printed as follows:

```
data.head()
data.tail()
```

The output will be as follows:

`data.head()`

	id	flag_tsunami	year	month	day	hour	minute	second	focal_depth	eq_primary	...	longitude	region_code
0	338.0	No	1048.0	NaN	NaN	NaN	NaN	NaN	NaN	NaN	...	NaN	120
1	771.0	Tsu	1580.0	4.0	6.0	NaN	NaN	NaN	33.0	6.2	...	1.309	120
2	7889.0	Tsu	1757.0	7.0	15.0	NaN	NaN	NaN	NaN	NaN	...	-6.320	120
3	6697.0	Tsu	1500.0	NaN	NaN	NaN	NaN	NaN	NaN	NaN	...	NaN	150
4	6013.0	Tsu	1668.0	4.0	13.0	NaN	NaN	NaN	NaN	NaN	...	-71.050	150

5 rows × 28 columns

`data.tail()`

	id	flag_tsunami	year	month	day	hour	minute	second	focal_depth	eq_primary	...	longitude	region_code
6067	5360.0	Tsu	1993.0	8.0	8.0	8.0	34.0	24.9	59.0	7.8	...	144.801	170
6068	5009.0	No	1983.0	12.0	22.0	1.0	2.0	2.4	26.0	6.4	...	151.868	170
6069	10307.0	No	2018.0	2.0	25.0	17.0	44.0	43.0	23.0	7.5	...	142.768	170
6070	5498.0	No	1998.0	7.0	9.0	5.0	19.0	7.3	10.0	6.2	...	-28.626	130
6071	5459.0	No	1997.0	4.0	22.0	9.0	31.0	23.2	5.0	6.7	...	-60.892	90

5 rows × 28 columns

Figure 2.3: The first and last five rows

We can see in these outputs that there are 28 columns, but not all of them are displayed. Only the first 10 and last 10 columns are displayed, with the ellipses representing the fact that there are columns in between that are not displayed.

4. Use **data.describe()** to find the summary statistics of the dataset. Run **data.describe().T**:

```
data.describe().T
```

Here, **.T** indicates that we're taking a transpose of the DataFrame to which it is applied, that is, turning the columns into rows and vice versa. Applying it to the **describe()** function allows us to see the output more easily with each row in the transposed DataFrame now corresponding to the statistics for a single feature.

We should get an output like this:

	count	mean	std	min	25%	50%	75%	max
id	6072.0	4658.426219	2924.650010	1.000	2142.75000	4608.5	6475.25000	10378.000
year	6072.0	1802.307477	377.924931	-2150.000	1818.00000	1927.0	1986.00000	2018.000
month	5667.0	6.510852	3.450167	1.000	4.00000	7.0	9.00000	12.000
day	5515.0	15.734361	8.752862	1.000	8.00000	16.0	23.00000	31.000
hour	4044.0	11.308605	7.033485	0.000	5.00000	11.0	17.00000	23.000
minute	3838.0	28.855915	17.151545	0.000	14.00000	30.0	44.00000	59.000
second	2721.0	29.740243	17.132196	0.100	14.80000	29.7	44.50000	59.900
focal_depth	3120.0	41.680769	71.258782	0.000	11.00000	26.0	40.00000	675.000
eq_primary	4286.0	6.471419	1.043968	1.600	5.70000	6.5	7.30000	9.500
eq_mag_mw	1216.0	6.526562	0.937869	3.600	5.80000	6.5	7.20000	9.500
eq_mag_ms	2916.0	6.574451	0.989850	2.100	5.80000	6.6	7.30000	9.100
eq_mag_mb	1786.0	5.797592	0.716809	2.100	5.30000	5.8	6.30000	8.200
intensity	2748.0	8.325328	1.800089	2.000	7.00000	8.0	10.00000	12.000
latitude	6018.0	22.537909	22.787934	-62.877	9.87175	32.2	38.77825	73.122
longitude	6022.0	37.985633	86.726852	-179.984	-8.00000	43.3	115.50000	180.000
injuries	1169.0	2293.579127	27095.202227	1.000	10.00000	42.0	200.00000	799000.000
damage_millions_dollars	478.0	1715.606259	12157.409978	0.013	3.62500	20.9	204.35000	220000.000
total_injuries	1184.0	2510.967061	28273.298405	1.000	10.00000	42.5	200.00000	799000.000
total_damage_millions_dollars	418.0	1978.743206	12988.187606	0.010	4.31000	28.0	300.00000	220085.456

Figure 2.4: Summary statistics

NOTE

To access the source code for this specific section, please refer to https://packt.live/2YI5qer.

You can also run this example online at https://packt.live/2V3I76D. You must execute the entire Notebook in order to get the desired result.

Notice here that the **describe()** function only shows the statistics for columns with numerical values. This is because we cannot calculate the statistics for the columns having non-numerical values (although we can visualize their values, as we will see later).

MISSING VALUES

When there is no value (that is, a null value) recorded for a particular feature in a data point, we say that the data is missing. Having missing values in a real dataset is inevitable; no dataset is ever perfect. However, it is important to understand why the data is missing, and whether there is a factor that has affected the loss of data. Appreciating and recognizing this allows us to handle the remaining data in an appropriate manner. For example, if the data is missing randomly, then it's highly likely that the remaining data is still representative of the population. However, if the missing data is not random in nature and we assume that it is, it could bias our analysis and subsequent modeling.

Let's look at the common reasons (or mechanisms) for missing data:

- **Missing Completely at Random (MCAR)**: Values in a dataset are said to be MCAR if there is no correlation whatsoever between the value missing and any other recorded variable or external parameter. This means that the remaining data is still representative of the population, though this is rarely the case and taking missing data to be completely random is usually an unrealistic assumption.

  For example, in a study that involves determining the reason for obesity among K12 children, MCAR is when the parents forgot to take their children to the clinic for the study.

- **Missing at Random (MAR)**: If the case where the data is missing is related to the data that was recorded rather than the data that was not, then the data is said to be MAR. Since it's unfeasible to statistically verify whether data is MAR, we'd have to depend on whether it's a reasonable possibility.

  Using the K12 study, missing data in this case is due to parents moving to a different city, hence the children had to leave the study; *missingness* has nothing to do with the study itself.

- **Missing Not at Random (MNAR)**: Data that is neither MAR nor MCAR is said to be MNAR. This is the case of a non-ignorable non-response, that is, the value of the variable that's missing is related to the reason it is missing.

  Continuing with the example of the case study, data would be MNAR if the parents were offended by the nature of the study and did not want their children to be bullied, so they withdrew their children from the study.

FINDING MISSING VALUES

So, now that we know why it's important to familiarize ourselves with the reasons behind why our data is missing, let's talk about how we can find these missing values in a dataset. For a pandas DataFrame, this is most commonly executed using the `.isnull()` method on a DataFrame to create a mask of the null values (that is, a DataFrame of Boolean values) indicating where the null values exist—a **True** value at any position indicates a null value, while a **False** value indicates the existence of a valid value at that position.

> **NOTE**
>
> The `.isnull()` method can be used interchangeably with the `.isna()` method for pandas DataFrames. Both these methods do exactly the same thing—the reason there are two methods to do the same thing is pandas DataFrames were originally based on R DataFrames, and hence have reproduced much of the syntax and ideas of the latter.

It may not be immediately obvious whether the missing data is random or not. Discovering the nature of missing values across features in a dataset is possible through two common visualization techniques:

- **Nullity matrix**: This is a data-dense display that lets us quickly visualize the patterns in data completion. It gives us a quick glance at how the null values within a feature (and across features) are distributed, how many there are, and how often they appear with other features.

- **Nullity-correlation heatmap**: This heatmap visually describes the nullity relationship (or a data completeness relationship) between each pair of features; that is, it measures how strongly the presence or absence of one variable affects the presence of another.

  Akin to regular correlation, nullity correlation values range from -1 to 1, the former indicating that one variable appears when the other definitely does not, and the latter indicating the simultaneous presence of both variables. A value of 0 implies that one variable having a null value has no effect on the other being null.

EXERCISE 2.02: VISUALIZING MISSING VALUES

Let's analyze the nature of the missing values by first looking at the count and percentage of missing values for each feature, and then plotting a nullity matrix and correlation heatmap using the **missingno** library in Python. We will be using the same dataset from the previous exercises.

Please note that this exercise is a continuation of *Exercise 2.01: Summarizing the Statistics of Our Dataset*.

The following steps will help you complete this exercise to visualize the missing values in the dataset:

1. Calculate the count and percentage of missing values in each column and arrange these in decreasing order. We will use the **.isnull()** function on the DataFrame to get a mask. The count of null values in each column can then be found using the **.sum()** function over the DataFrame mask. Similarly, the fraction of null values can be found using **.mean()** over the DataFrame mask and multiplied by 100 to convert it to a percentage.

    Then, we combine the total and percentage of null values into a single DataFrame using the **pd.concat()** function, and subsequently sort the rows by percentage of missing values and print the DataFrame:

```
mask = data.isnull()
total = mask.sum()
percent = 100*mask.mean()

missing_data = pd.concat([total, percent], axis=1,join='outer', \
                          keys=['count_missing', 'perc_missing'])
missing_data.sort_values(by='perc_missing', ascending=False, \
                          inplace=True)
missing_data
```

The output will be as follows:

	count_missing	perc_missing
state	5764	94.927536
total_damage_millions_dollars	5654	93.115942
damage_millions_dollars	5594	92.127800
injuries	4903	80.747694
total_injuries	4888	80.500659
eq_mag_mw	4856	79.973650
injuries_description	4723	77.783267
total_injuries_description	4715	77.651515
eq_mag_mb	4286	70.586298
second	3351	55.187747
intensity	3324	54.743083
eq_mag_ms	3156	51.976285
focal_depth	2952	48.616601
total_damage_description	2924	48.155468
minute	2234	36.791831
hour	2028	33.399209

Figure 2.5: The count and percentage of missing values in each column

Here, we can see that the **state**, **total_damage_millions_dollars**, and **damage_millions_dollars** columns have over 90% missing values, which means that data for fewer than 10% of the data points in the dataset are available for these columns. On the other hand, **year**, **flag_tsunami**, **country**, and **region_code** have no missing values.

2. Plot the nullity matrix. First, we find the list of columns that have any null values in them using the `.any()` function on the DataFrame mask from the previous step. Then, we use the **missingno** library to plot the nullity matrix for a random sample of 500 data points from our dataset, for only those columns that have missing values:

```
nullable_columns = data.columns[mask.any()].tolist()
msno.matrix(data[nullable_columns].sample(500))
plt.show()
```

The output will be as follows:

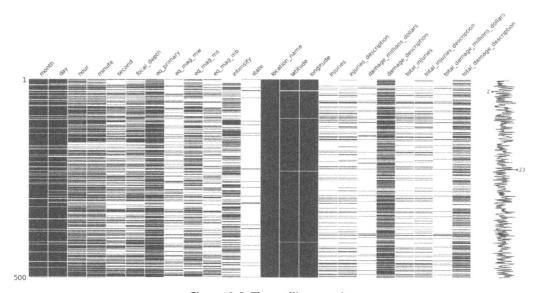

Figure 2.6: The nullity matrix

Here, black lines represent non-nullity while the white lines indicate the presence of a null value in that column. At a glance, **location_name** appears to be completely populated (we know from the previous step that there is, in fact, only one missing value in this column), while **latitude** and **longitude** seem mostly complete, but spottier.

The spark line on the right summarizes the general shape of the data completeness and points out the rows with the maximum and minimum nullity in the dataset. Note that this is only for the sample of 500 points.

3. Plot the nullity correlation heatmap. We will plot the nullity correlation heatmap using the **missingno** library for our dataset, for only those columns that have missing values:

```
msno.heatmap(data[nullable_columns], figsize=(18,18))
plt.show()
```

The output will be as follows:

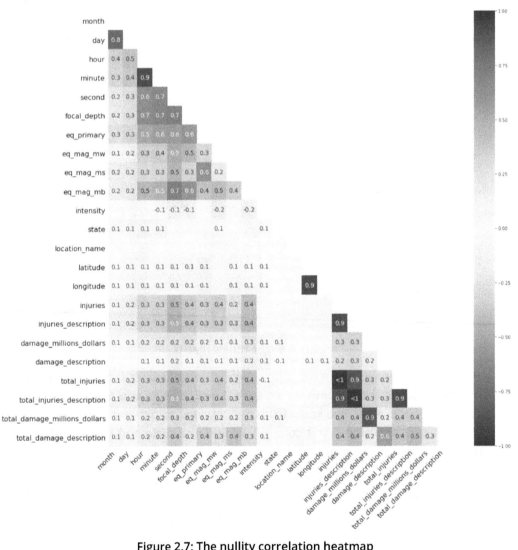

Figure 2.7: The nullity correlation heatmap

Here, we can also see some boxes labeled **<1**: this just means that the correlation values in those cases are all close to 1.0, but still not quite perfectly so. We can see a value of **<1** between `injuries` and `total_injuries`, which means that the missing values in each category are correlated. We would need to dig deeper to understand whether the missing values are correlated because they are based upon the same or similar information, or for some other reason.

> **NOTE**
>
> To access the source code for this specific section, please refer to https://packt.live/2YSXq3k.
>
> You can also run this example online at https://packt.live/2Yn3Us7. You must execute the entire Notebook in order to get the desired result.

IMPUTATION STRATEGIES FOR MISSING VALUES

There are multiple ways of dealing with missing values in a column. The simplest way is to simply delete rows having missing values; however, this can result in the loss of valuable information from other columns. Another option is to impute the data, that is, replace the missing values with a valid value inferred from the known part of the data. The common ways in which this can be done are listed here:

- Create a new value that is distinct from the other values to replace the missing values in the column so as to differentiate those rows altogether. Then, use a non-linear machine learning algorithm (such as ensemble models or support vectors) that can separate the values out.

- Use an appropriate central value from the column (mean, median, or mode) to replace the missing values.

- Use a model (such as a K-nearest neighbors or a Gaussian mixture model) to learn the best value with which to replace the missing values.

Python has a few functions that are useful for replacing null values in a column with a static value. One way to do this is to use the inherent pandas `.fillna(0)` function: there is no ambiguity in imputation here—the static value with which to substitute the null data point in the column is the argument being passed to the function (the value in the brackets).

However, if the number of null values in a column is significant and it's not immediately obvious what the appropriate central value is that can be used to replace each null value, then we can either delete the rows having null values or delete the column altogether from the modeling perspective, as it may not add any significant value. This can be done by using the `.dropna()` function on the DataFrame. The parameters that can be passed to the function are as follows:

- **axis**: This defines whether to drop rows or columns, which is determined by assigning the parameter a value of **0** or **1**, respectively.

- **how**: A value of **all** or **any** can be assigned to this parameter to indicate whether the row/column should contain all null values to drop the column, or whether to drop the column if there is at least one null value.

- **thresh**: This defines the minimum number of null values the row/column should have in order to be dropped.

Additionally, if an appropriate replacement for a null value for a categorical feature cannot be determined, a possible alternative to deleting the column is to create a new category in the feature that can represent the null values.

> **NOTE**
>
> If it is immediately obvious how a null value for a column can be replaced from an intuitive understanding or domain knowledge, then we can replace the value on the spot. Keep in mind that any such data changes should be made in your code and never directly on the raw data. One reason for this is that it allows the strategy to be updated easily in the future. Another reason is that it makes it visible to others who may later be reviewing the work where changes were made. Directly changing raw data can lead to data versioning problems and make it impossible for others to reproduce your work. In many cases, inferences become more obvious at later stages in the exploration process. In these cases, we can substitute null values as and when we find an appropriate way to do so.

EXERCISE 2.03: PERFORMING IMPUTATION USING PANDAS

Let's look at missing values and replace them with zeros in time-based (continuous) features having at least one null value (month, day, hour, minute, and second). We do this because, for cases where we do not have recorded values, it would be safe to assume that the events take place at the beginning of the time duration. This exercise is a continuation of *Exercise 2.02: Visualizing Missing Values*:

1. Create a list containing the names of the columns whose values we want to impute:

```
time_features = ['month', 'day', 'hour', 'minute', 'second']
```

2. Impute the null values using `.fillna()`. We will replace the missing values in these columns with **0** using the inherent pandas `.fillna()` function and pass **0** as an argument to the function:

```
data[time_features] = data[time_features].fillna(0)
```

3. Use the `.info()` function to view null value counts for the imputed columns:

```
data[time_features].info()
```

The output will be as follows:

```
<class 'pandas.core.frame.DataFrame'>
RangeIndex: 6072 entries, 0 to 6071
Data columns (total 5 columns):
month     6072 non-null float64
day       6072 non-null float64
hour      6072 non-null float64
minute    6072 non-null float64
second    6072 non-null float64
dtypes: float64(5)
memory usage: 237.3 KB
```

Figure 2.8: Null value counts

As we can now see, all values for our features in the DataFrame are now non-null.

> **NOTE**
>
> To access the source code for this specific section, please refer to
> https://packt.live/2V9nMx3.
>
> You can also run this example online at https://packt.live/2BqoZZM.
> You must execute the entire Notebook in order to get the desired result.

EXERCISE 2.04: PERFORMING IMPUTATION USING SCIKIT-LEARN

In this exercise, you will replace the null values in the description-related categorical features using scikit-learn's **SimpleImputer** class. In *Exercise 2.02: Visualizing Missing Values*, we saw that almost all of these features comprised more than 50% of null values in the data. Replacing these null values with a central value might bias any model we try to build using the features, deeming them irrelevant. Let's instead replace the null values with a separate category, having the value **NA**. This exercise is a continuation of *Exercise 2.02: Visualizing Missing Values*:

1. Create a list containing the names of the columns whose values we want to impute:

```
description_features = ['injuries_description', \
                        'damage_description', \
                        'total_injuries_description', \
                        'total_damage_description']
```

2. Create an object of the **SimpleImputer** class. Here, we first create an **imp** object of the **SimpleImputer** class and initialize it with parameters that represent how we want to impute the data. The parameters we will pass to initialize the object are as follows:

   missing_values: This is the placeholder for the missing values, that is, all occurrences of the values in the **missing_values** parameter will be imputed.

   strategy: This is the imputation strategy, which can be one of **mean**, **median**, **most_frequent** (that is, the mode), or **constant**. While the first three can only be used with numeric data and will replace missing values using the specified central value along each column, the last one will replace missing values with a constant as per the **fill_value** parameter.

fill_value: This specifies the value with which to replace all occurrences of **missing_values**. If left to the default, the imputed value will be **0** when imputing numerical data and the **missing_value** string for strings or object data types:

```
imp = SimpleImputer(missing_values=np.nan, \
                    strategy='constant', \
                    fill_value='NA')
```

3. Perform the imputation. We will use **imp.fit_transform()** to actually perform the imputation. It takes the DataFrame with null values as input and returns the imputed DataFrame:

```
data[description_features] = \
imp.fit_transform(data[description_features])
```

4. Use the **.info()** function to view null value counts for the imputed columns:

```
data[description_features].info()
```

The output will be as follows:

```
<class 'pandas.core.frame.DataFrame'>
RangeIndex: 6072 entries, 0 to 6071
Data columns (total 4 columns):
injuries_description          6072 non-null object
damage_description            6072 non-null object
total_injuries_description    6072 non-null object
total_damage_description      6072 non-null object
dtypes: object(4)
memory usage: 189.9+ KB
```

Figure 2.9: The null value counts

NOTE

To access the source code for this specific section, please refer to https://packt.live/3ervLgk.

You can also run this example online at https://packt.live/3doEX3G.
You must execute the entire Notebook in order to get the desired result.

In the last two exercises, we looked at two ways to use pandas and scikit-learn methods to impute missing values. These methods are very basic methods we can use if we have little or no information about the underlying data. Next, we'll look at more advanced techniques we can use to fill in missing data.

EXERCISE 2.05: PERFORMING IMPUTATION USING INFERRED VALUES

Let's replace the null values in the continuous **damage_millions_dollars** feature with information from the categorical **damage_description** feature. Although we may not know the exact dollar amount that was incurred, the categorical feature gives us information on the range of the amount that was incurred due to damage from the earthquake. This exercise is a continuation of *Exercise 2.04: Performing Imputation Using scikit-learn*:

1. Find how many rows have null **damage_millions_dollars** values, and how many of those have non-null **damage_description** values:

```
print(data[pd.isnull(data.damage_millions_dollars)].shape[0])
print(data[pd.isnull(data.damage_millions_dollars) \
        & (data.damage_description != 'NA')].shape[0])
```

The output will be as follows:

```
5594
3849
```

As we can see, 3,849 of 5,594 null values can be easily substituted with the help of another variable. For example, we know that all variables having column names ending with **_description** are a descriptor field containing estimates for data that may not be available in the original numerical column. For **deaths**, **injuries**, and **total_injuries**, the corresponding categorical values represent the following:

0 = None

1 = Few (~1 to 50 deaths)

2 = Some (~51 to 100 deaths)

3 = Many (~101 to 1,000 deaths)

4 = Very Many (~1,001 or more deaths)

As regards **damage_millions_dollars**, the corresponding categorical values represent the following:

0 = None

1 = Limited (roughly corresponding to less than 1 million dollars)

2 = Moderate (~1 to 5 million dollars)

3 = Severe (~>5 to 24 million dollars)

4 = Extreme (~25 million dollars or more)

2. Find the mean **damage_millions_dollars** value for each category. Since each of the categories in **damage_description** represents a range of values, we find the mean **damage_millions_dollars** value for each category from the non-null values already available. These provide a reasonable estimate for the most likely value for that category:

```
category_means = data[['damage_description', \
                       'damage_millions_dollars']]\
                 .groupby('damage_description').mean()
category_means
```

The output will be as follows:

damage_description	damage_millions_dollars
1	0.417211
2	3.078840
3	13.818806
4	3574.998799
NA	NaN

Figure 2.10: The mean damage_millions_dollars value for each category

Note that the first three values make intuitive sense given the preceding definitions: 0.42 is between 0 and 1, 3.1 is between 1 and 5, and 13.8 is between 5 and 24. The last category is defined as 25 million or more; it transpires that the mean of these extreme cases is very high (3,575!).

3. Store the mean values as a dictionary. In this step, we will convert the DataFrame containing the mean values to a dictionary (a Python **dict** object), so that accessing them is convenient.

Additionally, since the value for the newly created **NA** category (the imputed value in the previous exercise) was **NaN**, and the value for the **0** category was absent (no rows had **damage_description** equal to **0** in the dataset), we explicitly added these values to the dictionary as well:

```
replacement_values = category_means\
                    .damage_millions_dollars.to_dict()
replacement_values['NA'] = -1
replacement_values['0'] = 0
replacement_values
```

The output will be as follows:

```
{'1': 0.4172105263157895,
 '2': 3.0788402777777772,
 '3': 13.818805970149256,
 '4': 3574.9987991266385,
 'NA': -1,
 '0': 0}
```

Figure 2.11: The dictionary of mean values

4. Create a series of replacement values. For each value in the **damage_description** column, we map the categorical value onto the mean value using the **map** function. The **.map()** function is used to map the keys in the column to the corresponding values for each element from the **replacement_values** dictionary:

```
imputed_values = data.damage_description.map(replacement_values)
```

5. Replace null values in the column. We do this by using **np.where** as a ternary operator: the first argument is the mask, the second is the series from which to take the value if the mask is positive, and the third is the series from which to take the value if the mask is negative.

This ensures that the array returned by **np.where** only replaces the null values in **damage_millions_dollars** with values from the **imputed_values** series:

```
data['damage_millions_dollars'] = \
np.where(data.damage_millions_dollars.isnull(), \
data.damage_description.map(replacement_values), \
data.damage_millions_dollars)
```

6. Use the **.info()** function to view null value counts for the imputed columns:

```
data[['damage_millions_dollars']].info()
```

The output will be as follows:

```
<class 'pandas.core.frame.DataFrame'>
RangeIndex: 6072 entries, 0 to 6071
Data columns (total 1 columns):
damage_millions_dollars    6072 non-null float64
dtypes: float64(1)
memory usage: 47.6 KB
```

Figure 2.12: The null value counts

We can see that, after replacement, there are no null values in the **damage_millions_dollars** column.

> **NOTE**
>
> To access the source code for this specific section, please refer to https://packt.live/3fMRqQo.
>
> You can also run this example online at https://packt.live/2YkBgYC. You must execute the entire Notebook in order to get the desired result.

In this section, we have looked at replacing missing values in more than one way. In one case, we replaced values with zeros; in another case, we looked at more information about the dataset to reason that we could replace missing values with a combination of information from a descriptive field and the means of values we did have. These sorts of decisions and steps are extremely common when working with real data. We also noted that, occasionally, when we have sufficient data and the instances with missing values are few, we can just drop them. In the following activity, we'll use a different dataset for you to practice and reinforce these methods.

ACTIVITY 2.01: SUMMARY STATISTICS AND MISSING VALUES

In this activity, we'll revise some of the summary statistics and missing value exploration we have looked at thus far in this chapter. We will be using a new dataset, *House Prices: Advanced Regression Techniques*, available on Kaggle.

> **NOTE**
>
> The original dataset is available at https://www.kaggle.com/c/house-prices-advanced-regression-techniques/data or on our GitHub repository at https://packt.live/2TjU9aj.

While the Earthquakes dataset used in the exercises is aimed at solving a classification problem (when the target variable has only discrete values), the dataset we will use in the activities will be aimed at solving a regression problem (when the target variable takes on a range of continuous values). We will use **pandas** functions to generate summary statistics and visualize missing values using a nullity matrix and nullity correlation heatmap.

The steps to be performed are as follows:

1. Read the data (**house_prices.csv**).

2. Use pandas' **.info()** and **.describe()** methods to view the summary statistics of the dataset.

The output of the **info()** method will be as follows:

```
<class 'pandas.core.frame.DataFrame'>
RangeIndex: 1460 entries, 0 to 1459
Data columns (total 81 columns):
Id              1460 non-null int64
MSSubClass      1460 non-null int64
MSZoning        1460 non-null object
LotFrontage     1201 non-null float64
LotArea         1460 non-null int64
Street          1460 non-null object
Alley           91 non-null object
LotShape        1460 non-null object
LandContour     1460 non-null object
Utilities       1460 non-null object
LotConfig       1460 non-null object
LandSlope       1460 non-null object
Neighborhood    1460 non-null object
Condition1      1460 non-null object
Condition2      1460 non-null object
```

Figure 2.13: The output of the info() method (abbreviated)

The output of the **describe()** method will be as follows:

	count	mean	std	min	25%	50%	75%	max
Id	1460.0	730.500000	421.610009	1.0	365.75	730.5	1095.25	1460.0
MSSubClass	1460.0	56.897260	42.300571	20.0	20.00	50.0	70.00	190.0
LotFrontage	1201.0	70.049958	24.284752	21.0	59.00	69.0	80.00	313.0
LotArea	1460.0	10516.828082	9981.264932	1300.0	7553.50	9478.5	11601.50	215245.0
OverallQual	1460.0	6.099315	1.382997	1.0	5.00	6.0	7.00	10.0
OverallCond	1460.0	5.575342	1.112799	1.0	5.00	5.0	6.00	9.0
YearBuilt	1460.0	1971.267808	30.202904	1872.0	1954.00	1973.0	2000.00	2010.0
YearRemodAdd	1460.0	1984.865753	20.645407	1950.0	1967.00	1994.0	2004.00	2010.0
MasVnrArea	1452.0	103.685262	181.066207	0.0	0.00	0.0	166.00	1600.0
BsmtFinSF1	1460.0	443.639726	456.098091	0.0	0.00	383.5	712.25	5644.0
BsmtFinSF2	1460.0	46.549315	161.319273	0.0	0.00	0.0	0.00	1474.0
BsmtUnfSF	1460.0	567.240411	441.866955	0.0	223.00	477.5	808.00	2336.0
TotalBsmtSF	1460.0	1057.429452	438.705324	0.0	795.75	991.5	1298.25	6110.0
1stFlrSF	1460.0	1162.626712	386.587738	334.0	882.00	1087.0	1391.25	4692.0
2ndFlrSF	1460.0	346.992466	436.528436	0.0	0.00	0.0	728.00	2065.0

Figure 2.14: The output of the describe() method (abbreviated)

NOTE

The outputs of the `info()` and `describe()` methods have been truncated for presentation purposes. You can find the outputs in their entirety here: https://packt.live/2TjZSgi

3. Find the total count and total percentage of missing values in each column of the DataFrame and display them for columns having at least one null value, in descending order of missing percentages.

4. Plot the nullity matrix and nullity correlation heatmap.

The nullity matrix will be as follows:

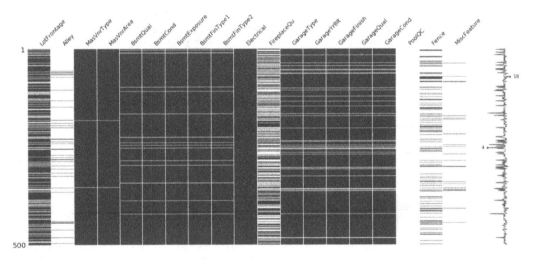

Figure 2.15: Nullity matrix

The nullity correlation heatmap will be as follows:

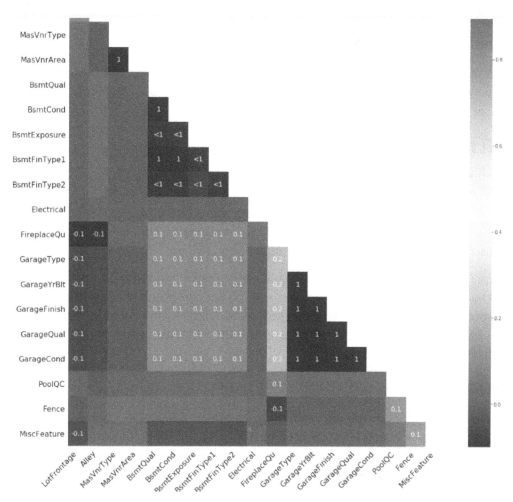

Figure 2.16: Nullity correlation heatmap

5. Delete the columns having more than 80% of their values missing.

6. Replace null values in the **FireplaceQu** column with **NA** values.

> **NOTE**
>
> The solution to this activity can be found on page 406.

You should now be comfortable using the approaches we've learned to investigate missing values in any type of tabular data.

DISTRIBUTION OF VALUES

In this section, we'll look at how individual variables behave—what kind of values they take, what the distribution across those values is, and how those distributions can be represented visually.

TARGET VARIABLE

The target variable can either have values that are continuous (in the case of a regression problem) or discrete (as in the case of a classification problem). The problem statement we're looking at in this chapter involves predicting whether an earthquake caused a tsunami, that is, the **flag_tsunami** variable, which takes on two discrete values only—making it a classification problem.

One way of visualizing how many earthquakes resulted in tsunamis and how many didn't involves the use of a bar chart, where each bar represents a single discrete value of the variable, and the height of the bars is equal to the count of the data points having the corresponding discrete value. This gives us a good comparison of the absolute counts of each category.

EXERCISE 2.06: PLOTTING A BAR CHART

Let's look at how many of the earthquakes in our dataset resulted in a tsunami. We will do this by using the **value_counts()** method over the column and using the **.plot(kind='bar')** function directly on the returned **pandas** series. This exercise is a continuation of *Exercise 2.05: Performing Imputation Using Inferred Values*:

1. Use **plt.figure()** to initiate the plotting:

```
plt.figure(figsize=(8,6))
```

2. Next, type in our primary plotting command:

```
data.flag_tsunami.value_counts().plot(kind='bar', \
                                       color = ('grey', \
                                       'black'))
```

3. Set the display parameters and display the plot:

```
plt.ylabel('Number of data points')
plt.xlabel('flag_tsunami')
plt.show()
```

The output will be as follows:

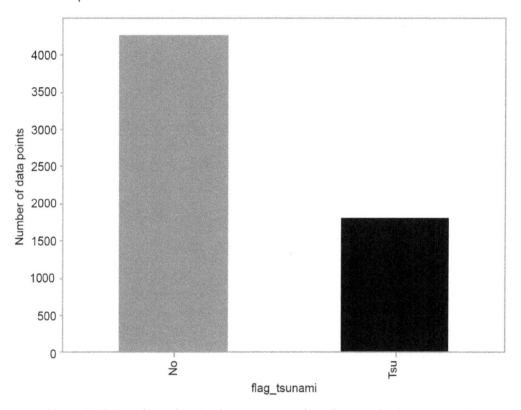

Figure 2.17: Bar chart showing how many earthquakes resulted in a tsunami

From this bar plot, we can see that most of the earthquakes did not result in tsunamis and that fewer than one-third of the earthquakes actually did. This shows us that the dataset is slightly imbalanced.

> **NOTE**
>
> To access the source code for this specific section, please refer to
> https://packt.live/2Yn4UfR.
>
> You can also run this example online at https://packt.live/37QvoJI.
> You must execute the entire Notebook in order to get the desired result.

Let's look more closely at what these Matplotlib commands do:

- `plt.figure(figsize=(8,6))`: This command defines how big our plot should be, by providing width and height values. This is always the first command before any plotting command is written.

- `plt.xlabel()` and `plt.ylabel()`: These commands take a string as input and allow us to specify what the labels for the X and Y axes on the plot should be.

- `plt.show()`: This is the final command that is written when plotting a visualization that displays the plot inline within the Jupyter notebook.

CATEGORICAL DATA

Categorical variables are ones that take discrete values representing different categories or levels of observation that can either be string objects or integer values. For example, our target variable, **flag_tsunami**, is a categorical variable with two categories, **Tsu** and **No**.

Categorical variables can be of two types:

- **Nominal variables**: Variables in which the categories are labeled without any order of precedence are called nominal variables. An example of a nominal variable from our dataset would be **location_name**. The values that this variable takes cannot be said to be ordered, that is, one location is not *greater* than the other. Similarly, more examples of such a variable would be color, types of footwear, ethnicity type, and so on.

- **Ordinal variables**: Variables that have some order associated with them are called ordinal variables. An example from our dataset would be **damage_ description** since each value represents an increasing value of damage incurred. Another example could be days of the week, which would have values from Monday to Sunday, which have some order associated with them and we know that Thursday comes after Wednesday but before Friday.

  Although ordinal variables can be represented by object data types, they are often represented as numerical data types as well, often making it difficult to differentiate between them and continuous variables.

One of the major challenges faced when dealing with categorical variables in a dataset is high cardinality, that is, a large number of categories or distinct values with each value appearing a relatively small number of times. For example, **location_ name** has a large number of unique values, with each value occurring a small number of times in the dataset.

Additionally, non-numerical categorical variables will always require some form of preprocessing to be converted into a numerical format so that they can be ingested for training by a machine learning model. It can be a challenge to encode categorical variables numerically without losing out on contextual information that, despite being easy for humans to interpret (due to domain knowledge or otherwise just plain common sense), would be hard for a computer to automatically understand. For example, a geographical feature such as country or location name by itself would give no indication of the geographical proximity of different values, but that might just be an important feature—what if earthquakes that occur at locations in South East Asia trigger more tsunamis than those that occur in Europe? There would be no way of capturing that information by merely encoding the feature numerically.

EXERCISE 2.07: IDENTIFYING DATA TYPES FOR CATEGORICAL VARIABLES

Let's establish which variables in our Earthquake dataset are categorical and which are continuous. As we now know, categorical variables can also have numerical values, so having a numeric data type doesn't guarantee that a variable is continuous. This exercise is a continuation of *Exercise 2.05: Performing Imputation Using Inferred Values*:

1. Find all the columns that are numerical and object types. We use the `.select_dtypes()` method on the DataFrame to create a subset DataFrame having numeric (`np.number`) and categorical (`np.object`) columns, and then print the column names for each. For numeric columns, use this command:

    ```
    numeric_variables = data.select_dtypes(include=[np.number])
    numeric_variables.columns
    ```

    The output will be as follows:

    ```
    Index(['id', 'year', 'month', 'day', 'hour', 'minute', 'second', 'focal_depth',
           'eq_primary', 'eq_mag_mw', 'eq_mag_ms', 'eq_mag_mb', 'intensity',
           'latitude', 'longitude', 'injuries', 'damage_millions_dollars',
           'total_injuries', 'total_damage_millions_dollars'],
          dtype='object')
    ```

    Figure 2.18: All columns that are numerical

    For categorical columns, use this command:

    ```
    object_variables = data.select_dtypes(include=[np.object])
    object_variables.columns
    ```

The output will be as follows:

```
Index(['flag_tsunami', 'country', 'state', 'location_name', 'region_code',
       'injuries_description', 'damage_description',
       'total_injuries_description', 'total_damage_description'],
      dtype='object')
```

Figure 2.19: All columns that are object types

Here, it is evident that the columns that are object types are categorical variables. To differentiate between the categorical and continuous variables from the numeric columns, let's see how many unique values there are for each of these features.

2. Find the number of unique values for numeric features. We use the **select_dtypes** method on the DataFrame to find the number of unique values in each column and sort the resulting series in ascending order. For numeric columns, use this command:

```
numeric_variables.nunique().sort_values()
```

The output will be as follows:

```
intensity                       11
month                           12
hour                            24
day                             31
eq_mag_mb                       47
eq_mag_mw                       54
eq_mag_ms                       55
minute                          60
eq_primary                      64
focal_depth                    197
total_damage_millions_dollars  233
damage_millions_dollars        248
injuries                       338
total_injuries                 344
second                         575
year                           946
latitude                      2885
longitude                     3654
id                            6072
dtype: int64
```

Figure 2.20: Number of unique values for numeric features

For categorical columns, use this command:

```
object_variables.nunique().sort_values()
```

The output will be as follows:

```
flag_tsunami                    2
injuries_description            5
damage_description              5
total_injuries_description      5
total_damage_description        5
region_code                    18
state                          29
country                       155
location_name                3821
dtype: int64
```

Figure 2.21: Number of unique values for categorical columns

> **NOTE**
>
> To access the source code for this specific section, please refer to
> https://packt.live/2YlSmFt.
>
> You can also run this example online at https://packt.live/31hnuIr.
> You must execute the entire Notebook in order to get the desired result.

For the numeric variables, we can see that the top nine have significantly fewer unique values than the remaining rows, and it's likely that these are categorical variables. However, we must keep in mind that it is possible that some of them might just be continuous variables with a low range of rounded-up values. Also, **month** and **day** would not be considered categorical variables here.

EXERCISE 2.08: CALCULATING CATEGORY VALUE COUNTS

For columns with categorical values, it would be useful to see what the unique values (categories) of the feature are, along with what the frequencies of these categories are, that is, how often does each distinct value occur in the dataset. Let's find the number of occurrences of each **0** to **4** label and **NaN** values for the **injuries_description** categorical variable. This exercise is a continuation of *Exercise 2.07: Identifying Data Types for Categorical Variables*:

1. Use the **value_counts()** function on the **injuries_description** column to find the frequency of each category. Using **value_counts** gives us the frequencies of each value in decreasing order in the form of a pandas series:

```
counts = data.injuries_description.value_counts(dropna=False)
counts
```

The output should be as follows:

```
NA      4723
1        666
3        347
2        193
4        143
Name: injuries_description, dtype: int64
```

Figure 2.22: Frequency of each category

2. Sort the values in increasing order of the ordinal variable. If we want the frequencies in the order of the values themselves, we can reset the index to give us a DataFrame and sort values by the index (that is, the ordinal variable):

```
counts.reset_index().sort_values(by='index')
```

The output will be as follows:

	index	injuries_description
1	1	666
3	2	193
2	3	347
4	4	143
0	NA	4723

Figure 2.23: Sorted values

> **NOTE**
>
> To access the source code for this specific section, please refer to
> https://packt.live/2Yn5URj.
>
> You can also run this example online at https://packt.live/314dYlr.
> You must execute the entire Notebook in order to get the desired result.

EXERCISE 2.09: PLOTTING A PIE CHART

Since our target variable in our sample data is categorical, the example in *Exercise 2.06: Plotting a Bar Chart*, showed us one way of visualizing how the categorical values are distributed (using a bar chart). Another plot that can make it easy to see how each category functions as a fraction of the overall dataset is a pie chart. Let's plot a pie chart to visualize the distribution of the discrete values of the **damage_description** variable. This exercise is a continuation of *Exercise 2.08, Calculating Category Value Counts*:

1. Format the data into the form that needs to be plotted. Here, we run **value_counts()** over the column and sort the series by index:

```
counts = data.damage_description.value_counts()
counts = counts.sort_index()
```

2. Plot the pie chart. The **plt.pie()** category plots the pie chart using the count data. We will use the same three steps for plotting as described in *Exercise 2.06: Plotting a Bar Chart*:

```
fig, ax = plt.subplots(figsize=(10,10))
slices = ax.pie(counts, \
                labels=counts.index, \
                colors = ['white'], \
                wedgeprops = {'edgecolor': 'black'})
patches = slices[0]
hatches =  ['/', '\\', '|', '-', '+', 'x', 'o', 'O', '\.', '*']
for patch in range(len(patches)):
    patches[patch].set_hatch(hatches[patch])
plt.title('Pie chart showing counts for\ndamage_description '\
          'categories')
plt.show()
```

The output will be as follows:

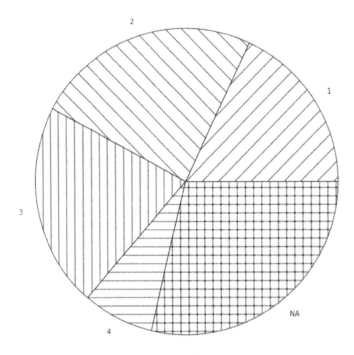

Pie chart showing counts for
damage_description categories

Figure 2.24: Pie chart showing counts for damage_description categories

> **NOTE**
>
> To access the source code for this specific section, please refer to
> https://packt.live/37Ovj9s.
>
> You can also run this example online at https://packt.live/37OvotM.
> You must execute the entire Notebook in order to get the desired result.

Figure 2.24 tells us the relative number of items in each of the five damage description categories. Note that it would be good practice to do the extra work to change the uninformative labels to the categories—recall from the EDA discussion that:

  0 = NONE

  1 = LIMITED (roughly corresponding to less than $1 million)

  2 = MODERATE (~$1 to $5 million)

  3 = SEVERE (~>$5 to $24 million)

  4 = EXTREME (~$25 million or more)

In addition, while the pie chart gives us a quick visual impression of which are the largest and smallest categories, we get no idea of the actual quantities, so adding those labels would increase the value of the chart. You can use the code in the repository for this book to update the chart.

CONTINUOUS DATA

Continuous variables can take any number of values and are usually integer (for example, number of deaths) or float data types (for example, the height of a mountain). It's useful to get an idea of the basic statistics of the values in the feature: the minimum, maximum, and percentile values we see from the output of the `describe()` function gives us a fair estimate of this.

However, for continuous variables, it is also very useful to see how the values are distributed in the range they operate in. Since we cannot simply find the counts of individual values, instead, we order the values in ascending order, group them into evenly-sized intervals, and find the counts for each interval. This gives us the underlying frequency distribution and plotting this gives us a histogram, which allows us to examine the shape, central values, and amount of variability in the data.

Histograms give us an easy view of the data that we're looking at. They tell us about the behavior of the values at a glance in terms of the underlying distribution (for example, a normal or exponential distribution), the presence of outliers, skewness, and more.

> **NOTE**
>
> It is easy to get confused between a bar chart and a histogram. The major difference is that a histogram is used to plot continuous data that has been binned to visualize the frequency distribution, while bar charts can be used for a variety of other use cases, including to represent categorical variables as we have done. Additionally, with histograms, the number of bins is something we can vary, so the range of values in a bin is determined by the number of bins, as is the height of the bars in the histogram. In a bar chart, the width of the bars does not generally convey meaning, and the height is usually a property of the category, like a count.

One of the most common frequency distributions is a **Gaussian** (or normal) distribution. This is a symmetric distribution that has a bell-shaped curve, which indicates that the values near the middle of the range have the highest occurrences in the dataset with a symmetrically decreasing frequency of occurrences as we move away from the middle. You almost certainly have seen examples of Gaussian distributions, because many natural and man-made processes generate values that vary nearly like the Gaussian distribution. Thus, it is extremely common to see data compared to the Gaussian distribution.

It is a probability distribution and the area under the curve equals one, as shown in *Figure 2.25*:

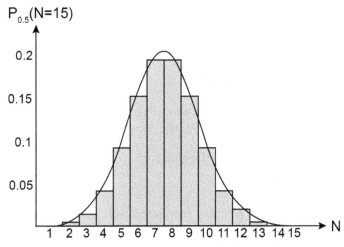

Figure 2.25: Gaussian (normal) distribution

A symmetric distribution like normal distribution can be characterized entirely by two parameters—the mean (μ) and the standard deviation (σ). In *Figure 2.25*, the mean is at 7.5, for example. However, there are significant amounts of real data that do not follow a normal distribution and may be asymmetric. The asymmetry of data is often referred to as a skew.

SKEWNESS

A distribution is said to be skewed if it is not symmetric in nature, and skewness measures the asymmetry of a variable about its mean. The value can be positive or negative (or undefined). In the former case, the tail is on the right-hand side of the distribution, while the latter indicates that the tail is on the left-hand side.

However, it must be noted that a thick and short tail would have the same effect on the value of skewness as a long, thin tail.

KURTOSIS

Kurtosis is a measure of the *tailedness* of the distribution of a variable and is used to measure the presence of outliers in one tail versus the other. A high value of kurtosis indicates a fatter tail and the presence of outliers. In a similar way to the concept of skewness, kurtosis also describes the shape of the distribution.

EXERCISE 2.10: PLOTTING A HISTOGRAM

Let's plot the histogram for the **eq_primary** feature using the Seaborn library. This exercise is a continuation of *Exercise 2.09, Plotting a Pie Chart*:

1. Use **plt.figure()** to initiate the plotting:

```
plt.figure(figsize=(10,7))
```

2. **sns.distplot()** is the primary command that we will use to plot the histogram. The first parameter is the one-dimensional data over which to plot the histogram, while the **bins** parameter defines the number and size of the bins. Use this as follows:

```
sns.distplot(data.eq_primary.dropna(), \
            bins=np.linspace(0,10,21))
```

3. Display the plot using **plt.show()**:

```
plt.show()
```

The output will be as follows:

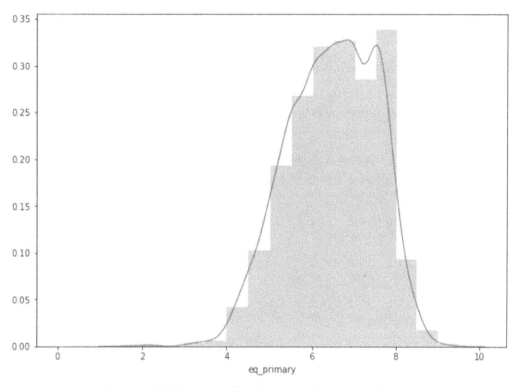

Figure 2.26: Histogram for the example primary feature

The plot gives us a normed (or normalized) histogram, which means that the area under the bars of the histogram equals unity. Additionally, the line over the histogram is the **kernel density estimate**, which gives us an idea of what the probability distribution for the variable would look like.

> **NOTE**
>
> To access the source code for this specific section, please refer to https://packt.live/2BwZrdj.
>
> You can also run this example online at https://packt.live/3fMSxj2.
> You must execute the entire Notebook in order to get the desired result.

From the plot, we can see that the values of **eq_primary** lie mostly between 5 and 8, which means that most earthquakes had a magnitude with a moderate to high value, with barely any earthquakes having a low or very high magnitude.

EXERCISE 2.11: COMPUTING SKEW AND KURTOSIS

Let's calculate the skew and kurtosis values for all of the features in the dataset using the core pandas functions available to us. This exercise is a continuation of *Exercise 2.10, Plotting a Histogram*:

1. Use the `.skew()` DataFrame method to calculate the skew for all features and then sort the values in ascending order:

```
data.skew().sort_values()
```

The output will be as follows:

```
year                             -3.859655
latitude                         -1.038393
region_code                      -0.539048
longitude                        -0.457442
intensity                        -0.442065
eq_primary                       -0.295823
eq_mag_ms                        -0.243581
eq_mag_mb                        -0.058037
day                              -0.008719
month                            -0.006291
second                            0.016618
hour                              0.033799
minute                            0.040519
eq_mag_mw                         0.154842
id                                0.300563
focal_depth                       5.866408
total_damage_millions_dollars    13.227907
total_injuries                   22.191856
injuries                         24.428284
damage_millions_dollars          47.532464
dtype: float64
```

Figure 2.27: Skew values for all the features in the dataset

2. Use the `.kurt()` DataFrame method to calculate the kurtosis for all features:

```
data.kurt()
```

The output will be as follows:

```
id                             -0.866617
year                           19.532730
month                          -1.211339
day                            -1.172021
hour                           -1.225769
minute                         -1.154498
second                         -1.196864
focal_depth                    40.911649
eq_primary                     -0.327067
eq_mag_mw                      -0.593857
eq_mag_ms                      -0.486214
eq_mag_mb                       0.432798
intensity                       0.072622
latitude                        0.384692
longitude                      -0.777352
region_code                    -1.324200
injuries                      672.946635
damage_millions_dollars      2725.970362
total_injuries                569.624067
total_damage_millions_dollars 202.895621
dtype: float64
```

Figure 2.28: Kurtosis values for all the features in the dataset

Here, we can see that the kurtosis values for some variables deviate significantly from 0. This means that these columns have a long tail. But the values that are at the tail end of these variables (which indicate the number of people dead, injured, and the monetary value of damage), in our case, may be outliers that we may need to pay special attention to. Larger values might, in fact, indicate an additional force that added to the devastation caused by an earthquake, that is, a tsunami.

> **NOTE**
>
> To access the source code for this specific section, please refer to https://packt.live/2Yklmh0.
>
> You can also run this example online at https://packt.live/37PcMdj.
> You must execute the entire Notebook in order to get the desired result.

ACTIVITY 2.02: REPRESENTING THE DISTRIBUTION OF VALUES VISUALLY

In this activity, we will implement what we learned in the previous section by creating different plots such as histograms and pie charts. Furthermore, we will calculate the skew and kurtosis for the features of the dataset. Here, will use the same dataset we used in *Activity 2.01: Summary Statistics and Missing Values*, that is, *House Prices: Advanced Regression Techniques*. We'll use different types of plots to visually represent the distribution of values for this dataset. This activity is a continuation of *Activity 2.01: Summary Statistics and Missing Values*:

The steps to be performed are as follows:

1. Plot a histogram using Matplotlib for the target variable, **SalePrice**.

    The output will be as follows:

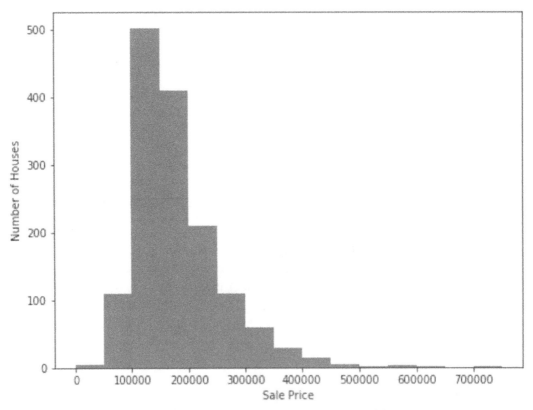

Figure 2.29: Histogram for the target variable

2. Find the number of unique values within each column having an object type.

3. Create a DataFrame representing the number of occurrences for each categorical value in the **HouseStyle** column.

4. Plot a pie chart representing these counts.

   The output will be as follows:

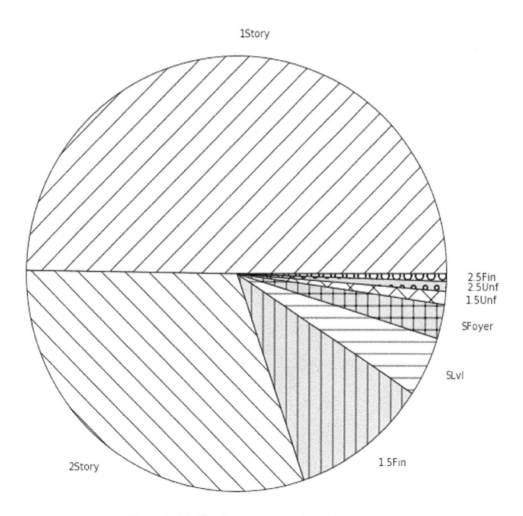

Figure 2.30: Pie chart representing the counts

5. Find the number of unique values within each column having a number type.

6. Plot a histogram using seaborn for the **LotArea** variable.

   The output will be as follows:

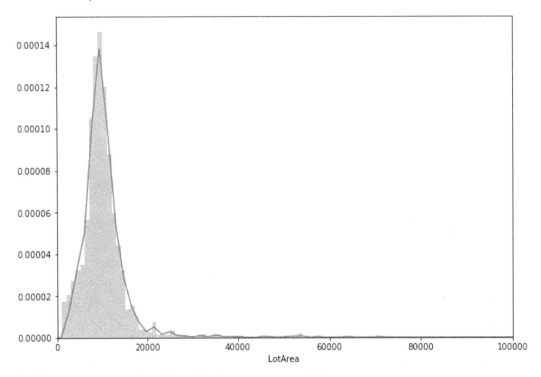

Figure 2.31: Histogram for the LotArea variable

7. Calculate the skew and kurtosis values for the values in each column.

The output for skew values will be:

```
GarageYrBlt        -0.649415
YearBuilt          -0.613461
YearRemodAdd       -0.503562
GarageCars         -0.342549
Id                  0.000000
FullBath            0.036562
YrSold              0.096269
GarageArea          0.179981
BedroomAbvGr        0.211790
MoSold              0.212053
OverallQual         0.216944
BsmtFullBath        0.596067
Fireplaces          0.649565
HalfBath            0.675897
TotRmsAbvGrd        0.676341
OverallCond         0.693067
2ndFlrSF            0.813030
BsmtUnfSF           0.920268
GrLivArea           1.366560
1stFlrSF            1.376757
MSSubClass          1.407657
TotalBsmtSF         1.524255
WoodDeckSF          1.541376
BsmtFinSF1          1.685503
SalePrice           1.882876
LotFrontage         2.163569
OpenPorchSF         2.364342
MasVnrArea          2.669084
EnclosedPorch       3.089872
BsmtHalfBath        4.103403
ScreenPorch         4.122214
BsmtFinSF2          4.255261
KitchenAbvGr        4.488397
LowQualFinSF        9.011341
3SsnPorch          10.304342
LotArea            12.207688
PoolArea           14.828374
MiscVal            24.476794
dtype: float64
```

Figure 2.32: Skew values for each column

The output for kurtosis values will be:

```
Id                   -1.200000
MSSubClass            1.580188
LotFrontage          17.452867
LotArea             203.243271
OverallQual           0.096293
OverallCond           1.106413
YearBuilt            -0.439552
YearRemodAdd         -1.272245
MasVnrArea           10.082417
BsmtFinSF1           11.118236
BsmtFinSF2           20.113338
BsmtUnfSF             0.474994
TotalBsmtSF          13.250483
1stFlrSF              5.745841
2ndFlrSF             -0.553464
LowQualFinSF         83.234817
GrLivArea             4.895121
BsmtFullBath         -0.839098
BsmtHalfBath         16.396642
FullBath             -0.857043
HalfBath             -1.076927
BedroomAbvGr          2.230875
KitchenAbvGr         21.532404
TotRmsAbvGrd          0.880762
Fireplaces           -0.217237
GarageYrBlt          -0.418341
GarageCars            0.220998
GarageArea            0.917067
WoodDeckSF            2.992951
OpenPorchSF           8.490336
EnclosedPorch        10.430766
3SsnPorch           123.662379
ScreenPorch          18.439068
PoolArea            223.268499
MiscVal             701.003342
MoSold               -0.404109
YrSold               -1.190601
SalePrice             6.536282
dtype: float64
```

Figure 2.33: Kurtosis values for each column

NOTE

The solution to this activity can be found on page 412.

We have seen how to look into the nature of data in more detail, in particular, by beginning to understand the distribution of the data using histograms or density plots, relative counts of data using pie charts, as well as inspecting the skew and kurtosis of the variables as a first step to finding potentially problematic data, outliers, and so on.

By now, you should have a comfort level handling various statistical measures of data such as summary statistics, counts, and the distribution of values. Using tools such as histograms and density plots, you can explore the shape of datasets, and augment that understanding by calculating statistics such as skew and kurtosis. You should be developing some intuition for some flags that warrant further investigation, such as large skew or kurtosis values.

RELATIONSHIPS WITHIN THE DATA

There are two reasons why it is important to find relationships between variables in the data:

- Establishing which features are potentially important can be deemed essential, since finding ones that have a strong relationship with the target variable will aid in the feature selection process.

- Finding relationships between different features themselves can be useful since variables in the dataset are usually never completely independent of every other variable and this can affect our modeling in a number of ways.

Now, there are a number of ways in which we can visualize these relationships, and this really depends on the types of variable we are trying to find the relationship between, and how many we are considering as part of the equation or comparison.

RELATIONSHIP BETWEEN TWO CONTINUOUS VARIABLES

Establishing a relationship between two continuous variables is basically seeing how one varies as the value of the other is increased. The most common way to visualize this would be to use a scatter plot, in which we take each variable along a single axis (the X and Y axes in a two-dimensional plane when we have two variables) and plot each data point using a marker in the X-Y plane. This visualization gives us a good idea of whether any kind of relationship exists between the two variables at all.

If we want to quantize the relationship between the two variables, however, the most common method is to find the correlation between them. If the target variable is continuous and it has a high degree of correlation with another variable, this is an indication that the feature would be an important part of the model.

PEARSON'S COEFFICIENT OF CORRELATION

Pearson's Coefficient of Correlation is a correlation coefficient that is commonly used to show the linear relationship between a pair of variables. The formula returns a value between -1 and +1, where:

- +1 indicates a strong positive relationship

- -1 indicates a strong negative relationship

- 0 indicates no relationship at all

It's also useful to find correlations between pairs of features themselves. In some models, highly correlated features can cause issues, including coefficients that vary strongly with small changes in data or modal parameters. In the extreme case, perfectly correlated features (such as $X2 = 2.5 * X1$) cause some models, including linear regression, to return undefined coefficients (values of **Inf**).

> ### NOTE
>
> When fitting a linear model, having features that are highly correlated to one another can result in an unpredictable and widely varying model. This is because the coefficients of each feature in a linear model can be interpreted as the unit change in the target variable, keeping all other features constant. When a set of features is not independent (that is, are correlated), however, we cannot determine the effect of the independent changes on the target variable due to each feature, resulting in widely varying coefficients.

To find the pairwise correlation for every numeric feature in a DataFrame with every other feature, we can use the `.corr()` function on the DataFrame.

EXERCISE 2.12: PLOTTING A SCATTER PLOT

Let's plot a scatter plot between the primary earthquake magnitude on the *X* axis and the corresponding number of injuries on the *Y* axis. This exercise is a continuation of *Exercise 2.11, Computing Skew and Kurtosis*:

1. Filter out the null values. Since we know that there are null values in both columns, let's first filter the data to include only the non-null rows:

```
data_to_plot = data[~pd.isnull(data.injuries) \
                & ~pd.isnull(data.eq_primary)]
```

2. Create and display the scatter plot. We will use Matplotlib's **plt. scatter(x=..., y=...)** command as the primary command for plotting the data. The **x** and **y** parameters state which feature is to be considered along which axis. They take a single-dimensional data structure such as a list, a tuple, or a pandas series. We can also send the **scatter** function more parameters that define, say, the icon to use to plot an individual data point. For example, to use a red cross as the icon, we would need to send the parameters **marker='x', c='r'**:

```
plt.figure(figsize=(12,9))
plt.scatter(x=data_to_plot.eq_primary, y=data_to_plot.injuries)
plt.xlabel('Primary earthquake magnitude')
plt.ylabel('No. of injuries')
plt.show()
```

The output will be as follows:

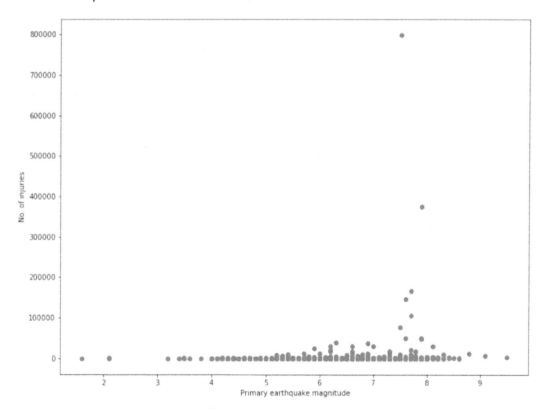

Figure 2.34: Scatter plot

From the plot, we can infer that although there doesn't appear to be a trend between the number of people who were injured and the earthquake magnitude, there is an increasing number of earthquakes with large injury counts as the magnitude increases. However, for the majority of earthquakes, there does not seem to be a relationship.

> **NOTE**
>
> To access the source code for this specific section, please refer to https://packt.live/314eupR.
>
> You can also run this example online at https://packt.live/2YWtbsm. You must execute the entire Notebook in order to get the desired result.

EXERCISE 2.13: PLOTTING A CORRELATION HEATMAP

Let's plot a correlation heatmap between all the numeric variables in our dataset using seaborn's **sns.heatmap()** function on the inter-feature correlation values in the dataset. This exercise is a continuation of *Exercise 2.12, Plotting a Scatter Plot*.

The optional parameters passed to the **sns.heatmap()** function are **square** and **cmap**, which indicate that the plot should be such that each pixel is square and specify which color scheme to use, respectively:

1. Plot a basic heatmap with all the features:

```
plt.figure(figsize = (12,10))
sns.heatmap(data.corr(), square=True, cmap="YlGnBu")
plt.show()
```

The output will be as follows:

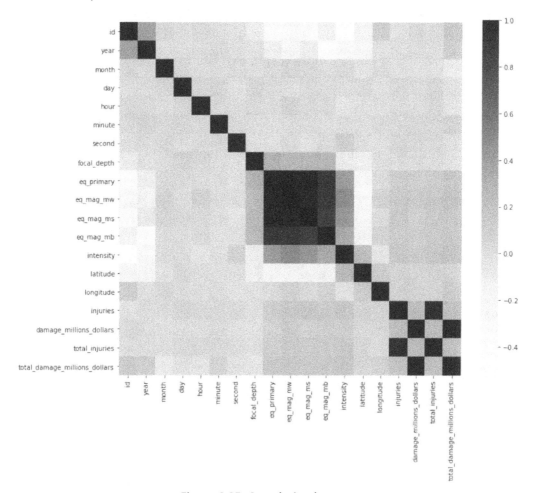

Figure 2.35: Correlation heatmap

We can see from the color bar on the right of the plot that the minimum value, around **-0.2**, is the lightest shade, which is a misrepresentation of the correlation values, which vary from **-1** to **1**.

2. Plot a subset of features in a more customized heatmap. We will specify the upper and lower limits using the **vmin** and **vmax** parameters and plot the heatmap again with annotations specifying the pairwise correlation values on a subset of features. We will also change the color scheme to one that can be better interpreted—while the neutral white will represent no correlation, increasingly darker shades of blue and red will represent higher positive and negative correlation values, respectively:

```
feature_subset = ['focal_depth', 'eq_primary', 'eq_mag_mw', \
                  'eq_mag_ms', 'eq_mag_mb', 'intensity', \
                  'latitude', 'longitude', 'injuries', \
                  'damage_millions_dollars','total_injuries', \
                  'total_damage_millions_dollars']


plt.figure(figsize = (12,10))
sns.heatmap(data[feature_subset].corr(), square=True, \
            annot=True, cmap="RdBu", vmin=-1, vmax=1)
plt.show()
```

The output will be as follows:

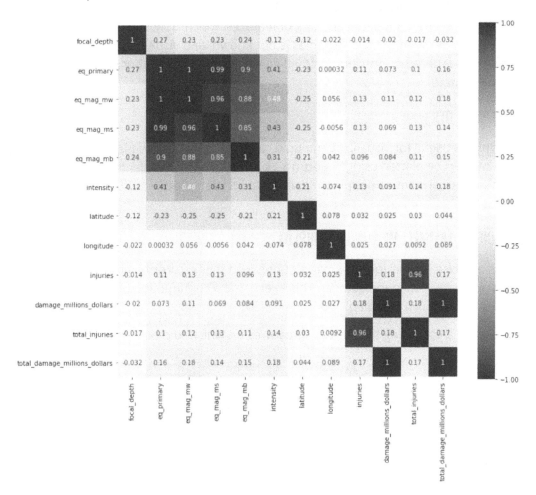

Figure 2.36: Customized correlation heatmap

NOTE

To access the source code for this specific section, please refer to https://packt.live/2Z1IPUB.

You can also run this example online at https://packt.live/2YntBc8.
You must execute the entire Notebook in order to get the desired result.

Now, while we can calculate the value of correlation, this only gives us an indication of a linear relationship. To better judge whether there's a possible dependency, we could plot a scatter plot between pairs of features, which is mostly useful when the relationship between the two variables is not known, and visualizing how the data points are scattered or distributed could give us an idea of whether (and how) the two may be related.

USING PAIRPLOTS

A pairplot is useful for visualizing multiple relationships between pairs of features at once and can be plotted using Seaborn's `.pairplot()` function. In the following exercise, we will create a pairplot and visualize relations between the features in a dataset.

EXERCISE 2.14: IMPLEMENTING A PAIRPLOT

In this exercise, we will look at a pairplot between the features having the highest pairwise correlation in the dataset. This exercise is a continuation of *Exercise 2.13, Plotting a Correlation Heatmap*:

1. Define a list having the subset of features on which to create the pairplot:

    ```
    feature_subset = ['focal_depth', 'eq_primary', 'eq_mag_mw', \
                      'eq_mag_ms', 'eq_mag_mb', 'intensity',]
    ```

2. Create the pairplot using seaborn. The arguments sent to the plotting function are **kind='scatter'**, which indicates that we want each individual plot between the pair of variables in the grid to be represented as a scatter plot, and **diag_kind='kde'**, which indicates that we want the plots along the diagonal (where both the features in the pair are the same) to be a kernel density estimate.

    It should also be noted here that the plots symmetrically across the diagonal from one another will essentially be the same, just with the axes reversed:

    ```
    sns.pairplot(data[feature_subset].dropna(), kind ='scatter', \
                 diag_kind='kde')
    plt.show()
    ```

The output will be as follows:

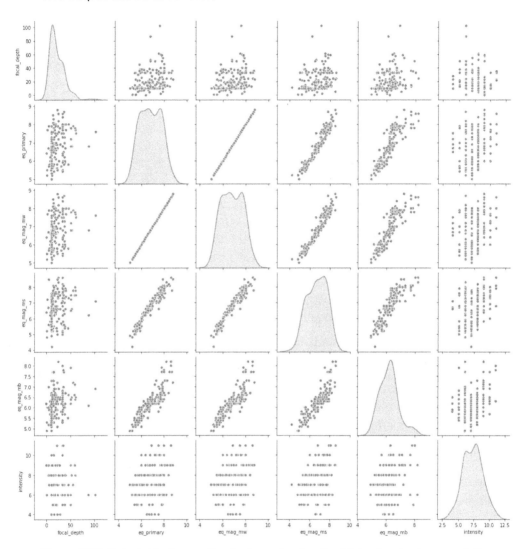

Figure 2.37: Pairplot between the features having the highest pairwise correlation

We have successfully visualized a pairplot to look at the features that have high correlation between them within a dataset.

> **NOTE**
>
> To access the source code for this specific section, please refer to https://packt.live/2Ni11T0.
>
> You can also run this example online at https://packt.live/3eol7aj. You must execute the entire Notebook in order to get the desired result.

RELATIONSHIP BETWEEN A CONTINUOUS AND A CATEGORICAL VARIABLE

A common way to view the relationship between two variables when one is categorical and the other is continuous is to use a bar plot or a box plot:

- A bar plot helps compare the value of a variable for a discrete set of parameters and is one of the most common types of plots. Each bar represents a categorical value and the height of the bar usually represents an aggregated value of the continuous variable over that category (such as average, sum, or count of the values of the continuous variable in that category).

- A box plot is a rectangle drawn to represent the distribution of the continuous variable for each discrete value of the categorical variable. It not only allows us to visualize outliers efficiently but also allows us to compare the distribution of the continuous variable across categories of the categorical variable. The lower and upper edges of the rectangle represent the first and third quartiles, respectively, the line down through the middle represents the median value, and the points (or fliers) above and below the rectangle represent outlier values.

EXERCISE 2.15: PLOTTING A BAR CHART

Let's visualize the total number of tsunamis created by earthquakes of each intensity level using a bar chart. This exercise is a continuation of *Exercise 2.14, Implementing a Pairplot*:

1. Preprocess the **flag_tsunami** variable. Before we can use the **flag_tsunami** variable, we need to preprocess it to convert the **No** values to zeros and the **Tsu** values to ones. This will give us the binary target variable. To do this, we set the values in the column using the **.loc** operator, with **:** indicating that values need to be set for all rows, and the second parameter specifying the name of the column for which values are to be set:

```
data.loc[:,'flag_tsunami'] = data.flag_tsunami\
                        .apply(lambda t: int(str(t) == 'Tsu'))
```

2. Remove all rows having null **intensity** values from the data we want to plot:

```
subset = data[~pd.isnull(data.intensity)][['intensity',\
                                           'flag_tsunami']]
```

3. Find the total number of tsunamis for each **intensity** level and display the DataFrame. To get the data in a format by means of which a bar plot can be visualized, we will need to group the rows by each intensity level, and then sum over the **flag_tsunami** values to get the total number of tsunamis for each intensity level:

```
data_to_plot = subset.groupby('intensity').sum()
data_to_plot
```

The output will be as follows:

	flag_tsunami
intensity	
2.0	0
3.0	8
4.0	19
5.0	38
6.0	63
7.0	91
8.0	119
9.0	132
10.0	130
11.0	58
12.0	4

Figure 2.38: Total number of tsunamis for each intensity level

4. Plot the bar chart, using Matplotlib's **plt.bar(x=..., height=...)** method, which takes two arguments, one specifying the **x** values at which bars need to be drawn, and the second specifying the height of each bar. Both of these are one-dimensional data structures that must have the same length:

```
plt.figure(figsize=(12,9))
plt.bar(x=data_to_plot.index, height=data_to_plot.flag_tsunami)
plt.xlabel('Earthquake intensity')
plt.ylabel('No. of tsunamis')
plt.show()
```

The output will be as follows:

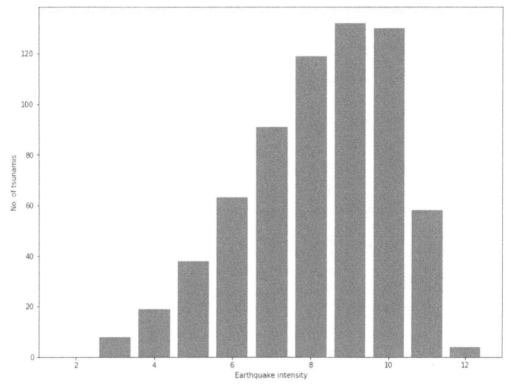

Figure 2.39: Bar chart

From this plot, we can see that as the earthquake intensity increases, the number of tsunamis caused also increases, but beyond an intensity of 9, the number of tsunamis seems to suddenly drop.

Think about why this could be happening. Perhaps it's just that there are fewer earthquakes with an intensity that high, and hence fewer tsunamis. Or it could be an entirely independent factor; maybe high-intensity earthquakes have historically occurred on land and couldn't trigger a tsunami. Explore the data to find out.

NOTE

To access the source code for this specific section, please refer to https://packt.live/3enFjsZ.

You can also run this example online at https://packt.live/2V5apxV. You must execute the entire Notebook in order to get the desired result.

EXERCISE 2.16: VISUALIZING A BOX PLOT

In this exercise, we'll plot a box plot that represents the variation in **eq_primary** over those countries with at least 100 earthquakes. This exercise is a continuation of *Exercise 2.15, Plotting a Bar Chart*:

1. Find countries with over 100 earthquakes. We will find the value counts for all the countries in the dataset. Then, we'll create a series comprising only those countries having a count greater than 100:

```
country_counts = data.country.value_counts()
top_countries = country_counts[country_counts > 100]
top_countries
```

The output will be as follows:

```
CHINA           590
JAPAN           403
INDONESIA       379
IRAN            377
ITALY           325
TURKEY          321
GREECE          260
USA             260
PHILIPPINES     210
MEXICO          198
CHILE           193
PERU            180
RUSSIA          149
Name: country, dtype: int64
```

Figure 2.40: Countries with over 100 earthquakes

2. Subset the DataFrame to filter in only those rows having countries in the preceding set. To filter the rows, we use the `.isin()` method on the pandas series to select those rows containing a value in the array-like object passed as a parameter:

```
subset = data[data.country.isin(top_countries.index)]
```

3. Create and display the box plot. The primary command for plotting the data is **sns.boxplot(x=..., y=..., data=..., order=)**. The **x** and **y** parameters are the names of the columns in the DataFrame to be plotted on each axis—the former is assumed to be the categorical variable and the latter the continuous. The **data** parameter takes the DataFrame from which to take the data and **order** takes a list of category names that indicates the order in which to display the categories on the *X* axis:

```
plt.figure(figsize=(15, 15))
sns.boxplot(x='country', y="eq_primary", data=subset, \
            order=top_countries.index)
plt.show()
```

The output will be as follows:

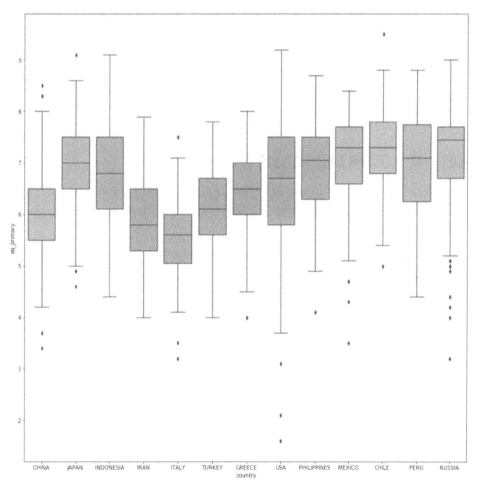

Figure 2.41: Box plot

> **NOTE**
>
> To access the source code for this specific section, please refer to
> https://packt.live/2zQHPZw.
>
> You can also run this example online at https://packt.live/3hPAzhN.
> You must execute the entire Notebook in order to get the desired result.

RELATIONSHIP BETWEEN TWO CATEGORICAL VARIABLES

When we are looking at only a pair of categorical variables to find a relationship between them, the most intuitive way to do this is to divide the data on the basis of the first category, and then subdivide it further on the basis of the second categorical variable and look at the resultant counts to find the distribution of data points. While this might seem confusing, a popular way to visualize this is to use stacked bar charts. As in a regular bar chart, each bar would represent a categorical value. But each bar would again be subdivided into color-coded categories that would provide an indication of what fraction of the data points in the primary category fall into each subcategory (that is, the second category). The variable with a larger number of categories is usually considered the primary category.

EXERCISE 2.17: PLOTTING A STACKED BAR CHART

In this exercise, we'll plot a stacked bar chart that represents the number of tsunamis that occurred for each intensity level. This exercise is a continuation of *Exercise 2.16, Visualizing a Box Plot* :

1. Find the number of data points that fall into each grouped value of **intensity** and **flag_tsunami**:

```
grouped_data = data.groupby(['intensity', \
                            'flag_tsunami']).size()

grouped_data
```

The output will be as follows:

```
intensity  flag_tsunami
2.0        0                    5
3.0        0                   10
           1                    8
4.0        0                   37
           1                   19
5.0        0                   74
           1                   38
6.0        0                  151
           1                   63
7.0        0                  342
           1                   91
8.0        0                  470
           1                  119
9.0        0                  356
           1                  132
10.0       0                  494
           1                  130
11.0       0                   79
           1                   58
12.0       0                   68
           1                    4
dtype: int64
```

Figure 2.42: Data points falling into each grouped value of intensity and flag_tsunami

2. Use the `.unstack()` method on the resultant DataFrame to get the level-1 index (**flag_tsunami**) as a column:

```
data_to_plot = grouped_data.unstack()
data_to_plot
```

The output will be as follows:

flag_tsunami	0	1
intensity		
2.0	5.0	NaN
3.0	10.0	8.0
4.0	37.0	19.0
5.0	74.0	38.0
6.0	151.0	63.0
7.0	342.0	91.0
8.0	470.0	119.0
9.0	356.0	132.0
10.0	494.0	130.0
11.0	79.0	58.0
12.0	68.0	4.0

Figure 2.43: The level-1 index

3. Create the stacked bar chart. We first use the **sns.set()** function to indicate that we want to use seaborn as our visualization library. Then, we can easily use the native **.plot()** function in pandas to plot a stacked bar chart by passing the **kind='bar'** and **stacked=True** arguments:

```
sns.set()
data_to_plot.plot(kind='bar', stacked=True, figsize=(12,8))
plt.show()
```

The output will be as follows:

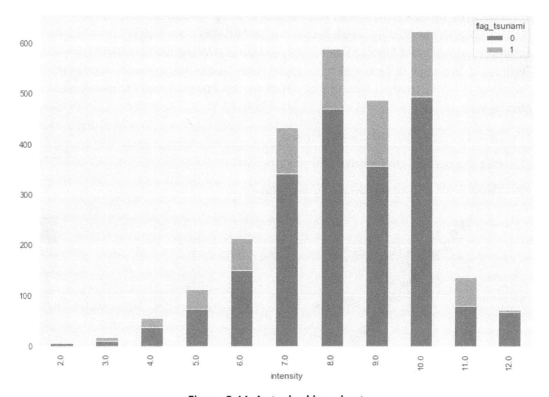

Figure 2.44: A stacked bar chart

> **NOTE**
>
> To access the source code for this specific section, please refer to
> https://packt.live/37SnqA8.
>
> You can also run this example online at https://packt.live/3dllvVx.
> You must execute the entire Notebook in order to get the desired result.

The plot now lets us visualize and interpret the fraction of earthquakes that caused tsunamis at each intensity level. In *Exercise 2.15: Plotting a Bar Chart*, we saw the number of tsunamis drop for earthquakes having an intensity of greater than 9. From this plot, we can now confirm that this was primarily because the number of earthquakes themselves dropped beyond level 10; the fraction of tsunamis even increased for level 11.

ACTIVITY 2.03: RELATIONSHIPS WITHIN THE DATA

In this activity, we will revise what we learned in the previous section about relationships between data. We will use the same dataset we used in *Activity 2.01: Summary Statistics and Missing Values*, that is, *House Prices: Advanced Regression Techniques*. We'll use different plots to highlight relationships between values in this dataset. This activity is a continuation of *Activity 2.01: Summary Statistics and Missing Values*:

The steps to be performed are as follows:

1. Plot the correlation heatmap for the dataset.

    The output should be similar to the following:

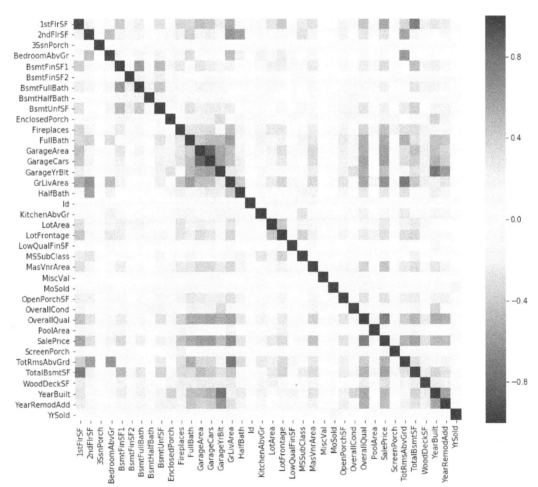

Figure 2.45: Correlation Heatmap for the Housing dataset

2. Plot a more compact heatmap having annotations for correlation values using the following subset of features:

```
feature_subset = ['GarageArea','GarageCars','GarageCond', \
                   'GarageFinish','GarageQual','GarageType', \
                   'GarageYrBlt','GrLivArea','LotArea', \
                   'MasVnrArea','SalePrice']
```

The output should be similar to the following:

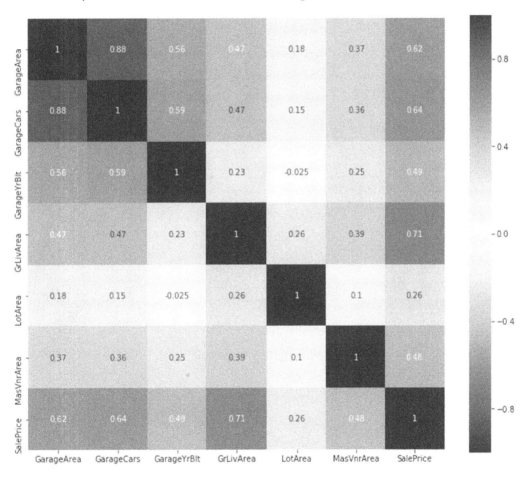

Figure 2.46: Correlation heatmap for selected variables of the Housing dataset

3. Display the pairplot for the same subset of features, with the KDE plot on the diagonals and the scatter plot elsewhere.

The output will be as follows:

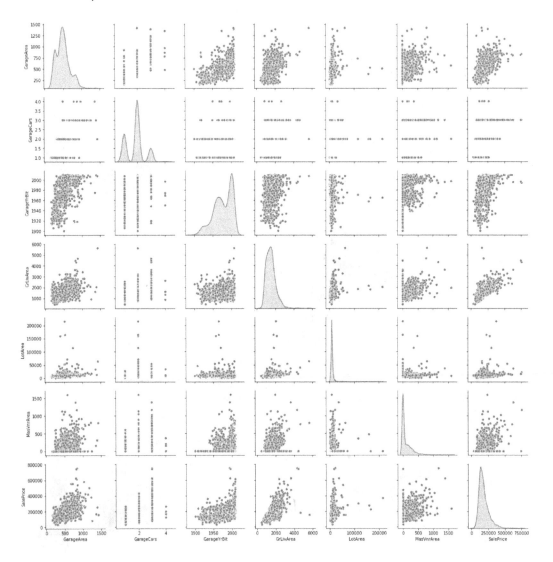

Figure 2.47: Pairplot for the same subset of features

4. Create a boxplot to show the variation in **SalePrice** for each category of **GarageCars**:

The output will be as follows:

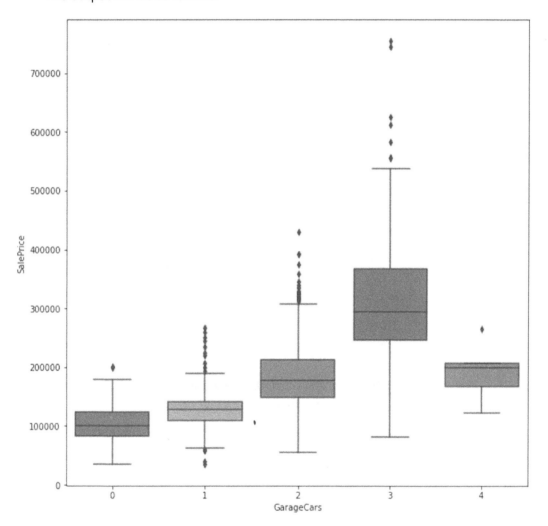

Figure 2.48: Boxplot showing variation in SalePrice for each category of GarageCars

5. Plot a line graph using seaborn to show the variation in **SalePrice** for older and more recently built homes:

    The output will be as follows:

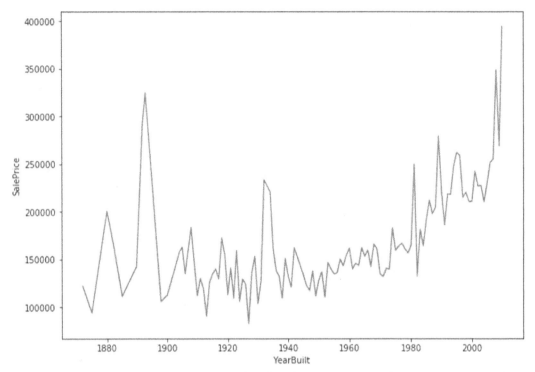

Figure 2.49: Line graph showing the variation in SalePrice
for older to more recently built homes

NOTE

The solution to this activity can be found on page 419.

You have learned how to use more advanced methods from the seaborn package to visualize large numbers of variables at once, using charts such as the correlation heatmap, pairplot, and boxplots. With boxplots, you learned how to visualize the range of one variable segmented across another, categorical variable. The boxplot further directly visualizes the quantiles and outliers, making it a powerful tool in your EDA toolkit. You have also created some preliminary line and scatter plots that are helpful in visualizing continuous data that trends over time or some other variable.

SUMMARY

In this chapter, we started by talking about why data exploration is an important part of the modeling process and how it can help in not only preprocessing the dataset for the modeling process but also help us engineer informative features and improve model accuracy. This chapter focused on not only gaining a basic overview of the dataset and its features but also gaining insights by creating visualizations that combine several features. We looked at how to find the summary statistics of a dataset using core functionality from pandas. We looked at how to find missing values and talked about why they're important while learning how to use the `Missingno` library to analyze them and the pandas and scikit-learn libraries to impute the missing values. Then, we looked at how to study the univariate distributions of variables in the dataset and visualize them for both categorical and continuous variables using bar charts, pie charts, and histograms. Lastly, we learned how to explore relationships between variables, and about how they can be represented using scatter plots, heatmaps, box plots, and stacked bar charts, to name but a few.

In the following chapters, we will start exploring supervised machine learning algorithms. Now that we have an idea of how to explore a dataset that we have, we can proceed to the modeling phase. The next chapter will introduce regression, a class of algorithms that are primarily used to build models for continuous target variables.

3

LINEAR REGRESSION

OVERVIEW

This chapter covers regression problems and analysis, introducing us to linear regression, as well as multiple linear regression and gradient descent. By the end of this chapter, you will be able to distinguish between regression and classification problems. You will be able to implement gradient descent in linear regression problems, and also apply it to other model architectures. You will also be able to use linear regression to construct a linear model for data in an *x-y* plane, evaluate the performance of linear models, and use the evaluation to choose the best model. In addition, you will be able to execute feature engineering to create dummy variables for constructing complicated linear models.

INTRODUCTION

In *Chapter 1, Fundamentals*, and *Chapter 2, Exploratory Data Analysis and Visualization*, we introduced the concept of supervised machine learning in Python and the essential techniques required for loading, cleaning, exploring, and visualizing raw data sources. We discussed the importance of fully understanding the data before moving on to further analysis, as well as how the initial data preparation process can sometimes account for the majority of the time spent on the project as a whole. In particular, we considered correlations among all the variables, finding and addressing missing values, and understanding the shape of data via histograms, bar plots, and density plots. In this chapter, we will delve into the model building process and will construct our first supervised machine learning solution using linear regression.

REGRESSION AND CLASSIFICATION PROBLEMS

We discussed two distinct methods, supervised learning and unsupervised learning, in *Chapter 1, Fundamentals*. Supervised learning problems aim to map input information to a known output value or label, but there are two further subcategories to consider. Supervised learning problems can be further divided into regression or classification problems. Regression problems, which are the subject of this chapter, aim to predict or model continuous values, for example, predicting the temperature tomorrow in degrees Celsius, from historical data, or forecasting future sales of a product on the basis of its sales history. In contrast, classification problems, rather than returning a continuous value, predict membership of one or more of a specified number of classes or categories. The example supervised learning problem in *Chapter 1, Fundamentals*, where we wanted to determine or predict whether a hairstyle was from the 1960s or 1980s, is a good example of a supervised classification problem. There, we attempted to predict whether a hairstyle was from one of two distinct groups or classes, class 1 being the 1960s and class 2 being the 1980s. Other classification problems include predicting whether a passenger of the Titanic survived, or the classic MNIST problem (http://yann.lecun.com/exdb/mnist/). (MNIST is a database of 70,000 labeled images of handwritten digits 0 through 9. The task in classifying examples from MNIST is to take one of the 70,000 input images and predict or classify which digit, 0-9, is written in the image. The model must predict the membership of the image in one of 10 different classes.)

THE MACHINE LEARNING WORKFLOW

Before we begin with regression problems, we will first look at the six major stages involved in creating any machine learning model, supervised regression or otherwise. These stages are as follows:

1. Business understanding

2. Data understanding

3. Data preparation

4. Modeling

5. Evaluation

6. Deployment

This workflow is described by a well-known open industry standard called CRISP-DM (cross-industry standard process for data mining) and can be viewed as follows:

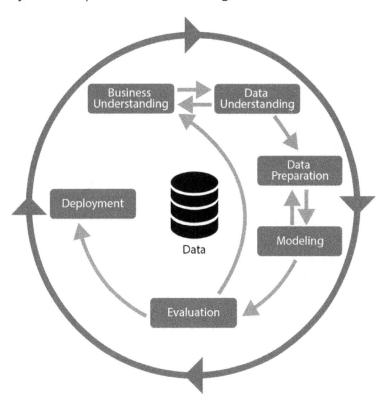

Figure 3.1: CRISP-DM Workflow

It is advised that you ensure you are completely confident in your understanding of this pipeline and of what is described in this section, as each of these stages is critical in achieving good model performance as well as meeting the needs of the business. Here, we review the key aspects of each stage.

BUSINESS UNDERSTANDING

The first stage of any data analysis and modeling project is not to jump into the data or building, but rather to understand why we are analyzing the data and what the impact of our models and conclusions on the business will be. As an individual working with the data, you may not have all the domain knowledge needed for this stage; the solution is to spend time engaging with the stakeholders in the business who know the pain points and business goals. It's very important not to underestimate this stage. Also note from the flowchart that there is feedback between the business understanding and data understanding stages, as well as from the evaluation stage to the business understanding stage. In other words, these are ongoing stages and you should endeavor to continuously discover as much as you can about the business aspects of the problem on which you are working. In the initial work in this phase, you should also formulate a preliminary overall plan for the project.

DATA UNDERSTANDING

In most real projects, there are multiple potential data sources that may vary over time. This stage is intended to acquire data and understand it enough to choose data for the solution of the problem. This could result in determining a need for more data. The basic steps are to determine what data is available initially and make a data inventory. Then, review the data, which may include reading it into Python and doing an assessment of the data quality; the common issues of missing values, anomalous values, and so on can be uncovered here and discussed with the business team to determine the best actions. Although methods to impute (fill in by means of a calculation) missing values are widely described in popular literature, you should not jump immediately to applying tools to "fix" problems in the data—the goal here is to understand them and review the appropriate actions with the business stakeholders. Note that it may be more appropriate to discard data instances with missing values than to impute them or undertake a process to find the missing values.

In addition to the data inventory, a key output of this stage is a report describing the data, what has been found, and expected actions. To get to that output, some EDA (Exploratory Data Analysis) is needed, as was described in *Chapter 2, Exploratory Data Analysis and Visualization*.

DATA PREPARATION

In data preparation, we use the data determined to be appropriate from the prior stage and apply any cleaning and transformations that are needed for it to be used in modeling. This was the focus of a significant component of *Chapter 1, Fundamentals*, and thus will not be the subject of further analysis in this section. It is important, however, that the criticality of the data specification, collection, and cleaning/tidying process is well understood. We cannot expect to produce a high-performing system if the input data is sub-optimal. One common phrase that you should always remember with regard to data quality is *garbage in, garbage out*. If you use poor quality data, you are going to produce poor quality results. In our hairstyle example, we are looking for a sample size at least in the order of hundreds, ideally thousands that has been correctly labeled as either from the 1960s or 1980s. We do not want samples that have been incorrectly labeled or are even from either era.

Note that during data preparation, it is entirely possible to discover additional aspects of the data and that additional visualization may be required during the process to get to the dataset for modeling.

MODELING

The modeling stage is comprised of two sub-stages: model architecture specification and model training.

- Model architecture specification: These may be iteratively related in more complex projects. In many cases, there are multiple possible model types (such as linear regression, artificial neural network, gradient boosting, and others) that may be applicable to the problem at hand. Thus, it is sometimes beneficial to investigate more than one model architecture and to do that, the models must be trained and compared in terms of their predictive capability.

- Training: The second sub-stage of modeling is training, wherein we use the existing data and known outcomes in a process to "learn" the parameters of the candidate model. Here, we must establish the design and execution of the training process; the details of that will vary, depending on the model architecture chosen and the scale of the input data. For example, for very large datasets, we may have to stream or flow the data through the training process as the data is too large for the computer memory, while for smaller data, we can simply use the data all at once.

EVALUATION

The next stage of the workflow is the evaluation of the model, which yields the final performance metric. This is the mechanism through which we know whether the model is worth publishing, is better than a previous version, or whether it has been effectively translated across programming languages or development environments. We will cover some of these metrics in more detail in *Chapter 7, Model Evaluation*, and, as such, this will not be discussed in detail at this stage. Just keep in mind that whatever approach is used, it needs to be capable of consistently reporting and independently measuring the performance of the model against the metric using an appropriate sample from the data.

DEPLOYMENT

In a complete data analytics workflow, most models, once developed, need to be deployed in order to be used. Deployment is critical in some applications, such as where a model might underlie a recommendation system on an e-commerce site, and the model has to be redeployed to the web application each time it is updated. Deployment can take many forms, from simply sharing a Jupyter notebook, to automated code updates to a website on a code commit, to a master repository. Although important, deployment is beyond the scope of this book and we won't address it much going forward.

Before moving on to regression modeling, let's do some final data preparation exercises. For this purpose, we have created a synthetic dataset of recorded air temperatures from the years 1841 to 2010, which is available in the accompanying code bundle of this book or on GitHub at https://packt.live/2Pu850C. This dataset is composed of values designed to demonstrate the subject matter of this chapter and should not be mistaken for data collected from a scientific study.

EXERCISE 3.01: PLOTTING DATA WITH A MOVING AVERAGE

As we discussed in *Chapter 1, Fundamentals*, and in the preceding section, a thorough understanding of the dataset being used is critical if a high-performing model is to be built. So, with this in mind, let's use this exercise to load, plot, and interrogate the data source:

1. Import the **numpy**, **pandas**, and **matplotlib** packages:

```
import numpy as np
import pandas as pd
import matplotlib.pyplot as plt
```

2. Use the pandas **read_csv** function to load the CSV file containing the **synth_temp.csv** dataset, and then display the first five lines of data:

```
df = pd.read_csv('../Datasets/synth_temp.csv')
df.head()
```

The output will be as follows:

	Region	Year	RgnAvTemp
0	A	1841	12.557395
1	B	1841	13.267048
2	E	1841	12.217463
3	F	1841	13.189420
4	A	1842	13.462887

Figure 3.2: The first five rows

3. For our purposes, we don't want to use all this data, but let's look at how many points there are per year. Create a **print** statement to output the number of points for the years 1841, 1902, and 2010, and make a simple plot of the number of points per year:

```
# take a quick look at the number of data points per year
print('There are ' + str(len(df.loc[df['Year'] == 1841])) \
        + ' points in 1841\n' + 'and ' \
        + str(len(df.loc[df['Year'] == 2010])) \
        + ' points in 2010\n' + 'and ' \
        + str(len(df.loc[df['Year'] == 1902])) \
        + ' points in 1902')
# seeing there are different numbers of points, let's do a quick chart
fig, ax = plt.subplots()
ax.plot(df['Year'].unique(), [len(df.loc[df['Year'] == i]) \
        for i in df['Year'].unique()])
plt.show()
```

The output will be as follows:

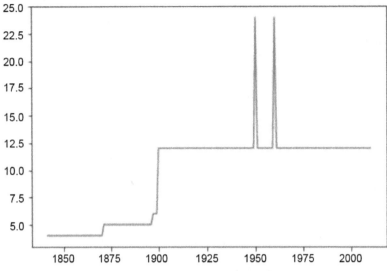

Figure 3.3: Different number of points per year

We see varying numbers of points per year. Also note that we don't have the information on exactly when in each year the various points were measured. If that were important, we would want to ask the appropriate business stakeholder if the information could be obtained.

4. Let's slice the DataFrame to remove all rows through 1901, as we can see that there is much less data in those years:

```
# slice 1902 and forward
df = df.loc[df.Year > 1901]
df.head()
```

The output will be as follows:

	Region	Year	RgnAvTemp
292	A	1902	17.021583
293	B	1902	17.590253
294	C	1902	17.493082
295	D	1902	18.706166
296	E	1902	17.390903

Figure 3.4: Subset of data from 1902 onward

5. Make a quick plot to visualize the data:

```
# quick plot to understand what we have so far
fig, ax = plt.subplots()
ax.scatter(df.Year, df.RgnAvTemp)
plt.show()
```

The output will be as follows:

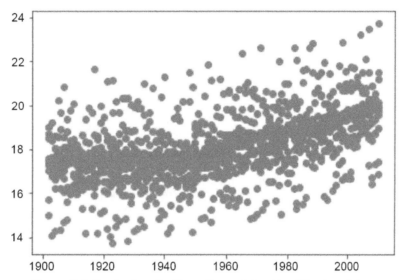

Figure 3.5: Basic visualization of raw data after filtering dates

6. We can see that there is quite a range for each year. Group the data by year and use the **agg** method of the DataFrame to create annual averages. This works around the issue that we have multiple points at unknown dates in each year, but uses all the data:

```
# roll up by year
df_group_year = (df.groupby('Year').agg('mean')\
                .rename(columns = {'RgnAvTemp' : 'AvgTemp'}))
print(df_group_year.head())
print(df_group_year.tail())
```

The output will be as follows:

```
            AvgTemp
Year
1902   17.385044
1903   17.222163
1904   17.217215
1905   17.817502
1906   17.386445
            AvgTemp
Year
2006   19.904999
2007   19.820224
2008   19.245558
2009   19.537290
2010   19.919115
```

Figure 3.6: Yearly average data

As before, perform a quick visualization, as follows:

```
# visualize result of averaging over each year
fig, ax = plt.subplots()
ax.scatter(df_group_year.index, df_group_year['AvgTemp'])
plt.show()
```

The data will now appear as follows:

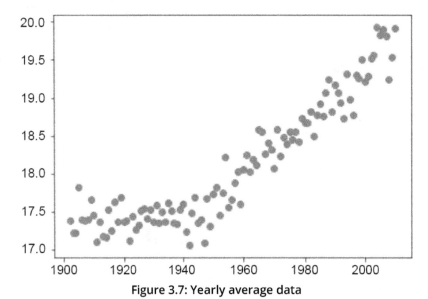

Figure 3.7: Yearly average data

7. Given that the data is still noisy, a moving average filter can provide a useful indicator of the overall trend. A moving average filter simply computes the average over the last *N* values and assigns this average to the Nth sample. Compute the values for a moving average signal for the temperature measurements using a window of 10 years:

```
window = 10
smoothed_df = \
pd.DataFrame(df_group_year.AvgTemp.rolling(window).mean())
smoothed_df.colums = 'AvgTemp'
print(smoothed_df.head(14))
print(smoothed_df.tail())
```

We will obtain the following output:

```
             AvgTemp
Year
1902             NaN
1903             NaN
1904             NaN
1905             NaN
1906             NaN
1907             NaN
1908             NaN
1909             NaN
1910             NaN
1911       17.401761
1912       17.398872
1913       17.394177
1914       17.388443
1915       17.358825
             AvgTemp
Year
2006       19.531170
2007       19.583102
2008       19.581256
2009       19.584580
2010       19.654919
```

Figure 3.8: 10-year moving average temperatures

Notice that the first 9 samples are **NaN**, which is because of the size of the moving average filter window. The window size is 10, hence, 9 (10-1) samples are required to generate the first average, and thus the first 9 samples are **NaN**. There are additional options to the `rolling()` method that can extend the values to the left or right, or allow the early values to be based on fewer points. In this case, we'll just filter them out:

```
# filter out the NaN values
smoothed_df = smoothed_df[smoothed_df['AvgTemp'].notnull()]
# quick plot to understand what we have so far
fig, ax = plt.subplots()
ax.scatter(smoothed_df.index, smoothed_df['AvgTemp'])
plt.show()
```

The output will be as follows:

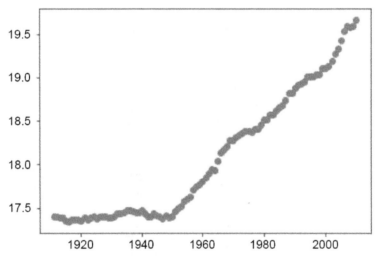

Figure 3.9: Visualization of preprocessed temperature data

8. Finally, plot the measurements by year along with the moving average signal:

```
fig = plt.figure(figsize=(10, 7))
ax = fig.add_axes([1, 1, 1, 1]);
# Raw data
raw_plot_data = df[df.Year > 1901]
ax.scatter(raw_plot_data.Year, \
            raw_plot_data.RgnAvTemp, \
            label = 'Raw Data', c = 'blue', s = 1.5)
# Annual averages
annual_plot_data = df_group_year\
```

```
                      .filter(items = smoothed_df.index, axis = 0)
ax.scatter(annual_plot_data.index, \
           annual_plot_data.AvgTemp, \
           label = 'Annual average', c = 'k')
# Moving averages
ax.plot(smoothed_df.index, smoothed_df.AvgTemp, \
        c = 'r', linestyle = '--', \
        label = f'{window} year moving average')
ax.set_title('Mean Air Temperature Measurements', fontsize = 16)
# make the ticks include the first and last years
tick_years = [1902] + list(range(1910, 2011, 10))
ax.set_xlabel('Year', fontsize = 14)
ax.set_ylabel('Temperature ($^\circ$C)', fontsize = 14)
ax.set_xticks(tick_years)
ax.tick_params(labelsize = 12)
ax.legend(fontsize = 12)
plt.show()
```

The output will be as follows:

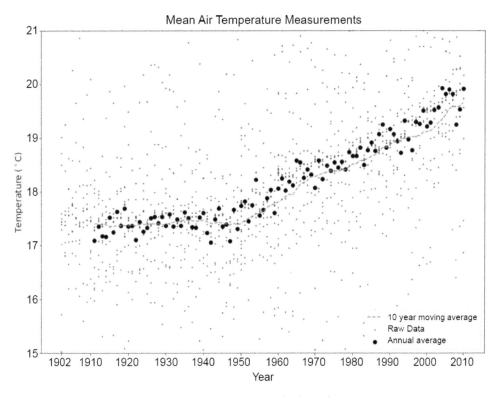

Figure 3.10: Annual average temperature overlaid on the 10-year moving average

9. We can improve the plot by focusing on the part we are most interested in, the annual average values, by adjusting the *y* scale. This is an important aspect of most visualizations in that the scale should be optimized to convey the most information to the reader:

```python
fig = plt.figure(figsize=(10, 7))
ax = fig.add_axes([1, 1, 1, 1]);
# Raw data
raw_plot_data = df[df.Year > 1901]
ax.scatter(raw_plot_data.Year, raw_plot_data.RgnAvTemp, \
           label = 'Raw Data', c = 'blue', s = 1.5)
# Annual averages
annual_plot_data = df_group_year\
                   .filter(items = smoothed_df.index, axis = 0)
ax.scatter(annual_plot_data.index, annual_plot_data.AvgTemp, \
           label = 'Annual average', c = 'k')
# Moving averages
ax.plot(smoothed_df.index, smoothed_df.AvgTemp, c = 'r', \
        linestyle = '--', \
        label = f'{window} year moving average')
ax.set_title('Mean Air Temperature Measurements', fontsize = 16)
# make the ticks include the first and last years
tick_years = [1902] + list(range(1910, 2011, 10))
ax.set_xlabel('Year', fontsize = 14)
ax.set_ylabel('Temperature ($^\circ$C)', fontsize = 14)
ax.set_ylim(17, 20)
ax.set_xticks(tick_years)
ax.tick_params(labelsize = 12)
ax.legend(fontsize = 12)
plt.show()
```

The final plot should appear as follows:

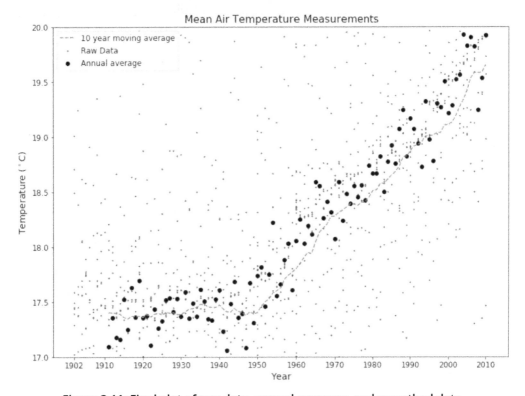

Figure 3.11: Final plot of raw data, annual averages, and smoothed data

Looking at *Figure 3.11*, we can immediately make a few interesting observations. First, the temperature remained relatively consistent from the year 1902 to about 1950, after which there is an increasing trend through to the end of the data. Second, there is scatter or noise in the measurements, even after averaging within each year. Third, there appears to be a shift at 1960, which might represent a change in measurement methods or some other factor; we might want to follow up with the business team to understand this more fully.

Finally, note that the moving average values tend to be to the right of the raw data during periods in which there are trends. This is a direct result of the default parameters in the **rolling()** method; each moving average value is the average of 9 points to the left and the current point.

> **NOTE**
>
> To access the source code for this specific section, please refer to https://packt.live/316S0o6.
>
> You can also run this example online at https://packt.live/2CmpJPZ. You must execute the entire Notebook in order to get the desired result.

ACTIVITY 3.01: PLOTTING DATA WITH A MOVING AVERAGE

For this activity, we have acquired a dataset of weather information from Austin, Texas (**austin_weather.csv**), available in the accompanying source code, and will be looking at the changes in average daily temperature. We will plot a moving average filter for this dataset.

> **NOTE**
>
> The original dataset can be found here: https://www.kaggle.com/grubenm/austin-weather

The steps to be performed are as follows:

1. Import **pandas** and **matplotlib.pyplot.**

2. Load the dataset into a pandas DataFrame from the CSV file.

3. We only need the **Date** and **TempAvgF** columns; remove all others from the dataset.

4. Initially, we will only be interested in the first year's data, so we need to extract that information only.

   Create a column in the DataFrame for the **year** value and extract the year value as an integer from the strings in the **Date** column and assign these values to the **Year** column.

5. Repeat this process to extract the month values and store the values as integers in the **Month** column.

6. Repeat this process one more time to store the day values as integers in the **Day** column.

7. Copy the first year's worth of data to a DataFrame.

8. Compute a 20-day moving average filter.

9. Plot the raw data and moving average signal, with the x axis being the day number in the year.

The output should be as follows:

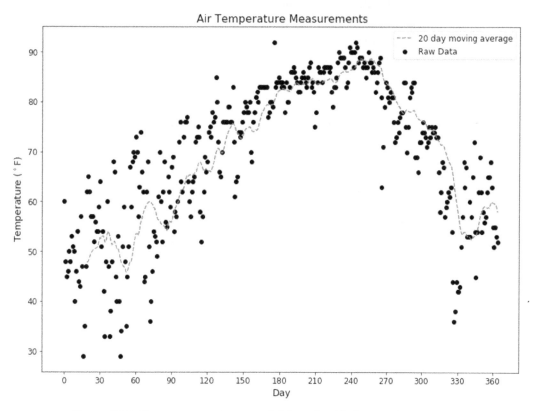

Figure 3.12: Temperature data overlaid on the 20-day moving average

NOTE

The solution to this activity can be found on page 426.

You have learned how to load data from a CSV file, how to remove columns that are not required, how to extract information from text fields containing dates as strings, how to smooth data using a moving average, and how to visualize the results.

LINEAR REGRESSION

We will start our investigation into regression models with the selection of a linear model. Linear models, while being a great first choice due to their intuitive nature, are also very powerful in their predictive power, assuming datasets contain some degree of linear or polynomial relationship between the input features and values. The intuitive nature of linear models often arises from the ability to view data as plotted on a graph and observe a trending pattern in the data with, say, the output (the y-axis value for the data) trending positively or negatively with the input (the x-axis value). The fundamental components of linear regression models are also often learned during high school mathematics classes. You may recall that the equation of a straight line is defined as follows:

$$y = \beta_0 + \beta_1 * x$$

Figure 3.13: Equation of a straight line

Here, x is the input value and y is the corresponding output or predicted value. The parameters of the model are the slope of the line (the change in the y values divided by the change in x, also called the gradient), noted by β_1 in the equation, as well as the y-intercept value, β_1, which indicates where the line crosses the y axis. With such a model, we can provide values for the β_1 and β_0 parameters to construct a linear model.

For example, $y = 1 + 2 * x$ has a slope of 2, indicating that the changes in the y values are at a rate of twice that of x; the line crosses the y intercept at 1, as you can see in the following diagram:

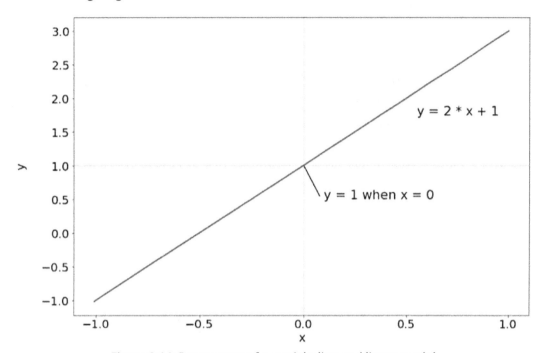

Figure 3.14: Parameters of a straight line and linear model

So, we have an understanding of the parameters that are required to define a straight line, but this isn't really doing anything particularly interesting. We just dictated the parameters of the model to construct a line. What we want to do is take a dataset and construct a model that best describes a dataset. In terms of the previous section, we want to choose the model architecture as a linear model, and then train the model to find the best values of β_0 and β_1. As mentioned before, this dataset needs to have something that approximates a linear relationship between the input features and output values for a linear model to be a good choice.

LEAST SQUARES METHOD

Many of the various techniques used in machine learning actually significantly pre-date the use of machine learning as a description. Some embody elements of statistics, and others have been used in the sciences to "fit" data for a very long time. The least squares method of finding the equation of a straight line that best represents a set of data is one of these, originally created in the early 1800s. The method can be used to illustrate many key ideas of the supervised learning of regression models, and so we'll start with it here.

The least squares method focuses on minimizing the square of the error between the predicted y values and the actual y values. The idea of minimizing an error is fundamental in machine learning and is the basis for essentially all learning algorithms.

Although simple linear regression using the least squares method can be written down as simple algebraic expressions, most packages (like scikit-learn) will have more general optimization methods "under the hood."

THE SCIKIT-LEARN MODEL API

The scikit-learn API uses a similar code pattern irrespective of the type of model being constructed. The general flow is:

1. Import the class for the model type you want to use.

    Here, we will use **from sklearn.linear_model import LinearRegression**.

2. Instantiate an instance of the model class. This is where hyperparameters are set. For simple linear regression, we can use defaults.

3. Use the **fit** method with the x and y data we want to model.

4. Inspect the results, get metrics, and then visualize them.

Let's use this workflow to create a linear regression model in the next exercise.

EXERCISE 3.02: FITTING A LINEAR MODEL USING THE LEAST SQUARES METHOD

In this exercise, we will construct our first linear regression model using the least squares method to visualize the air temperatures over a yearly timeframe and evaluate the performance of the model using evaluation metrics:

> **NOTE**
>
> We will be using the same **synth_temp.csv** dataset as in *Exercise 3.01: Plotting Data with a Moving Average.*

1. Import the **LinearRegression** class from the **linear_model** module of scikit-learn, along with the other packages we need:

```
import pandas as pd
import matplotlib.pyplot as plt
from sklearn.linear_model import LinearRegression
```

2. Load the data. For this exercise, we'll use the same synthetic temperature data as was used previously:

```
# load the data
df = pd.read_csv('../Datasets/synth_temp.csv')
```

3. Repeat the preprocessing of the data from before:

```
# slice 1902 and forward
df = df.loc[df.Year > 1901]
# roll up by year
df_group_year = df.groupby(['Year']).agg({'RgnAvTemp' : 'mean'})
df_group_year.head(12)
# add the Year column so we can use that in a model
df_group_year['Year'] = df_group_year.index
df_group_year = \
df_group_year.rename(columns = {'RgnAvTemp' : 'AvTemp'})
df_group_year.head()
```

The data should appear as follows:

	AvTemp	Year
Year		
1902	17.385044	1902
1903	17.222163	1903
1904	17.217215	1904
1905	17.817502	1905
1906	17.386445	1906

Figure 3.15: Data after preprocessing

4. Instantiate the **LinearRegression** class. Then, we can fit the model using our data. Initially, we will just fit the temperature data to the years. In the following code, note that the method requires the *x* data to be a 2D array and that we are passing only the year. We also need to use the **reshape** method and, in the **(-1, 1)** parameters, **-1** means that "the value is inferred from the length of the array and remaining dimensions":

```
# construct the model and inspect results
linear_model = LinearRegression(fit_intercept = True)
linear_model.fit(df_group_year['Year'].values.reshape((-1, 1)), \
                 df_group_year.AvTemp)
print('model slope = ', linear_model.coef_[0])
print('model intercept = ', linear_model.intercept_)
r2 = linear_model.score(df_group_year['Year']\
                        .values.reshape((-1, 1)), \
                        df_group_year.AvTemp)
print('r squared = ', r2)
```

> **NOTE**
>
> Refer to the following link for more reading on scikit-learn: https://scikit-learn.org/stable/modules/generated/sklearn.linear_model.LinearRegression.html

The output will be as follows:

```
model slope =  0.02352237024970654
model intercept =  -27.88736502793287
r squared =  0.84384992946671093
```

Figure 3.16: Results from using the fit method

Note the use of the **score** method, which is a method of the **model** object, to obtain the r^2 value. This metric, called the coefficient of determination, is a widely used metric for linear regression. The closer r^2 is to 1, the more closely our model is predicting the data. There are multiple formulas that can be used to compute r^2. Here is an example:

$$r^2 = 1 - \frac{\sum_i (y_i - \hat{y})^2}{\sum_i (y_i - \bar{y})^2}$$

Figure 3.17: Calculation of r2

From *Figure 3.17*, you can get some understanding of r^2 by noting that the numerator sums the errors from the predictions, while the denominator sums the variation of the data from the mean. Thus, r^2 increases as the prediction errors get smaller. It's important to emphasize here that r^2 is just a measure of "goodness of fit"—in this case, how well a simple straight line fits the given data. In more complex, real-world supervised learning problems, we would use a more robust approach to optimize the model and choose the best/final model. In particular, in general, we evaluate the model on data *not* used to train it, because evaluating it on the training data would give an overly optimistic measure of performance. This will be discussed in *Chapter 7, Model Evaluation*.

5. To visualize the results, we need to pass some data to the **predict** method of the model. A simple way to do that is to just reuse the data we used to fit the model:

```
# generate predictions for visualization
pred_X = df_group_year.loc[:, 'Year']
pred_Y = linear_model.predict(df_group_year['Year']\
                              .values.reshape((-1, 1)))
```

6. Now, we have everything we need to visualize the result:

```
fig = plt.figure(figsize=(10, 7))
ax = fig.add_axes([1, 1, 1, 1]);
# Raw data
raw_plot_data = df[df.Year > 1901]
ax.scatter(raw_plot_data.Year, raw_plot_data.RgnAvTemp, \
           label = 'Raw Data', c = 'red', s = 1.5)
# Annual averages
ax.scatter(df_group_year.Year, df_group_year.AvTemp, \
           label = 'Annual average', c = 'k', s = 10)
# linear fit
ax.plot(pred_X, pred_Y, c = "blue", linestyle = '-.', \
        linewidth = 4, label = 'linear fit')
ax.set_title('Mean Air Temperature Measurements', fontsize = 16)
# make the ticks include the first and last years
tick_years = [1902] + list(range(1910, 2011, 10))
ax.set_xlabel('Year', fontsize = 14)
ax.set_ylabel('Temperature ($^\circ$C)', fontsize = 14)
ax.set_ylim(15, 21)
ax.set_xticks(tick_years)
ax.tick_params(labelsize = 12)
ax.legend(fontsize = 12)
plt.show()
```

The output will be as follows:

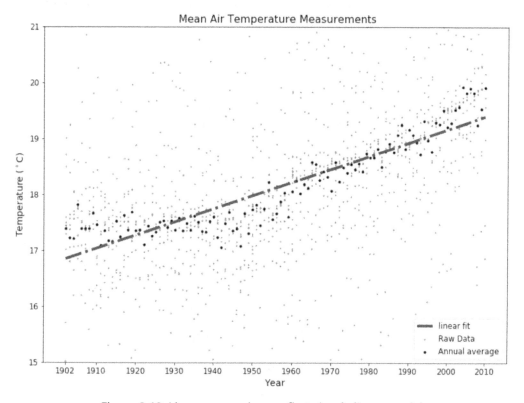

Figure 3.18: Linear regression – a first simple linear model

From *Figure 3.18*, it's evident that a straight line isn't a very good model of the data. We'll return to this issue after an activity.

> **NOTE**
>
> To access the source code for this specific section, please refer to https://packt.live/2NwANg1.
>
> You can also run this example online at https://packt.live/2Z1qQfT. You must execute the entire Notebook in order to get the desired result.

We have seen how to load in some data, import the **LinearRegression** class from scikit-learn, and use the **fit**, **score**, and **predict** methods to construct a model, look at a performance metric, and then visualize the results. Along the way, we introduced the least squares method, gave some of the mathematical background, and showed how some of the calculations work.

We saw that for our synthetic temperature data, a linear model doesn't fit the data all that well. That's okay. In most cases, it is good practice to generate a baseline model early on in the project to serve as a benchmark against which the performance of more sophisticated models can be compared. So we can consider the linear model we developed here to be a naïve baseline model.

Before continuing, it is important to note that when reporting the performance of machine learning models, the data used to train the model is *not* to be used to evaluate it, as it will give an optimistic view of the model's performance. We will cover the concept of validation, which includes evaluating and reporting model performance, in *Chapter 7, Model Evaluation*. For the purpose of this chapter, however, we will use the training data to check the model's performance; just remember that once you have completed *Chapter 7, Model Evaluation*, you will know better.

ACTIVITY 3.02: LINEAR REGRESSION USING THE LEAST SQUARES METHOD

For this activity, we will use the Austin, Texas weather dataset that we used in the previous activity. We will plot a linear regression model using the least squares method for the dataset.

The steps to be performed are as follows:

1. Import the requisite packages, classes, and suchlike. Refer to *Exercise 3.02: Fitting a Linear Model Using the Least Squares Method* if necessary.

2. Load the data from the csv (**austin_weather.csv**).

3. Inspect the data (using the **head()** and **tail()** methods).

The output for **df.head()** will be as follows:

```
          Date  TempHighF  TempAvgF  TempLowF  DewPointHighF  DewPointAvgF  \
0   2013-12-21         74        60        45             67            49
1   2013-12-22         56        48        39             43            36
2   2013-12-23         58        45        32             31            27
3   2013-12-24         61        46        31             36            28
4   2013-12-25         58        50        41             44            40

   DewPointLowF  HumidityHighPercent  HumidityAvgPercent  HumidityLowPercent  ...  \
0            43                   93                  75                  57  ...
1            28                   93                  68                  43  ...
2            23                   76                  52                  27  ...
3            21                   89                  56                  22  ...
4            36                   86                  71                  56  ...

   SeaLevelPressureAvgInches  SeaLevelPressureLowInches  VisibilityHighMiles  \
0                      29.68                      29.59                   10
1                      30.13                      29.87                   10
2                      30.49                      30.41                   10
3                      30.45                       30.3                   10
4                      30.33                      30.27                   10

   VisibilityAvgMiles  VisibilityLowMiles  WindHighMPH  WindAvgMPH  WindGustMPH  \
0                   7                   2           20           4           31
1                  10                   5           16           6           25
2                  10                  10            8           3           12
3                  10                   7           12           4           20
4                  10                   7           10           2           16

   PrecipitationSumInches                  Events
0                     0.46  Rain , Thunderstorm
1                        0
2                        0
3                        0
4                        T

[5 rows x 21 columns]
```

Figure 3.19: Output for df.head()

The output for **df.tail()** will be as follows:

```
         Date  TempHighF  TempAvgF  TempLowF  DewPointHighF  DewPointAvgF  \
1314  2017-07-27       103        89        75             71            67
1315  2017-07-28       105        91        76             71            64
1316  2017-07-29       107        92        77             72            64
1317  2017-07-30       106        93        79             70            68
1318  2017-07-31        99        88        77             66            61

      DewPointLowF  HumidityHighPercent  HumidityAvgPercent  HumidityLowPercent  \
1314            61                   82                  54                  25
1315            55                   87                  54                  20
1316            55                   82                  51                  19
1317            63                   69                  48                  27
1318            54                   64                  43                  22

      ...  SeaLevelPressureAvgInches  SeaLevelPressureLowInches  \
1314  ...                      29.97                      29.88
1315  ...                       29.9                      29.81
1316  ...                      29.86                      29.79
1317  ...                      29.91                      29.87
1318  ...                      29.97                      29.91

      VisibilityHighMiles  VisibilityAvgMiles  VisibilityLowMiles  WindHighMPH  \
1314                   10                  10                  10           12
1315                   10                  10                  10           14
1316                   10                  10                  10           12
1317                   10                  10                  10           13
1318                   10                  10                  10           12

      WindAvgMPH  WindGustMPH  PrecipitationSumInches  Events
1314           5           21                       0
1315           5           20                       0
1316           4           17                       0
1317           4           20                       0
1318           4           20                       0

[5 rows x 21 columns]
```

Figure 3.20: Output for df.tail()

4. Drop everything except the **Date** and **TempAvgF** columns.

5. Create new **Year**, **Month**, and **Day** columns and populate them by parsing the **Date** column.

6. Create a new column for a moving average and populate it with a 20-day moving average of the **TempAvgF** column.

7. Slice one complete year of data to use in a model. Ensure the year doesn't have missing data due to the moving average. Also, create a column for **Day_of_Year** (it should start at 1).

8. Create a scatterplot of the raw data (the original **TempAvgF** column) and overlay it with a line for the 20-day moving average.

    The plot will be as follows:

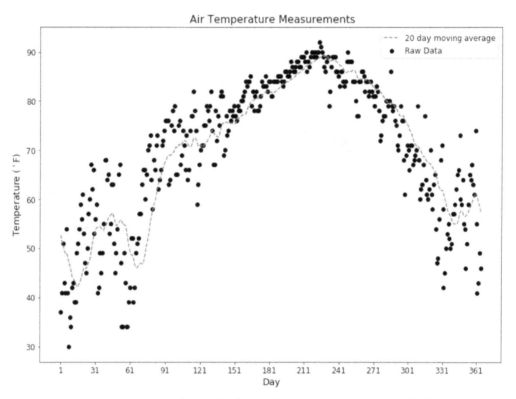

Figure 3.21: Raw data with the 20-day moving average overlaid

9. Create a linear regression model using the default parameters, that is, calculate a y intercept for the model and do not normalize the data.

10. Now fit the model, where the input data is the day number for the year (1 to 365) and the output is the average temperature. Print the parameters of the model and the r^2 value.

The results should be as follows:

```
model slope: [0.04304568]
model intercept: 62.23496914044859
model r squared: 0.09549593659736466
```

11. Generate predictions from the model using the same *x* data.

12. Create a new scatterplot, as before, adding an overlay of the predictions of the model.

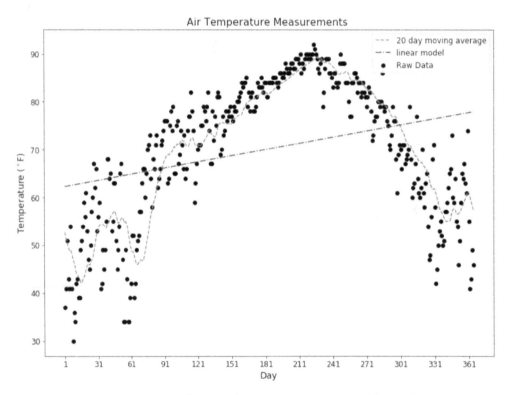

Figure 3.22: Raw data, 20-day moving average, and linear fit

NOTE

The solution to this activity can be found on page 429.

Building on the previous exercise, you have seen how to load and use the **LinearRegression** class from scikit-learn and the **fit**, **score**, and **predict** methods. Not surprisingly, a simple linear model that produces a straight line isn't the best model for this data. In later exercises, we will investigate ways in which we might address that.

You have learned how to load data, structure it for the scikit-learn API, and use the **LinearRegression** class to fit a simple line to the data. It is evident that this is a poor model for this data, so we will explore ways to improve our model, beginning with the next topic, *Linear Regression with Categorical Variables*.

LINEAR REGRESSION WITH CATEGORICAL VARIABLES

There is an aspect of the model architecture selection phase that somewhat overlaps the data preparation phase: feature engineering. Broadly, feature engineering involves creating additional features (columns in our case) and using them in the model to improve model performance. Features may be engineered by transforming existing features (such as taking the logarithm and square root) or may be generated in some way and added to the dataset. As an example of the latter, we can extract the month, the day of the month, the day of the week, and so on from the date information in a dataset. Although a new feature such as the month could be a numeric value, in the majority of cases in supervised learning, simply using a numeric value of such a feature is not best practice. A simple idea would be as follows: if we code January to December as 1 to 12, a model might give more weight to December since it is 12 times larger than January. Also, when the date changes from December back to January, there would be an artificial step change in the value. Thus, such a feature is considered to be nominal categorical. Nominal categorical variables are features with multiple possible values but where the ordering of the values does not contain any information, and could even be misleading. There are also categorical variables that do have an implied order, which are called ordinal categorical variables. Examples include "tiny," "small," "medium," "large," "extra-large," and "huge."

To handle either type of categorical data in most machine learning models, we still have to convert it to numbers. The general approach to such a conversion is called encoding. A very powerful but easy to understand encoding method is to convert a categorical feature using **one-hot encoding**.

When using one-hot encoding, each possible value of the categorical feature becomes a column. In the column corresponding to a given value, a **1** is entered if that instance of data had the feature at that value, otherwise, a **0** is entered. An example will make this much clearer, as seen in the following figure:

Case_ID	avg_calories	weight	age_at_death	breed
1970887	450	10	12	miniature dachshund
1232378	1800	71	13	german shepherd
1106164	1700	65	15	Boxer
1325790	250	7	13	Chihuahua
.	.	.	.	.
.	.	.	.	.
.	.	.	.	.
1962648	1150	35	17	Beagle
1623065	425	8	15	miniature dachshund
1290069	1550	57	14	Collie
1301688	1900	79	12	boxer
1018806	2350	95	11	german shepherd

breeds →

beagle
boxer
chihuahua
collie
german shepherd
miniature dachshund
6 unique values

Replace 'breed' column with 6 new columns:

Case_ID	avg_calories	weight	age_at_death	beagle	boxer	chihuahua	collie	german shepherd	miniature dachshund
1970887	450	10	12	0	0	0	0	0	1
1232378	1800	71	13	0	0	0	0	1	0
1106164	1700	65	15	0	1	0	0	0	0
1325790	250	7	13	0	0	1	0	0	0
.	.	.	.	.	.	.	.	.	.
.	.	.	.	.	.	.	.	.	.
.	.	.	.	.	.	.	.	.	.
1962648	1150	35	17	1	0	0	0	0	0
1623065	425	8	15	0	0	0	0	0	1
1290069	1550	57	14	0	0	0	1	0	0
1301688	1900	79	12	0	1	0	0	0	0
1018806	2350	95	11	0	0	0	0	1	0

Figure 3.23: One-hot encoding of a nominal categorical column

So, by creating these columns and inserting the ones in the appropriate locations, we let the model "know" about the presence of the nominal categorical variable, but don't give extra weight to any given value. In the example in *Figure 3.23*, if we were trying to model dog life expectancy, before using one-hot encoding, we only had diet and weight as predictors. After applying one-hot encoding, we would expect to get a better model, since our intuition would be that some breeds live longer than others, all other factors being equal. In the following exercise, we'll see how to use encoding to leverage the power of linear models to model complex behavior.

> **NOTE**
>
> There are a number of other possible ways to encode categorical variables; see, for example, *A Comparative Study of Categorical Variable Encoding Techniques for Neural Network Classifiers*: https://pdfs.semanticscholar.org/0c43/fb9cfea23e15166c58e24106ce3605b20229.pdf

In some cases, the best method may depend on the type of model being used. For example, linear regression has a requirement that none of the features are linearly dependent on any others (we will discuss this further later in this chapter). One-hot encoding actually introduces this problem, because the nth category can actually be determined from the other n-1 categories—intuitively, in *Figure 3.23*, if beagle, boxer, chihuahua, collie, and german shepherd are all 0, then miniature dachshund will be 1 (note that we are assuming that an instance may not have more than one valid category). Thus, in linear regression, we use a slightly different encoding called dummy variables. The only difference between dummy variables and one-hot encoding is that we drop one of the **n** columns to eliminate the dependence.

EXERCISE 3.03: INTRODUCING DUMMY VARIABLES

In this exercise, we will introduce dummy variables into our linear regression model to improve its performance.

We will be using the same **synth_temp** dataset as was used in the previous exercise:

1. Import the required packages and classes:

```
import pandas as pd
import numpy as np
import matplotlib.pyplot as plt
from sklearn.linear_model import LinearRegression
```

2. Load the data:

```
# load data
df = pd.read_csv('../Datasets/synth_temp.csv')
```

3. Slice the DataFrame from 1902 onward, and then compute yearly averages:

```
# slice 1902 and forward
print(df.head())
df = df.loc[df.Year > 1901]
print(df.head())
```

The output will be as follows:

```
    Region  Year  RgnAvTemp
0        A  1841  12.557395
1        B  1841  13.267048
2        E  1841  12.217463
3        F  1841  13.189420
4        A  1842  13.462887
      Region  Year  RgnAvTemp
292        A  1902  17.021583
293        B  1902  17.590253
294        C  1902  17.493082
295        D  1902  18.706166
296        E  1902  17.390903
```

Figure 3.24: Output after slicing 1902

```
# roll up by year
df_group_year = df.groupby(['Year', 'Region'])\
                .agg({'RgnAvTemp':'mean'})
"""
note that the .droplevel() method removes the multiindex
added by the .agg() method() to make things simpler
later on in our analysis
"""
print(df_group_year.head(12))
print(df_group_year.tail(12))
```

The data should appear as follows:

```
                  RgnAvTemp
Year  Region
1902  A           17.021583
      B            17.590253
      C            17.493082
      D            18.706166
      E            17.390903
      F            17.438122
      G            18.494440
      H            15.708989
      I            19.012183
      J            17.292191
      K            15.020913
      L            17.451698
                  RgnAvTemp
Year  Region
2010  A           19.732301
      B            20.161722
      C            19.922963
      D            21.221710
      E            19.571958
      F            19.903760
      G            21.511489
      H            16.867440
      I            23.772483
      J            18.982479
      K            17.462226
      L            19.918854
```

Figure 3.25: Annual average temperature by region

4. Add a **Year** column using the index (which is in calendar years) level **0**, and the **Region** column using the index level **1**:

```
# add the region column so we can use that for dummy variables
df_group_year['Region'] = df_group_year.index.get_level_values(1)
# add the Year column so we can use that in a model
df_group_year['Year'] = df_group_year.index.get_level_values(0)
# reset the index on the long axis
df_group_year = df_group_year.droplevel(0, axis = 0)
df_group_year = df_group_year.reset_index(drop = True)
```

5. Perhaps the temperature levels or variation differs by region. Let's look at the overall average temperatures for each region:

```
# inspect data by region
region_temps = df_group_year.groupby('Region').
agg({'RgnAvTemp':'mean'})
colors = ['red', 'green', 'blue', 'black', 'lightcoral', \
          'palegreen','skyblue', 'lightslategray', 'magenta', \
          'chartreuse', 'lightblue', 'olive']
fig = plt.figure(figsize=(10, 7))
ax = fig.add_axes([1, 1, 1, 1])
ax.bar(region_temps.index, region_temps.RgnAvTemp, \
       color = colors, alpha = 0.5)
ax.set_title('Mean Air Temperature Measurements', fontsize = 16)
ax.set_xlabel('Region', fontsize = 14)
ax.set_ylabel('Temperature ($^\circ$C)', fontsize = 14)
ax.tick_params(labelsize = 12)
plt.show()
```

The result should appear as follows:

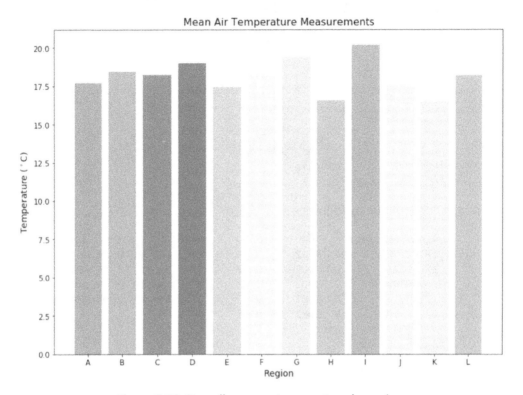

Figure 3.26: Overall average temperature by region

We see that, on average, the regions vary from one another by as many as 5 degrees. Thus, it might benefit the model to take the region into account. To do that, we will create dummy variables from the **Region** column.

6. Pandas has a DataFrame method called **get_dummies()** that we can use for our needs. First, we create a new DataFrame with the new columns. Note that they are already populated with zeros and ones. We then concatenate the dummy variable columns to our data and drop the **Region** column as it is now redundant:

```
# convert the categorical variable 'region' to dummy vars
dummy_cols = pd.get_dummies(df_group_year.Region, \
                          drop_first = True)
df_group_year = pd.concat([df_group_year, dummy_cols], axis = 1)
print(df_group_year.head())
print(df_group_year.tail())
```

The result should be as follows:

```
     RgnAvTemp Region  Year  B  C  D  E  F  G  H  I  J  K  L
0    17.021583      A  1902  0  0  0  0  0  0  0  0  0  0  0
1    17.590253      B  1902  1  0  0  0  0  0  0  0  0  0  0
2    17.493082      C  1902  0  1  0  0  0  0  0  0  0  0  0
3    18.706166      D  1902  0  0  1  0  0  0  0  0  0  0  0
4    17.390903      E  1902  0  0  0  1  0  0  0  0  0  0  0
     RgnAvTemp Region  Year  B  C  D  E  F  G  H  I  J  K  L
1303 16.867440      H  2010  0  0  0  0  0  0  1  0  0  0  0
1304 23.772483      I  2010  0  0  0  0  0  0  0  1  0  0  0
1305 18.982479      J  2010  0  0  0  0  0  0  0  0  1  0  0
1306 17.462226      K  2010  0  0  0  0  0  0  0  0  0  1  0
1307 19.918854      L  2010  0  0  0  0  0  0  0  0  0  0  1
```

Figure 3.27: Addition of dummy variables for the region

Note that in the **get_dummies** method, we set the **drop_first = True** parameter to remove one of the columns, as discussed earlier.

7. We now create a linear model, as before, using the **Year** column and all the dummy columns:

```
linear_model = LinearRegression(fit_intercept = True)
linear_model.fit(df_group_year.loc[:, 'Year':'L'], \
                df_group_year.RgnAvTemp)
r2 = linear_model.score(df_group_year.loc[:, 'Year':'L'], \
                df_group_year.RgnAvTemp)
print('r squared ', r2)
```

The output will be as follows:

```
r squared 0.7778768442731825
```

8. The r^2 value is much higher than before, which looks promising. Generate predictions from the DataFrame with the dummy variables, and then visualize everything on a plot:

```
# construct data to predict from model
pred_X = df_group_year.drop(['RgnAvTemp', 'Region'], axis = 1)
pred_Y = linear_model.predict(pred_X.values)
preds = pd.concat([df_group_year.RgnAvTemp, \
                   df_group_year.Region, \
                   pred_X,  pd.Series(pred_Y)], axis = 1)
preds.rename(columns = {0 : 'pred_temp'}, inplace = True)
print(preds.head())
```

The data should appear as follows:

	RgnAvTemp	Region	Year	B	C	D	E	F	G	H	I	J	K	L	pred_temp
0	17.021583	A	1902	0	0	0	0	0	0	0	0	0	0	0	16.441468
1	17.590253	B	1902	1	0	0	0	0	0	0	0	0	0	0	17.188189
2	17.493082	C	1902	0	1	0	0	0	0	0	0	0	0	0	16.977391
3	18.706166	D	1902	0	0	1	0	0	0	0	0	0	0	0	17.732365
4	17.390903	E	1902	0	0	0	1	0	0	0	0	0	0	0	16.195227

Figure 3.28: Predictions from the new model

9. For plotting, we'll reduce the clutter by sampling from the predictions:

```
# define a sample of the raw data and predictions
# set a seed so results are repeatable
np.random.seed(42)
plot_data = preds.sample(n = 100)
fig = plt.figure(figsize=(10, 7))
ax = fig.add_axes([1, 1, 1, 1])
# Raw data
raw_plot_data = plot_data
ax.scatter(raw_plot_data.Year, raw_plot_data.RgnAvTemp, \
           label = 'Raw Data', c = 'red', s = 1.5)
# Annual averages
annual_plot_data = df_group_year.groupby('Year').agg('mean')
ax.scatter(annual_plot_data.index, annual_plot_data.RgnAvTemp, \
           label = 'Annual average', c = 'k', s = 10)
```

10. Let's also visualize the linear fit results:

```
fit_data = plot_data
for i in range(len(plot_data.Region.unique())):
    region = plot_data.Region.unique()[i]
    plot_region = fit_data.loc[fit_data.Region == region, :]
    ax.scatter(plot_region.Year, plot_region.pred_temp, \
               edgecolor = colors[i], facecolor = "none", \
               s = 80, label = region)
# draw faint lines connecting the raw to the predicted
for i in fit_data.index:
    ax.plot([fit_data.Year[i], fit_data.Year[i]], \
            [fit_data.pred_temp[i], fit_data.RgnAvTemp[i]], \
            '-', linewidth = 0.1, c = "red")
ax.set_title('Mean Air Temperature Measurements', fontsize = 16)
# make the ticks include the first and last years
tick_years = [1902] + list(range(1910, 2011, 10))
ax.set_xlabel('Year', fontsize = 14)
ax.set_ylabel('Temperature ($^\circ$C)', fontsize = 14)
ax.set_ylim(15, 21)
ax.set_xticks(tick_years)
ax.tick_params(labelsize = 12)
ax.legend(fontsize = 12)
plt.show()
```

NOTE

For error-free execution, you should run the cell only after writing the code for both *steps 9* and *10*.

The plot should appear as follows:

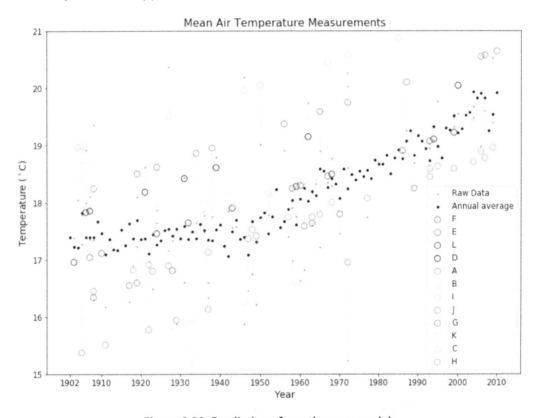

Figure 3.29: Predictions from the new model

What we can see is that the model is predicting different levels for different regions, which, while still not wholly following the trend, accounts for much more of the variation than before.

11. Let's now finish by plotting just one region to get a feel for how well the model works:

```
# let's plot just one region
region_B = preds.loc[preds.B == 1, :]
np.random.seed(42)
plot_data = region_B.sample(n = 50)
fig = plt.figure(figsize=(10, 7))
ax = fig.add_axes([1, 1, 1, 1])
# Raw data
ax.scatter(plot_data.Year, plot_data.RgnAvTemp, \
           label = 'Raw Data', c = 'red', s = 1.5)
ax.scatter(plot_data.Year, plot_data.pred_temp, \
           label = "Predictions", facecolor = "none", \
           edgecolor = "blue", s = 80)
```

12. Draw faint lines connecting the raw to the predicted values:

```
for i in plot_data.index:
    ax.plot([plot_data.Year[i], plot_data.Year[i]], \
            [plot_data.pred_temp[i], plot_data.RgnAvTemp[i]], \
            '-', linewidth = 0.1, c = "red")
# make the ticks include the first and last years
tick_years = [1902] + list(range(1910, 2011, 10))
ax.set_xlabel('Year', fontsize = 14)
ax.set_ylabel('Temperature ($^\circ$C)', fontsize = 14)
ax.set_ylim(16, 21)
ax.set_xticks(tick_years)
ax.tick_params(labelsize = 12)
ax.legend(fontsize = 12)
plt.show()
```

NOTE

For error-free execution, you should run the cell only after writing the code for both *steps 11* and *12*.

The result should be as follows:

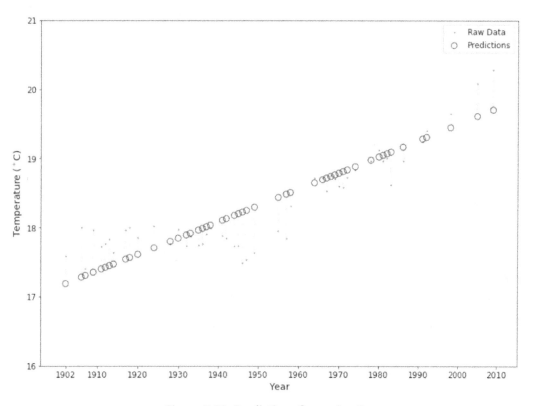

Figure 3.30: Predictions for region B

> **NOTE**
>
> To access the source code for this specific section, please refer to https://packt.live/2YogxDt.
>
> You can also run this example online at https://packt.live/311LDCx. You must execute the entire Notebook in order to get the desired result.

We now have an improved model that follows much of the variation in the data. However, we can see that we have still not captured the change in trend that is apparent around 1960. To address that, we'll explore using linear regression to fit a model by using the powers of the *x* data, known as a polynomial model. First, you will practice using dummy variables using the Austin temperature dataset.

ACTIVITY 3.03: DUMMY VARIABLES

For this activity, we will use the Austin, Texas, weather dataset that we used in the previous activity. In this activity, we will use dummy variables to enhance our linear regression model for this dataset.

The steps to be performed are as follows:

1. Load the **LinearRegression** class from scikit-learn, along with the **fit**, **score**, and **predict** methods, as well as **pandas** and **matplotlib. pyplot**.

2. Load the **austin_weather.csv** dataset, drop all but the **Date** and **TempAvgF** columns, and create **Year**, **Month**, and **Day** columns from the data.

3. Create a 20-day moving average column and populate it, and then slice the first complete year of data (days 1 through 365—this will be the year 2015). After slicing, reset the index of the DataFrame (**Pandas** core method, **reset_index**). Now, create a **Day_of_Year** column and populate it (keep in mind that the first day should be **1**, not **0**).

4. Plot the raw data and moving average against **Day_of_Year**.

    The plot should appear as follows:

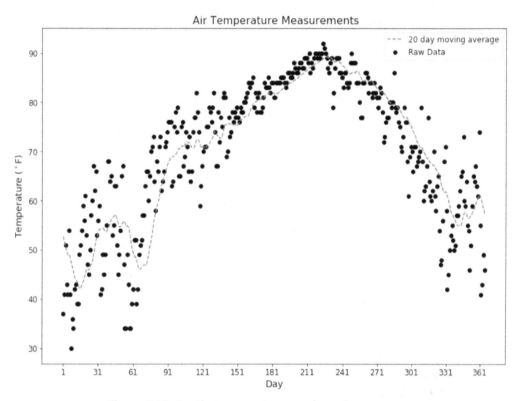

Figure 3.31: Austin temperatures and moving average

Now, investigate whether adding the month to the model could improve the model. To do this, create a **dummy_vars** DataFrame using the pandas **get_dummies** method on the **Month** column of the DataFrame, and then rename the dummy columns **Jan** through **Dec**. Now, concatenate **dummy_vars** to the DataFrame in a new DataFrame called **df_one_year**.

Display the DataFrame and confirm that the dummy columns are present.

5. Use a least squares linear regression model and fit the model to the **Day_of_Year** values and the dummy variables to predict **TempAvgF**.

6. Get the model parameters and the r^2 value. The r^2 value should be much larger than in the previous activity.

7. Using the **Day_of_Year** values and the dummy variables, predict the temperature for the **df_one_year** data.

8. Plot the raw data, the 20-day moving average, and the new prediction.

The output will be as follows:

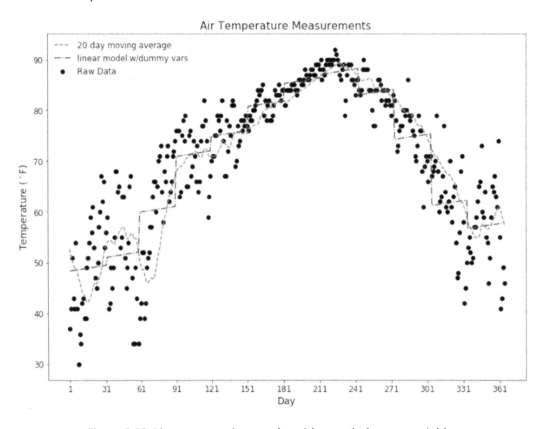

Figure 3.32: Linear regression results with month dummy variables

NOTE

The solution to this activity can be found on page 439.

You have learned how to use the scikit-learn API with the **LinearRegression** class to fit data augmented with dummy variables. The **get_dummies** pandas method was used to generate additional variable columns encoding the months to improve the model. A useful property of the new model is that it accounts for the seasonal variation in temperature, as well as any overall trend. However, it is rather piecewise, which may or may not meet the business needs for prediction.

At this stage, you should be comfortable with basic linear regression as well as using the scikit-learn interface and the **get_dummies** pandas method. We have also touched on a few visualization points and introduced the idea of feature engineering in the context of using dummy variables. We will now move on to polynomial regression, which takes feature engineering in a different direction while still leveraging the power of linear regression.

POLYNOMIAL MODELS WITH LINEAR REGRESSION

Linear regression models are not constrained to straight-line linear models. We can fit some more complicated models using the exact same techniques. In the synthetic temperature data, we can see an upward curve in the trend. Therefore, in addition to any overall (linear in time) trend, there may be a trend related to a positive power of time. If we build a model using integer powers of the independent variable, this is called polynomial regression. For powers up to 2, the equation would be as follows. Note that we refer to the order of the polynomial as the highest power, so this is a polynomial of order 2:

$$y = \beta_0 + \beta_1 * x + \beta_2 * x^2$$

Figure 3.33: Equation of a polynomial of order 2

The addition of this squared term transforms the trendline from a straight line to one that has curvature. In general, polynomial models can be very powerful to fit given data, but they may not extrapolate very well outside the range of the data. This would be an example of overfitting and is especially true as the order of the polynomial increases.

Therefore, in general, you should make limited use of polynomial regression and keep the order low, unless there is a clear business case or a known underlying model that indicates doing otherwise:

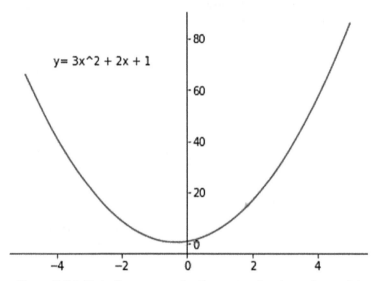

Figure 3.34: Plot of y versus x for the second order polynomial

Note that here, we are looking at a simple model where there is only one feature, the variable *x*. In more complex cases, we might have several features. The number of terms in the equation will increase quickly as the number of features increases. To construct a polynomial, regression packages such as scikit-learn offer methods to automatically generate polynomial features (for example, **sklearn.preprocessing.PolynomialFeatures**). Here, we will build a simple polynomial model manually to illustrate the approach.

EXERCISE 3.04: POLYNOMIAL MODELS WITH LINEAR REGRESSION

In order to fit a polynomial model using linear regression, we need to create the features raised to the desired powers. Recall the earlier discussion on feature engineering; we are going to engineer new features, which are the original independent variables raised to a power:

1. Beginning with the **synth_temp.csv** data, load the packages and classes, and then preprocess the data as before:

```
import pandas as pd
import matplotlib.pyplot as plt
from sklearn.linear_model import LinearRegression
```

```
# load the data
df = pd.read_csv('../Datasets/synth_temp.csv')
# slice 1902 and forward
df = df.loc[df.Year > 1901]
# roll up by year
df_group_year = df.groupby(['Year']).agg({'RgnAvTemp' : 'mean'})
```

2. Now, we add the **Year** column using the index, and then calculate a **Year2** column by raising the **Year** column to the power of 2:

```
# add the Year column so we can use that in a model
df_group_year['Year'] = df_group_year.index
df_group_year = df_group_year\
                .rename(columns = {'RgnAvTemp' : 'AvTemp'})
# add a Year**2 column to build a polynomial model of degree 2
df_group_year['Year2'] = df_group_year['Year']**2
print(df_group_year.head())
print(df_group_year.tail())
```

The result is as follows:

```
         AvTemp   Year      Year2
Year
1902   17.385044   1902   3617604
1903   17.222163   1903   3621409
1904   17.217215   1904   3625216
1905   17.817502   1905   3629025
1906   17.386445   1906   3632836
         AvTemp   Year      Year2
Year
2006   19.904999   2006   4024036
2007   19.820224   2007   4028049
2008   19.245558   2008   4032064
2009   19.537290   2009   4036081
2010   19.919115   2010   4040100
```

Figure 3.35: Yearly temperature data with the year and the year to the second power

3. Fit the data to the model. This time, we will need to provide two sets of values as the inputs to the model, **Year** and **Year2**, which is equivalent to passing x and x^2 to the polynomial equation. As we are providing two columns of data, we do not need to reshape the input data as it will be provided as an $N \times 2$ array by default. The target y value remains the same:

```
# construct the model and inspect results
linear_model = LinearRegression(fit_intercept = True)
linear_model.fit(df_group_year.loc[:, ['Year', 'Year2']], \
                 df_group_year.AvTemp)
print('model coefficients = ', linear_model.coef_)
print('model intercept = ', linear_model.intercept_)
r2 = linear_model.score(df_group_year.loc[:, ['Year', 'Year2']], \
                        df_group_year.AvTemp)
print('r squared = ', r2)
```

The output will be as follows:

```
model coefficients =   [-1.02981369e+00  2.69257683e-04]
model intercept =   1002.0087338444181
r squared =   0.9313996496373635
```

4. The model has improved on the dummy variable method, but let's visualize the results to see whether it is a more reasonable fit. First, generate predictions. Here, we take an additional step to extend the predictions out to the next 10 years to see whether those predictions appear reasonable. In most supervised learning problems, the end goal is to predict values for previously unknown data. As our model simply uses the **Year** and **Year2** variables, we can generate a list of year values and then square them as before, for the next 10 years:

```
# generate predictions for visualization
pred_X = df_group_year.loc[:, ['Year', 'Year2']]
pred_Y = linear_model.predict(pred_X)
# generate predictions for the next 10 years
pred_X_future = pd.DataFrame(list(range(2011, 2021)))\
                            .rename(columns = {0 : 'Year'})
pred_X_future['Year2'] = pred_X_future['Year']**2
pred_Y_future = linear_model.predict(pred_X_future)
```

5. Now, create a visualization:

```
fig = plt.figure(figsize=(10, 7))
ax = fig.add_axes([1, 1, 1, 1]);
# Raw data
raw_plot_data = df
ax.scatter(raw_plot_data.Year, raw_plot_data.RgnAvTemp, \
           label = 'Raw Data', c = 'red', s = 1.5)
# Annual averages
ax.scatter(df_group_year.Year, df_group_year.AvTemp, \
           label = 'Annual average', c = 'k', s = 10)
# linear fit
ax.plot(pred_X.Year, pred_Y, c = "blue", linestyle = '-.', \
        linewidth = 4, label = 'linear fit')
```

6. Visualize the future predictions:

```
ax.plot(pred_X_future.Year, pred_Y_future, c = "purple", \
        linestyle = '--', linewidth = 4, \
        label = 'future predictions')
ax.set_title('Mean Air Temperature Measurements', fontsize = 16)
# make the ticks include the first and last years
tick_years = [1902] + list(range(1910, 2021, 10))
ax.set_xlabel('Year', fontsize = 14)
ax.set_ylabel('Temperature ($^\circ$C)', fontsize = 14)
ax.set_ylim(15, 21)
ax.set_xticks(tick_years)
ax.tick_params(labelsize = 12)
ax.legend(fontsize = 12)
plt.show()
```

The result is as follows:

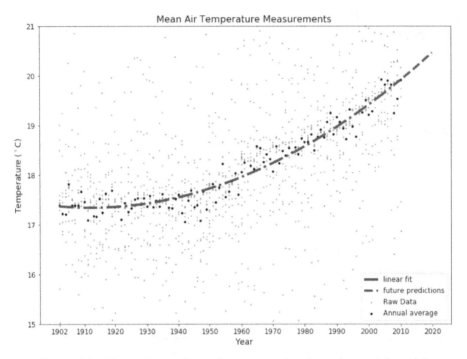

Figure 3.36: Linear regression using a second order polynomial model

> **NOTE**
>
> To access the source code for this specific section, please refer to https://packt.live/3fSusaR.
>
> You can also run this example online at https://packt.live/2BulmCd. You must execute the entire Notebook in order to get the desired result.

Referring to *Figure 3.36,* we can see the performance benefit in using the polynomial model, with the trendline almost following the 10-year moving average. This is a reasonably good fit given the amount of noise in the yearly average raw data. In such a case, it should not be expected that the model will fit the data perfectly. If our model was to perfectly fit the observed examples, there would be a very strong case for overfitting the data, leading to poor predictive power with unseen examples. As an example, imagine we fitted a 10th order polynomial to this data. The resulting model would wiggle up and down and might be moving up or down very steeply at the last data point, which would lead to poor predictions. In this case, using order 2, we see that the future trend seems reasonable, although that remains to be demonstrated.

ACTIVITY 3.04: FEATURE ENGINEERING WITH LINEAR REGRESSION

We have tried a standard linear model as well as a model including dummy variables. In this activity, we will create some periodic features to try and get a better fit for the data. Periodic features are derived from functions that repeat over some range of the independent variable. In *Figure 3.37*, we can see that the data at the beginning of the year is near the same values and, in between, the temperature increases and then decreases. This is intuitively reasonable because we know that in temperate climates, there is an annual temperature cycle. Thus, we might improve the model if we include features that are periodic on a time scale of 1 year. We can construct sine and cosine functions that have the desired behavior.

When fitting a model with engineered periodic features, we face an additional challenge to determine how to line up the periodic cycle of the features to the actual data. You can think of this as a time offset in this case, which we don't know a priori. You could also think of the offset as a hyperparameter—fitting the model does not give us the value so we have to find the best value in some other way. In the following diagram, the needed offset is Δt:

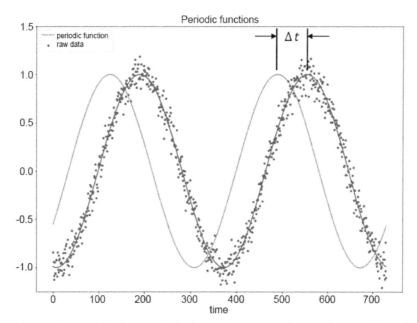

Figure 3.37: Some data exhibiting periodic behavior versus time and a candidate function to fit to the data

Fortunately, if we use sine and cosine functions for our features, there is a way to address this. It is a mathematical fact that any given sine function at a single period, such as the raw data in *Figure 3.37*, can be expressed as a linear combination of a sine and cosine function of the same period. In the next figure, we show a sine and cosine function, each with a period of 365 days, and the raw data from *Figure 3.37*. We also show a linear combination of the sine and cosine function that matches the raw data very well. Thus, to fit a sine (or cosine) function to our data, we simply need to engineer two features, one as the sine of the time, and the other as the cosine of the time. The linear regression will then find the best coefficients just like any other feature. Note that this implies we know the period:

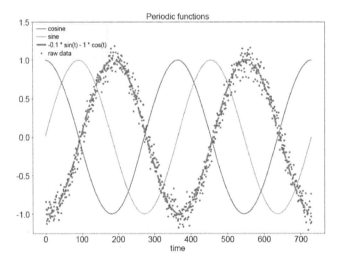

Figure 3.38: A linear combination of a sine and cosine function will match a sine function shifted by an unknown time offset

The last thing we need to know is how to formulate the sine and cosine functions. For this, we can use the NumPy methods, **sin** and **cos**. We know we want a period of 1 year, and our data is in days. The correct way to write a sine function with a 365-day period is as follows:

$$\sin_{365} = \sin\left(2 * \pi * \frac{time}{365}\right)$$

Figure 3.39: A sine function with a period of 365 days

Alternatively, in Python a sine function with a 365-day period is as follows:

```
sin_365 = np.sin(2 * np.pi * df_one_year['day_of_year'] / 365
```

Figure 3.40: A Python series with a period of 365 days

Now, let's proceed with the activity to use a periodic function to fit the Austin temperature data. The steps to be performed are as follows:

1. Load the packages and classes (**numpy**, **pandas**, **LinearRegression**, and **matplotlib**).

2. Perform the preprocessing as before, through to the step where the **Day_of_Year** column is created.

3. Add a column for the sine of **Day_of_Year** and another for the cosine of **Day_of_Year**.

4. Perform a linear regression of the average temperature versus the **Day_of_Year** and the sine and cosine features.

5. Print the parameters of the model and the r² score.

6. Generate predictions using the new features.

7. Visualize the raw data and the new model.

8. The output will be as follows:

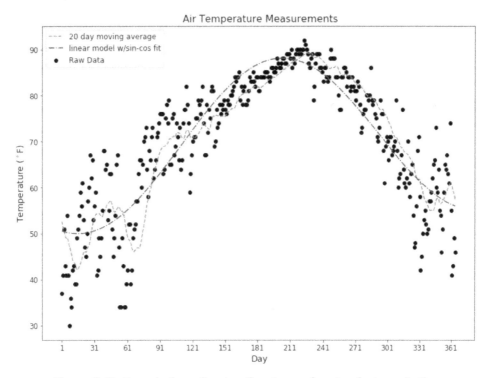

Figure 3.41: Expected result using the sine and cosine features in the
linear regression model

You have by now learned that we can engineer features by applying functions to existing features, such as polynomial functions or periodic functions. You have seen how to construct period functions using sine and cosine functions to fit an arbitrary sine or cosine function. In this case, we assumed a period of 365 days, which is reasonable based on the annual weather cycle of temperate regions on Earth. In an actual business case, we may not be certain of the period, or there might be more than one cycle occurring at the same time (such as weekly, monthly, and quarterly cycles in sales). In addition, using functions such as polynomials and sines/cosines can easily lead to overfitting, resulting in very poor extrapolation.

> **NOTE**
>
> The solution to this activity can be found on page 448.

In *Figure 3.41*, we see that the new model smoothly varies during the year, returning at the end of the year to a value near the beginning. Since we already knew that there is an overall trend during the year, this model, because it includes the **Day_of_Year** feature, shows that the temperature at the end of the year is somewhat higher than at the beginning. In terms of feature engineering, we could consider using the date (converting it to, say, an integer) and fitting the model over more than 1 year's worth of data to try and capture longer-term trends.

GENERIC MODEL TRAINING

The least squares method of constructing a linear regression model is a useful and accurate method of training, assuming that the dimensionality of the dataset is low and that the system memory is sufficiently large to be able to manage the dataset.

In recent times, large datasets have become more readily available, with universities, governments, and even some companies releasing large datasets for free online; as such, it may be relatively easy to exceed system memory when using the least squares method of regression modeling. In this situation, we will need to employ a different method of training the algorithm, such as gradient descent, which is not as susceptible to high dimensionality, allows large datasets to be trained, and avoids the use of memory-intensive matrix operations.

Before we look at gradient descent in a little more detail, we will revisit the process of training a model in a more general form, as most training methods, including gradient descent, adhere to this generic process. The following is an overview of the parameter update loop of the model training process:

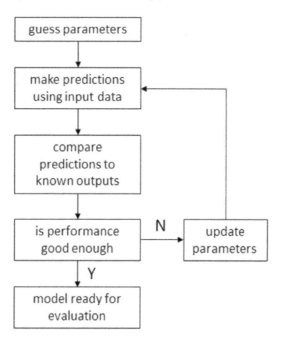

Figure 3.42: Generic model parameter update loop

The training process involves the repeated exposure of the model and its parameters (including hyperparameters) to a set of sample training data and passing the predicted values issued by the model to a specified cost or error function. The cost function is, with some of the hyperparameters, what determines how to calculate the updates in the "update parameters" block in *Figure 3.42*.

The cost function is used to determine how close the model is to its target values and a measure of progress throughout the training process. However, the cost function is also used to determine the parameter updates, in combination with some of the hyperparameters. For example, in our linear regression case, the cost function is the mean squared error.

The least squares method, which we showed as a method to build a linear regression model, minimizes the MSE, hence, least squares. We can therefore update our diagram of the training process to the following:

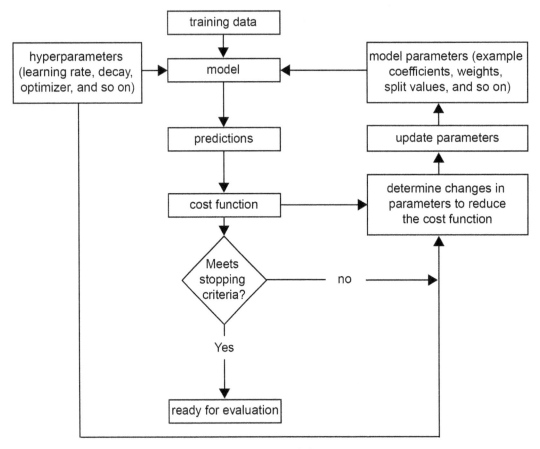

Figure 3.43: Generic training process

GRADIENT DESCENT

The process of gradient descent can be summarized as a means of updating the parameters of the model proportionally and in response to an error within the system, as defined by the cost function. There are a number of cost functions that can be selected, depending on the type of model being fitted or the problem being solved. We will select the simple, but effective, mean squared error cost function.

Recall that the equation of a straight line can be written as follows:

$$y = \beta_0 + \beta_1 * x$$

Figure 3.44: Equation of a straight line

The following figure is a plot of the cost function, J, for ranges of values, β_0 and β_1. The optimal set of parameters are those for which the cost function is a minimum, and this point is called the global minima of the cost function. We can then make an analogy with trying to find the lowest point in a valley while hiking. Intuitively, wherever we are standing, if we are not at the bottom, then we are on a slope, and to get to the bottom, we would head downhill. Thus, the slope is the gradient, and finding the minimum is gradient descent:

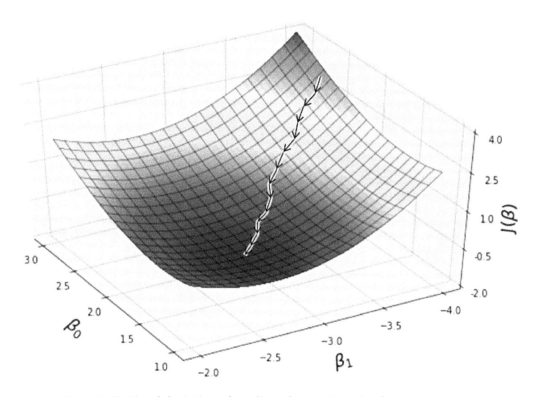

Figure 3.45: Visual depiction of gradient descent in a simple two-parameter linear regression case

As you can see in the preceding figure, on each training cycle, the parameters β_0 and β_1 are updated to move in the direction of the steepest slope (the gradient), and eventually, the minimum of $J(\beta)$ is found.

Let's look at the gradient descent algorithm in greater detail:

1. Gradient descent starts by taking an initial, random guess at the values for all β. Note that in some models, this step, called initialization, may be constrained by choosing a particular distribution from which the initial values are sampled. The choice of initialization may be considered a hyperparameter and can affect the final outcome, especially in complicated models such as artificial neural networks. Most methods implemented in Python have good defaults, and it is common to use the defaults.

2. A prediction for each of the samples in the training set is made using the random values for β, and the cost function $J(\beta)$ is then computed.

3. The values for β are then updated, making a small adjustment proportional to the error, in an attempt to minimize the error. In general, it is not the best approach to try to move all the way from the current β values to the values that would minimize $J(\beta)$ because the loss surface may not be smooth as shown in *Figure 3.45*. Most real loss surfaces, even in three dimensions, have multiple peaks and valleys. For more complicated cost function surfaces, there are multiple minima, called local minima, and the lowest of all the minima is the global minima. Non-convex cost functions may present challenges in finding the global minima, and a lot of effort in the research community has been devoted to finding ways to efficiently find the global minima of non-convex surfaces. The hyperparameter **learning rate**, denoted by y, is used to adjust the step size on each pass of the training.

This process is visualized in the following graph, simplified to two dimensions:

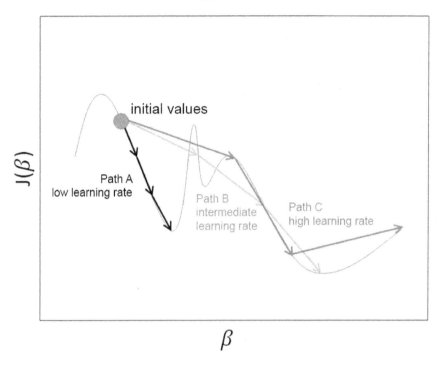

Figure 3.46: Gradient descent process

In this simplified case, using a low learning rate leads to Path A, and we get stuck in a local minimum. Path C results from a very high learning rate and does not converge. Path B uses an intermediate learning rate value and converges to the global minimum.

As a general hint for setting the learning rate, start larger, say around 0.1, and if a solution cannot be found, that is, the error is an **NaN** or is varying wildly, reduce the learning rate by a factor of 10. Once a learning rate is found that allows a relatively smooth decrease of the cost function versus epochs, other hyperparameters, including the learning rate, can be tested to achieve the best results.

While this process may sound complicated, it isn't anywhere near as scary as it looks. Gradient descent can be summarized by making a one-time-only guess at the values for the parameters, calculating the error in the guess, making small adjustments to the parameters, and continually repeating the process until the error converges at a minimum value. To reinforce our understanding, let's look at a more concrete example. We will use gradient descent to train the original linear regression model we constructed in *Exercise 3.02: Fitting a Linear Model Using the Least Squares Method*, replacing the least squares method with gradient descent.

EXERCISE 3.05: LINEAR REGRESSION WITH GRADIENT DESCENT

In this exercise, we will implement a gradient descent algorithm manually. We will start with the **synth_temp.csv** data, as before:

1. Import the packages and classes as before:

```
import pandas as pd
import numpy as np
import matplotlib.pyplot as plt
from sklearn.metrics import r2_score
```

Before we can start the gradient descent process, we need to implement some key functions.

2. Write a function to define our linear model. This is where the advantage of using the shortened form of the linear model comes in handy. We can use linear algebra multiplication between the parameters (β) and the input values, *x*:

```
# model function
def h_x(Beta, X):
# calculate the matrix dot product of X and the Betas
    return np.dot(Beta, X).flatten()
```

3. We also need to write a function to evaluate the cost function, $J(\beta)$:

```
# cost function
def J_beta(pred, true):
```

```
# mean squared error
    return np.mean((pred - true) ** 2)
```

4. Finally, we need to implement the function to update the parameters:

```
# update function
def update(pred, true, X, gamma):
    return gamma * np.sum((true - pred) * X, axis = 1)
```

5. Next, load the data, slicing from 1902 forward, computing the annual averages, and adding the **Year** column:

```
# load the data
df = pd.read_csv('../Datasets/synth_temp.csv')
# slice 1902 and forward
df = df.loc[df.Year > 1901]
# roll up by year
df_group_year = df.groupby(['Year']).agg({'RgnAvTemp' : 'mean'})
# add the Year column so we can use that in a model
df_group_year['Year'] = df_group_year.index
df_group_year = \
df_group_year.rename(columns = {'RgnAvTemp' : 'AvTemp'})
```

6. Now, we will build the training data. First, we need to scale the data to between **0** and **1** before using gradient descent. Some machine learning algorithms can work well with raw data (such as regular linear regression), but when using gradient descent, if the variables have very different scales, then the gradient values will be much larger in the axes of some of the parameters than others. Left unscaled, the data in raw form could distort the descent along the cost function surface, skewing the results. Intuitively, in our case, the **Year** data is in the order of thousands, while the **AvTemp** data is in the order of tens. Thus, the **Year** variable would dominate in terms of its influence on the parameters.

    There are a variety of scaling methods used in machine learning. Examples are normalization to a specific range (such as (0, 1) or (-1, 1)), and standardization (where the data is scaled to a mean of 0 and standard deviation of 1). Here, we will normalize both the **x** and **y** data to the range (0, 1):

```
# scale the data and add the X0 series
X_min = df_group_year.Year.min()
X_range = df_group_year.Year.max() - df_group_year.Year.min()
Y_min = df_group_year.AvTemp.min()
```

```
Y_range = df_group_year.AvTemp.max() - df_group_year.AvTemp.min()
scale_X = (df_group_year.Year - X_min) / X_range
train_X = pd.DataFrame({'X0' : np.ones(df_group_year.shape[0]), \
                        'X1' : scale_X}).transpose()
train_Y = (df_group_year.AvTemp - Y_min) / Y_range

print(train_X.iloc[:, :5])
print(train_Y[:5])
```

The output should appear as follows:

```
Year 1902       1903       1904       1905       1906
X0    1.0   1.000000   1.000000   1.000000   1.000000
X1    0.0   0.009259   0.018519   0.027778   0.037037
Year
1902      0.114676
1903      0.058017
1904      0.056296
1905      0.265110
1906      0.115164
Name: AvTemp, dtype: float64
```

Figure 3.47: Normalized data for gradient descent

Note that the **train_Y** values are the true values, also called *ground truth*.

7. As we have learned, we need to initialize the parameter values. Note that we use the NumPy **random.seed()** method with a constant value. Setting **random.seed** will reproduce the same results every time you run the notebook. This is useful during model development and while exploring hyperparameters so that you can see the impact of changes you make versus the impact of the random initialization. The **reshape()** method is used to put the data into the correct matrix form:

```
# initialize Beta and the learning rate gamma
np.random.seed(42)
Beta = np.random.randn(2).reshape((1, 2)) * 0.1
print('initial Beta\n', Beta)
```

The values should look something like the following:

```
initial Beta [[ 0.04967142 -0.01382643]]
```

8. We also need to set a couple of hyperparameters, the learning rate, gamma, and the maximum number of times that we will go through the training cycle (epochs):

```
gamma = 0.0005
max_epochs = 100
```

9. Make an initial prediction and calculate the error or cost in that prediction using the defined **h_x** and **J_beta** functions:

```
y_pred = h_x(Beta, train_X)
print('Initial cost J(Beta) = ' + str(J_beta(y_pred, train_Y)))
```

The output will be as follows:

```
Initial cost J(Beta) = 0.18849128813354338
```

10. We are now ready to use a loop to iterate through the training. Here, we are storing the **epoch** and **cost** values so that we can visualize them later. Also, we are printing out the **cost** function and **epoch** every 10 epochs:

```
epochs = []
costs = []
for epoch in range(max_epochs):
    Beta += update(y_pred, train_Y, train_X, gamma)
    y_pred = h_x(Beta, train_X)
    cost = J_beta(y_pred, train_Y)
    if epoch % 10 == 0:
        print('New cost J(Beta) = ' + str(round(cost, 3)) \
                + ' at epoch ' + str(epoch))
    epochs.append(epoch)
    costs.append(cost)
```

The output will be as follows:

```
New cost J(Beta) = 0.171 at epoch 0
New cost J(Beta) = 0.083 at epoch 10
New cost J(Beta) = 0.06 at epoch 20
New cost J(Beta) = 0.052 at epoch 30
New cost J(Beta) = 0.048 at epoch 40
New cost J(Beta) = 0.046 at epoch 50
New cost J(Beta) = 0.043 at epoch 60
New cost J(Beta) = 0.041 at epoch 70
New cost J(Beta) = 0.039 at epoch 80
New cost J(Beta) = 0.037 at epoch 90
```

Figure 3.48: Training results every 10 epochs

Observe in *Figure 3.48* the relatively rapid decrease in the cost function in the first 20 cycles, before the improvement slows down. This is a very typical pattern for gradient descent training when the learning rate is at a reasonable value.

11. Visualize the training history:

```
# plot training history
fig = plt.figure(figsize=(10, 7))
ax = fig.add_axes([1, 1, 1, 1])
ax.plot(epochs, costs)
ax.tick_params(labelsize = 14)
ax.set_ylabel('Cost Function J(' + r'$\theta$' + ')', \
              fontsize = 18)
ax.set_xlabel('Epoch', fontsize = 18)
plt.show()
```

The output will be as follows:

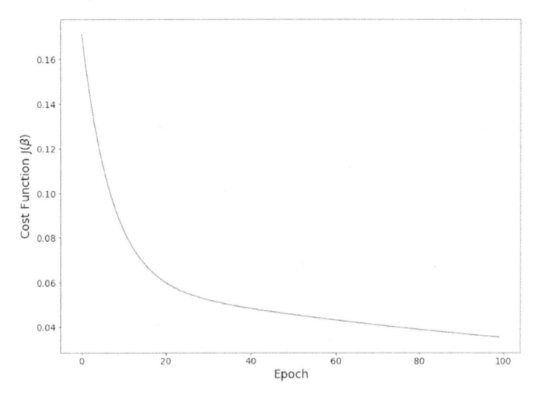

Figure 3.49: Plot of the cost function versus epoch for the first 100 epochs

In *Figure 3.49*, we can see that the cost function was still decreasing when we stopped the updates. Thus, we could rerun the training with a larger **max_epochs** hyperparameter and see whether the results improved.

12. Use the **r2_score** function from **sklearn.metrics**, which we imported earlier, to compute the R-squared score for the model trained using gradient descent:

```
# calculate the r squared value
r2 = r2_score(train_Y, y_pred)
print('r squared = ', r2)
```

The output should be similar to the following:

```
r squared =  0.5488427996385263
```

Note that you could vary the learning rate and max epochs parameters to see the impact on the training history and the r^2 value.

13. Now, we generate predictions using the training data so that we can visualize the resulting model. In this cell, we first predict using the scaled training data since the model coefficients are based on the scaled inputs, and then we scale the results back to "real" values using the (**Y_min** and **Y_range**) values we saved earlier in the scaling process. Note the use of our model function, **h_x**, to generate the predictions. Also, for convenience, we replace **pred_X** with the original year values for use in visualization:

```
# generate predictions for visualization
pred_X = train_X
# make predictions
pred_Y = h_x(Beta, pred_X)
# scale predictions back to real values
pred_Y = (pred_Y * Y_range) + Y_min
# replace the X with the original values
pred_X = df_group_year['Year']
```

14. One impact of doing the regression with scaled data is that the β values are relative to the scaled data, not the original data. In many cases, we would like to obtain the unscaled parameter values. In particular, in linear regression, the unscaled coefficients are interpretable as the unit change in the dependent variable for a unit change in the variable associated with the parameter. Specifically, in our case here, β_1 is the "slope" of the line and represents the change in average annual temperature for a change of 1 year. We can now calculate the parameters of the unscaled model:

```
# scale the coefficients back to real values
Beta0 = (Y_min + Y_range * Beta[0, 0] \
            - Y_range * Beta[0, 1] * X_min / X_range)
Beta1 = Y_range * Beta[0, 1] / X_range
```

15. Visualize the results:

```
fig = plt.figure(figsize=(10, 7))
ax = fig.add_axes([1, 1, 1, 1])
# Raw data
raw_plot_data = df
ax.scatter(raw_plot_data.Year, raw_plot_data.RgnAvTemp, \
            label = 'Raw Data', c = 'red', s = 1.5)
# Annual averages
ax.scatter(df_group_year.Year, df_group_year.AvTemp, \
            label = 'Annual average', c = 'k', s = 10)
# linear fit
ax.plot(pred_X, pred_Y, c = "blue", linestyle = '-.', \
            linewidth = 4, label = 'linear fit')
```

16. Put the model on the plot:

```
ax.text(1902, 20, 'Temp = ' + str(round(Beta0, 2)) \
            +' + ' + str(round(Beta1, 4)) + ' * Year', \
            fontsize = 16, backgroundcolor = 'white')
ax.set_title('Mean Air Temperature Measurements', fontsize = 16)
# make the ticks include the first and last years
tick_years = [1902] + list(range(1910, 2011, 10))
ax.set_xlabel('Year', fontsize = 14)
ax.set_ylabel('Temperature ($^\circ$C)', fontsize = 14)
ax.set_ylim(15, 21)
ax.set_xticks(tick_years)
ax.tick_params(labelsize = 12)
ax.legend(fontsize = 12)
plt.show()
```

NOTE

For error-free execution, you should run the cell only after writing the code for both *steps 15* and *16*.

The output will be as follows:

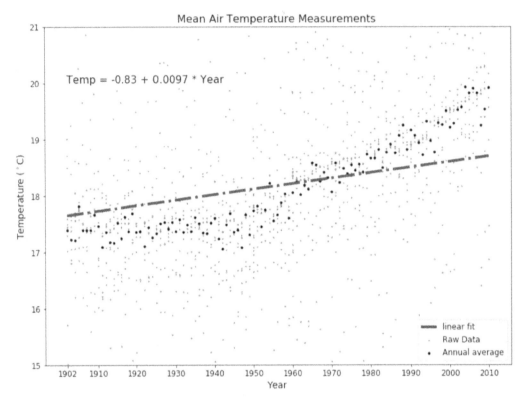

Figure 3.50: Mean air temperature measurements using gradient descent

> **NOTE**
>
> To access the source code for this specific section, please refer to
> https://packt.live/3diOR76.
>
> You can also run this example online at https://packt.live/2YWvviZ.
> You must execute the entire Notebook in order to get the desired result.

You have just trained your first model with gradient descent. This is an important step as this simple tool can be used to construct more complicated models such as logistic regression and neural network models. We must first, however, note one important observation: the r-squared value produced by the gradient descent model is not as high as the least squares model, and the equation of the line is different.

That being said, there are many more options available to modify the gradient descent process, including different types of gradient descent algorithms and more advanced uses of learning rate and the way the data is supplied during training. These modifications fall outside the scope of this book, as an entire book could be written on the gradient descent process and methods for improving performance. With enough experimentation, we would be able to match the two results to any arbitrary level of precision, but in this case, that would not be an effective use of time.

In this exercise, we implemented gradient descent directly; however, we would not typically use this implementation, but instead leverage an existing, highly optimized package. The scikit-learn method of gradient descent contains a number of optimizations and can be used in only a few lines of code. The following is from the scikit-learn documentation (refer to https://scikit-learn.org/stable/modules/generated/sklearn.linear_model.SGDRegressor.html): "SGD stands for Stochastic Gradient Descent: the gradient of the loss is estimated each sample at a time and the model is updated along the way with a decreasing strength schedule (aka learning rate)."

In our examples so far, we have used all the data directly in the linear regression method or used all the data for every update in our implementation by means of gradient descent. However, with gradient descent, we have total control over when to update our estimates of the parameters.

EXERCISE 3.06: OPTIMIZING GRADIENT DESCENT

In this exercise, we will use the scikit-learn module **SGDRegressor**, which utilizes stochastic gradient descent to train models.

In this exercise, we start with the **synth_temp.csv** data, as before:

1. Import the packages and classes as before, adding **SGDRegressor**:

```
import pandas as pd
import numpy as np
import matplotlib.pyplot as plt
from sklearn.metrics import r2_score
from sklearn.linear_model import SGDRegressor
```

2. Load the data and carry out the same preprocessing and scaling as before:

```
# load the data
df = pd.read_csv('../Datasets/synth_temp.csv')
# slice 1902 and forward
```

```
df = df.loc[df.Year > 1901]
# roll up by year
df_group_year = df.groupby(['Year']).agg({'RgnAvTemp' : 'mean'})
# add the Year column so we can use that in a model
df_group_year['Year'] = df_group_year.index
df_group_year = df_group_year\
                .rename(columns = {'RgnAvTemp' : 'AvTemp'})
# scale the data
X_min = df_group_year.Year.min()
X_range = df_group_year.Year.max() - df_group_year.Year.min()
Y_min = df_group_year.AvTemp.min()
Y_range = df_group_year.AvTemp.max() - df_group_year.AvTemp.min()
scale_X = (df_group_year.Year - X_min) / X_range
train_X = scale_X.ravel()
train_Y = ((df_group_year.AvTemp - Y_min) / Y_range).ravel()
```

3. We instantiate the model by calling **SGDRegressor**, and pass the hyperparameters. Here, we set the NumPy **random.seed** method and, as we are not passing a seed or method to **SGDRegressor**, it uses the NumPy random generator:

```
# create the model object
np.random.seed(42)
model = SGDRegressor(loss = 'squared_loss', max_iter = 100, \
                     learning_rate = 'constant', eta0 = 0.0005, \
                     tol = 0.00009, penalty = 'none')
```

4. We fit the model by calling the **fit** method of the model object:

```
# fit the model
model.fit(train_X.reshape((-1, 1)), train_Y)
```

The output should be as follows, echoing the parameters used in the call:

```
SGDRegressor(alpha=0.0001, average=False, early_stopping=False, epsilon=0.1,
            eta0=0.0005, fit_intercept=True, l1_ratio=0.15,
            learning_rate='constant', loss='squared_loss', max_iter=100,
            n_iter_no_change=5, penalty='none', power_t=0.25,
            random_state=None, shuffle=True, tol=0.001,
            validation_fraction=0.1, verbose=0, warm_start=False)
```

Figure 3.51: Output from calling the fit method on the model object

5. We now want to retrieve the coefficients from the model and rescale them as in the previous exercise so that we can compare the results directly:

```
Beta0 = (Y_min + Y_range * model.intercept_[0] \
         - Y_range * model.coef_[0] * X_min / X_range)
Beta1 = Y_range * model.coef_[0] / X_range
print(Beta0)
print(Beta1)
```

The output should be as follows:

```
-0.5798539884018439
0.009587734834970016
```

6. As before, we now generate predictions, and then use the **r2_score** function to calculate r^2. Note that since we are using a scikit-learn method, we use the **predict** method on the model object to return predictions:

```
# generate predictions
pred_X = df_group_year['Year']
pred_Y = model.predict(train_X.reshape((-1, 1)))
# calculate the r squared value
r2 = r2_score(train_Y, pred_Y)
print('r squared = ', r2)
```

The result will be something similar to the following:

```
r squared = 0.5436475116024911
```

7. Finally, we rescale the predictions back to actual temperatures for visualization:

```
# scale predictions back to real values
pred_Y = (pred_Y * Y_range) + Y_min
```

8. Now, visualize the results:

```
fig = plt.figure(figsize=(10, 7))
ax = fig.add_axes([1, 1, 1, 1])
# Raw data
raw_plot_data = df
ax.scatter(raw_plot_data.Year, raw_plot_data.RgnAvTemp, \
           label = 'Raw Data', c = 'red', s = 1.5)
# Annual averages
ax.scatter(df_group_year.Year, df_group_year.AvTemp, \
           label = 'Annual average', c = 'k', s = 10)
```

```
# linear fit
ax.plot(pred_X, pred_Y, c = "blue", linestyle = '-.', \
        linewidth = 4, label = 'linear fit')
# put the model on the plot
ax.text(1902, 20, 'Temp = ' + str(round(Beta0, 2)) +' + ' \
        + str(round(Beta1, 4)) + ' * Year', fontsize = 16)
ax.set_title('Mean Air Temperature Measurements', fontsize = 16)
# make the ticks include the first and last years
tick_years = [1902] + list(range(1910, 2011, 10))
ax.set_xlabel('Year', fontsize = 14)
ax.set_ylabel('Temperature ($^\circ$C)', fontsize = 14)
ax.set_ylim(15, 21)
ax.set_xticks(tick_years)
ax.tick_params(labelsize = 12)
ax.legend(fontsize = 12)
plt.show()
```

The output will be as follows:

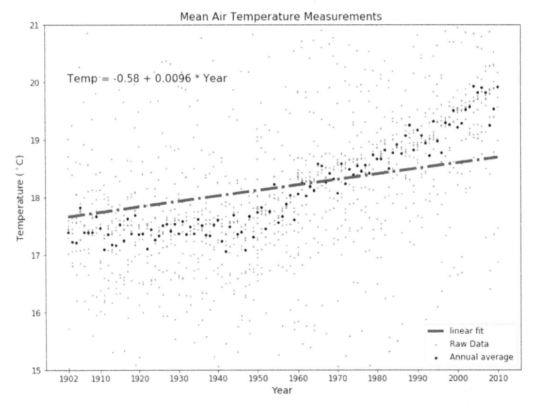

Figure 3.52: Gradient descent results of linear fit using the scikit-learn interface

> **NOTE**
>
> To access the source code for this specific section, please refer to
> https://packt.live/2zWladm.
>
> You can also run this example online at https://packt.live/3eqhroj.
> You must execute the entire Notebook in order to get the desired result.

Compare this graph to the one constructed using the manual implementation of gradient descent. Notice the similarities: this provides us with confidence that both implementations of gradient descent are correct. However, we now have the use of all the power of the scikit-learn implementation of SGD. For more complex problems, this could be critical to success. For example, you may have noticed that **SGDRegressor** supports regularization methods, but we did not use them. Some regularization methods add an adjustment to the cost function equation to apply a penalty (a factor to make a parameter smaller) to parameter values that are large in comparison to others. There are other methods available specific to some models (for example, artificial neural networks have several additional regularization approaches that can be used). One important use of regularization is to reduce overfitting, which we have touched on but has not been present in the simple models we have used so far. Further discussion relating to regularization can be found in *Chapter 6, Ensemble Modeling*.

ACTIVITY 3.05: GRADIENT DESCENT

In this activity, we will implement the same model as *Activity 3.02: Linear Regression Using the Least Squares Method*; however, we will use the gradient descent process.

The steps to be performed are as follows:

1. Import the modules and classes; in this case:

```
import pandas as pd
import numpy as np
import matplotlib.pyplot as plt
from sklearn.metrics import r2_score
from sklearn.linear_model import SGDRegressor
```

2. Load the data (**austin_weather.csv**) and preprocess up to the point of creating the **Day_of_Year** column and slicing one full year (2015).

3. Create scaled *X* and *Y* data, scaling between 0 and 1 in each case.

4. Instantiate a model using **SGDRegressor**. Remember to set the NumPy **random.seed()** method.

5. Fit the model.

6. Extract the rescaled model coefficients, **Theta0** and **Theta1**, and print them.

7. Generate predictions using the scaled data, use the **r2_score** method to get the r^2 value of the fit, and then print out r^2.

8. Rescale the predictions to use for plotting.

9. Create a visualization with the raw data, the 20-day moving averages, and the new linear fit line. Include the model equation on the chart.

The output should be as follows:

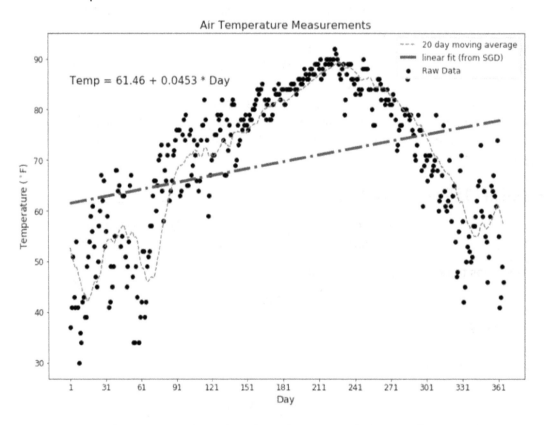

Figure 3.53: Optimized gradient descent predicted trendline

> **NOTE**
>
> The solution to this activity can be found on page 452.

By now, you should be comfortable using the scikit-learn **SGDRegressor** interface as well as understanding the basic process of gradient descent. You should also have some idea as to when using SGD is preferred over, say, standard linear regression.

We have now covered data smoothing and simple linear regression, have developed a gradient descent algorithm by hand, and used the scikit-learn **SGDRegressor** interface to apply gradient descent to linear regression. You've seen how to do some feature engineering with dummy variables, polynomial features, and sine/cosine features. You may have noticed along the way that most of the code is used to prepare the data and visualize results. This is not unusual for machine learning—understanding and working with data is generally the largest task, and critical to success. We'll now move on to another application of regression, multiple linear regression.

MULTIPLE LINEAR REGRESSION

We have already covered regular linear regression, as well as linear regression with polynomial and other terms, and considered training them with both the least squares method and gradient descent. This section of the chapter considers an additional type of linear regression: multiple linear regression, where more than one variable (or feature) is used to construct the model. In fact, we have already used multiple linear regression without calling it as such—when we added dummy variables, and again when we added the sine and cosine terms, we were fitting multiple x variables to predict the single y variable.

Let's consider a simple example of where multiple linear regression naturally arises as a modeling solution. Suppose you were shown the following chart, which is the total annual earnings of a hypothetical tech worker over a long career. You can see that over time, their pay increased, but there are some odd jumps and changes in the data slope:

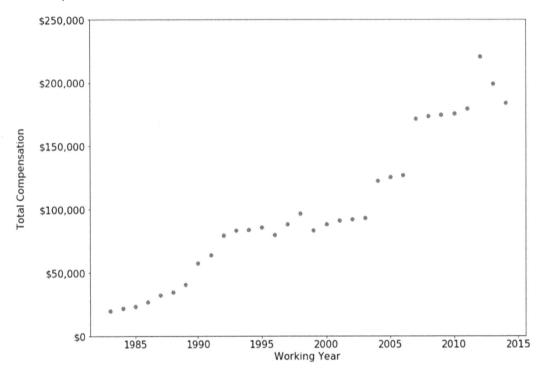

Figure 3.54: Earnings over the career of a hypothetical worker

You might guess that this worker changed jobs from time to time, causing some of the jumps. However, suppose from the data we are given, the compensation is the multiplication of their average hours per week each year and an hourly rate. Well, intuitively, the total in each year would be the product of the total hours worked and the rate. Instead of a simple linear model of income versus year, we could build a multiple linear model using year, rate, and hours per week to predict the totals. In this hypothetical case, using multiple linear regression versus simple linear regression results in the following chart:

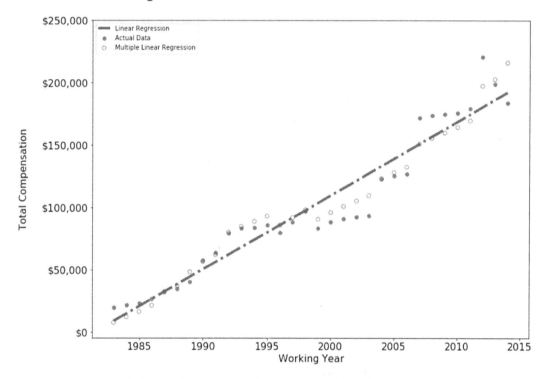

Figure 3.55: Simple linear regression versus multiple linear regression on a hypothetical dataset

The red circles appear to be a more satisfying model than the simple blue line. There are still features in the data not explained—perhaps there were bonuses or retirement fund matches in some years, and perhaps there are other things we are unaware of in relation to the data. Nonetheless, it makes sense to use multiple *x* variables in such a case.

Before moving on, let's cover a few details. We will be using the **corr()** method in pandas, which takes a DataFrame and calculates the pairwise correlation among all the variables. There are two key things that we will be investigating in the following exercise. First, when executing regression with multiple *x* variables, if any of the variables are highly correlated, this can cause issues with the model. This problem is known as **multicollinearity** and can cause the coefficient estimates to be unstable to small changes in the data or the model. In an extreme case, where one variable is actually a linear combination of other variables, the model can become singular; in some methods, the coefficient for one of the linearly dependent variables may be returned as **Inf**, or other errors may result. Secondly, we would also like to know whether the variables will have any impact on predictions. Let's solve an exercise to understand this better.

EXERCISE 3.07: MULTIPLE LINEAR REGRESSION

For this exercise, we will use a UCI dataset that has the power output of a combined cycle power plant and several possible explanatory variables:

> **NOTE**
>
> The original data and description are available from
> https://archive.ics.uci.edu/ml/datasets/Combined+Cycle+Power+Plant
>
> Alternatively, you can find the data in our repository here:
> https://packt.live/2Pu850C

1. Load the modules and classes; note that we are adding seaborn here to be used in some visualizations:

```
import pandas as pd
import numpy as np
import matplotlib.pyplot as plt
import seaborn as sns
from sklearn.linear_model import LinearRegression
```

2. Load and inspect the data:

> **NOTE**
>
> The triple-quotes (""") shown in the code snippet below are used to denote the start and end points of a multi-line code comment. Comments are added into code to help explain specific bits of logic.

```
"""
load and inspect data
from the description file
(https://archive.ics.uci.edu/ml/machine-learning-databases/00294/)
the variables are:
note: some var names are incorrect in the description file
Ambient Temperature (AT)
Ambient Pressure (AP)
Relative Humidity (RH)
Exhaust Vacuum (V)
and the dependent variable is
net hourly electrical energy output (PE)
"""
power_data = pd.read_csv\
            ('../Datasets/combined_cycle_power_plant.csv')
print(power_data.shape)
print(power_data.head())
missings = power_data.isnull().sum()
print(missings)
```

The result should appear as follows:

```
(9568, 5)
        AT       V        AP      RH        PE
0     8.34   40.77   1010.84   90.01   480.48
1    23.64   58.49   1011.40   74.20   445.75
2    29.74   56.90   1007.15   41.91   438.76
3    19.07   49.69   1007.22   76.79   453.09
4    11.80   40.66   1017.13   97.20   464.43
AT      0
V       0
AP      0
RH      0
PE      0
dtype: int64
```

Figure 3.56: The combined power cycle dataset has no missing values

3. Since we have not used this data before, let's do some very quick EDA. First, we'll look at the correlation among all the variables:

```
"""
quick EDA
correlation analysis
"""
corr = power_data.corr()
# mask for heatmap in seaborn
mask = np.ones((power_data.shape[1], power_data.shape[1]))
mask = [[1 if j< i else 0 \
        for j in range(corr.shape[0])] \
        for i in range(corr.shape[1])]
fig, ax = plt.subplots(figsize = (10, 7))
"""
plot the correlation matrix as a heatmap
blanking out the upper triangle (duplicates)
"""
sns.heatmap(corr, cmap = 'jet_r', square = True, linewidths = 0.5, \
            center = 0, annot = True, mask = mask, \
            annot_kws = {"size" : 12}, \
            xticklabels = power_data.columns, \
            yticklabels = power_data.columns)
plt.show()
```

The chart should appear as follows:

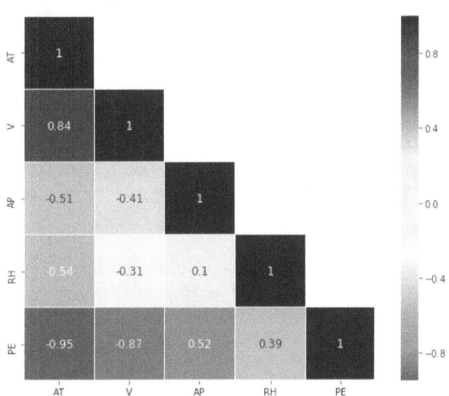

Figure 3.57: Correlation chart of variables

In the preceding data, the strongest correlation among the *x* variables is the `0.84` between **V** and **AT**. Hence, there should be no multicollinearity here.

We would like some indication that the *x* variables will impact on the thing we are trying to predict, **PE**. In the last row of the chart, we can see a significant correlation between **PE** and all the other variables, which is a good indicator they will all be valuable in the model. If there were a very large number of features, we might be interested in dropping variables that are less important in terms of reducing noise in the model. However, these correlation coefficients are only pairwise and even if we saw a low correlation, more work would be required to justify removing a variable.

Regarding the visualization, we are using the seaborn **heatmap** function to generate the plot. Because the correlation values are symmetric, the correlation between, say, **AT** and **V** is the same as **V** and **AT**. Therefore, the upper-right triangle of the grid would mirror the lower-left triangle, so the **heatmap** method provides a way to blank any squares we want. This is accomplished with the **mask** variable in the call, which takes a matrix the same shape as the correlation matrix, and blanks any squares corresponding to **False** values in the **mask**. We used a nested list comprehension to put the **False** values (integer **0**) into the **mask**.

Finally, note that the values along the diagonal are all **1**; by definition, a variable is perfectly correlated to itself. You might see examples where these squares are used to plot the variable distributions or other valuable information, as well as using the upper-right (or lower-left) triangle squares for additional information, such as the plots in the next step.

4. Use the seaborn pairplot to visualize the pairwise relationships among all the variables. This information augments the correlation plot and, as noted, is sometimes combined with it in a single grid:

```
# (2) look at the pairwise variable relationships
plot_grid = sns.pairplot(power_data)
```

The result should appear as follows:

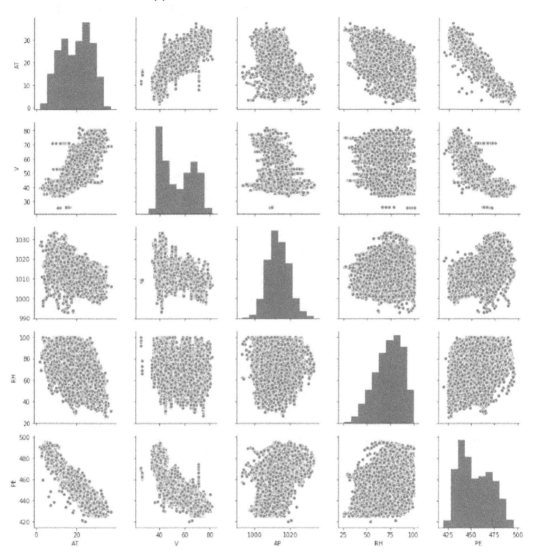

Figure 3.58: Seaborn pairplot of the data

By default, this chart shows the scatterplot of each variable against the other variables and the distributions of each variable along the diagonal. Note that the upper-right triangle is the mirror image of the lower-right triangle, and that the axes are flipped on each chart.

Along the diagonal, we see the distributions of all the variables. We can see that the **RH** variable is skewed to the left; we could consider applying a transform to that column, such as **numpy.log(power_data['RH'])** or **numpy. sqrt(power_data['RH'])**. For this exercise, we will leave them as is.

The other thing we can observe from this chart is the scatterplots along the bottom row; note that **AT**, which has the largest negative correlation to **PE**, shows a clear negative trend of **PE** versus **AT**, which intuitively makes sense. As we move to the right, the correlations become less strong, and that is consistent with the scatterplots. In the third chart, **PE** versus **AP**, we can see some indication of the positive correlation.

5. Now, we structure the data for the linear regression model, fit the model, and get predictions and the r^2 value. This is done in the same way as we did it in the previous exercises:

```
# structure data
X_train = power_data.drop('PE', axis = 1)
Y_train = power_data['PE']
# fit the model
model = LinearRegression()
model.fit(X_train, Y_train)
# get predictions
Y_pred = model.predict(X_train)
r2 = model.score(X_train, Y_train)
print('model coefficients ' + str(model.coef_))
print('r2 value ' + str(round(r2, 3)))
```

The output should appear as follows:

```
model coefficients [-1.97751311 -0.23391642  0.06208294 -0.1580541 ]
r2 value 0.929
```

Figure 3.59: Results of the multiple linear regression fit

The relatively high r^2 value is a good sign that the model may be effective at predicting **PE**.

6. With multiple linear regression, we can't visualize the results easily as a plot of the predicted variable versus an *x* variable. However, a very powerful visualization that can be used in almost any situation is simply to plot the predicted value against the true value. It's best to make this plot symmetric (the axis limits should be the same for *x* and *y*) for ease of interpretation—perfect predictions would then lie along the diagonal. We add a diagonal line to aid in visual interpretation:

```
fig, ax = plt.subplots(figsize=(10, 10))
# set some limits
PE_range = max(power_data.PE) - min(power_data.PE)
plot_range = [min(power_data.PE) - 0.05 * PE_range, \
              max(power_data.PE) + 0.05 * PE_range]
ax.scatter(Y_train, Y_pred)
ax.set_xlim(plot_range)
ax.set_ylim(plot_range)
ax.set_xlabel('Actual PE value', fontsize = 14)
ax.set_ylabel('Predicted PE value', fontsize = 14)
ax.plot(plot_range, plot_range, c = "black")
plt.show()
```

The result is as follows:

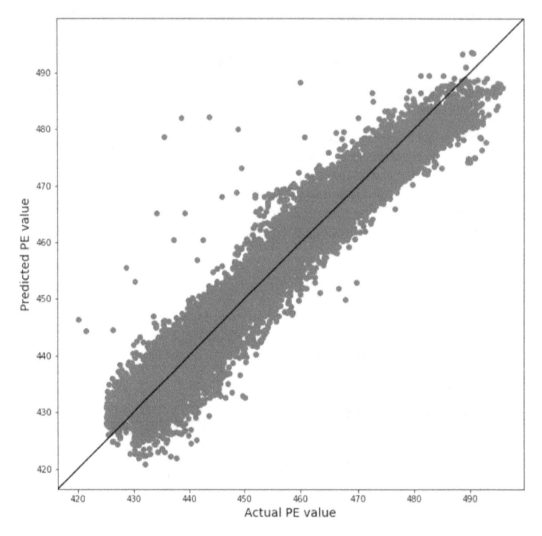

Figure 3.60: Predicted versus actual PE from multiple linear regression

Figure 3.60 indicates that the majority of predictions are along the diagonal. There are a few values that are predicted significantly higher than most, and we might want to investigate those particular points. In addition, at the highest values, the prediction tends to be too low on average, which may indicate that there is some feature engineering or other data we need in the model. Recall that we did not transform any of the variables; that would be useful to try here to see whether results subsequently improved. We will not pursue this further here.

> **NOTE**
>
> To access the source code for this specific section, please refer to
> https://packt.live/2CwflzZ.
>
> You can also run this example online at https://packt.live/37UzZuK.
> You must execute the entire Notebook in order to get the desired result.

We have seen that using multiple linear regression is a powerful addition to the toolset, and is a very easy extension to methods we have already mastered. In fact, multiple linear regression can often perform as well or better than more complex models on regression problems. Although we are not covering it here, a benefit of using multiple linear regression versus, let's say, an artificial neural network is that the coefficients of the multiple linear regression model can be interpreted as the estimates of the effects on the predicted variable of each x variable; there are times when that interpretation is extremely valuable.

SUMMARY

In this chapter, we took our first big leap into constructing machine learning models and making predictions with labeled datasets. We began our analysis by looking at a variety of different ways to construct linear models, starting with the precise least squares method, which is very good when modeling small amounts of data that can be processed using the available computer memory. The performance of linear models can be improved using dummy variables, which we created from categorical variables, adding additional features and context to the model. We then used linear regression analysis with a polynomial model to further improve performance, fitting a more natural curve to the dataset, and we investigated other non-linear feature engineering with the addition of sine and cosine series as predictors.

As a generalization from explicit linear regression, we implemented the gradient descent algorithm, which we noted, while not as precise as the least squares method (for a given number of iterations or epochs), would be able to process arbitrarily large datasets and larger numbers of variables. In addition, using generalized gradient descent introduces a number of other parameters, so-called hyperparameters, that can be optimized by us, the data scientists, to improve model performance. We deferred further investigation of model optimization to *Chapter 7, Model Evaluation*.

Now that we have a sound understanding of linear regression, we will look at autoregression models in depth in the next chapter.

AUTOREGRESSION

OVERVIEW

This chapter will teach you how to implement autoregression as a method for forecasting values depending on past values. By the end of this chapter, you will be able to create an autoregression model and construct time series regression models using autoregression. You will be fully equipped to use autoregressors to model datasets and predict future values.

INTRODUCTION

In the previous chapter, we studied the different methods used to construct linear regression models. We learned how to use the least squares method to develop linear models. We made use of dummy variables to improve the performance of these linear models. We also performed linear regression analysis with a polynomial model to improve the model's performance. Next, we implemented the gradient descent algorithm, which handles large datasets and large numbers of variables with ease.

In this chapter, we will be developing autoregression models. Autoregression is a special type of regression that can be used to predict future values based on the experience of previous data in the set.

AUTOREGRESSION MODELS

Autoregression models are classical or "standard" modeling methods used on time series data (that is, any dataset that changes with time) and can complement the linear regression techniques covered previously. Autoregression models are often used for forecasting in the economics and finance industry as they are useful with univariate time series (where there are no x variables other than time) and with very large datasets (such as streaming data or high-frequency sensor data) where the linear algebra operations might run into memory or performance issues on very large datasets. The "auto" part of autoregression refers to the fact that these models leverage correlation of a time series to itself in the past, hence autoregression. In addition, many systems do not have an associated causal model—the time series data is said to be stochastic. An example is stock price data over time. Although many attempts have been made, and continue to be made, to develop predictive causal models of stock market behavior, very few have been successful. Thus, we can treat a given stock symbol price over time as a stochastic series and use autoregression to attempt to model it.

> **NOTE**
>
> To illustrate autoregression, we will use the S&P daily closing prices from 1986 to 2018, which are available in the repository associated with this book (https://packt.live/2w3ZkDw).
>
> The original dataset can be found here:
>
> https://www.kaggle.com/pdquant/sp500-daily-19862018

A graphical view of this data is shown in the following figure:

Figure 4.1: S&P 500 Daily Closing Price

The main principle behind autoregression models is that, given enough previous observations, a reasonable prediction for the future can be made; that is, we are essentially constructing a model using the dataset as a regression against itself, using past values as the predictors. A key factor in choosing an autoregression model is that there is enough correlation of the future values to past values at specific lag times. Lag time refers to how far into the past the model uses data to predict the future.

EXERCISE 4.01: CREATING AN AUTOREGRESSION MODEL

In this exercise, we will use autoregression and attempt to predict the S&P 500 closing price 1 year into the future:

> **NOTE**
>
> This exercise will work on an earlier version of pandas, ensure that you downgrade the version of pandas using the command:
>
> `pip install pandas==0.24.2`

1. Import the necessary packages and classes. In this exercise, we introduce the **statsmodels** package, which includes a wide range of statistical and modeling functions, including autoregression. If you have not previously installed **statsmodels** from a terminal prompt, use the following command:

   ```
   conda install -c anaconda statsmodels
   ```

   If you are not using Anaconda (or Miniconda) and instead install via **pip**, use the following command:

   ```
   pip install -U statsmodels
   ```

   Once **statsmodels** is installed on your system, load the following:

   ```
   import pandas as pd
   import numpy as np
   from statsmodels.tsa.ar_model import AR
   from statsmodels.graphics.tsaplots import plot_acf
   import matplotlib.pyplot as plt
   ```

2. Load the S&P 500 data (**spx.csv**) and convert the **date** column into a **datetime** data type:

   ```
   df = pd.read_csv('../Datasets/spx.csv')
   df['date'] = pd.to_datetime(df['date'])
   print(df.head())
   print(df.tail())
   ```

We'll get the following output:

```
             date    close
0  1986-01-02  209.59
1  1986-01-03  210.88
2  1986-01-06  210.65
3  1986-01-07  213.80
4  1986-01-08  207.97
                date    close
8187  2018-06-25  2717.07
8188  2018-06-26  2723.06
8189  2018-06-27  2699.63
8190  2018-06-28  2716.31
8191  2018-06-29  2718.37
```

Figure 4.2: S&P 500 historical data

If you look carefully at the data in *Figure 4.2*, you might see that some data is missing—for example, there is no data on **1/4/1986** and **1/5/1986**. These are weekend dates during which the market is closed. An autoregression model, especially one containing a lot of data, will not be sensitive to the missing values for at least two reasons. First, since the model moves forward one period at a time and, in higher-order models, uses multiple past values, the prediction will be less sensitive to missing values compared to a model that was, say, based on a single lag value. Second, in the case such as here, where most missing values are periodic (Saturdays repeat every 7 days, Sundays repeat every 7 days, and so on), then, if we have a lot of data, the model will automatically account for those days. However, as we will see, the uncertainty of predicting far beyond the end of existing data can become large for autoregression models.

3. Plot the raw dataset versus the **date** data type:

```
fig, ax = plt.subplots(figsize = (10, 7))
ax.plot(df.date, df.close)
ax.set_title('S&P 500 Daily Closing Price', fontsize = 16)
ax.set_ylabel('Price ($)', fontsize = 14)
ax.tick_params(axis = 'both', labelsize = 12)
plt.show()
```

The output will be as follows:

Figure 4.3: Plot of the S&P 500 closing prices

4. Before constructing an autoregression model, we should first check to see whether the model is able to be used as a regression against itself. As we noted earlier, the success of an autoregression model depends on the ability to use past values in a linear model to predict future values. That means the future values should be strongly correlated to past values. We can investigate this using the **statsmodels plot_acf** function (plotting the autocorrelation function). We mentioned before that how far back we look into the past is called the lag; we will override the default maximum value of **plot_acf** and plot lags from 0 days to 4,000 days:

```
max_lag = 4000
fig, ax = plt.subplots(figsize = (10, 7))
acf_plot = plot_acf(x = df.close, ax = ax, lags = max_lag, \
                    use_vlines = False, alpha = 0.9, \
                    title = 'Autocorrelation of SPX vs. lag')
```

```
ax.grid(True)
ax.text(1000, 0.01, '90% confidence interval')
ax.set_xlabel('Lag', fontsize = 14)
ax.tick_params(axis = 'both', labelsize = 12)
plt.show()
```

The result should appear as follows:

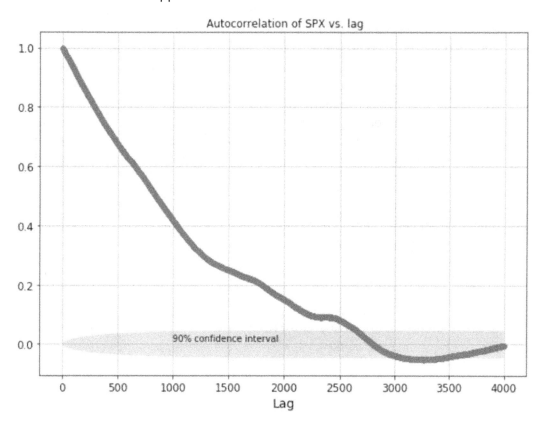

Figure 4.4: Autocorrelation plot of the S&P 500 closing price versus lag (days)

We can understand this chart as follows. First, by definition at 0 lag, a series is perfectly correlated to itself so the **autocorrelation function (ACF)** value is 1.0. Then, we see that as we increase the lag, the series is less and less correlated, meaning each data point farther back in time has less information about the value we are predicting. This is very typical of stochastic or random series (note that periodic series will have peaks and valleys in the ACF plot—we will see this later). Also, by choosing the value in the function call, we plotted a 90% confidence interval shaded in blue. The meaning of this interval is that any lag outside the interval is considered statistically significant—in other words, the correlation is statistically valid. To build an autocorrelation model, we must have ACF values outside the confidence interval to be successful. In this case, we have a fairly high correlation from 0 to some number of days, which we can use in the model (more on that shortly). Finally, we can see that at lags above about 2,750 days, the correlation is negative—that is, the past values predict the opposite to the future. However, in this case, those long-term negative lags are not very significant.

5. To get some intuition for the ACF results, let's choose a fairly short lag of 100 days and plot both the original data and the lagged data on one chart. We can do that using the **pandas.shift()** function:

```
spx_shift_100 = df.copy()
spx_shift_100['close'] = df.close.shift(100)
fix, ax = plt.subplots(figsize = (10, 7))
ax.plot(df.date, df.close, c = "blue")
ax.plot(spx_shift_100.date, spx_shift_100.close, c = "red")
plt.show()
```

The output will be as follows:

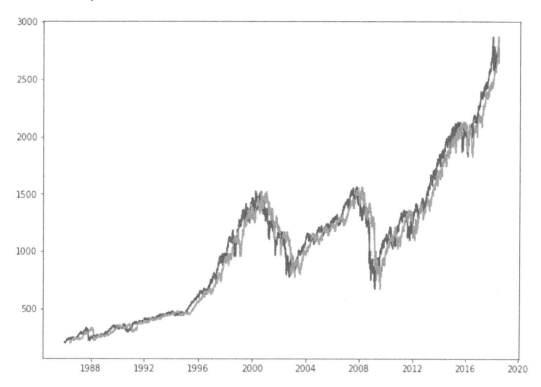

Figure 4.5: S&P 500 closing price (blue) and with a lag of 100 days (red)

In *Figure 4.5*, the red line indicates the values from 100 days ago, as compared to the blue line, which indicates actual (present) values for a given date. We see that during periods when the value is increasing, the past values are below the actual, and when the value is decreasing, the opposite is true. This makes intuitive sense. Importantly, during large portions of the time period covered, the vertical space between the two curves looks about constant. That means, intuitively, that the relationship of the past to the present is roughly similar. If you think about these curves for some time, you will also see the limitation of autoregression—the predictions will always look like the recent history, so when things change, the predictions will be less accurate until the model "catches up" with the new behavior.

6. There is one more way in which we can visualize the correlation we are analyzing. In the multiple linear regression case, we introduced a chart where we plotted the predicted values against the actual values; perfect prediction was along the diagonal. Similarly, if, instead of plotting the lagged values and the actual values, both versus time, we could plot the lagged values against the actual values. Let's see what this would look like:

```
print(spx_shift_100.head(), '\n', spx_shift_100.tail())
fig, ax = plt.subplots(figsize = (7, 7))
ax.scatter(df.loc[100:, 'close'], spx_shift_100.loc[100:, 'close'])
ax.set_xlim(0, 3000)
ax.set_ylim(0, 3000)
plt.show()
```

The output will be as follows:

```
        date  close
0 1986-01-02    NaN
1 1986-01-03    NaN
2 1986-01-06    NaN
3 1986-01-07    NaN
4 1986-01-08    NaN
           date    close
8187 2018-06-25  2823.81
8188 2018-06-26  2821.98
8189 2018-06-27  2762.13
8190 2018-06-28  2648.94
8191 2018-06-29  2695.14
```

The plot will be as follows:

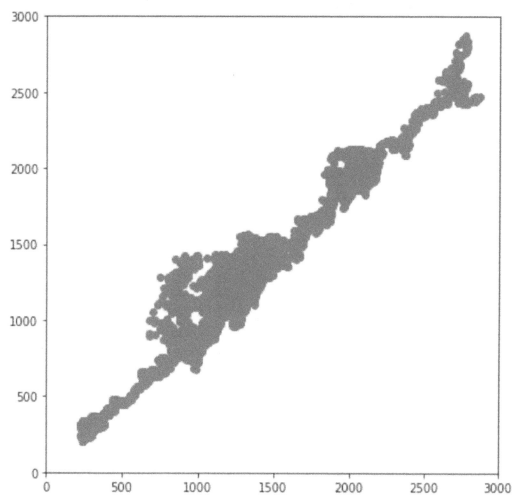

Figure 4.6: S&P closing value with a lag of 100 days versus actual values

Figure 4.6 shows that most of the values with a lag of 100 days are along a diagonal line, meaning that the relationship between the lagged values and the present values is similar across all actual values.

7. We could create plots like *Figure 4.6* across a range of lag times to try to understand which lags would be useful in a model and which would not be useful. Before we do that, it would be useful to have the values of the ACF from *Figure 4.6*, so we could relate what we see in the lag plots to the correlation function value. The **plot_acf** function of **statsmodels** is based upon an underlying **numpy** function, **correlate**. We can use that to get the values shown in *Figure 4.6*:

```
"""
the statsmodels plot_acf is based upon the numpy correlate
function, so we can generate the actual values for
illustration and so we can label some later plots
the standard presentation of an acf plot has the value at
lag 0 == 1; the correlate function returns unscaled
values so we get the first value for scaling to 1
the values to be tested in the function must have
the mean of the un-shifted series subtracted from
both series
"""
corr0 = np.correlate(df.close[0: ] - df.close.mean(), \
                     df.close[0: ] - df.close.mean(), \
                     mode = 'valid')
corrs = [np.correlate(df.close[:(df.close.shape[0] - i)] \
                     - df.close.mean(), df.close[i: ] \
                     - df.close.mean(), mode = 'valid')
         for i in range(max_lag)] / corr0
```

Note that we subtract the mean of the underlying series (**df.close**) from every value used in the **correlate** function. This is a mathematical subtlety to be consistent with the output of the **plot_act** function output.

8. Now, rather than creating many charts by hand at different lag values, let's create a function to generate a grid of plots that we can use with various lag ranges, numbers of plots, and so on. We will pass the **df.close** series to the function, along with the preceding **corrs** values, and with parameters to control the plots:

```
"""
utility function to plot out a range of
plots depicting self-correlation
"""
def plot_lag_grid(series, corrs, axis_min, axis_max, \
                  num_plots, total_lag, n_rows, n_cols):
    lag_step = int(total_lag / num_plots)
    fig = plt.figure(figsize = (18, 16))
    for i in range(num_plots):
        corr = corrs[lag_step * i]
        ax = fig.add_subplot(n_rows, n_cols, i + 1)
        ax.scatter(series, series.shift(lag_step * i))
        ax.set_xlim(axis_min, axis_max)
        ax.set_ylim(axis_min, axis_max)
        ax.set_title('lag = ' + str(lag_step * i))
        ax.text(axis_min + 0.05 * (axis_max - axis_min), \
                axis_max - 0.05 * (axis_max - axis_min), \
                'correlation = ' + str(round(corr[0], 3)))
    fig.tight_layout()
    plt.show()
```

9. We are now prepared to get a deeper understanding of how the correlation relates to the lag plots. We'll call the function:

```
"""
create a grid to see how well the data at increasing
lags correlates to the original data
'perfect' correlation will appear as a diagonal line
the farther from the line, the poorer the correlation
"""
plot_lag_grid(df.close, corrs, df.close.min(), df.close.max(), \
              num_plots = 16, total_lag = 480, \
              n_rows = 4, n_cols = 4)
```

This will produce the following:

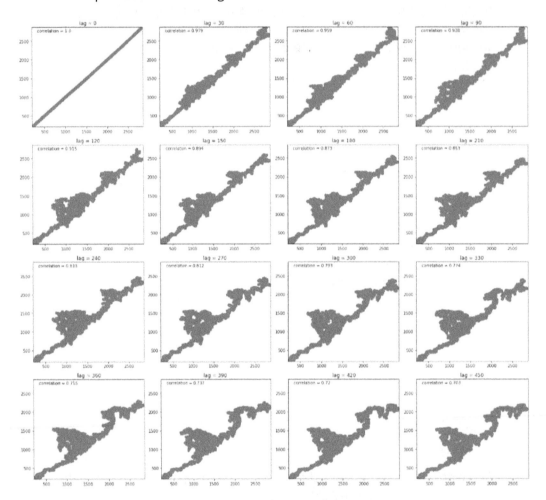

Figure 4.7: Lag plots at various values

In *Figure 4.7*, we can see a gradual degradation in lag chart appearance in direct relation to the ACF function value shown on each plot. This gives us the idea that trying to use longer lags will add noise to the model, which looks like it would be fairly large by lag 60, and not too large at lag 30. Now, we can use another **statsmodels** function to develop a model and see how that fits in with our idea.

10. The **statsmodels** function, **AR**, along with the associated **fit** method, builds an autoregression model. Used with the defaults, it will determine the max lag, return all the parameters from lag 1 to the max lag, and allow us to predict both in the range of the existing data and into the future:

```
"""
statsmodels AR function builds an autoregression model
using all the defaults, it will determine the max lag
and provide all the model coefficients
"""
model = AR(df.close)
model_fit = model.fit()
# model fit now contains all the model information
max_lag = model_fit.k_ar
"""
note that by using defaults, the maximum lag is
computed as round(12*(nobs/100.)**(1/4.))
see https://www.statsmodels.org/devel/generated/statsmodels.tsa.ar_
model.AR.fit.html#statsmodels.tsa.ar_model.AR.fit
"""
print('Max Lag: ' + str(max_lag))
print('Coefficients: \n' + str(model_fit.params))
```

The output will be as follows:

```
Max Lag: 36
Coefficients:
const        0.114237
L1.close     0.944153
L2.close     0.008452
L3.close     0.046900
L4.close    -0.014887
L5.close    -0.024734
L6.close     0.025849
L7.close    -0.004821
L8.close     0.009209
L9.close    -0.010451
L10.close    0.033449
L11.close   -0.029657
L12.close    0.052843
L13.close   -0.031489
L14.close   -0.023010
L15.close   -0.018195
L16.close    0.060165
L17.close    0.004425
L18.close   -0.057269
L19.close    0.025184
L20.close    0.008416
L21.close   -0.020273
L22.close    0.024271
L23.close   -0.010330
L24.close    0.004574
L25.close   -0.016035
L26.close    0.005954
L27.close    0.032375
L28.close   -0.037643
L29.close    0.024265
L30.close   -0.006099
L31.close   -0.018106
L32.close    0.005761
L33.close   -0.002750
L34.close   -0.037882
L35.close    0.046765
L36.close    0.000887
dtype: float64
```

Figure 4.8: Lag coefficients from the statsmodels AR function

Note that there are 36 coefficients for each of the weights and one constant—
the function determined that the maximum lag to use in the model is 36 days. It
is easy to make predictions and visualize the result:

```
# how far into the future we want to predict
max_forecast = 365
# generate predictions from the model
pred_close = pd.DataFrame({'pred_close': \
                           model_fit.predict(start = max_lag, \
                                             end = df.shape[0] \
                                             + max_forecast - 1)})
# attach the dates for visualization
pred_close['date'] = df.loc[pred_close.index, 'date'].reindex()
pred_close.loc[(max(df.index) + 1):, 'date'] = \
pd.to_datetime([max(df.date) \
               + pd.Timedelta(days = i) \
               for i in range(1, max_forecast + 1)])
"""
visualize the predictions overlaid on the real data
as well as the extrapolation to the future
"""
fig, ax = plt.subplots(figsize = (10, 7))
ax.plot(df.date, df.close, c = "blue", linewidth = 4, \
        label = 'actual SPX close')
ax.plot(pred_close.loc[0 : len(df.close), 'date'], \
        pred_close.loc[0 : len(df.close), 'pred_close'], \
        c = "yellow", linewidth = 0.5, \
        label = 'predicted SPX close')
ax.plot(pred_close.loc[len(df.close):, 'date'], \
        pred_close.loc[len(df.close):, 'pred_close'], \
        c = "red", linewidth = 2, label = 'forecast SPX close')
ax.set_xlabel('Date', fontsize = 14)
ax.tick_params(axis = 'both', labelsize = 12)
ax.legend()
plt.show()
```

The result will look as follows:

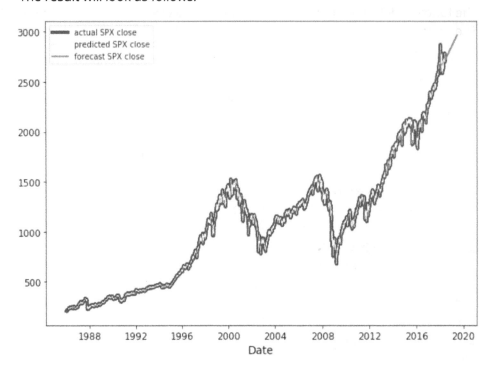

Figure 4.9: S&P 500 closing vales, predicted values, and forecasted (future) values from the autoregression model with order 36

Note that the predictions do an excellent job of following the dataset, and that after the dataset has ended, the predictions are relatively linear. Given that the model is constructed from a linear model of the previous samples, and that, after y_{t+1}, the predictions are less and less certain as they become based on past predictions, each of which has some error.

11. The fit is quite good. We can use the same approach as for linear regression to compare the predictions versus the actual values. We have to do a little work to deal with the fact that the predicted values don't start until the maximum lag beyond the start date of the original data—we need at least the maximum lag number of past values to predict the next one—in this case, 36 values. The result is that we need to offset the index of the datasets we want to compare, which we did not have to do in the linear regression case:

```
# compare predicted vs. actual
fig, ax = plt.subplots(figsize = (10, 7))
ax.scatter(df.loc[max_lag:(df.shape[0] - 1), 'close'], \
           pred_close.loc[max_lag:(df.shape[0] - 1), 'pred_close'])
```

```
ax.tick_params(axis = 'both', labelsize = 12)
ax.set_xlabel('SPX actual value', fontsize = 14)
ax.set_ylabel('SPX predicted value', fontsize = 14)
plt.show()
```

This provides the following plot:

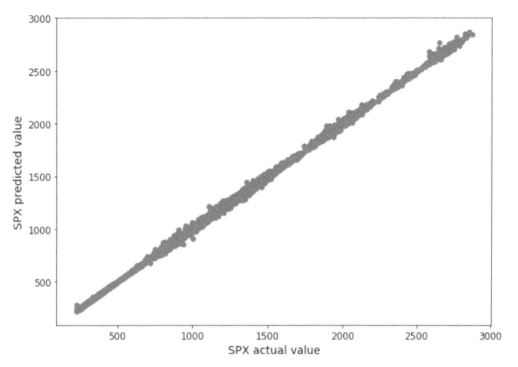

Figure 4.10: Predicted S&P 500 closing values versus the actual values

In *Figure 4.10*, it appears as if the predictions are good across all values. We can, however, dig a little deeper by looking at the residuals, which are the differences between the actual and predicted values:

12. Calculate the residuals using the same approach as used previously, to account for the date offsets:

```
fig, ax = plt.subplots(figsize = (10, 7))
residuals = pd.DataFrame({'date' : (df.loc[max_lag:\
                                     (df.shape[0] - 1), 'date']),
                          'residual' : df.loc[max_lag:\
                                       (df.shape[0] - 1), 'close'] \
                                       - pred_close.loc\
                                       [max_lag:(df.shape[0] - 1), \
                                       'pred_close']})
```

```
ax.scatter(residuals.date, residuals.residual)
ax.tick_params(axis = 'both', labelsize = 12)
ax.set_xlabel('Date', fontsize = 14)
ax.set_ylabel('residual (' + r'$SPX_{act} - SPX_{pred}$' \
              + ')', fontsize = 14)
plt.show()
```

This produces the following plot:

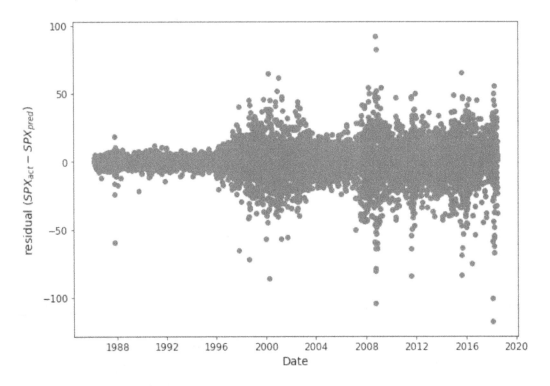

**Figure 4.11: Residual values versus time for the autoregression model
of the S&P 500 closing price**

Figure 4.11 shows that the residuals are uniformly spread around 0, meaning that there appears to be minimal bias in the model, and they seem to increase somewhat over time. This latter characteristic isn't automatically an indication of an issue—it is better to view this data as a percentage of the actual value— intuitively, the residual for an equally accurate model would be larger as the value gets larger. We can convert the data into a percent and look at that.

13. Calculate the percentage of residuals simply by dividing by the actual value (and multiplying by 100). Note that percent values have issues if the actual values are near zero, but, in this case, that is not an issue:

```
fig, ax = plt.subplots(figsize = (10, 7))
pct_residuals = pd.DataFrame({'date' : residuals.date, \
                              'pct_residual' : 100 \
                              * residuals.residual \
                              / df.loc[max_lag:(df.shape[0] - 1), \
                                       'close']})
ax.scatter(pct_residuals.date, pct_residuals.pct_residual)
ax.tick_params(axis = 'both', labelsize = 12)
ax.set_xlabel('Date', fontsize = 14)
ax.set_ylabel('% residual 100 *(' \
              + r'$SPX_{act} - SPX_{pred}$' + ') / ' \
              + r'$SPX_{act}$', fontsize = 14)
plt.show()
```

The output will be as follows:

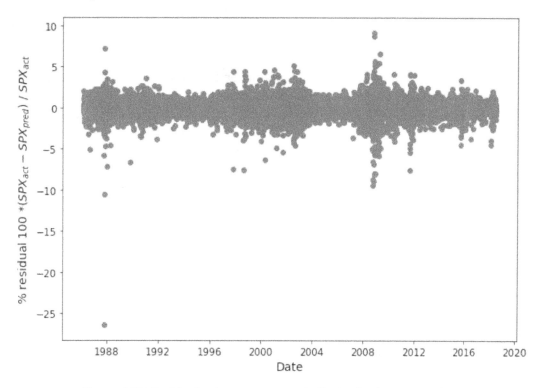

Figure 4.12: Residual values as a percent of actual value versus time

> **NOTE**
>
> To access the source code for this specific section, please refer to
> https://packt.live/3eAi6DG.
>
> You can also run this example online at https://packt.live/2Z0uEh4.
> You must execute the entire Notebook in order to get the desired result.
>
> Now that the exercise is successfully completed, upgrade the version of
> pandas to continue to smoothly run the exercises and activities present in
> the rest of the book. To upgrade pandas, run:
>
> ```
> pip install pandas==1.0.3
> ```

We now see that the percent error is very similar across the entire period, with a few periods where it gets larger. Excluding one outlier in 1987, most of the values are within 10 percent, and the vast majority are within 5 percent. We would conclude that this seems to be a fairly good model. However, we should reserve judgment until we see future results—predictions beyond the data we used in the model. We saw in *Figure 4.12* that the future prediction was a fairly linear upward trend after the end of the data.

We'll leave it as an exercise for you to go and get more recent S&P 500 closing data and compare this data with the one year prediction from this model. Also, we must stress that fully qualifying such a model requires separating out training, validation, and test data and performing tests such as cross-validation, which will be covered in *Chapter 6, Ensemble Modeling*. As a teaser, the worst error over the year after the data was about 20%, the average error 1.4%, and the error at the very end of the forecast period was 0.8%. We must *stress* that it is very challenging to predict stock markets and it might be fortuitous that the forecast period was somewhat uniformly positive.

From this exercise using an autoregression model, we can see that there is significant predictive power in using these models even when there is missing data. The autoregression model shown for the S&P 500 dataset was able to effectively provide predictions within the range of observed samples. However, outside of this range, when predicting future values for which no measurements have been taken, the predictive power may be somewhat limited. In this particular case, the future predictions seem reasonable. Let's now do an exercise that may be more challenging for this type of model.

ACTIVITY 4.01: AUTOREGRESSION MODEL BASED ON PERIODIC DATA

In this activity, we will now use an autoregression model to fit the Austin weather dataset and predict future values. This data has different characteristics to the stock market data and will illustrate some of the challenges associated with applying autoregression.

The steps to be performed are as follows:

1. Import the packages and classes needed. As in the stock market exercise, we need **pandas**, **numpy**, the **AR** function from **statsmodels.tsa.ar_model**, the **plot_acf** function from **statsmodels.graphics.tsaplots**, and, of course, **matplotlib.pyplot**.

2. Load the Austin weather data (**austin_weather.csv**) and convert the **Date** column to **datetime** as before.

3. Plot the complete set of average temperature values (**df.TempAvgF**) with **Date** on the *x* axis.

    The output should be as follows:

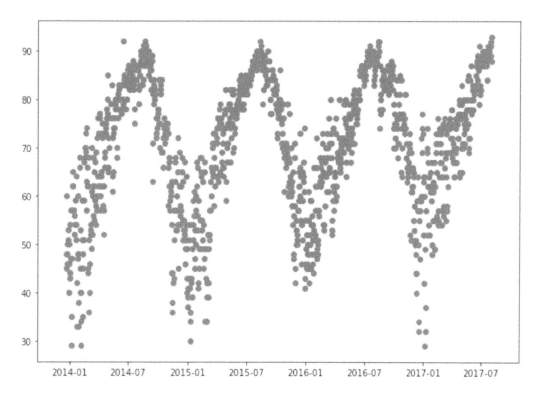

Figure 4.13: Plot of Austin temperature data over several years

4. Construct an autocorrelation plot to see whether the average temperature can be used with an autoregression model. Consider how this plot is different from *Exercise 4.01, Creating an Autoregression Model* and why.

   The plot should be as follows:

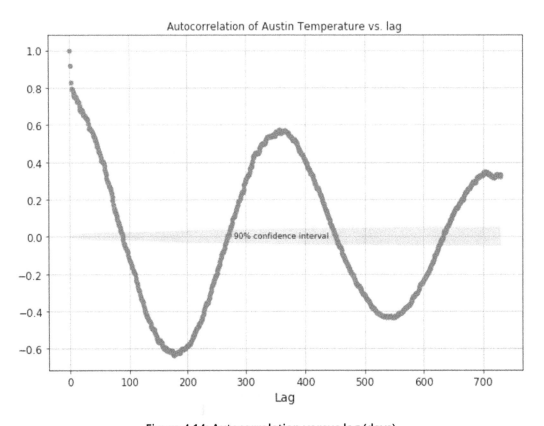

Figure 4.14: Autocorrelation versus lag (days)

5. Extract the actual ACF values using the **numpy.correlate()** function as in *Exercise 4.01, Creating an Autoregression Model*.

6. Use the same **plot_lag_grid** function to investigate the correlation versus the lag plots at various correlation values. Consider the fact that the raw data obviously repeats on a period of around 365 days, but also that an autocorrelation model might not be effective at such long lags. Look at both short and long lags and understand the data.

The output for short lags will be as follows:

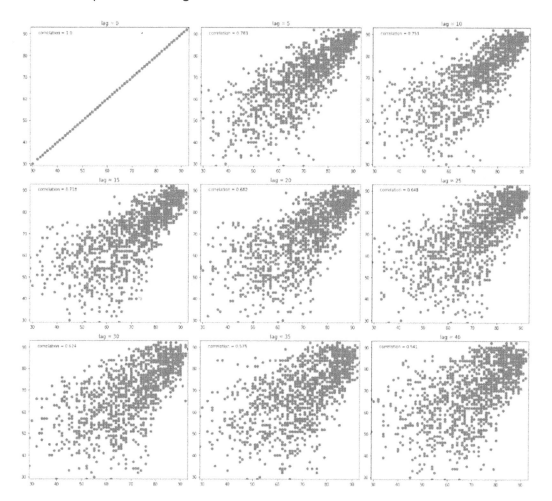

Figure 4.15: Lag plots with short lags

The output for longer lags will be as follows:

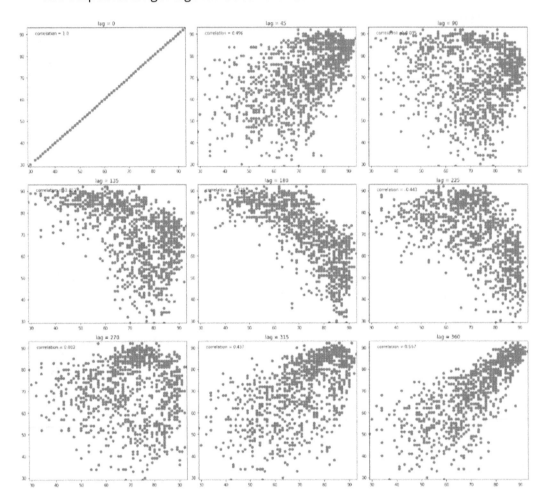

Figure 4.16: Lag plots with longer lags

7. Use the **statsmodels AR** function and the **model.fit()** method to model the data. Get the maximum model lag from the **model.fit()** method. Print the coefficients. How many terms are used (by default) in this case?

8. Use a maximum forecast period of 365 days (ask—why is this reasonable?) and generate predictions from the model. Using the same methods as before, match the correct dates to the predictions so that we can visualize them on the same plot as the raw data.

9. Plot the predictions (including the 365-day forecast), as well as the original dataset.

The results should look as follows:

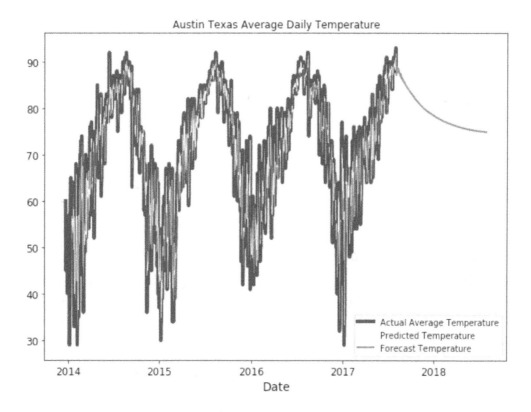

Figure 4.17: Austin temperature data, in-data predictions, and out-of-data forecast

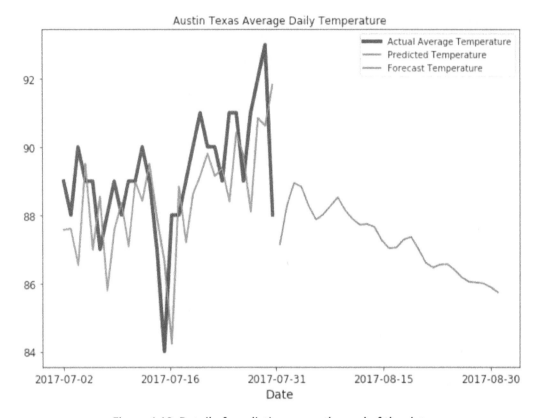

Figure 4.18: Detail of predictions near the end of the data

We can see from *Figure 4.18* that, as in the stock market case, the predictions in the range of the data used to fit the model are good. However, the future predictions don't seem nearly as good. They start on a reasonable trend, but then level off to a value that clearly isn't correct for some of the forecast period. This is a great example of the limits of autoregression models; they may be very effective for hard-to-predict series over short time periods, but the long term may be significantly in error. The only way to rigorously evaluate such a model before trusting it in production is to use the methods in *Chapter 6, Ensemble Modeling*.

> **NOTE**
>
> The solution to this activity can be found on page 457.

In this section, we've used a variety of tools such as autocorrelation, lag plots, and autoregression to build a predictive model for a time series. Such models are fast to build, can work well on univariate data (where we have no *x* values other than time), and can provide good short-range predictions.

We have explored autoregression models as an alternative to linear regression models for time series data. Autoregression models can be very useful for univariate time series where we don't have any underlying model, or obvious predictors we can use for the *x* variables. Autoregression is most widely used in time series, and particularly in economic or financial modeling where we consider the series to be stochastic or a random variable. We have seen that, in certain cases, autoregression models can be extremely powerful, but that these models can be limited in cases where there is periodic or other non-constant behaviors versus time. Fundamentally, this limitation is due to autoregression being a linear combination of past values, so the future predictions are always reflective of the recent past. In general, autoregression models are most useful for relatively short-term predictions, although the definition of short term can be quite relative.

SUMMARY

In this chapter, we have investigated the use of autoregression models, which predict future values based on the temporal behavior of prior data in the series. Using autoregression modeling, we were able to accurately model the closing price of the S&P 500 over the years 1986 to 2018 and a year into the future. On the other hand, the performance of autoregression modeling to predict annually periodic temperature data for Austin, Texas, seemed more limited.

Now that we have experience with regression problems, we will turn our attention to classification problems in the next chapter.

5

CLASSIFICATION TECHNIQUES

OVERVIEW

This chapter introduces classification problems, classification using linear and logistic regression, K-nearest neighbors, and decision trees. You will also be briefly introduced to artificial neural networks as a type of classification technique.

By the end of this chapter, you will be able to implement logistic regression and explain how it can be used to classify data into specific groups or classes. You will also be able to use the k-nearest neighbors algorithm for classification and decision trees for data classification, including the ID3 algorithm. Additionally, you will be able to identify the entropy within data and explain how decision trees such as ID3 aim to reduce entropy.

INTRODUCTION

In the previous chapters, we began our supervised machine learning journey using regression techniques, predicting the continuous variable output on a given set of input data. We will now turn to the other type of machine learning problem: classification. Recall that classification tasks aim to classify given input data into two or more specified number of classes.

So, while regression is a task of estimating a continuous value for given input data (for example, estimating the price of a house given its location and dimensions as input data), classification is about predicting a (discrete) label for given input data. For example, a well-known machine learning classification task is the spam detection of emails, where the task is to predict whether a given email is *spam* or *not_spam*. Here, *spam* and *not_spam* are the labels for this task and the input data is the email, or rather the textual data contained in the different fields of the email, such as subject, body, and receiver. The textual data would be preprocessed into numerical features in order to be usable for a classification model. Because there are only two labels in this task, it is known as a binary classification task. And if there are more than two labels in a classification task, it is called a multiclass classification task.

There are various kinds of classification models with different learning algorithms, each having their pros and cons. But essentially, all models are trained using a labeled dataset and, once trained, can predict labels for unlabeled data samples. In this chapter, we will extend the concepts learned in *Chapter 3*, *Linear Regression*, and *Chapter 4*, *Autoregression*, and will apply them to a dataset labeled with classes, rather than continuous values, as output. We will discuss some of the well-known classification models and apply them to some example labeled datasets.

ORDINARY LEAST SQUARES AS A CLASSIFIER

We covered **ordinary least squares** (**OLS**) as linear regression in the context of predicting continuous variable output in the previous chapter, but it can also be used to predict the class that a set of data is a member of. OLS-based classifiers are not as powerful as other types of classifiers that we will cover in this chapter, but they are particularly useful in understanding the process of classification. To recap, an OLS-based classifier is a non-probabilistic, linear binary classifier. It is non-probabilistic because it does not generate any confidence over the prediction such as, for example, logistic regression. It is a linear classifier as it has a linear relationship with respect to its parameters/coefficient.

Now, let's say we had a fictional dataset containing two separate groups, Xs and Os, as shown in *Figure 5.1*. We could construct a linear classifier by first using OLS linear regression to fit the equation of a straight line to the dataset. For any value that lies above the line, the *X* class would be predicted, and for any value beneath the line, the *O* class would be predicted. Any dataset that can be separated by a straight line is known as linearly separable (as in our example), which forms an important subset of data types in machine learning problems. The straight line, in this case, would be called the decision boundary. More generally, the decision boundary is defined as the hyperplane separating the data. In this case, the decision boundary is linear. There could be cases where a decision boundary can be non-linear. Datasets such as the one in our example can be learned by **linear classifiers** such as an OLS-based classifier, or **support vector machines (SVMs)** with linear kernels.

However, this does not mean that a linear model can only have a linear decision boundary. A linear classifier/model is a model that is linear with respect to the parameters/weights (β) of the model, but not necessarily with respect to inputs (**x**). Depending on the input, a linear model may have a linear or non-linear decision boundary. As mentioned before, examples of linear models include OLS, SVM, and logistic regression, while examples of non-linear models include KNN, random forest, decision tree, and ANN. We will cover more of these models in the later parts of this chapter:

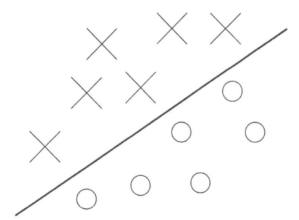

Figure 5.1: OLS as a classifier

EXERCISE 5.01: ORDINARY LEAST SQUARES AS A CLASSIFIER

This exercise contains a contrived example of using OLS as a classifier. In this exercise, we will use a completely fictional dataset, and test how the OLS model fares as a classifier. In order to implement OLS, we will use the **LinearRegression** API of **sklearn**. The dataset is composed of manually selected x and y values for a scatterplot which are approximately divided into two groups. The dataset has been specifically designed for this exercise, to demonstrate how linear regression can be used as a classifier, and this is available in the accompanying code files for this book, as well as on GitHub, at https://packt.live/3a7oAY8:

1. Import the required packages:

```
import matplotlib.pyplot as plt
import matplotlib.lines as mlines
import numpy as np
import pandas as pd
from sklearn.linear_model import LinearRegression
from sklearn.model_selection import train_test_split
```

2. Load the **linear_classifier.csv** dataset into a pandas DataFrame:

```
df = pd.read_csv('../Datasets/linear_classifier.csv')
df.head()
```

The output will be as follows:

	x	y	labels
0	1	13	x
1	8	18	o
2	9	25	x
3	5	25	x
4	4	17	x

Figure 5.2: First five rows

Looking through the dataset, each row contains a set of x, y coordinates, as well as the label corresponding to which class the data belongs to, either a cross (**x**) or a circle (**o**).

3. Produce a scatterplot of the data with the marker for each point as the corresponding class label:

```
plt.figure(figsize=(10, 7))
for label, label_class in df.groupby('labels'):
    plt.scatter(label_class.values[:,0], label_class.values[:,1], \
                label=f'Class {label}', marker=label, c='k')
plt.legend()
plt.title("Linear Classifier");
```

We'll get the following scatterplot:

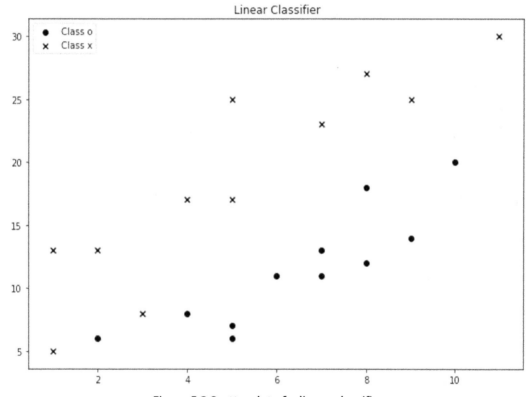

Figure 5.3 Scatterplot of a linear classifier

4. In order to impartially evaluate the model, we should split the training dataset into a training and a test set. We make that train/test split in the ratio 60:40 in the following step:

```
df_train, df_test = train_test_split(df.copy(), test_size=0.4, \
                                     random_state=12)
```

5. Using the scikit-learn **LinearRegression** API from the previous chapter, fit a linear model to the **x**, **y** coordinates of the training dataset and print out the linear equation:

```
# Fit a linear regression model
model = LinearRegression()
model.fit(df_train.x.values.reshape((-1, 1)), \
          df_train.y.values.reshape((-1, 1)))

# Print out the parameters
print(f'y = {model.coef_[0][0]}x + {model.intercept_[0]}')
```

The output will be as follows:

```
y = 1.2718120805369124x + 8.865771812080538
```

> **NOTE**
>
> Throughout the exercises and activities in this chapter, owing to randomization, there could be a minor variation in the outputs presented here and those that you might obtain.

6. Plot the fitted trendline over the test dataset:

```
# Plot the trendline
trend = model.predict(np.linspace(0, 10).reshape((-1, 1)))

plt.figure(figsize=(10, 7))
for label, label_class in df_test.groupby('labels'):
    plt.scatter(label_class.values[:,0], label_class.values[:,1], \
                label=f'Class {label}', marker=label, c='k')
plt.plot(np.linspace(0, 10), trend, c='k', label='Trendline')
plt.legend()
plt.title("Linear Classifier");
```

The output will be as follows:

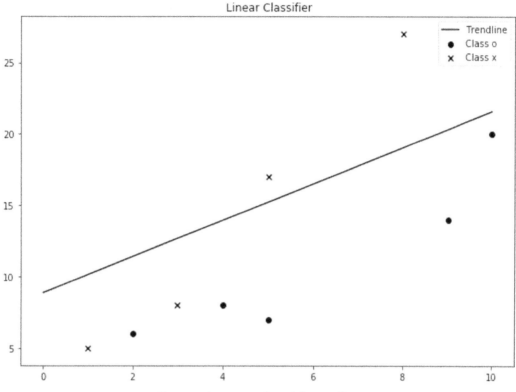

Figure 5.4: Scatterplot with trendline

7. With the fitted trendline, the classifier can then be applied. For each row in the test dataset, determine whether the *x, y* point lies above or below the linear model (or trendline). If the point lies below the trendline, the model predicts the **o** class; if above the line, the **x** class is predicted. Include these values as a column of predicted labels:

```
# Make predictions
y_pred = model.predict(df_test.x.values.reshape((-1, 1)))
pred_labels = []

for _y, _y_pred in zip(df_test.y, y_pred):
    if _y < _y_pred:
        pred_labels.append('o')
```

```
        else:
            pred_labels.append('x')
    df_test['Pred Labels'] = pred_labels
    df_test.head()
```

The output will be as follows:

	x	y	labels	Pred Labels
7	4	8	o	o
10	5	17	x	x
21	3	8	x	o
15	1	5	x	o
14	9	14	o	o

Figure 5.5: First five rows

8. Plot the points with the corresponding ground truth labels. For those points where the labels were correctly predicted, plot the corresponding class. For those incorrect predictions, plot a diamond:

```
plt.figure(figsize=(10, 7))
for idx, label_class in df_test.iterrows():
    if label_class.labels != label_class['Pred Labels']:
        label = 'D'
        s=70
    else:
        label = label_class.labels
        s=50
    plt.scatter(label_class.values[0], label_class.values[1], \
                label=f'Class {label}', marker=label, c='k', s=s)

plt.plot(np.linspace(0, 10), trend, c='k', label='Trendline')
plt.title("Linear Classifier");

incorrect_class = mlines.Line2D([], [], color='k', marker='D', \
                            markersize=10, \
                            label='Incorrect Classification');
plt.legend(handles=[incorrect_class]);
```

The output will be as follows:

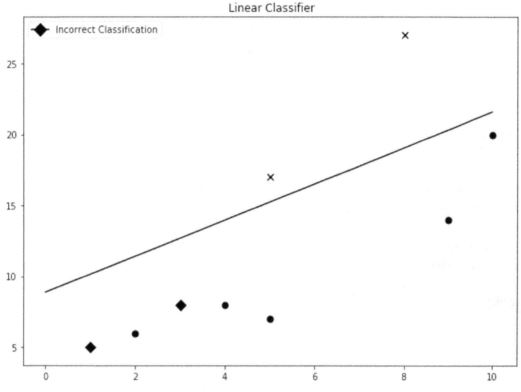

Figure 5.6: Scatterplot showing incorrect predictions

We can see that, in this plot, the linear classifier made two incorrect predictions in this completely fictional dataset, one at *x = 1*, and another at *x = 3*.

> **NOTE**
>
> To access the source code for this specific section, please refer to
> https://packt.live/3hT3Fwy.
>
> You can also run this example online at https://packt.live/3fECHai.
> You must execute the entire Notebook in order to get the desired result.

But what if our dataset is not linearly separable and we cannot classify the data using a straight-line model, which is very frequently the case. Furthermore, the preceding approach doesn't give us a measure of confidence regarding the predictions. To cope with these challenges, we turn to other classification methods, many of which use different models, but the process logically flows from our simplified linear classifier model.

LOGISTIC REGRESSION

The logistic, or logit, model is a linear model that has been effectively used for classification tasks in a number of different domains. Recalling the definition of the OLS model from the previous section, the logistic regression model takes as input a linear combination of the input features. In this section, we will use it to classify images of handwritten digits. In understanding the logistic model, we also take an important step in understanding the operation of a particularly powerful machine learning model – artificial neural networks. So, what exactly is the logistic model? Like the OLS model, which is composed of a linear or straight-line function, the logistic model is composed of the standard logistic function, which, in mathematical terms, looks something like this:

$$p(x) = \frac{1}{1 + e^{-(\beta_0 + \beta_1 x)}}$$

Figure 5.7: Logistic function

In practical terms, when trained, this function returns the probability of the input information belonging to a particular class or group. In the preceding equation, **x** is the input feature vector (an array of numbers, each representing a feature of the input data), β_1 is the parameter vector of the model that has to be learned by training the model, β_0 is the bias term or offset term (yet another parameter) that helps the model to deal with any constant value offsets in the relationship between input (**x**) and output (**y**), and **p(x)** is the output probability of the data sample **x** belonging to a certain class. For example, if we have two classes, A and B, then **p(x)** is the probability of class A and **1-p(x)** is the probability of class B.

So, how did we arrive at the logistic function? Well, the logistic regression model arises from the desire to model the log of odds in favor of a data point to belong to class A of the two classes (A and B) via linear functions in **x**. The model has the following form:

$$\log \frac{p(\text{class} = A)}{p(\text{class} = B)} = \beta_0 + \beta_1 X; -\infty < X < +\infty$$

Figure 5.8: Logistic function for the logistic regression model

We are considering the case of binary classification here, with just two classes, A and B, although we could easily extend the discussion to multiclass classification as well using the one-versus-all classification trick. More on that will be discussed in a subsequent section. But for now, because we know there are only two classes, we know that:

$$p(\text{class} = A) + p(\text{class} = B) = 1$$

Figure 5.9: Summation of the probability distribution

Using the preceding two equations, we can get:

$$\log \frac{p(\text{class} = A)}{1 - p(\text{class} = A)} = \beta_0 + \beta_1 X; -\infty < X < +\infty$$

Figure 5.10: Logistic function for the logistic regression model with binary classification

And now, if we consider class A as our target class, we can replace **p(class=A)** with **y** (target output):

$$\log \frac{y}{1 - y} = \beta_0 + \beta_1 X; -\infty < X < +\infty$$

Figure 5.11: Logistic function for the logistic regression model by replacing p(class=A)

The left-hand side of the preceding equation is popularly known as log-odds, as it is the logarithm of the odds ratio, which is the ratio of the probability of class A to the probability of class B. So, why is this important? For a linear model such as logistic regression, the fact that the log-odds of this model is linear with respect to the input **x** implies the linearity of the model.

By rearranging the preceding equation slightly, we get the logistic function:

$$y = \frac{1}{1 + e^{-(\beta_0 + \beta_1 x)}}; \ 0 \le y \le 1, \ -\infty < x < \infty$$

Figure 5.12: Logistic function

Notice the exponents of **e**, that is, $\beta_0 + \beta_1 x$, and that this relationship is a linear function of the two training parameters or *weights*, β_0 and β_1, as well as the input feature vector, *x*. If we were to assume $\beta_0 = 0$ and $\beta_1 = 1$, and plot the logistic function over the range **(-6, 6)**, we would get the following result:

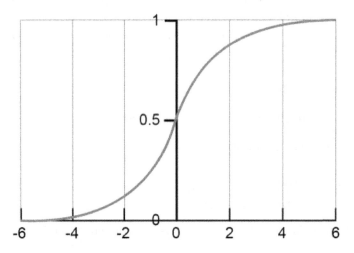

Figure 5.13: Logistic function curve

> **NOTE**
>
> The sigmoid curve centers around the point x = -β_0, so, if β_0 is nonzero, the curve would not center around the point x=0, as shown in the preceding figure.

Examining *Figure 5.13*, we notice some important aspects of classification. The first thing to note is that, if we look at the probability values on the **y** axis at the extremes of the function, the values are almost at zero when **x** $=$ **−6** and at one when **x** $=$ **6**. While it looks like the values are in fact **0** and **1**, this is not exactly the case. The logistic function approaches zero and one at these extremes and will only equal zero and one when **x** is at a positive or negative infinity. In practical terms, what this means is that the logistic function will never return a probability of greater than or equal to one, or less than or equal to zero, which is perfect for a classification task. In any event, we could never have a probability of greater than one since, by definition, a probability of one is a certainty of an event occurring. Likewise, we cannot have a probability of less than zero since, by definition, a probability of zero is a certainty of the event not occurring. The fact that the logistic function approaches but never equals one or zero means that there is always some uncertainty in the outcome or the classification.

The final aspect to notice regarding the logistic function is that at **x** $=$ **0**, the probability is 0.5, which, if we were to get this result, would indicate that the model is equally uncertain about the outcome of the corresponding class; that is, it really has no idea.

> **NOTE**
>
> It is very important to correctly understand and interpret the probability information provided by classification models such as logistic regression. Consider this probability score as the chance of the input information belonging to a particular class given the variability in the information provided by the training data. One common mistake is to use this probability score as an objective measure of whether the model can be trusted regarding its prediction; unfortunately, this isn't necessarily the case. For example, *a model can provide a probability of 99.99% that some data belongs to a particular class and might still be absolutely wrong.*

What we do use the probability value for is selecting the predicted class by the classifier. Between the model outputting the probability and us deciding the predicted class lies the probability threshold value. We need to decide a threshold value, τ, between 0 and 1, such that the two classes (say, A and B) can then be defined as:

- Data samples with a model output probability between 0 and τ belong to class A.

- Data samples with a model output probability between τ and 1 belong to class B.

Now, say we had a model that was to predict whether some set of data belonged to class A or class B, and we decided the threshold to be 0.5 (which is actually a very common choice). If the logistic model returned a probability of 0.7, then we would return class B as the predicted class for the model. If the probability was only 0.2, the predicted class for the model would be class A.

EXERCISE 5.02: LOGISTIC REGRESSION AS A CLASSIFIER – BINARY CLASSIFIER

For this exercise, we will be using a sample of the famous MNIST dataset (available at http://yann.lecun.com/exdb/mnist/ or on GitHub at https://packt.live/3a7oAY8), which is a sequence of images of handwritten code digits, 0 through 0, with corresponding labels. The MNIST dataset is comprised of 60,000 training samples and 10,000 test samples, where each sample is a grayscale image with a size of 28 x 28 pixels. In this exercise, we will use logistic regression to build a classifier. The first classifier we will build is a binary classifier, where we will determine whether the image is a handwritten 0 or a 1:

1. For this exercise, we will need to import a few dependencies. Execute the following import statements:

```
import struct
import numpy as np
import gzip
import urllib.request
import matplotlib.pyplot as plt
from array import array
from sklearn.linear_model import LogisticRegression
```

2. We will also need to download the MNIST datasets. You will only need to do this once, so after this step, feel free to comment out or remove these cells. Download the image data, as follows:

```
request = \
urllib.request.urlopen('http://yann.lecun.com/exdb'\
                       '/mnist/train-images-idx3-ubyte.gz')

with open('../Datasets/train-images-idx3-ubyte.gz', 'wb') as f:
    f.write(request.read())

request = \
urllib.request.urlopen('http://yann.lecun.com/exdb'\
                       '/mnist/t10k-images-idx3-ubyte.gz')

with open('../Datasets/t10k-images-idx3-ubyte.gz', 'wb') as f:
    f.write(request.read())
```

3. Download the corresponding labels for the data:

```
request = \
urllib.request.urlopen('http://yann.lecun.com/exdb'\
                       '/mnist/train-labels-idx1-ubyte.gz')

with open('../Datasets/train-labels-idx1-ubyte.gz', 'wb') as f:
    f.write(request.read())

request = \
urllib.request.urlopen('http://yann.lecun.com/exdb'\
                       '/mnist/t10k-labels-idx1-ubyte.gz')

with open('../Datasets/t10k-labels-idx1-ubyte.gz', 'wb') as f:
    f.write(request.read())
```

4. Once all the files have been successfully downloaded, unzip the files in the local directory using the following command (for Windows):

```
!ls *.gz #!dir *.gz for windows
```

The output will be as follows:

```
t10k-images-idx3-ubyte.gz    train-images-idx3-ubyte.gz
t10k-labels-idx1-ubyte.gz    train-images-idx1-ubyte.gz
```

> **NOTE**
>
> For Linux and macOS, check out the files in the local directory using the
> `!ls *.gz` command.

5. Load the downloaded data. Don't worry too much about the exact details of reading the data, as these are specific to the MNIST dataset:

```
with gzip.open('../Datasets/train-images-idx3-ubyte.gz', 'rb') as f:
    magic, size, rows, cols = struct.unpack(">IIII", f.read(16))
    img = np.array(array("B", f.read())).reshape((size, rows, cols))

with gzip.open('../Datasets/train-labels-idx1-ubyte.gz', 'rb') as f:
    magic, size = struct.unpack(">II", f.read(8))
    labels = np.array(array("B", f.read()))

with gzip.open('../Datasets/t10k-images-idx3-ubyte.gz', 'rb') as f:
    magic, size, rows, cols = struct.unpack(">IIII", f.read(16))

    img_test = np.array(array("B", f.read()))\
                    .reshape((size, rows, cols))

with gzip.open('../Datasets/t10k-labels-idx1-ubyte.gz', 'rb') as f:
    magic, size = struct.unpack(">II", f.read(8))
    labels_test = np.array(array("B", f.read()))
```

6. As always, having a thorough understanding of the data is key, so create an image plot of the first 10 images in the training sample. Notice the grayscale images and the fact that the corresponding labels are the digits 0 through 9:

```
for i in range(10):
    plt.subplot(2, 5, i + 1)
    plt.imshow(img[i], cmap='gray');
    plt.title(f'{labels[i]}');
    plt.axis('off')
```

The output will be as follows:

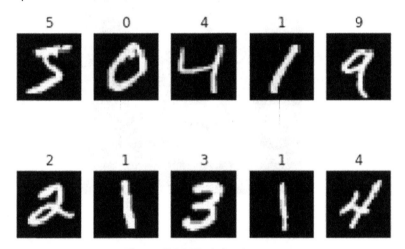

Figure 5.14: Training images

7. As the initial classifier is aiming to classify either images of zeros or images of ones, we must first select these samples from the dataset:

```
samples_0_1 = np.where((labels == 0) | (labels == 1))[0]
images_0_1 = img[samples_0_1]
labels_0_1 = labels[samples_0_1]

samples_0_1_test = np.where((labels_test == 0) | (labels_test == 1))
images_0_1_test = img_test[samples_0_1_test]\
                    .reshape((-1, rows * cols))
labels_0_1_test = labels_test[samples_0_1_test]
```

8. Visualize one sample from the 0 selection and another from the handwritten 1 digits to ensure that we have correctly allocated the data.

Here is the code for 0:

```
sample_0 = np.where((labels == 0))[0][0]
plt.imshow(img[sample_0], cmap='gray');
```

The output will be as follows:

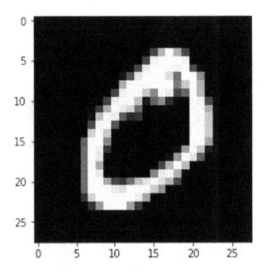

Figure 5.15: First handwritten image

Here is the code for 1:

```
sample_1 = np.where((labels == 1))[0][0]
plt.imshow(img[sample_1], cmap='gray');
```

The output will be as follows:

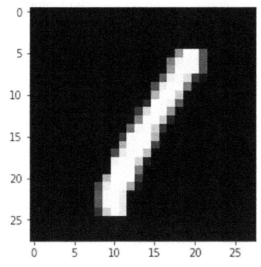

Figure 5.16: Second handwritten image

9. We are almost at the stage where we can start building the model. However, as each sample is an image and has data in a matrix format, we must first rearrange each of the images. The model needs the images to be provided in vector form, that is, all the information for each image is stored in one row. Execute this as follows:

```
images_0_1 = images_0_1.reshape((-1, rows * cols))
images_0_1.shape
```

10. Now, we can build and fit the logistic regression model with the selected images and labels:

```
model = LogisticRegression(solver='liblinear')
model.fit(X=images_0_1, y=labels_0_1)
```

The output will be as follows:

```
LogisticRegression(C=1.0, class_weight=None, dual=False, fit_intercept=True,
                intercept_scaling=1, l1_ratio=None, max_iter=100,
                multi_class='warn', n_jobs=None, penalty='l2',
                random_state=None, solver='liblinear', tol=0.0001, verbose=0,
                warm_start=False)
```

Figure 5.17: Logistic regression model

Note how the scikit-learn API calls for logistic regression are consistent with that of linear regression. There is an additional argument, **solver**, which specifies the type of optimization process to be used. We have provided this argument here with the default value to suppress a future warning in this version of scikit-learn that requires **solver** to be specified. The specifics of the **solver** argument are beyond the scope of this chapter and have only been included to suppress the warning message.

11. Check the performance of this model against the corresponding training data:

```
model.score(X=images_0_1, y=labels_0_1)
```

The output will be as follows:

```
1.0
```

In this example, the model was able to predict the training labels with 100% accuracy.

12. Display the first two predicted labels for the training data using the model:

```
model.predict(images_0_1)[:2]
```

The output will be as follows:

```
array([0, 1], dtype=uint8)
```

13. How is the logistic regression model making the classification decisions? Look at some of the probabilities produced by the model for the training set:

```
model.predict_proba(images_0_1)[:2]
```

The output will be as follows:

```
array([[9.99999999e-01, 9.89532857e-10],
       [4.56461358e-09, 9.99999995e-01]])
```

We can see that, for each prediction made, there are two probability values. For the prediction of each image, the first value is the probability that it is an image of digit **0**, and the second value is the probability of digit **1**. These two values add up to 1. We can see that, in the first example, the prediction probability is 0.9999999 for digit **0** and, hence, the prediction is digit **0**. Similarly, the inverse is true for the second example.

> **NOTE**
>
> The probabilities should ideally add up to 1 but, due to computational limits and truncation errors, it is almost 1.

14. Compute the performance of the model against the test set to check its performance against data that it has not seen:

```
model.score(X=images_0_1_test, y=labels_0_1_test)
```

The output will be as follows:

```
0.9995271867612293
```

> **NOTE**
>
> Refer to *Chapter 7*, *Model Evaluation*, for better methods of objectively measuring the model's performance.

We can see here that logistic regression is a powerful classifier that is able to distinguish between handwritten samples of 0 and 1.

> **NOTE**
>
> To access the source code for this specific section, please refer to https://packt.live/3dqqEvH.
>
> You can also run this example online at https://packt.live/3hT6FJm. You must execute the entire Notebook in order to get the desired result.

Now that we have trained a logistic regression model on a binary classification problem, let's extend the model to multiple classes. Essentially, we will be using the same dataset and, instead of classifying into just two classes or digits, 0 and 1, we classify into all 10 classes, or digits 0–9. In essence, multiclass classification for logistic regression works as one-versus-all classification. That is, for classification into the 10 classes, we will be training 10 binary classifiers. Each classifier will have 1 digit as the first class, and all the other 9 digits as the second class. In this way, we get 10 binary classifiers that are then collectively used to make predictions. In other words, we get the prediction probabilities from each of the 10 binary classifiers and the final output digit/class is one whose classifier gave the highest probability.

EXERCISE 5.03: LOGISTIC REGRESSION – MULTICLASS CLASSIFIER

In the previous exercise, we examined using logistic regression to classify between one of two groups. Logistic regression, however, can also be used to classify a set of input information to **k** different groups and it is this multiclass classifier we will be investigating in this exercise. The process for loading the MNIST training and test data is identical to the previous exercise:

1. Import the required packages:

```
import struct
import numpy as np
import gzip
import urllib.request
import matplotlib.pyplot as plt
from array import array
from sklearn.linear_model import LogisticRegression
```

2. Load the training/test images and the corresponding labels:

```
with gzip.open('../Datasets/train-images-idx3-ubyte.gz', 'rb') as f:
    magic, size, rows, cols = struct.unpack(">IIII", f.read(16))
    img = np.array(array("B", f.read()))\
        .reshape((size, rows, cols))

with gzip.open('../Datasets/train-labels-idx1-ubyte.gz', 'rb') as f:
    magic, size = struct.unpack(">II", f.read(8))
    labels = np.array(array("B", f.read()))

with gzip.open('../Datasets/t10k-images-idx3-ubyte.gz', 'rb') as f:
    magic, size, rows, cols = struct.unpack(">IIII", f.read(16))
```

```
        img_test = np.array(array("B", f.read()))\
                    .reshape((size, rows, cols))

    with gzip.open('../Datasets/t10k-labels-idx1-ubyte.gz', 'rb') as f:
        magic, size = struct.unpack(">II", f.read(8))
        labels_test = np.array(array("B", f.read()))
```

3. Visualize a sample of the data:

```
for i in range(10):
    plt.subplot(2, 5, i + 1)
    plt.imshow(img[i], cmap='gray');
    plt.title(f'{labels[i]}');
    plt.axis('off')
```

The output will be as follows:

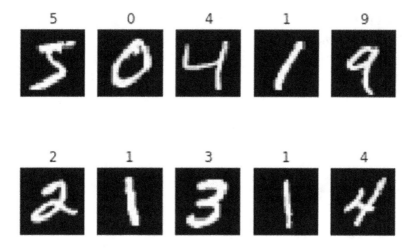

Figure 5.18: Sample data

4. Given that the training data is so large, we will select a subset of the overall data to reduce the training time as well as the system resources required for the training process:

```
np.random.seed(0) # Give consistent random numbers
selection = np.random.choice(len(img), 5000)
selected_images = img[selection]
selected_labels = labels[selection]
```

Note that, in this example, we are using data from all 10 classes, not just classes 0 and 1, so we are making this example a multiclass classification problem.

5. Again, reshape the input data in vector form for later use:

```
selected_images = selected_images.reshape((-1, rows * cols))
selected_images.shape
```

The output will be as follows:

```
(5000, 784)
```

6. The next cell is intentionally commented out. Leave this code commented out for the moment:

```
# selected_images = selected_images / 255.0
# img_test = img_test / 255.0
```

7. Construct the logistic model. There are a few extra arguments, as follows: the **lbfgs** value for **solver** is geared up for multiclass problems, with additional **max_iter** iterations required for converging on a solution. The **multi_class** argument is set to **multinomial** to calculate the loss over the entire probability distribution:

```
model = LogisticRegression(solver='lbfgs', \
                           multi_class='multinomial', \
                           max_iter=500, tol=0.1)
model.fit(X=selected_images, y=selected_labels)
```

The output will be as follows:

```
LogisticRegression(C=1.0, class_weight=None, dual=False, fit_intercept=True,
                   intercept_scaling=1, l1_ratio=None, max_iter=500,
                   multi_class='multinomial', n_jobs=None, penalty='l2',
                   random_state=None, solver='lbfgs', tol=0.1, verbose=0,
                   warm_start=False)
```

Figure 5.19: Logistic regression model

> **NOTE**
>
> Refer to the documentation at https://scikit-learn.org/stable/modules/generated/sklearn.linear_model.LogisticRegression.html for more information on the arguments.

8. Determine the accuracy score against the training set:

```
model.score(X=selected_images, y=selected_labels)
```

The output will be as follows:

```
1.0
```

9. Determine the first two predictions for the training set and plot the images with the corresponding predictions:

```
model.predict(selected_images)[:2]
```

The output will be as follows:

```
array([4, 1], dtype-uint8)
```

10. Show the images for the first two samples of the training set to see whether we are correct:

```
plt.subplot(1, 2, 1)
plt.imshow(selected_images[0].reshape((28, 28)), cmap='gray');
plt.axis('off');
plt.subplot(1, 2, 2)
plt.imshow(selected_images[1].reshape((28, 28)), cmap='gray');
plt.axis('off');
```

The output will be as follows:

Figure 5.20: Plotting the two selected images

11. Again, print out the probability scores provided by the model for the first sample of the training set. Confirm that there are 10 different values for each of the 10 classes in the set:

```
model.predict_proba(selected_images)[0]
```

The output will be as follows:

```
array([2.53877306e-43, 1.05847372e-86, 5.44376165e-35, 3.02366979e-69,
       1.00000000e+00, 3.61108748e-54, 3.61751648e-37, 1.69034999e-50,
       4.64785509e-32, 1.30058462e-38])
```

Figure 5.21: Array of predicted values

Notice that, in the probability array of the first sample, the fifth (index four) sample is the highest probability, thereby indicating a prediction of **4**.

12. Compute the accuracy of the model against the test set. This will provide a reasonable estimate of the model's *in the wild* performance, as it has never seen the data in the test set. It is expected that the accuracy rate of the test set will be slightly lower than the training set, given that the model has not been exposed to this data:

```
model.score(X=img_test.reshape((-1, rows * cols)), y=labels_test)
```

The output will be as follows:

```
0.878
```

When checked against the test set, the model produced an accuracy level of 87.8%. When applying a test set, a performance drop is expected, as this is the very first time the model has seen these samples; while, during training, the training set was repeatedly shown to the model.

13. Find the cell with the commented-out code, as shown in *Step 4*. Uncomment the code in this cell:

```
selected_images = selected_images / 255.0
img_test = img_test / 255.0
```

This cell simply scales all the image values to between 0 and 1. Grayscale images are comprised of pixels with values between and including 0–255, where 0 is black and 255 is white.

14. Click **Restart** & **Run-All** to rerun the entire notebook.

15. Find the training set error:

```
model.score(X=selected_images, y=selected_labels)
```

We'll get the following score:

```
0.986
```

16. Find the test set error:

```
model.score(X=img_test.reshape((-1, rows * cols)), y=labels_test)
```

We'll get the following score:

```
0.9002
```

> **NOTE**
>
> To access the source code for this specific section, please refer to
> https://packt.live/2B1CNKe.
>
> You can also run this example online at https://packt.live/3fQU4Vd.
> You must execute the entire Notebook in order to get the desired result.

What effect did normalizing the images have on the overall performance of the system? The training error is worse! We went from 100% accuracy in the training set to 98.6%. Yes, there was a reduction in the performance of the training set, but an increase in the test set accuracy from 87.8% to 90.02%. The test set performance is of more interest, as the model has not seen this data before, and so it is a better representation of the performance that we could expect once the model is in the field. So, why do we get a better result?

Recall what we discussed about normalization and data scaling methods in *Chapter 2, Exploratory Data Analysis and Visualization*. And now let's review *Figure 5.13*, and notice the shape of the curve as it approaches -6 and +6. The curve saturates or flattens at almost 0 and almost 1, respectively. So, if we use an image (or **x** values) of between 0 and 255, the class probability defined by the logistic function is well within this flat region of the curve. Predictions within this region are unlikely to change much, as they will need to have very large changes in **x** values for any meaningful change in **y**. Scaling the images to be between 0 and 1 initially puts the predictions closer to $p(x)$ = 0.5, and so, changes in **x** can have a bigger impact on the value for **y**. This allows for more sensitive predictions and results in getting a couple of predictions in the training set wrong, but more in the test set right. It is recommended, for your logistic regression models, that you scale the input values to be between either 0 and 1 or -1 and 1 prior to training and testing.

The following function is one way of scaling values of a NumPy array between 0 and 1:

```
def scale_input(x):
    normalized = (x-min(x))/(max(x)-min(x))
    return normalized
```

The preceding method of scaling is called min-max scaling, as it is based on scaling with respect to the minimum and maximum values of the array. Z-scaling and mean scaling are other well-known scaling methods.

Thus, we have successfully solved a multiclass classification problem using the logistic regression model. Let's now proceed toward an activity where, similar to *Exercise 5.02: Logistic Regression as a Classifier – Binary Classifier*, we will solve a binary classification problem. This time, however, we will use a simpler model – a linear regression classifier.

ACTIVITY 5.01: ORDINARY LEAST SQUARES CLASSIFIER – BINARY CLASSIFIER

In this activity, we will build a two-class OLS (linear regression)-based classifier using the MNIST dataset to classify between two digits, 0 and 1.

The steps to be performed are as follows:

1. Import the required dependencies:

```
import struct
import numpy as np
import gzip
import urllib.request
import matplotlib.pyplot as plt
from array import array
from sklearn.linear_model import LinearRegression
```

2. Load the MNIST data into memory.

3. Visualize a sample of the data.

4. Construct a linear classifier model to classify the digits 0 and 1. The model we are going to create is to determine whether the samples are either the digits 0 or 1. To do this, we first need to select only those samples.

5. Visualize the selected information with images of one sample of 0 and one sample of 1.

6. In order to provide the image information to the model, we must first flatten the data out so that each image is 1 x 784 pixels in shape.

7. Let's construct the model; use the **LinearRegression** API and call the **fit** function.

8. Determine the accuracy against the training set.

9. Determine the label predictions for each of the training samples, using a threshold of 0.5. Values greater than 0.5 classify as 1; values less than, or equal to, 0.5 classify as 0.

10. Compute the classification accuracy of the predicted training values versus the ground truth.

11. Compare the performance against the test set.

> **NOTE**
>
> The solution to this activity can be found on page 470.

An interesting point to note here is that the test set performance here is worse than that in *Exercise 5.02: Logistic Regression as a Classifier – Binary Classifier*. The dataset is exactly the same in both cases, but the models are different. And, as expected, the linear regression classifier, being a simpler model, leads to poorer test set performance compared to a stronger, logistic regression model.

SELECT K BEST FEATURE SELECTION

Now that we have established how to train and test the linear regression and logistic regression models on the MNIST dataset, we will now solve another multiclass classification problem on a different dataset using the logistic regression model. As a prerequisite for the next exercise, let's quickly discuss a particular kind of feature selection method – select k best feature selection. In this method, we select features according to the k highest scores. The scores are derived based on a scoring function, which takes in the input feature (**X**) and target (**y**), and returns scores for each feature. An example of such a function could be a function that computes the ANOVA F-value between label (**y**) and feature (**X**). An implementation of this scoring function is available with scikit-learn: https://scikit-learn.org/stable/modules/generated/sklearn.feature_selection.f_classif.html#sklearn.feature_selection.f_classif. The features are then sorted based on the decreasing order of scores, and we choose the top k features out of this ordered list. An implementation of the select k best feature selection method is available with scikit-learn: https://scikit-learn.org/stable/modules/generated/sklearn.feature_selection.SelectKBest.html. Furthermore, the following is an example code to demonstrate how this method is used in scikit-learn:

```
>>> from sklearn.datasets import load_digits
>>> from sklearn.feature_selection import SelectKBest, chi2
>>> X, y = load_digits(return_X_y=True)
>>> X.shape
(1797, 64)
>>> X_new = SelectKBest(chi2, k=20).fit_transform(X, y)
>>> X_new.shape
(1797, 20)
```

And now we move on to our next exercise, where we solve a multiclass classification problem.

EXERCISE 5.04: BREAST CANCER DIAGNOSIS CLASSIFICATION USING LOGISTIC REGRESSION

In this exercise, we will be using the Breast Cancer Diagnosis dataset (available at https://archive.ics.uci.edu/ml/datasets/Breast+Cancer+Wisconsin+%28Diagnostic%29) or on GitHub at https://packt.live/3a7oAY8). This dataset is a part of the UCI Machine Learning Repository (https://archive.ics.uci.edu/ml/index.php). The dataset contains characteristics of the cell nuclei present in the digitized image of a **Fine Needle Aspirate** (**FNA**) of a breast mass, with the labels of malignant and benign for each cell nucleus. Characteristics are features (30 in total), such as the mean radius, radius error, worst radius, mean texture, texture error, and worst texture of the cell nuclei. In this exercise, we will use the features provided in the dataset to classify between malignant and benign cells.

The steps to be performed are as follows:

1. Import the required packages. For this exercise, we will require the pandas package to load the data, the Matplotlib package for plotting, and scikit-learn for creating the logistic regression model. Import all the required packages and relevant modules for these tasks:

```
import pandas as pd
import matplotlib.pyplot as plt
from sklearn.linear_model import LogisticRegression
from sklearn.feature_selection import SelectKBest
from sklearn.model_selection import train_test_split
```

2. Load the Breast Cancer Diagnosis dataset using pandas and examine the first five rows:

```
df = pd.read_csv('../Datasets/breast-cancer-data.csv')
df.head()
```

The output will be as follows:

	mean radius	mean texture	mean perimeter	mean area	mean smoothness	mean compactness	mean concavity	mean concave points	mean symmetry	mean fractal dimension	...	worst texture	worst perimeter	worst area	worst smoothness
0	17.99	10.38	122.80	1001.0	0.11840	0.27760	0.3001	0.14710	0.2419	0.07871	...	17.33	184.60	2019.0	0.1622
1	20.57	17.77	132.90	1326.0	0.08474	0.07864	0.0869	0.07017	0.1812	0.05667	...	23.41	158.80	1956.0	0.1238
2	19.69	21.25	130.00	1203.0	0.10960	0.15990	0.1974	0.12790	0.2069	0.05999	...	25.53	152.50	1709.0	0.1444
3	11.42	20.38	77.58	386.1	0.14250	0.28390	0.2414	0.10520	0.2597	0.09744	...	26.50	98.87	567.7	0.2098
4	20.29	14.34	135.10	1297.0	0.10030	0.13280	0.1980	0.10430	0.1809	0.05883	...	16.67	152.20	1575.0	0.1374

5 rows × 31 columns

Figure 5.22: Top five rows of the breast cancer dataset

Additionally, dissect the dataset into input (X) and output (y) variables:

```
X, y = df[[c for c in df.columns if c != 'diagnosis']], df.diagnosis
```

3. The next step is feature engineering. We use scikit-learn's select k best features sub-module under its feature selection module. Basically, this examines the power of each feature against the target output based on a scoring function. You can read about the details here: https://scikit-learn.org/stable/modules/generated/sklearn.feature_selection.SelectKBest.html:

```
"""
restricting to 2 best features so that
we can visualize them on a plot
"""
skb_model = SelectKBest(k=2)
X_new = skb_model.fit_transform(X, y)


# get the k - best column names
mask = skb_model.get_support() #list of booleans
selected_features = [] # The list of your K best features

for bool, feature in zip(mask, df.columns):
    if bool:
        selected_features.append(feature)
print(selected_features)
```

The output will be as follows:

```
['worst perimeter', 'worst concave points']
```

4. And now let's visualize how these two most important features correlate with the target (diagnosis) and how well they separate the two classes of diagnosis:

```
markers = {'benign': {'marker': 'o'}, \
           'malignant': {'marker': 'x'},}
plt.figure(figsize=(10, 7))
for name, group in df.groupby('diagnosis'):
    plt.scatter(group[selected_features[0]], \
                group[selected_features[1]], label=name, \
                marker=markers[name]['marker'],)


plt.title(f'Diagnosis Classification {selected_features[0]} vs \
{selected_features[1]}');
```

```
plt.xlabel(selected_features[0]);
plt.ylabel(selected_features[1]);
plt.legend();
```

The output will be as follows:

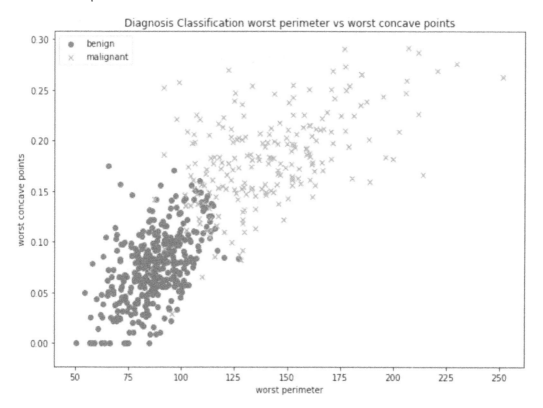

Figure 5.23: Scatterplot for feature selection

5. Before we can construct the model, we must first convert the **diagnosis** values into labels that can be used within the model. Replace the **benign** diagnosis string with the value **0**, and the **malignant** diagnosis string with the value **1**:

```
diagnoses = ['benign', 'malignant',]
output = [diagnoses.index(diag) for diag in df.diagnosis]
```

6. Also, in order to impartially evaluate the model, we should split the training dataset into a training and a validation set:

```
train_X, valid_X, \
train_y, valid_y = train_test_split(df[selected_features], output, \
                                    test_size=0.2, random_state=123)
```

7. Create the model using the **selected_features** and the assigned **diagnosis** labels:

```
model = LogisticRegression(solver='liblinear')
model.fit(df[selected_features], output)
```

The output will be as follows:

```
LogisticRegression(C=1.0, class_weight=None, dual=False, fit_
intercept=True,
                   intercept_scaling=1, l1_ratio=None, max_iter=100,
                   multi_class='warn', n_jobs=None, penalty='l2',
                   random_state=None, solver='liblinear', tol=0.0001,
                   verbose=0,
                   warm_start=False)
```

8. Compute the accuracy of the model against the validation set:

```
model.score(valid_X, valid_y)
```

The output will be as follows:

```
0.9385964912280702
```

9. Construct another model using a random choice of **selected_features** and compare performance:

```
selected_features = ['mean radius', # List features here \
                     'mean texture', 'compactness error']

train_X, valid_X, \
train_y, valid_y = train_test_split(df[selected_features], output, \
                   test_size=0.2, random_state=123)

model = LogisticRegression(solver='liblinear')
model.fit(train_X, train_y)

model.score(valid_X, valid_y)
```

The output will be as follows:

```
0.8859649122807017
```

This reduced accuracy shows that indeed, using the two most important features renders a more powerful model than using three randomly chosen features.

10. Construct another model using all the available information and compare performance:

```
selected_features = [feat for feat in df.columns \
                    if feat != 'diagnosis' # List features here
]

train_X, valid_X, \
train_y, valid_y = train_test_split(df[selected_features], output, \
                    test_size=0.2, random_state=123)

model = LogisticRegression(solver='liblinear')
model.fit(train_X, train_y)

model.score(valid_X, valid_y)
```

The output will be as follows:

```
0.9824561403508771
```

> **NOTE**
>
> To access the source code for this specific section, please refer to https://packt.live/2YWxjIN.
>
> You can also run this example online at https://packt.live/2Bx8NWt.
> You must execute the entire Notebook in order to get the desired result.

This improvement in performance by using all the features shows that even those features that are not among the most important ones do still play a role in improving model performance.

CLASSIFICATION USING K-NEAREST NEIGHBORS

Now that we are comfortable with creating multiclass classifiers using logistic regression and are getting reasonable performance with these models, we will turn our attention to another type of classifier: the K-nearest neighbors (KNN) classifier. KNN is a non-probabilistic, non-linear classifier. It does not predict the probability of a class. Also, as it does not learn any parameters, there is no linear combination of parameters and, thus, it is a non-linear model:

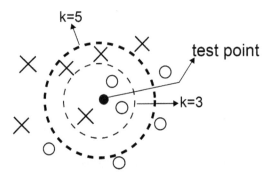

Figure 5.24: Visual representation of KNN

Figure 5.24 represents the workings of a KNN classifier. The two different symbols, **X** and **O**, represent data points belonging to two different classes. The solid circle at the center is the test point requiring classification, the inner dotted circle shows the classification process where **k=3**, while the outer dotted circle shows the classification process where **k=5**. What we mean here is that, if **k=3**, we only look at the three data points nearest to the test point, which gives us the impression of that dotted circle encompassing those three nearest data points.

KNN is one of the simplest "learning" algorithms available for data classification. The use of learning in quotation marks is explicit, as KNN doesn't really learn from the data and encode these learnings in parameters or weights like other methods, such as logistic regression. KNN uses instance-based or lazy learning in that it simply stores or memorizes all the training samples and the corresponding classes. It derives its name, k-nearest neighbors, from the fact that, when a test sample is provided to the algorithm for class prediction, it uses a majority vote of the k-nearest points to determine the corresponding class. If we look at *Figure 5.24* and if we assume **k=3**, the nearest three points lie within the inner dotted circle, and, in this case, the classification would be a hollow circle (**O**).

If, however, we were to take **k=5**, the nearest five points lie within the outer dotted circle and the classification would be a cross (**X**) (three crosses to two hollow circles). So, how do we select **k**? Academically, we should plot the KNN model performance (error) as a function of **k**. Look for an elbow in this plot, and the moment when an increase in **k** does not change the error significantly; this means that we have found an optimal value for **k**. More practically, the choice of **k** depends on the data, with larger values of **k** reducing the effect of noise on the classification, but thereby making boundaries between classes less distinct.

The preceding figure highlights a few characteristics of KNN classification that should be considered:

1. As mentioned previously, the selection of **k** is quite important. In this simple example, switching **k** from three to five flipped the class prediction due to the proximity of both classes. As the final classification is taken by a majority vote, it is often useful to use odd numbers of **k** to ensure that there is a winner in the voting process. If an even value of **k** is selected, and a tie in the vote occurs, then there are a number of different methods available for breaking the tie, including:

    Reducing **k** by one until the tie is broken

    Selecting the class on the basis of the smallest Euclidean distance to the nearest point

    Applying a weighting function to bias the test point toward those neighbors that are closer

2. KNN models have the ability to form extremely complex non-linear boundaries, which can be advantageous in classifying images or datasets with highly non-linear boundaries. Considering that, in *Figure 5.24*, the test point changes from a hollow circle classification to a cross with an increase in **k**, we can see here that a complex boundary could be formed.

3. KNN models can be highly sensitive to local features in the data, given that the classification process is only really dependent on the nearby points.

4. As KNN models memorize all the training information to make predictions, they can struggle with generalizing to new, unseen data.

There is another variant of KNN, which, rather than specifying the number of nearest neighbors, specifies the size of the radius around the test point at which to look. This method, known as the radius neighbors classification, will not be considered in this chapter, but, in understanding KNN, you will also develop an understanding of the radius neighbors classification and how to use the model through scikit-learn.

> **NOTE**
>
> Our explanation of KNN classification and the next exercise examines modeling data with two features or two dimensions, as it enables simpler visualization and a greater understanding of the KNN modeling process. And then we will classify a dataset with a greater number of dimensions in *Activity 5.02: KNN Multiclass Classifier*, wherein we'll classify MNIST using KNN. Remember, just because there are too many dimensions to plot, this doesn't mean it cannot be classified with *N* dimensions.

To allow visualization of the KNN process, we will turn our attention in the following exercise to the Breast Cancer Diagnosis dataset. This dataset is provided as part of the accompanying code files for this book.

EXERCISE 5.05: KNN CLASSIFICATION

In this exercise, we will be using the KNN classification algorithm to build a model on the Breast Cancer Diagnosis dataset and evaluate its performance by calculating its accuracy:

1. For this exercise, we need to import pandas, Matplotlib, and the **KNeighborsClassifier** and **train_test_split** sub-modules of scikit-learn. We will use the shorthand notation **KNN** for quick access:

```
import pandas as pd
import matplotlib.pyplot as plt
from sklearn.neighbors import KNeighborsClassifier as KNN
from sklearn.model_selection import train_test_split
```

2. Load the Breast Cancer Diagnosis dataset and examine the first five rows:

```
df = pd.read_csv('../Datasets/breast-cancer-data.csv')
df.head()
```

The output will be as follows:

	mean radius	mean texture	mean perimeter	mean area	mean smoothness	mean compactness	mean concavity	mean concave points	mean symmetry	mean fractal dimension	...	worst texture	worst perimeter	worst area	worst smoothness	comp
0	17.99	10.38	122.80	1001.0	0.11840	0.27760	0.3001	0.14710	0.2419	0.07871	...	17.33	184.60	2019.0	0.1622	
1	20.57	17.77	132.90	1326.0	0.08474	0.07864	0.0869	0.07017	0.1812	0.05667	...	23.41	158.80	1956.0	0.1238	
2	19.69	21.25	130.00	1203.0	0.10960	0.15990	0.1974	0.12790	0.2069	0.05999	...	25.53	152.50	1709.0	0.1444	
3	11.42	20.38	77.58	386.1	0.14250	0.28390	0.2414	0.10520	0.2597	0.09744	...	26.50	98.87	567.7	0.2098	
4	20.29	14.34	135.10	1297.0	0.10030	0.13280	0.1980	0.10430	0.1809	0.05883	...	16.67	152.20	1575.0	0.1374	

5 rows × 31 columns

Figure 5.25: First five rows

3. At this stage, we need to choose the most appropriate features from the dataset for use with the classifier. We could simply select all 30 features. However, as this exercise is designed to allow visualization of the KNN process, we will arbitrarily only select the mean radius and worst radius. Construct a scatterplot for mean radius versus worst radius for each of the classes in the dataset with the corresponding diagnosis type:

```
markers = {'benign': {'marker': 'o', 'facecolor': 'g', \
                       'edgecolor': 'g'}, \
           'malignant': {'marker': 'x', 'facecolor': 'r', \
                         'edgecolor': 'r'},}
plt.figure(figsize=(10, 7))
for name, group in df.groupby('diagnosis'):
    plt.scatter(group['mean radius'], group['worst radius'], \
                label=name, marker=markers[name]['marker'], \
                facecolors=markers[name]['facecolor'], \
                edgecolor=markers[name]['edgecolor'])

plt.title('Breast Cancer Diagnosis Classification Mean Radius '\
          'vs Worst Radius');
plt.xlabel('Mean Radius');
plt.ylabel('Worst Radius');
plt.legend();
```

The output will be as follows:

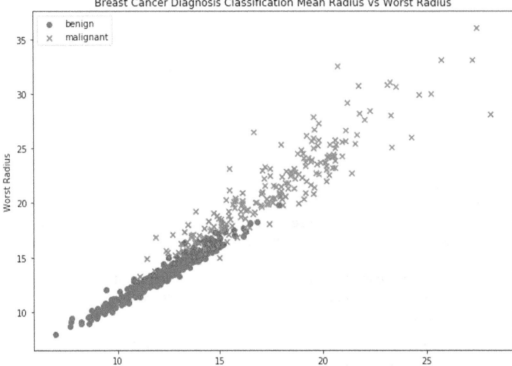

Figure 5.26: Scatterplot of cancer data

4. Before actually going into training a model, let's split the training dataset further into a training and a validation set in the ratio 80:20 to be able to impartially evaluate the model performance later using the validation set:

```
train_X, valid_X, \
train_y, valid_y = train_test_split(df[['mean radius', \
                                        'worst radius']], \
                                    df.diagnosis, test_size=0.2, \
                                    random_state=123)
```

5. Construct a KNN classifier model with **k = 3** and fit it to the training data:

```
model = KNN(n_neighbors=3)
model.fit(X=train_X, y=train_y)
```

The output will be as follows:

```
KNeighborsClassifier(algorithm='auto', leaf_size=30, metric='minkowski',
                     metric_params=None, n_jobs=None, n_neighbors=3, p=2,
                     weights='uniform')
```

Figure 5.27: K Neighbor classifier

6. Check the performance of the model against the validation set:

```
model.score(X=valid_X, y=valid_y)
```

The output will show the performance score:

```
0.9385964912280702
```

As we can see, the accuracy is over 93% on the validation set. Next, by means of an exercise, we will try to understand what decision boundaries are formed by the KNN model during the training process. We will draw the boundaries in the exercise.

> **NOTE**
>
> To access the source code for this specific section, please refer to https://packt.live/3dovRUH.
>
> You can also run this example online at https://packt.live/2V5hYEP. You must execute the entire Notebook in order to get the desired result.

EXERCISE 5.06: VISUALIZING KNN BOUNDARIES

To visualize the decision boundaries produced by the KNN classifier, we need to sweep over the prediction space, that is, the minimum and maximum values for the mean radius and worst radius, and determine the classifications made by the model at those points. Once we have this sweep, we can then plot the classification decisions made by the model:

1. Import all the relevant packages. We will also need NumPy for this exercise:

```
import numpy as np
import pandas as pd
import matplotlib.pyplot as plt
from matplotlib.colors import ListedColormap
from sklearn.neighbors import KNeighborsClassifier as KNN
```

2. Load the dataset into a pandas DataFrame:

```
df = pd.read_csv('../Datasets/breast-cancer-data.csv')
df.head()
```

The output will be as follows:

mean concavity	mean concave points	mean symmetry	mean fractal dimension	...	worst texture	worst perimeter	worst area	worst smoothness	worst compactness	worst concavity	worst concave points	worst symmetry	worst fractal dimension	diagnosis
0.3001	0.14710	0.2419	0.07871	...	17.33	184.60	2019.0	0.1622	0.6656	0.7119	0.2654	0.4601	0.11890	malignant
0.0869	0.07017	0.1812	0.05667	...	23.41	158.80	1956.0	0.1238	0.1866	0.2416	0.1860	0.2750	0.08902	malignant
0.1974	0.12790	0.2069	0.05999	...	25.53	152.50	1709.0	0.1444	0.4245	0.4504	0.2430	0.3613	0.08758	malignant
0.2414	0.10520	0.2597	0.09744	...	26.50	98.87	567.7	0.2098	0.8663	0.6869	0.2575	0.6638	0.17300	malignant
0.1980	0.10430	0.1809	0.05883	...	16.67	152.20	1575.0	0.1374	0.2050	0.4000	0.1625	0.2364	0.07678	malignant

Figure 5.28: First five rows

3. While we could use the diagnosis strings to create the model in the previous exercise, in plotting the decision boundaries, it would be more useful to map the diagnosis to separate integer values. To do this, create a list of the labels for later reference and iterate through this list, replacing the existing label with the corresponding index in the list:

```
labelled_diagnoses = ['benign', 'malignant',]

for idx, label in enumerate(labelled_diagnoses):
    df.diagnosis = df.diagnosis.replace(label, idx)
df.head()
```

The output will be as follows:

mean concavity	mean concave points	mean symmetry	mean fractal dimension	...	worst texture	worst perimeter	worst area	worst smoothness	worst compactness	worst concavity	worst concave points	worst symmetry	worst fractal dimension	diagnosis
0.3001	0.14710	0.2419	0.07871	...	17.33	184.60	2019.0	0.1622	0.6656	0.7119	0.2654	0.4601	0.11890	1
0.0869	0.07017	0.1812	0.05667	...	23.41	158.80	1956.0	0.1238	0.1866	0.2416	0.1860	0.2750	0.08902	1
0.1974	0.12790	0.2069	0.05999	...	25.53	152.50	1709.0	0.1444	0.4245	0.4504	0.2430	0.3613	0.08758	1
0.2414	0.10520	0.2597	0.09744	...	26.50	98.87	567.7	0.2098	0.8663	0.6869	0.2575	0.6638	0.17300	1
0.1980	0.10430	0.1809	0.05883	...	16.67	152.20	1575.0	0.1374	0.2050	0.4000	0.1625	0.2364	0.07678	1

Figure 5.29: First five rows

Notice the use of the **enumerate** function in the **for** loop definition. When iterating through the **for** loop, the **enumerate** function provides the index of the value in the list as well as the value itself through each iteration. We assign the index of the value to the **idx** variable and the value to **label**. Using **enumerate** in this way provides an easy way to replace the species strings with a unique integer label.

4. Construct a KNN classification model, again using three nearest neighbors and fit to the mean radius and worst radius with the newly labeled diagnosis data:

```
model = KNN(n_neighbors=3)
model.fit(X=df[['mean radius', 'worst radius']], y=df.diagnosis)
```

The output will be as follows:

```
KNeighborsClassifier(algorithm='auto', leaf_size=30, metric='minkowski',
                     metric_params=None, n_jobs=None, n_neighbors=3, p=2,
                     weights='uniform')
```

Figure 5.30: K-neighbors classifier

5. To visualize our decision boundaries, we need to create a mesh or range of predictions across the information space, that is, all possible combinations of values of mean radius and worst radius. Starting with **1** unit less than the minimum for both the mean radius and worst radius, and finishing at **1** unit more than the maximum for mean radius and worst radius, use the **arange** function of NumPy to create a range of values between these limits in increments of **0.1** (spacing):

```
spacing = 0.1
mean_radius_range = np.arange(df['mean radius'].min() - 1, \
                              df['mean radius'].max() + 1, spacing)
worst_radius_range = np.arange(df['worst radius'].min() - 1, \
                               df['worst radius'].max() + 1, spacing)
```

6. Use the NumPy **meshgrid** function to combine the two ranges in a grid:

```
# Create the mesh
xx, yy = np.meshgrid(mean_radius_range, worst_radius_range)
```

Check out **xx**:

```
xx
```

The output will be as follows:

```
array([[ 5.981,   6.081,   6.181,  ...,  28.881, 28.981, 29.081],
       [ 5.981,   6.081,   6.181,  ...,  28.881, 28.981, 29.081],
       [ 5.981,   6.081,   6.181,  ...,  28.881, 28.981, 29.081],
       ...,
       [ 5.981,   6.081,   6.181,  ...,  28.881, 28.981, 29.081],
       [ 5.981,   6.081,   6.181,  ...,  28.881, 28.981, 29.081],
       [ 5.981,   6.081,   6.181,  ...,  28.881, 28.981, 29.081]])
```

Figure 5.31: Array of meshgrid xx values

7. Check out **yy**:

```
yy
```

The output will be as follows:

```
array([[ 6.93,   6.93,   6.93,  ...,   6.93,   6.93,   6.93],
       [ 7.03,   7.03,   7.03,  ...,   7.03,   7.03,   7.03],
       [ 7.13,   7.13,   7.13,  ...,   7.13,   7.13,   7.13],
       ...,
       [36.83, 36.83, 36.83,  ...,  36.83, 36.83, 36.83],
       [36.93, 36.93, 36.93,  ...,  36.93, 36.93, 36.93],
       [37.03, 37.03, 37.03,  ...,  37.03, 37.03, 37.03]])
```

Figure 5.32: Array of meshgrid yy values

8. Concatenate the mesh into a single NumPy array using **np.c_**:

```
pred_x = np.c_[xx.ravel(), yy.ravel()] # Concatenate the results
pred_x
```

The output will be as follows:

```
array([[ 5.981,   6.93 ],
       [ 6.081,   6.93 ],
       [ 6.181,   6.93 ],
       ...,
       [28.881, 37.03 ],
       [28.981, 37.03 ],
       [29.081, 37.03 ]])
```

Figure 5.33: Array of predicted values

While this function call looks a little mysterious, it simply concatenates the two separate arrays together (refer to https://docs.scipy.org/doc/numpy/reference/generated/numpy.c_.html) and is shorthand for concatenate.

9. Produce the class predictions for the mesh:

```
pred_y = model.predict(pred_x).reshape(xx.shape)
pred_y
```

The output will be as follows:

```
array([[0, 0, 0, ..., 1, 1, 1],
       [0, 0, 0, ..., 1, 1, 1],
       [0, 0, 0, ..., 1, 1, 1],
       ...,
       [1, 1, 1, ..., 1, 1, 1],
       [1, 1, 1, ..., 1, 1, 1],
       [1, 1, 1, ..., 1, 1, 1]], dtype=int64)
```

Figure 5.34: Array of predicted y values

10. To consistently visualize the boundaries, we will need two sets of consistent colors; a lighter set of colors for the decision boundaries, and a darker set of colors for the points of the training set themselves. Create two color maps using **ListedColormaps**:

```
# Create color maps
cmap_light = ListedColormap(['#6FF6A5', '#F6A56F',])
cmap_bold = ListedColormap(['#0EE664', '#E6640E',])
```

11. To highlight the decision boundaries, first plot the training data according to the diagnosis types, using the **cmap_bold** color scheme and different markers for each of the different diagnosis types:

```
markers = {'benign': {'marker': 'o', 'facecolor': 'g', \
                      'edgecolor': 'g'}, \
           'malignant': {'marker': 'x', 'facecolor': 'r', \
                         'edgecolor': 'r'},}
plt.figure(figsize=(10, 7))
for name, group in df.groupby('diagnosis'):
    diagnoses = labelled_diagnoses[name]
    plt.scatter(group['mean radius'], group['worst radius'], \
                c=cmap_bold.colors[name], \
                label=labelled_diagnoses[name], \
```

```
                    marker=markers[diagnoses]['marker'])

plt.title('Breast Cancer Diagnosis Classification Mean Radius '\
          'vs Worst Radius');
plt.xlabel('Mean Radius');
plt.ylabel('Worst Radius');
plt.legend();
```

The output will be as follows:

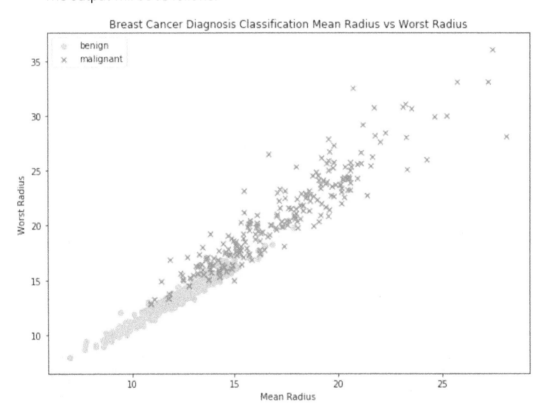

Figure 5.35: Scatterplot with highlighted decision boundaries

12. Using the prediction mesh made previously, plot the decision boundaries in addition to the training data:

```
plt.figure(figsize=(10, 7))
plt.pcolormesh(xx, yy, pred_y, cmap=cmap_light);
plt.scatter(df['mean radius'], df['worst radius'], c=df.diagnosis,
cmap=cmap_bold, edgecolor='k', s=20);
plt.title('Breast Cancer Diagnosis Decision Boundaries Mean Radius '\
          'vs Worst Radius');
plt.xlabel('Mean Radius');
```

```
plt.ylabel('Worst Radius');
plt.text(15, 12, 'Benign', ha='center',va='center', \
        size=20,color='k');
plt.text(15, 30, 'Malignant', ha='center',va='center', \
        size=20,color='k');
```

The output will be as follows:

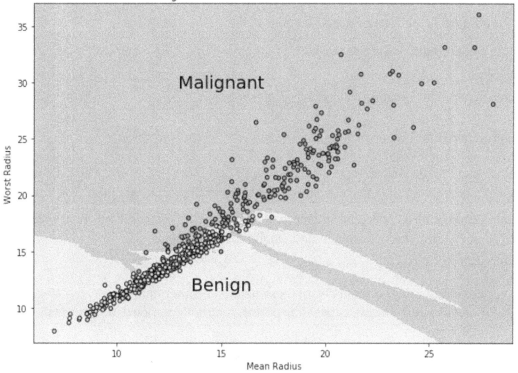

Figure 5.36: The decision boundary

> **NOTE**
>
> To access the source code for this specific section, please refer to
> https://packt.live/3dpxPnY.
>
> You can also run this example online at https://packt.live/3drmBPE.
> You must execute the entire Notebook in order to get the desired result.

We have thus both trained a KNN classifier and also understood how the knn decision boundaries are formed. Next, we will train a KNN multiclass classifier for a different dataset and evaluate its performance.

ACTIVITY 5.02: KNN MULTICLASS CLASSIFIER

In this activity, we will use the KNN model to classify the MNIST dataset into 10 different digit-based classes.

The steps to be performed are as follows:

1. Import the following packages:

```
import struct
import numpy as np
import gzip
import urllib.request
import matplotlib.pyplot as plt
from array import array
from sklearn.neighbors import KNeighborsClassifier as KNN
```

2. Load the MNIST data into memory; first the training images, then the training labels, then the test images, and, finally, the test labels.

3. Visualize a sample of the data.

4. Construct a KNN classifier, with three nearest neighbors to classify the MNIST dataset. Again, to save processing power, randomly sample 5,000 images for use in training.

5. In order to provide the image information to the model, we must first flatten the data out such that each image is 1 x 784 pixels in shape.

6. Build the KNN model with **k=3** and fit the data to the model. Note that, in this activity, we are providing 784 features or dimensions to the model, not just 2.

7. Determine the score against the training set.

8. Display the first two predictions for the model against the training data.

9. Compare the performance against the test set.

   The output will be as follows:

   ```
   0.9376
   ```

> **NOTE**
>
> The solution to this activity can be found on page 474.

If we compare the preceding test set performance with that in *Exercise 5.03, Logistic Regression – Multiclass Classifier*, we see that for the exact same dataset, the knn model outperforms the logistic regression classifier regarding this task. This doesn't necessarily mean that knn always outperforms logistic regression, but it does so for this task, for this dataset.

CLASSIFICATION USING DECISION TREES

Another powerful classification method that we will be examining in this chapter is decision trees, which have found particular use in applications such as natural language processing, for example. There are a number of different machine learning algorithms that fall within the overall umbrella of decision trees, such as **Iterative Dichotomiser 3 (ID3)** and **Classification and Regression Tree (CART)**. In this chapter, we will investigate the use of the ID3 method in classifying categorical data, and we will use the scikit-learn CART implementation as another method of classifying the dataset. So, what exactly are decision trees?

As the name suggests, decision trees are a learning algorithm that apply a sequential series of decisions based on input information to make the final classification. Recalling your childhood biology class, you may have used a process similar to decision trees in the classification of different types of animals via dichotomous keys. Just like the dichotomous key example shown, decision trees aim to classify information following the result of a number of decision or question steps:

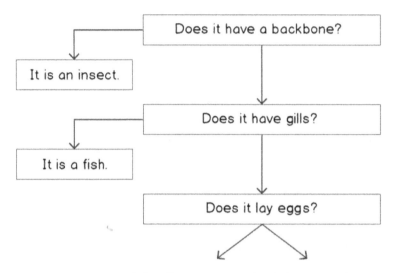

Figure 5.37: Animal classification using the dichotomous key

Depending upon the decision tree algorithm being used, the implementation of the decision steps may vary slightly, but we will be considering the implementation of the ID3 algorithm specifically. The ID3 algorithm aims to classify the data on the basis of each decision providing the largest information gain. To further understand this design, we also need to understand two additional concepts: entropy and information gain.

NOTE

The ID3 algorithm was first proposed by the Australian researcher Ross Quinlan in 1985 (https://doi.org/10.1007/BF00116251).

- Entropy: In simple terms, entropy shows the degree of uncertainty of the signal. For example, if a football (soccer) game is 5 minutes from finishing and if the score is 5-0, then we would say that the game has a low entropy, or, in other words, we are almost certain that the team with 5 goals will win. However, if the score is 1-1, then the game will be considered to have a high entropy (uncertainty). In the context of information theory, entropy is the average rate at which information is provided by a random source of data. Mathematically speaking, this entropy is defined as:

$$H(s) = - \sum_i P_i \log P_i$$

Figure 5.38: Entropy equation

In this scenario, when the random source of data produces a probability value of around 0.5, the event carries more information, as the final outcome is relatively uncertain compared to when the data source produces an extreme (high or low) probability value.

- Information gain: This quantifies the amount of uncertainty reduced if we have prior information about a variable **a** (the variable will be a feature in the case of machine learning models). In other words, how much information can variable a provide regarding an event. Given a dataset **S**, and an attribute to observe **a**, the information gain is defined mathematically as:

$$IG(S, a) = H(S) - H(S \mid a) = H(S) - \sum_{t \in T} p(t) H(t)$$

Figure 5.39: Information gain equation

The information gain of dataset **S**, for attribute **a**, is equal to the entropy of **S** minus the entropy of **S** conditional on attribute **a**, or the entropy of dataset *S* minus the ratio of number of elements in set **t** to the total number of elements in source **S**, times the entropy of **t**, where **t** is one of the categories in attribute **a**.

If at first you find the mathematics here a little daunting, don't worry, for it is far simpler than it seems. To clarify the ID3 process, we will walk through the process using the same dataset as was provided by Quinlan in the original paper.

EXERCISE 5.07: ID3 CLASSIFICATION

In this exercise, we will be performing ID3 classification on a dataset. In the original paper, Quinlan provided a small dataset of 10 weather observation samples labeled with either **P** to indicate that the weather was suitable for, say, a Saturday morning game of cricket, or baseball for our North American friends, or, if the weather was not suitable for a game, **N**. The example dataset described in the paper will be created in the exercise:

1. Import the required packages:

```
import pandas as pd
import numpy as np
import matplotlib.pyplot as plt
```

2. In a Jupyter notebook, create a pandas DataFrame of the following training set:

```
df = pd.DataFrame()
df['Outlook'] = ['sunny', 'sunny', 'overcast', 'rain', 'rain', \
                 'rain', 'overcast', 'sunny', 'sunny', 'rain', \
                 'sunny', 'overcast', 'overcast', 'rain']

df['Temperature'] = ['hot', 'hot', 'hot', 'mild', 'cool', 'cool', \
                     'cool', 'mild', 'cool', 'mild', 'mild', \
                     'mild', 'hot', 'mild',]

df['Humidity'] = ['high', 'high', 'high', 'high', 'normal', \
                  'normal', 'normal', 'high', 'normal', \
                  'normal', 'normal', 'high', 'normal', 'high']

df['Windy'] = ['Weak', 'Strong', 'Weak', 'Weak', 'Weak', 'Strong', \
               'Strong', 'Weak', 'Weak', 'Weak','Strong', 'Strong', \
               'Weak', 'Strong']

df['Decision'] = ['N', 'N', 'P', 'P', 'P', 'N', 'P', 'N', 'P', \
                  'P','P', 'P', 'P', 'N']
df
```

The output will be as follows:

	Outlook	Temperature	Humidity	Windy	Decision
0	sunny	hot	high	Weak	N
1	sunny	hot	high	Strong	N
2	overcast	hot	high	Weak	P
3	rain	mild	high	Weak	P
4	rain	cool	normal	Weak	P
5	rain	cool	normal	Strong	N
6	overcast	cool	normal	Strong	P
7	sunny	mild	high	Weak	N
8	sunny	cool	normal	Weak	P
9	rain	mild	normal	Weak	P
10	sunny	mild	normal	Strong	P
11	overcast	mild	high	Strong	P
12	overcast	hot	normal	Weak	P
13	rain	mild	high	Strong	N

Figure 5.40: pandas DataFrame

3. In the original paper, the ID3 algorithm starts by taking a small sample of the training set at random and fitting the tree to this window. This can be a useful method for large datasets, but given that ours is quite small, we will simply start with the entire training set. The first step is to calculate the entropy for the **Decision** column, where there are two possible values, or classes, **P** and **N**:

```
# Probability of P
p_p = len(df.loc[df.Decision == 'P']) / len(df)

# Probability of N
p_n = len(df.loc[df.Decision == 'N']) / len(df)

entropy_decision = -p_n * np.log2(p_n) - p_p * np.log2(p_p)
print(f'H(S) = {entropy_decision:0.4f}')
```

The output will be as follows:

```
H(S) = 0.94403
```

4. We will need to repeat this calculation, so wrap it in a function:

```
def f_entropy_decision(data):
    p_p = len(data.loc[data.Decision == 'P']) / len(data)
    p_n = len(data.loc[data.Decision == 'N']) / len(data)
    return -p_n * np.log2(p_n) - p_p * np.log2(p_p)
```

5. The next step is to calculate which attribute provides the highest information gain out of **Outlook**, **Temperature**, **Humidity**, and **Windy**. Starting with the **Outlook** parameter, determine the probability of each decision given sunny, overcast, and rainy conditions. We need to evaluate the following equation:

$$IG(S, a) = H(S) - H(S|a) = H(S) - \sum_{t \in T} p(t)H(t)$$

Figure 5.41: Information gain

6. Construct this equation in Python using the pandas **groupby** method:

```
IG_decision_Outlook = entropy_decision # H(S)

# Create a string to print out the overall equation
overall_eqn = 'Gain(Decision, Outlook) = Entropy(Decision)'

"""Iterate through the values for outlook and compute the
probabilities and entropy values
"""
for name, Outlook in df.groupby('Outlook'):
    num_p = len(Outlook.loc[Outlook.Decision == 'P'])
    num_n = len(Outlook.loc[Outlook.Decision != 'P'])
    num_Outlook = len(Outlook)
    print(f'p(Decision=P|Outlook={name}) = {num_p}/{num_Outlook}')
    print(f'p(Decision=N|Outlook={name}) = {num_n}/{num_Outlook}')
    print(f'p(Outlook={name}) = {num_Outlook}/{len(df)}')
    print(f'Entropy(Decision|Outlook={name}) = '\
        f'-{num_p}/{num_Outlook}.log2({num_p}/{num_Outlook}) - '\
        f'{num_n}/{num_Outlook}.log2({num_n}/{num_Outlook})')

    entropy_decision_outlook = 0
```

```
        # Cannot compute log of 0 so add checks
        if num_p != 0:
            entropy_decision_outlook -= (num_p / num_Outlook) \
                                    * np.log2(num_p / num_Outlook)


        # Cannot compute log of 0 so add checks
        if num_n != 0:
            entropy_decision_outlook -= (num_n / num_Outlook) \
                                    * np.log2(num_n / num_Outlook)


        IG_decision_Outlook -= (num_Outlook / len(df)) \
                            * entropy_decision_outlook
        print()
        overall_eqn += f' - p(Outlook={name}).'
        overall_eqn += f'Entropy(Decision|Outlook={name})'
    print(overall_eqn)
    print(f'Gain(Decision, Outlook) = {IG_decision_Outlook:0.4f}')
```

The output will be as follows:

```
p(Decision=P|Outlook=overcast) = 4/4
p(Decision=N|Outlook=overcast) = 0/4
p(Outlook=overcast) = 4/14
Entropy(Decision|Outlook=overcast) = -4/4.log2(4/4) - 0/4.log2(0/4)

p(Decision=P|Outlook=rain) = 3/5
p(Decision=N|Outlook=rain) = 2/5
p(Outlook=rain) = 5/14
Entropy(Decision|Outlook=rain) = -3/5.log2(3/5) - 2/5.log2(2/5)

p(Decision=P|Outlook=sunny) = 2/5
p(Decision=N|Outlook=sunny) = 3/5
p(Outlook=sunny) = 5/14
Entropy(Decision|Outlook=sunny) = -2/5.log2(2/5) - 3/5.log2(3/5)

Gain(Decision, Outlook) = Entropy(Decision) - p(Outlook=overcast).Entropy(Decision|Outlook=overcast) - p(Outlook=rai
n).Entropy(Decision|Outlook=rain) - p(Outlook=sunny).Entropy(Decision|Outlook=sunny)
Gain(Decision, Outlook) = 0.2467
```

Figure 5.42: Entropy and gain probabilities

7. The final gain equation for **Outlook** can be rewritten as:

$$G(Decision, Outlook) = H(Decision) - p(Outlook = overcast)H(Decision|Outlook = overcast)$$
$$- p(Outlook = sunny)H(Decision|Outlook = sunny) - p(Outlook = rain)H(Decision|Outlook = rain)$$

Figure 5.43: Equation of information gain

8. We need to repeat this process quite a few times, so wrap it in a function for ease of use later:

```
def IG(data, column, ent_decision=entropy_decision):
    IG_decision = ent_decision
    for name, temp in data.groupby(column):
        p_p = len(temp.loc[temp.Decision == 'P']) / len(temp)
        p_n = len(temp.loc[temp.Decision != 'P']) / len(temp)

        entropy_decision = 0

        if p_p != 0:
            entropy_decision -= (p_p) * np.log2(p_p)

        if p_n != 0:
            entropy_decision -= (p_n) * np.log2(p_n)

        IG_decision -= (len(temp) / len(df)) * entropy_decision
    return IG_decision
```

9. Repeat this process for each of the other columns to compute the corresponding information gain:

```
for col in df.columns[:-1]:
    print(f'Gain(Decision, {col}) = {IG(df, col):0.4f}')
```

The output will be as follows:

```
Gain(Decision, Outlook) = 0.2467
Gain (Decision, Temperature) = 0.0292
Gain(Decision, Humidity) = 0.1518
Gain(Decision, Windy) = 0.0481
```

10. This information provides the first decision of the tree. We want to split on the maximum information gain, so we split on **Outlook**. Look at the data splitting on **Outlook**:

```
for name, temp in df.groupby('Outlook'):
    print('-' * 15)
    print(name)
    print('-' * 15)
    print(temp)
    print('-' * 15)
```

The output will be as follows:

```
- - - - - - - - - - - - - - -
overcast
- - - - - - - - - - - - - - -
      Outlook Temperature Humidity  Windy Decision
2    overcast           hot      high    Weak        P
6    overcast          cool    normal  Strong        P
11   overcast          mild      high  Strong        P
12   overcast           hot    normal    Weak        P
- - - - - - - - - - - - -

- - - - - - - - - - - - -
rain
- - - - - - - - - - - - - -
      Outlook Temperature Humidity  Windy Decision
3      rain           mild      high    Weak        P
4      rain           cool    normal    Weak        P
5      rain           cool    normal  Strong        N
9      rain           mild    normal    Weak        P
13     rain           mild      high  Strong        N
- - - - - - - - - - - - - -

- - - - - - - - - - - - - -
sunny
- - - - - - - - - - - - - -
      Outlook Temperature Humidity  Windy Decision
0     sunny            hot      high    Weak        N
1     sunny            hot      high  Strong        N
7     sunny           mild      high    Weak        N
8     sunny           cool    normal    Weak        P
10    sunny           mild    normal  Strong        P
- - - - - - - - - - - - - -
```

Figure 5.44: Information gain

Notice that all the overcast records have a decision of **P**. This provides our first terminating leaf of the decision tree. If it is overcast, we are going to play, while if it is rainy or sunny, there is a chance we will not play. The decision tree so far can be represented as in the following figure:

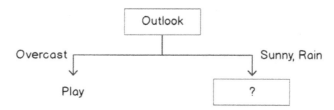

Figure 5.45: Decision tree

> **NOTE**
>
> This figure was created manually for reference and is not contained in, or obtained from, the accompanying source code.

11. We now repeat this process, splitting by information gain until all the data is allocated and all branches of the tree terminate. First, remove the overcast samples, as they no longer provide any additional information:

```
df_next = df.loc[df.Outlook != 'overcast']
df_next
```

The output will be as follows:

	Outlook	Temperature	Humidity	Windy	Decision
0	sunny	hot	high	Weak	N
1	sunny	hot	high	Strong	N
3	rain	mild	high	Weak	P
4	rain	cool	normal	Weak	P
5	rain	cool	normal	Strong	N
7	sunny	mild	high	Weak	N
8	sunny	cool	normal	Weak	P
9	rain	mild	normal	Weak	P
10	sunny	mild	normal	Strong	P
13	rain	mild	high	Strong	N

Figure 5.46: Data after removing the overcast samples

12. Now, we will turn our attention to the sunny samples and will rerun the gain calculations to determine the best way to split the sunny information:

```
df_sunny = df_next.loc[df_next.Outlook == 'sunny']
```

13. Recompute the entropy for the sunny samples:

```
entropy_decision = f_entropy_decision(df_sunny)
entropy_decision
```

The output will be as follows:

```
0.9709505944546686
```

14. Run the gain calculations for the sunny samples:

```
for col in df_sunny.columns[1:-1]:
    print(f'Gain(Decision, {col}) = \
{IG(df_sunny, col, entropy_decision):0.4f}')
```

The output will be as follows:

```
Gain(Decision, Temperature) = 0.8281
Gain(Decision, Humidity) = 0.9710
Gain(Decision, Windy) = 0.6313
```

15. Again, we select the largest gain, which is **Humidity**. Group the data by **Humidity**:

```
for name, temp in df_sunny.groupby('Humidity'):
    print('-' * 15)
    print(name)
    print('-' * 15)
    print(temp)
    print('-' * 15)
```

The output will be as follows:

```
---------------
high
---------------
   Outlook Temperature Humidity   Windy Decision
0    sunny         hot     high    Weak        N
1    sunny         hot     high  Strong        N
7    sunny        mild     high    Weak        N
---------------

---------------
normal
---------------
    Outlook Temperature Humidity   Windy Decision
8     sunny        cool   normal    Weak        P
10    sunny        mild   normal  Strong        P
---------------
```

Figure 5.47: After grouping data according to humidity

We can see here that we have two terminating leaves in that when the **Humidity** is high, there is a decision not to play, and, vice versa, when the **Humidity** is normal, there is the decision to play. So, updating our representation of the decision tree, we have:

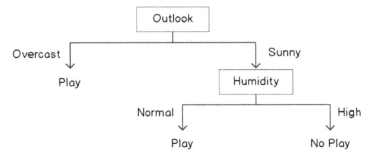

Figure 5.48: Decision tree with two values

16. So, the last set of data that requires classification is the rainy outlook data. Extract only the **rain** data and rerun the entropy calculation:

```
df_rain = df_next.loc[df_next.Outlook == 'rain']
entropy_decision = f_entropy_decision(df_rain)
entropy_decision
```

The output will be as follows:

```
0.9709505944546686
```

17. Repeat the gain calculation with the **rain** subset:

```
for col in df_rain.columns[1:-1]:
    print(f'Gain(Decision, {col}) = \
{IG(df_rain, col, entropy_decision):0.4f}')
```

The output will be as follows:

```
Gain(Decision, Temperature) = 0.6313
Gain(Decision,Humidity) = 0.6313
Gain(Decision, Windy) = 0.9710
```

18. Again, splitting on the attribute with the largest gain value requires splitting on the **Windy** values. So, group the remaining information by **Windy**:

```
for name, temp in df_rain.groupby('Windy'):
    print('-' * 15)
    print(name)
    print('-' * 15)
```

```
print(temp)
print('-' * 15)
```

The output will be as follows:

```
---------------
Strong
---------------
    Outlook Temperature Humidity  Windy Decision
5      rain        cool   normal Strong        N
13     rain        mild     high Strong        N
---------------

---------------
Weak
---------------
    Outlook Temperature Humidity Windy Decision
3      rain        mild     high  Weak        P
4      rain        cool   normal  Weak        P
9      rain        mild   normal  Weak        P
---------------
```

Figure 5.49: Data grouped according to Windy

19. Finally, we have all the terminating leaves required to complete the tree, as splitting on **Windy** provides two sets, all of which indicate either play (**P**) or no-play (**N**) values. Our complete decision tree is as follows:

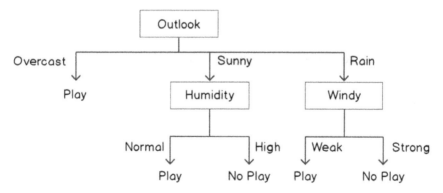

Figure 5.50: Final decision tree

> **NOTE**
>
> To access the source code for this specific section, please refer to https://packt.live/37Rh7fX.
>
> You can also run this example online at https://packt.live/3hTz4Px.
> You must execute the entire Notebook in order to get the desired result.

Decision trees, very much like KNN models, are discriminative models. Discriminative models are the models that aim to maximize the conditional probability of the class of data given the features. The opposite of discriminative models is generative models, which learn the joint probability of data classes and features and, hence, learn the distribution of data to generate artificial samples.

So, how do we make predictions with unseen information in the case of a decision tree? Simply follow the tree. Look at the decision being made at each node and apply the data from the unseen sample. The prediction will then end up being the label specified at the terminating leaf. Let's say we had a weather forecast for the upcoming Saturday and we wanted to predict whether we were going to play or not. The weather forecast is as follows:

Attribute	Value
Outlook	Rain
Temperature	Mild
Humidity	Normal
Windy	Strong

Figure 5.51: Weather forecast for the upcoming Saturday

The decision tree for this would be as follows (the dashed circles indicate selected leaves in the tree):

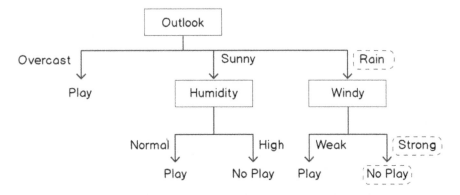

Figure 5.52: Making a new prediction using a decision tree

Now, hopefully, you have a reasonable understanding of the underlying concept of decision trees and the process of making sequential decisions. With the principles of decision trees in our toolkit, we will now look at applying a more complicated model using the functionality provided in scikit-learn.

CLASSIFICATION AND REGRESSION TREE

The scikit-learn decision tree methods implement the CART method, which provides the ability to use decision trees in both classification and regression problems. CART differs from ID3 in that the decisions are made by comparing the values of features against a calculated value. More precisely, we can see that in the ID3 algorithm, a decision is made based on the value of the feature that is present in the dataset. This serves the purpose well when data is categorical; however, once data becomes continuous, this method does not work well. In such cases, CART is used, which calculates the threshold value for comparison with a feature value. And because, in such comparisons, there can only be two possible outcomes – (a) the feature value is greater than (or equal to) the threshold value or, (b) the feature value is less than (or equal to) the threshold value – hence, CART results in binary trees.

On the contrary, ID3 creates multiway trees because, as mentioned earlier, in ID3, the decision is made based on existing feature values and if the feature is categorical, then the tree is going to branch into potentially as many branches as the number of categories. Another difference between ID3 and CART is, as opposed to ID3, which uses information gain as the metric to find the best split, CART uses another measure called the **gini impurity measure**. Mathematically, you will recall that we defined entropy as:

$$H(s) = - \sum_i P_i logP_i$$

Figure 5.53: Definition of entropy

And so, gini impurity is defined as:

$$I_G = \sum_i P_i(1 - P_i)$$

Figure 5.54: Definition of gini impurity

Conceptually, this is a measure of the following: if we randomly pick a data point in our dataset and if we randomly classify (label) it according to the class distribution in the dataset, then what is the probability of classifying the data point incorrectly?

Having discussed the CART- and ID3-based decision tree methodologies, let's now solve a classification problem using the CART methodology.

EXERCISE 5.08: BREAST CANCER DIAGNOSIS CLASSIFICATION USING A CART DECISION TREE

In this exercise, we will classify the Breast Cancer Diagnosis data using scikit-learn's decision tree classifier, which can be used in both classification and regression problems:

1. Import the required packages:

```
import numpy as np
import pandas as pd
import matplotlib.pyplot as plt
from sklearn.tree import DecisionTreeClassifier
from sklearn.model_selection import train_test_split
```

2. Load the Breast Cancer dataset:

```
df = pd.read_csv('../Datasets/breast-cancer-data.csv')
df.head()
```

The output will be as follows:

	mean radius	mean texture	mean perimeter	mean area	mean smoothness	mean compactness	mean concavity	mean concave points	mean symmetry	mean fractal dimension	...	worst texture	worst perimeter	worst area	worst smoothness
0	17.99	10.38	122.80	1001.0	0.11840	0.27760	0.3001	0.14710	0.2419	0.07871	...	17.33	184.60	2019.0	0.1622
1	20.57	17.77	132.90	1326.0	0.08474	0.07864	0.0869	0.07017	0.1812	0.05667	...	23.41	158.80	1956.0	0.1238
2	19.69	21.25	130.00	1203.0	0.10960	0.15990	0.1974	0.12790	0.2069	0.05999	...	25.53	152.50	1709.0	0.1444
3	11.42	20.38	77.58	386.1	0.14250	0.28390	0.2414	0.10520	0.2597	0.09744	...	26.50	98.87	567.7	0.2098
4	20.29	14.34	135.10	1297.0	0.10030	0.13280	0.1980	0.10430	0.1809	0.05883	...	16.67	152.20	1575.0	0.1374

5 rows × 31 columns

Figure 5.55: First five rows

3. Before actually going into training a model, let's further split the training dataset into a training and a validation set in the ratio 70:30 to be able to impartially evaluate the model performance later using the validation set:

```
train_X, valid_X, \
train_y, valid_y = train_test_split(df[set(df.columns)\
                                    -{'diagnosis'}], df.diagnosis, \
                                    test_size=0.3, random_state=123)
```

4. Fit the model to the training data and check the corresponding accuracy:

```
model = DecisionTreeClassifier()
model = model.fit(train_X, train_y)
model.score(train_X, train_y)
```

The output will be as follows:

```
1.0
```

Our model achieves 100% accuracy on the training set.

5. Check the performance against the test set:

```
model.score(valid_X, valid_y)
```

The output accuracy should be smaller than 1, ideally:

```
0.9415204678362573
```

6. One of the great things about decision trees is that we can visually represent the model and see exactly what is going on. Install the required dependency:

```
!conda install python-graphviz
```

7. Import the graphing package:

```
import graphviz
from sklearn.tree import export_graphviz
```

8. Plot the model:

```
dot_data = export_graphviz(model, out_file=None)
graph = graphviz.Source(dot_data)
graph
```

The output will be as follows:

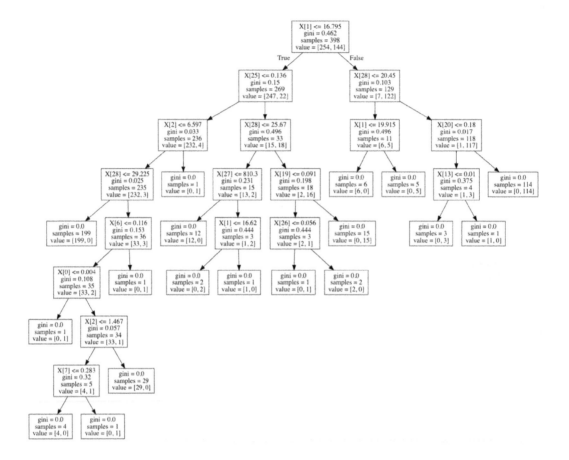

Figure 5.56: Decisions of the CART decision tree

This figure illustrates the decisions of the CART decision tree in the scikit-learn model. The first line of the node is the decision that is made at that step. The first node, *X[1]* *<= 16.795*, indicates that the training data is split on column 1 on the basis of being less than or equal to 16.795. Those samples with values on column 1 less than 16.795 (of which there are 254) are then further dissected on column 25. Similarly, samples with values on column 1 greater than or equal to 16.795 (of which there are 144) are then further dissected on column 28. This decision/branching process continues until the terminating condition is reached. The terminating condition can be defined in several ways. Some of them are as follows:

- The tree has been exhausted and all terminating leaves have been constructed/found.

- Impurity (the measure of the different number of classes that the elements in a node belong to) at a particular node is below a given threshold.

- The number of elements at a particular node is lower than a threshold number of elements.

> **NOTE**
>
> To access the source code for this specific section, please refer to https://packt.live/31btfY5.
>
> You can also run this example online at https://packt.live/37PJTO4.
> You must execute the entire Notebook in order to get the desired result.

Before we move on to the next topic, let's perform a binary classification task using the CART decision tree on the MNIST digits dataset. The task is to classify images of digits 0 and 1 into digits (or classes) 0 and 1.

ACTIVITY 5.03: BINARY CLASSIFICATION USING A CART DECISION TREE

In this activity, we will build a CART Decision Tree-based classifier using the MNIST dataset to classify between two digits: 0 and 1.

The steps to be performed are as follows:

1. Import the required dependencies:

```
import struct
import numpy as np
import pandas as pd
import gzip
import urllib.request
import matplotlib.pyplot as plt
from array import array
from sklearn.model_selection import train_test_split
from sklearn.tree import DecisionTreeClassifier
```

2. Load the MNIST data into memory.

3. Visualize a sample of the data.

4. Construct a CART Decision Tree classifier model to classify the digits 0 and 1. The model we are going to create is to determine whether the samples are either the digits 0 or 1. To do this, we first need to select only those samples.

5. Visualize the selected information with images of one sample of 0 and one sample of 1.

6. In order to provide the image information to the model, we must first flatten the data out so that each image is 1 x 784 pixels in shape.

7. Construct the model; use the **DecisionTreeClassifier** API and call the **fit** function.

8. Determine the training set accuracy.

9. Compare the performance against the test set.

    The output will be as follows:

```
0.9962174940898345
```

> **NOTE**
>
> The solution to this activity can be found on page 478.

An interesting point to note here is that the test set performance here is much better than that in *Activity 5.01: Ordinary Least Squares Classifier – Binary Classifier*. The dataset is exactly the same in both cases, but the models are different. This demonstrates the fact that the CART decision trees-based model performs better than the OLS-based model on this binary classification task.

Now that we have acquired an understanding of decision trees for classification, we will next discuss one of the most popular and powerful types of machine learning model that is widely used in the industry as well as in academia – artificial neural networks.

ARTIFICIAL NEURAL NETWORKS

The final type of classification model that we will be studying is **Artificial Neural Networks (ANNs)**. Firstly, this class of model is inspired by how the human brain functions. More specifically, we try to mathematically emulate the interconnected-neurons architecture, hence the name – neural networks. Essentially, an artificial neural network architecture looks something like that shown in *Figure 5.57*:

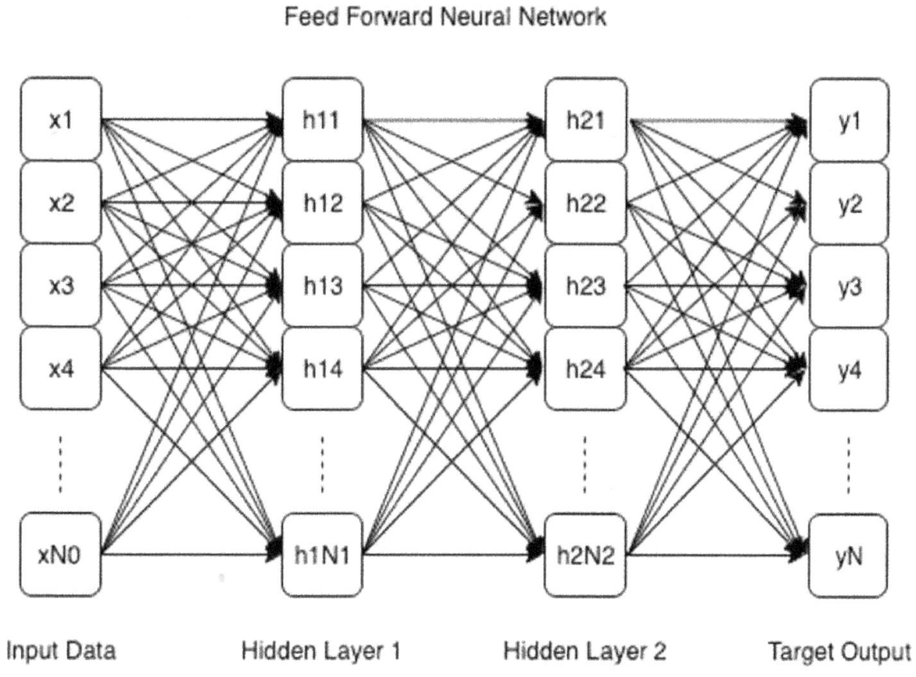

Figure 5.57: Neural network architecture example

To the extreme left is the input data *X*, expanded into the **N0** different feature dimensions. This example has two hidden layers, **h1** and **h2**, having **N1** and **N2** number of neurons, respectively. Wait, what is a neuron? The nomenclature is derived from the human brain analogy, and a neuron in the context of an artificial neural network is essentially a node in the network/graph. And finally, in the figure, there is the output layer, Y, which consists of the *N* number of classes for the example of a multiclass classification task. Each arrow in this figure represents a network weight or parameter. As you can see, these models can therefore have a large number of arrows/parameters, which essentially makes them complex and powerful. And the way these weights come into play is, for example, **h11** is the weighted sum of all the input features, **x1, x2 ... xN0**, passed through an activation function.

Wait, what then is an activation function? In neural networks, inside each neuron or node is an implicit non-linear function. This helps make the model non-linear (hence complex), and if we remove these non-linearities, then the several hidden layers will collapse (by virtue of a series of matrix multiplications) resulting in an extremely simple linear model. This linear model would imply that the output class of data can be represented as the weighted sum of input features, which is absolutely not the case with ANNs. Popular non-linear activation functions used in neural networks are **sigmoid, tanh** (hyperbolic tangent), and **Rectified Linear Unit (ReLU)** In fact, if we use sigmoid as the activation function and omit all the hidden layers and restrict the number of classes to two, we get the following neural network:

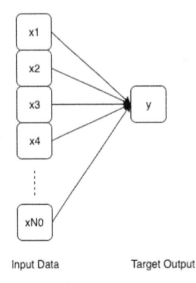

Feed Forward Neural Network
(binary classifier with no hidden layers)

Input Data   Target Output

Figure 5.58: Neural network binary classifier with no hidden layers

Does this look familiar? This model is precisely the same as our logistic regression model! First, we take the weighted sum of all the input features **x1**, **x2** .... **xN0**, and then apply the sigmoid or logistic function in order to get the final output. This output is then compared with the ground truth label to compute the loss. And, similar to linear regression models as discussed in the previous chapter, neural networks use gradient descent to derive the optimal set of weights or parameters by minimizing the loss. Although, since a neural network model is much more complex than a linear regression model, the way the parameters are updated in the former is much more sophisticated than the latter, and a technique called backpropagation is used to do so. Mathematical details of backpropagation are beyond the scope of this chapter, but we encourage readers to read further on that.

EXERCISE 5.09: NEURAL NETWORKS – MULTICLASS CLASSIFIER

Neural networks can be used for multiclass classification and are by no means restricted just to binary classification. In this exercise, we will be investigating a 10-class classification problem, in other words, the MNIST digits classification task. The process for loading the MNIST training and test data is identical to the previous exercises:

1. Import the required packages:

```
import struct
import numpy as np
import gzip
import urllib.request
import matplotlib.pyplot as plt
from array import array
from sklearn.neural_network import MLPClassifier
```

2. Load the training/test images and the corresponding labels:

```
with gzip.open('../Datasets/train-images-idx3-ubyte.gz', 'rb') as f:
    magic, size, rows, cols = struct.unpack(">IIII", f.read(16))
    img = np.array(array("B", f.read())).reshape((size, rows, cols))
with gzip.open('../Datasets/train-labels-idx1-ubyte.gz', 'rb') as f:
    magic, size = struct.unpack(">II", f.read(8))
    labels = np.array(array("B", f.read()))
with gzip.open('../Datasets/t10k-images-idx3-ubyte.gz', 'rb') as f:
    magic, size, rows, cols = struct.unpack(">IIII", f.read(16))
    img_test = np.array(array("B", f.read()))\
                .reshape((size, rows, cols))
```

```
with gzip.open('../Datasets/t10k-labels-idx1-ubyte.gz', 'rb') as f:
    magic, size = struct.unpack(">II", f.read(8))
    labels_test = np.array(array("B", f.read()))
```

3. Visualize a sample of the data:

```
for i in range(10):
    plt.subplot(2, 5, i + 1)
    plt.imshow(img[i], cmap='gray');
    plt.title(f'{labels[i]}');
    plt.axis('off')
```

The output will be as follows:

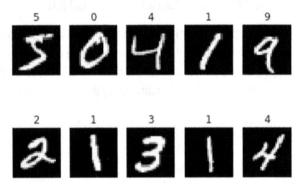

Figure 5.59: Sample data

4. Given that the training data is so large, we will select a subset of the overall data to reduce the training time as well as the system resources required for the training process:

```
np.random.seed(0) # Give consistent random numbers
selection = np.random.choice(len(img), 5000)
selected_images = img[selection]
selected_labels = labels[selection]
```

5. Again, reshape the input data in vector form for later use:

```
selected_images = selected_images.reshape((-1, rows * cols))
selected_images.shape
```

The output will be as follows:

```
(5000, 784)
```

6. Next, we normalize the image data. We scale all the image values between **0** and **1**. Originally, grayscale images are comprised of pixels with values between and including 0 to **255**, where **0** is black and **255** is white. Normalization is important because it helps the gradient descent algorithm perform effectively. Unnormalized data is more prone to diminishing/exploding values of gradients during weight updates and will, therefore, lead to negligible weight updates:

```
selected_images = selected_images / 255.0
img_test = img_test / 255.0
```

7. Construct the neural network (or the multilayer perceptron) model. There are a few extra arguments, as follows: the **sgd** value for **solver** tells the model to use stochastic gradient descent, with additional **max_iter** iterations required to converge on a solution. The **hidden_layer_sizes** argument essentially describes the model architecture, in other words, how many hidden layers there are and how many neurons there are in each hidden layer. For example, (20, 10, 5) would mean 3 hidden layers, with 20, 10, and 5 neurons in them, respectively. The **learning_rate_init** argument gives the initial learning rate for the gradient descent algorithm:

```
model = MLPClassifier(solver='sgd', hidden_layer_sizes=(100,), \
                      max_iter=1000, random_state=1, \
                      learning_rate_init=.01)
model.fit(X=selected_images, y=selected_labels)
```

The output will be as follows:

```
MLPClassifier(activation='relu', alpha=0.0001, batch_size='auto', beta_1=0.9,
              beta_2=0.999, early_stopping=False, epsilon=1e-08,
              hidden_layer_sizes=(100,), learning_rate='constant',
              learning_rate_init=0.01, max_iter=1000, momentum=0.9,
              n_iter_no_change=10, nesterovs_momentum=True, power_t=0.5,
              random_state=1, shuffle=True, solver='sgd', tol=0.0001,
              validation_fraction=0.1, verbose=False, warm_start=False)
```

Figure 5.60: Neural network model

NOTE

Refer to the documentation at https://scikit-learn.org/stable/modules/
generated/sklearn.neural_network.MLPClassifier.html#sklearn.neural_network.
MLPClassifier for more information on the arguments.

8. Determine the accuracy score against the training set:

```
model.score(X=selected_images, y=selected_labels)
```

The output will be as follows:

```
1.0
```

9. Determine the first two predictions for the training set and plot the images with the corresponding predictions:

```
model.predict(selected_images)[:2]
```

The output will be as follows:

```
array([4, 1], dtype=uint8)
```

10. Show the images for the first two samples of the training set to see whether we are correct:

```
plt.subplot(1, 2, 1)
plt.imshow(selected_images[0].reshape((28, 28)), cmap='gray');
plt.axis('off');
plt.subplot(1, 2, 2)
plt.imshow(selected_images[1].reshape((28, 28)), cmap='gray');
plt.axis('off');
```

The output will be as follows:

Figure 5.61: Sample images from the training dataset

11. Again, print out the probability scores provided by the model for the first sample of the training set. Confirm that there are 10 different values for each of the 10 classes in the set:

```
model.predict_proba(selected_images)[0]
```

The output will be as follows:

```
array([2.06600762e-08, 3.20511169e-12, 6.42583214e-07, 5.68539725e-12,
       9.99995240e-01, 4.93612091e-11, 1.28518030e-06, 2.63272729e-10,
       2.41742908e-06, 3.94211627e-07])
```

Figure 5.62: Array of predicted class probability

Notice that, in the probability array of the first sample, the fifth (digit **4**) number is the highest probability, thus indicating a prediction of **4**.

12. Compute the accuracy of the model against the test set. This will provide a reasonable estimate of the model's *in the wild* performance, as it has never seen the data in the test set. It is expected that the accuracy rate of the test set will be slightly lower than the training set, given that the model has not been exposed to this data:

```
model.score(X=img_test.reshape((-1, rows * cols)), y=labels_test)
```

The output will be as follows:

```
0.9384
```

If we compare these training and test set scores (1 and 0.9384) for the neural network model with those for the logistic regression model (0.986 and 0.9002) as obtained in *Exercise 5.03, Logistic Regression – Multiclass Classifier*, we can see that the neural network model expectedly outperforms the logistic regression model. This happens because there are many more parameters to be learned in a neural network compared to a logistic regression model, making neural networks more complex and hence powerful. Conversely, if we build a neural network binary classifier with no hidden layers and using sigmoidal activation functions, it essentially becomes the same as a logistic regression model.

> **NOTE**
>
> To access the source code for this specific section, please refer to https://packt.live/2NjfiyX.
>
> You can also run this example online at https://packt.live/3dowv4z. You must execute the entire Notebook in order to get the desired result.

Before we conclude this chapter, let's work out a last classification task using neural networks, this time, on the Breast Cancer Diagnosis classification dataset.

ACTIVITY 5.04: BREAST CANCER DIAGNOSIS CLASSIFICATION USING ARTIFICIAL NEURAL NETWORKS

In this activity, we will be using the Breast Cancer Diagnosis dataset (available at https://archive.ics.uci.edu/ml/datasets/Breast+Cancer+Wisconsin+%28Diagnostic%29 or on GitHub at https://packt.live/3a7oAY8). This dataset is a part of the UCI Machine Learning Repository (https://archive.ics.uci.edu/ml/index.php). The dataset contains characteristics of the cell nuclei present in the digitized image of a fine needle aspirate (FNA) of a breast mass, with the labels malignant and benign for each cell nucleus. Characteristics are features (30 in total) such as the mean radius, radius error, worst radius, mean texture, texture error, and worst texture of the cell nuclei. In this activity, we will use the features provided in the dataset to classify between malignant and benign cells.

The steps to be performed are as follows:

1. Import the required packages. For this activity, we will require the **pandas** package for loading the data, the **matplotlib** package for plotting, and scikit-learn for creating the neural network model, as well as to split the dataset into training and test sets. Import all the required packages and relevant modules for these tasks:

```
import pandas as pd
import matplotlib.pyplot as plt
from sklearn.neural_network import MLPClassifier
from sklearn.model_selection import train_test_split
from sklearn import preprocessing
```

2. Load the Breast Cancer Diagnosis dataset using pandas and examine the first five rows.

3. The next step is feature engineering. Different columns of this dataset have different scales of magnitude, hence, before constructing and training a neural network model, we normalize the dataset. For this, we use the **MinMaxScaler** API from **sklearn**, which normalizes each column's values between 0 and 1, as discussed in the *Logistic Regression* section of this chapter (see *Exercise 5.03, Logistic Regression – Multiclass Classifier*): https://scikit-learn.org/stable/modules/generated/sklearn.preprocessing.MinMaxScaler.html.

4. Before we can construct the model, we must first convert the **diagnosis** values into labels that can be used within the model. Replace the **benign** diagnosis string with the value **0**, and the **malignant** diagnosis string with the value **1**.

5. Also, in order to impartially evaluate the model, we should split the training dataset into a training and a validation set.

6. Create the model using the normalized dataset and the assigned `diagnosis` labels.

7. Compute the accuracy of the model against the validation set.

    The output will be similar to the following:

    ```
    0.9824561403508771
    ```

    > **NOTE**
    >
    > The solution to this activity can be found on page 482.

If we compare this validation set accuracy result with the result(s) from *Activity 5.02: KNN Multiclass Classifier*, we find artificial neural networks to be performing better than the logistic regression model on the exact same dataset. This is also expected, as the former is a more complex and powerful type of machine learning model than the latter.

SUMMARY

We covered a number of powerful and extremely useful classification models in this chapter, starting with the use of OLS as a classifier, and then we observed a significant increase in performance through the use of the logistic regression classifier. We then moved on to memorizing models, such as KNN, which, while simple to fit, was able to form complex non-linear boundaries in the classification process, even with images as input information into the model. Thereafter, we discussed decision trees and the ID3 algorithm. We saw how decision trees, like KNN models, memorize the training data using rules to make predictions with quite a high degree of accuracy. Finally, we concluded our introduction to classification problems with one of the most powerful classification models – artificial neural networks. We briefly covered the basics of a feedforward neural network and also showed through an exercise how it outperformed the logistic regression model on a classification task.

In the next chapter, we will be extending what we have learned in this chapter. It will cover ensemble techniques, including boosting, and the very effective random forest model.

6

ENSEMBLE MODELING

OVERVIEW

This chapter examines different ways of performing ensemble modeling, along with its benefits and limitations. By the end of the chapter, you will be able to recognize the underfitting and overfitting of data on machine learning models. You will also be able to devise a bagging classifier using decision trees and implement adaptive boosting and gradient boosting models. Finally, you will be able to build a stacked ensemble using a number of classifiers.

INTRODUCTION

In the previous chapters, we discussed the two types of supervised learning problems: regression and classification. We looked at a number of algorithms for each type and delved into how those algorithms worked.

But there are times when these algorithms, no matter how complex they are, just don't seem to perform well on the data that we have. There could be a variety of causes and reasons for this – perhaps the data is not good enough, perhaps there really is no trend where we are trying to find one, or perhaps the model itself is too complex.

Wait. What?! How can a model being too complex be a problem? If a model is too complex and there isn't enough data, the model could fit so well to the data that it learns even the noise and outliers, which is not what we want.

Often, where a single complex algorithm can give us a result that is way off from actual results, aggregating the results from a group of models can give us a result that's closer to the actual truth. This is because there is a high likelihood that the errors from all the individual models would cancel out when we take them all into account when making a prediction.

This approach of grouping multiple algorithms to give an aggregated prediction is what ensemble modeling is based on. The ultimate goal of an ensemble method is to combine several underperforming base estimators (that is, individual algorithms) in such a way that the overall performance of the system improves and the ensemble of algorithms results in a model that is more robust and can generalize well compared to an individual algorithm.

In the first half of this chapter, we will discuss how building an ensemble model can help us build a robust system that makes accurate predictions without increasing variance. We will start by talking about some reasons as to why a model may not perform well, and then move on to discussing the concepts of bias and variance, as well as overfitting and underfitting. We will introduce ensemble modeling as a solution for these performance issues and discuss different ensemble methods that could be used to overcome different types of problems when it comes to underperforming models.

We will discuss three types of ensemble methods; namely, bagging, boosting, and stacking. Each of these will be discussed right from the basic theory to discussions on which use cases each type deals with well and which use cases each type might not be a good fit for. We will also go through a number of exercises to implement the models using the scikit-learn library in Python.

Before diving deep into the topics, we shall first get familiar with a dataset that we will be using to demonstrate and understand the different concepts that are to be covered in this chapter. The next exercise enables us to do that. Before we delve into the exercise, it is necessary to become familiar with the concept of **one-hot encoding**.

ONE-HOT ENCODING

So, what is one-hot encoding? Well, in machine learning, we sometimes have categorical input features such as name, gender, and color. Such features contain label values rather than numeric values, such as John and Tom for name, male and female for gender, and red, blue, and green for color. Here, blue is one such label for the categorical feature – color. All machine learning models can work with numeric data, but many machine learning models cannot work with categorical data because of the way their underlying algorithms are designed. For example, decision trees can work with categorical data, but logistic regression cannot.

In order to still make use of categorical features with models such as logistic regression, we transform such features into a usable numeric format. *Figure 6.1* shows an example of what this transformation looks like:

red	blue	green
1	0	0
0	1	0
0	0	1

Figure 6.1: One-hot encoding

Figure 6.2 shows how one-hot encoding changes the dataset, once applied:

color
red
green
red
blue
green

color_red	color_blue	color_green
1	0	0
0	0	1
1	0	0
0	1	0
0	0	1

Figure 6.2: One-hot encoding applied

Basically, in this example, there are 3 categories of colors – red, blue, and green, and therefore 3 binary variables are needed – **color_red, color_blue**, and **color_green**. A **1** value is used to represent the binary variable for the color and **0** values for the other colors. These binary variables – **color_red, color_blue**, and **color_green** – are also known as **dummy** variables. Armed with this information, we can proceed to our exercise.

EXERCISE 6.01: IMPORTING MODULES AND PREPARING THE DATASET

In this exercise, we will import all the modules we will need for this chapter and get our dataset in shape for the exercises to come:

1. Import all the modules required to manipulate the data and evaluate the model:

```
import pandas as pd
import numpy as np
%matplotlib inline
import matplotlib.pyplot as plt

from sklearn.model_selection import train_test_split
from sklearn.metrics import accuracy_score
from sklearn.model_selection import KFold
```

The dataset that we will use in this exercise is the Titanic dataset, which was introduced in the previous chapters.

2. Read the dataset and print the first five rows:

```
data = pd.read_csv('titanic.csv')
data.head()
```

> **NOTE**
>
> The code snippet presented above assumes that the dataset is stored in the same folder as that of the Jupyter Notebook for this exercise. However, if this dataset is saved in the **Datasets** folder, you then need to use the following code: **data = pd.read_csv('../Datasets/titanic. csv')**

The output is as follows:

	PassengerId	Survived	Pclass	Name	Gender	Age	SibSp	Parch	Ticket	Fare	Cabin	Embarked
0	1	0	3	Braund, Mr. Owen Harris	male	22.0	1	0	A/5 21171	7.2500	NaN	S
1	2	1	1	Cumings, Mrs. John Bradley (Florence Briggs Th...	female	38.0	1	0	PC 17599	71.2833	C85	C
2	3	1	3	Heikkinen, Miss. Laina	female	26.0	0	0	STON/O2. 3101282	7.9250	NaN	S
3	4	1	1	Futrelle, Mrs. Jacques Heath (Lily May Peel)	female	35.0	1	0	113803	53.1000	C123	S
4	5	0	3	Allen, Mr. William Henry	male	35.0	0	0	373450	8.0500	NaN	S

Figure 6.3: The first five rows

3. In order to make the dataset ready for use, we will add a **preprocess** function, which will preprocess the dataset to get it into a format that is ingestible by the scikit-learn library.

    First, we create a **fix_age** function to preprocess the **age** column and get an integer value. If the age is **null**, the function returns a value of **-1** to differentiate it from the available values, otherwise it returns the value. We then apply this function to the **age** column.

    Then, we convert the **Gender** column into a binary variable with **1** for female and **0** for male values, and subsequently create dummy binary columns for the **Embarked** column using pandas' **get_dummies** function. Following this, we combine the DataFrame containing the dummy columns with the remaining numerical columns to create the final DataFrame, which is returned by the function:

```
def preprocess(data):
    def fix_age(age):
        if np.isnan(age):
            return -1
        else:
            return age
    data.loc[:, 'Age'] = data.Age.apply(fix_age)
    data.loc[:, 'Gender'] = data.Gender.apply(lambda s: \
                            int(s == 'female'))
    embarked = pd.get_dummies(data.Embarked, \
                      prefix='Emb')[['Emb_C',\
                              'Emb_Q','Emb_S']]
    cols = ['Pclass','Gender','Age','SibSp','Parch','Fare']
    return pd.concat([data[cols], embarked], axis=1).values
```

4. Split the dataset into training and validation sets.

    We split the dataset into two parts – one on which we will train the models during the exercises (**train**), and another on which we will make predictions to evaluate the performance of each of those models (**val**). We will use the function we wrote in the previous step to preprocess the training and validation datasets separately.

    Here, the **Survived** binary variable is the target variable that determines whether or not the individual in each row survived the sinking of the Titanic, so we create **y_train** and **y_val** as the dependent variable columns from both the splits:

    ```
    train, val = train_test_split(data, test_size=0.2, random_state=11)


    x_train = preprocess(train)
    y_train = train['Survived'].values


    x_val = preprocess(val)
    y_val = val['Survived'].values


    print(x_train.shape)
    print(y_train.shape)
    print(x_val.shape)
    print(y_val.shape)
    ```

    You should get the following output:

    ```
    (712, 9)
    (712,)
    (179, 9)
    (179,)
    ```

As we can see, the dataset is now split into 2 subsets, with the training set having **712** data points and the validation set having **179** data points.

> **NOTE**
>
> To access the source code for this specific section, please refer to https://packt.live/2Nm6KHM.
>
> You can also run this example online at https://packt.live/2YWh9zg. You must execute the entire Notebook in order to get the desired result.

In this exercise, we began by loading the data and importing the necessary Python modules. We then preprocessed different columns of our dataset to make it usable for training machine learning models. Finally, we split the dataset into two subsets. And now, before doing anything further with the dataset, we will try to understand two important concepts of machine learning – overfitting and underfitting.

OVERFITTING AND UNDERFITTING

Let's say we fit a supervised learning algorithm to our data and subsequently use the model to perform a prediction on a hold-out validation set. The performance of this model will be considered to be good based on how well it generalizes, that is, how well it makes predictions for data points in an independent validation dataset.

Sometimes, we find that the model is not able to make accurate predictions and gives poor performance on the validation data. This poor performance can be the result of a model that is too simple to model the data appropriately, or a model that is too complex to generalize to the validation dataset. In the former case, the model has a *high bias* and results in *underfitting*, while, in the latter case, the model has a *high variance* and results in *overfitting*.

Bias

The bias in the prediction of a machine learning model represents the difference between the predicted target value and the true target value of a data point. A model is said to have a high bias if the average predicted values are far off from the true values and is conversely said to have a low bias if the average predicted values are close to the true values.

A high bias indicates that the model cannot capture the complexity in the data and is unable to identify the relevant relationships between the inputs and outputs.

Variance

The variance in prediction of a machine learning model represents how scattered the predicted values are compared to the true values. A model is said to have high variance if the predictions are scattered and unstable and is conversely said to have low variance if the predictions are consistent and not very scattered.

A high variance indicates the model's inability to generalize and make accurate predictions on data points previously unseen by the model. As you can see in the following figure, the center of these circles represents the true target value of the data points. And the dots represent the predicted target value of the data points:

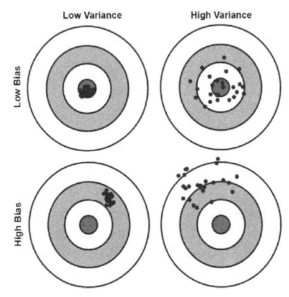

Figure 6.4: Visual representation of data points having high and low bias and variance

UNDERFITTING

Let's say that we fit a simple model on the training dataset, one with low model complexity, such as a simple linear model. We have fit a function that's able to represent the relationship between the **X** (input data) and **Y** (target output) data points in the training data to some extent, but we see that the training error is still high:

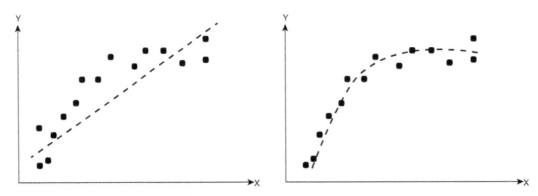

Figure 6.5: Underfitting versus an ideal fit in regression

For example, look at the two regression plots shown in *Figure 6.5*. While the first plot shows a model that fits a straight line to the data, the second plot shows a model that attempts to fit a relatively more complex polynomial to the data, one that seems to represent the mapping between **X** and **Y** quite well.

If we look closely at the first model (on the left in the figure), the straight line is usually far away from the individual data points, as opposed to the second model where the data points are quite close to the curve. According to the definition of bias that we made in the previous section, we can say that the first model has a high bias. And, if we refer to the definition of the variance of a model, the first model is quite consistent in its predictions in that it predicts a fixed straight line-based output for a given input. Hence, the first model has a low variance and we can say that the first model demonstrates underfitting, since it shows the characteristics of a high bias and low variance; that is, while it is unable to capture the complexity in the mapping between the inputs and outputs, it is consistent in its predictions. This model will have a high prediction error on both the training data and validation data.

OVERFITTING

Let's say that we trained a highly complex model that is able to make predictions on the training dataset almost perfectly. We have managed to fit a function to represent the relationship between the **X** and **Y** data points in the training data such that the predicted error on the training data is extremely low:

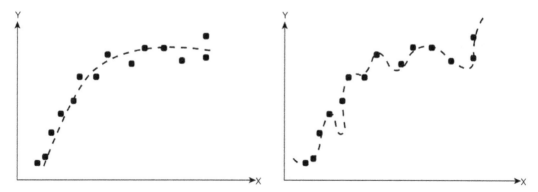

Figure 6.6: An ideal fit versus overfitting in regression

Looking at the two plots in *Figure 6.6*, we can see that the second plot shows a model that attempts to fit a highly complex function to the data points, compared to the plot on the left, which represents the ideal fit for the given data.

It is evident that, when we try to use the second-plot model to predict the **Y** values for **X** data points that did not appear in the training set, we will see that the predictions are way off from the corresponding true values. This is a case of overfitting, the phenomenon where the model fits the data too well so that it is unable to generalize to new data points, since the model learns even the random noise and outliers in the training data. This model shows the characteristics of high variance and low bias: while the average predicted values would be close to the true values, they would be quite scattered compared to the true values.

Another way in which overfitting can happen is when the number of data points is less than or equal to the degree of the polynomial that we are trying to fit to the model. We should, therefore, avoid a model where:

degree of polynomial > number of data points

With an extremely small dataset, trying to fit even a simple model can therefore also lead to overfitting.

OVERCOMING THE PROBLEM OF UNDERFITTING AND OVERFITTING

From the previous sections, we can see that, as we move from an overly simplistic to an overly complex model, we go from having an underfitting model with a high bias and low variance to an overfitting model with a low bias and high variance. The purpose of a supervised machine learning algorithm is to achieve a low bias with low variance and arrive at a place between underfitting and overfitting. This will also help the algorithm generalize well from the training data to validation data points, resulting in good prediction performance on data the model has never seen.

The best way to improve performance when the model underfits the data is to increase the model complexity so as to identify the relevant relationships in the data. This can be done by adding new features, or by creating an ensemble of high-bias models. However, in this case, adding more data to train on would not help, as the constraining factor is model complexity and more data will not help to reduce the model's bias.

Overfitting is, however, more difficult to tackle. Here are some common techniques used to overcome the problem posed by overfitting:

- **Getting more data**: A highly complex model can easily overfit to a small dataset, but will not be able to as easily on a larger dataset.

- **Dimensionality reduction**: Reducing the number of features can help make the model less complex.

- **Regularization**: A new term is added to the cost function to adjust the coefficients (especially the high-degree coefficients in linear regression) toward a low value.

- **Ensemble modeling**: Aggregating the predictions of several overfitting models can effectively eliminate high variance in prediction and perform better than individual models that overfit to the training data.

We will talk in more detail about ensemble modeling techniques in the following sections of this chapter. Some of the common types of ensembles are:

- **Bagging**: A shorter term for **Bootstrap Aggregation**, this technique is also used to decrease the model's variance and avoid overfitting. It involves taking a subset of features and data points at a time, training a model on each subset, and subsequently aggregating the results from all the models into a final prediction.

- **Boosting**: This technique is used to reduce bias rather than to reduce variance and involves incrementally training new models that focus on the misclassified data points in the previous model.

- **Stacking**: The aim of this technique is to increase the predictive power of the classifier, as it involves training multiple models and then using a combiner algorithm to make the final prediction by using the predictions from all these models' additional inputs.

Let's start with bagging, and then move on to boosting and stacking.

BAGGING

The term *bagging* is derived from a technique called bootstrap aggregation. In order to implement a successful predictive model, it's important to know in what situation we could benefit from using bootstrapping methods to build ensemble models. Such models are used extensively both in industry as well as academia.

One such application would be that these models can be used for the quality assessment of Wikipedia articles. Features such as `article_length`, `number_of_references`, `number_of_headings`, and `number_of_images` are used to build a classifier that classifies Wikipedia articles into low- or high-quality articles. Out of the several models that were tried for this task, the random forest model – a well-known bagging-based ensemble classifier that we will discuss in our next section – outperforms all other models such as SVM, logistic regression, and even neural networks, with the best precision and recall scores of **87.3%** and **87.2%**, respectively. This demonstrates the power of such models as well as their potential to be used in real-life applications.

In this section, we'll talk about a way to use bootstrap methods to create an ensemble model that minimizes variance and look at how we can build an ensemble of decision trees, that is, the random forest algorithm. But what is bootstrapping and how does it help us build robust ensemble models?

BOOTSTRAPPING

The bootstrap method essentially refers to drawing multiple samples (each known as a resample) from the dataset consisting of randomly chosen data points, where there can be an overlap in the data points contained in each resample and each data point has an equal probability of being selected from the overall dataset:

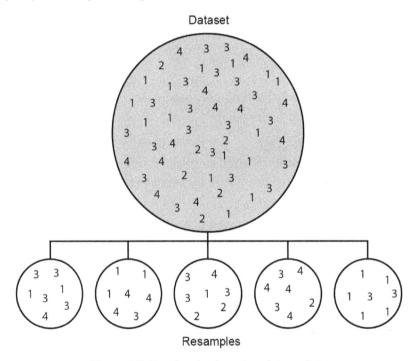

Figure 6.7: Randomly choosing data points

From the previous diagram, we can see that each of the five bootstrapped samples taken from the primary dataset is different and has different characteristics. As such, training models on each of these resamples would result in different predictions.

The following are the advantages of bootstrapping:

- Each resample can contain different characteristics from that of the entire dataset, allowing us a different perspective of how the data behaves.

- Algorithms that make use of bootstrapping are powerfully built and handle unseen data better, especially on smaller datasets that have a tendency to cause overfitting.

- The bootstrap method can test the stability of a prediction by testing models using datasets with different variations and characteristics, resulting in a model that is more robust.

Now that we are aware of what bootstrapping is, what exactly does a bagging ensemble do? In simple words, bagging means aggregating the outputs of parallel models, each of which is built by bootstrapping data. It is essentially an ensemble model that generates multiple versions of a predictor on each resample and uses these to get an aggregated predictor. The aggregation step gives us a *meta prediction*, which involves taking an average over the models when predicting a continuous numerical value for regression problems, while taking a *vote* when predicting a class for classification problems. Voting can be of two types:

- Hard voting (class-based)

- Soft voting (probabilistic)

In hard voting, we consider the majority among the classes predicted by the base estimators, whereas in soft voting, we average the probabilities of belonging to a class and then predict the class.

The following diagram gives us a visual representation of how a bagging estimator is built from the bootstrap sampling shown in *Figure 6.7*:

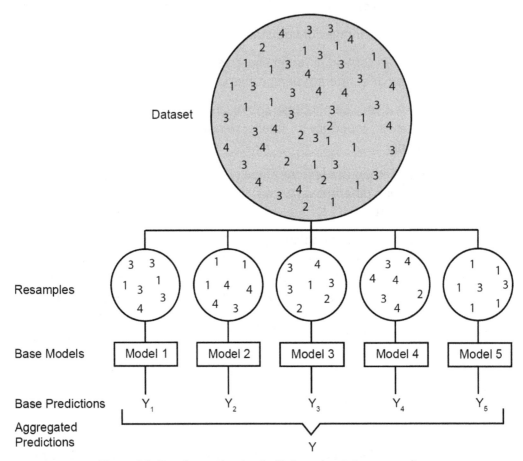

Figure 6.8: Bagging estimator built from bootstrap sampling

Since each model is essentially independent of the others, all the base models can be trained in parallel, considerably speeding up the training process as a resampled dataset is smaller in size than the original dataset, and therefore allowing us to take advantage of the computational power we have on our hands today.

Bagging essentially helps to reduce the variance of the entire ensemble. It does so by introducing randomization into its formulation procedure and is usually used with a base predictor that has a tendency to overfit the training data. The primary point of consideration here would be the stability (or lack thereof) of the training dataset: bagging proves effective in cases where a slight perturbation in data leads to a significant change in model results, that is, the model with high variance. This is how bagging helps in countering variance.

scikit-learn uses **BaggingClassifier** and **BaggingRegressor** to implement generic bagging ensembles for classification and regression tasks, respectively. The primary inputs to these are the base estimators to use on each resample, along with the number of estimators to use (that is, the number of resamples).

EXERCISE 6.02: USING THE BAGGING CLASSIFIER

In this exercise, we will use scikit-learn's bagging classifier as our ensemble, with **DecisionTreeClassifier** as the base estimator. We know that decision trees are prone to overfitting, and so will have a high variance and low bias, both being important characteristics for the base estimators to be used in bagging ensembles.

The dataset that we will use in this exercise is the Titanic dataset. Please complete *Exercise 6.01, Importing Modules and Preparing the Dataset,* before you embark on this exercise:

1. Import the base and ensemble classifiers:

```
from sklearn.tree import DecisionTreeClassifier
from sklearn.ensemble import BaggingClassifier
```

2. Specify the hyperparameters and initialize the model.

    Here, we will first specify the hyperparameters of the base estimator, for which we are using the decision tree classifier with the entropy or information gain as the splitting criterion. We will not specify any limits on the depth of the tree or size/number of leaves on each tree to grow fully. Following this, we will define the hyperparameters for the bagging classifier and pass the base estimator object to the classifier as a hyperparameter.

    We will take 50 base estimators for our example, which will run in parallel and utilize all the processes available in the machine (which is done by specifying **n_jobs=-1**). Additionally, we will specify **max_samples** as 0.5, indicating that the number of data points in the bootstrap should be half that in the total dataset. We will also set a random state (to any arbitrary value, which will stay constant throughout) to maintain the reproducibility of the results:

```
dt_params = {'criterion': 'entropy', 'random_state': 11}
dt = DecisionTreeClassifier(**dt_params)

bc_params = {'base_estimator': dt, 'n_estimators': 50, \
             'max_samples': 0.5, 'random_state': 11, 'n_jobs': -1}
bc = BaggingClassifier(**bc_params)
```

3. Fit the bagging classifier model to the training data and calculate the prediction accuracy.

Let's now fit the bagging classifier and find the meta predictions for both the training and validation sets. Following this, let's find the prediction accuracy on the training and validation datasets:

```
bc.fit(x_train, y_train)
bc_preds_train = bc.predict(x_train)
bc_preds_val = bc.predict(x_val)


print('Bagging Classifier:\n> Accuracy on training data = {:.4f}'\
        '\n> Accuracy on validation data = {:.4f}'\
        .format(accuracy_score(y_true=y_train, \
                                y_pred=bc_preds_train), \
                    accuracy_score(y_true=y_val, y_pred=bc_preds_val)))
```

The output is as follows:

```
Bagging Classifier:
> Accuracy on training data = 0.9270
> Accuracy on validation data = 0.8659
```

4. Fit the decision tree model to the training data to compare prediction accuracy.

Let's also fit the decision tree (from the object we initialized in *Step 2*) so that we will be able to compare the prediction accuracies of the ensemble with that of the base predictor:

```
dt.fit(x_train, y_train)
dt_preds_train = dt.predict(x_train)
dt_preds_val = dt.predict(x_val)


print('Decision Tree:\n> Accuracy on training data = {:.4f}'\
        '\n> Accuracy on validation data = {:.4f}'\
        .format(accuracy_score(y_true=y_train, \
                                y_pred=dt_preds_train), \
                    accuracy_score(y_true=y_val, y_pred=dt_preds_val)))
```

The output is as follows:

```
Decision Tree:
> Accuracy on training data = 0.9831
> Accuracy on validation data = 0.7709
```

Here, we can see that, although the decision tree has a much higher training accuracy than the bagging classifier, its accuracy on the validation dataset is lower, a clear signal that the decision tree is overfitting to the training data. The bagging ensemble, on the other hand, reduces the overall variance and results in a much more accurate prediction.

> **NOTE**
>
> To access the source code for this specific section, please refer to https://packt.live/37O6735.
>
> You can also run this example online at https://packt.live/2Nh3ayB. You must execute the entire Notebook in order to get the desired result.

Next, we will look at perhaps the most widely known bagging-based machine learning model there is, the random forest model. Random forest is a bagging ensemble model that uses a decision tree as the base estimator.

RANDOM FOREST

An issue that is commonly faced with decision trees is that the split on each node is performed using a **greedy** algorithm that minimizes the entropy of the leaf nodes. Keeping this in mind, the base estimator decision trees in a bagging classifier can still be similar in terms of the features they split on, and so can have predictions that are quite similar. However, bagging is only useful in reducing the variance in predictions if the predictions from the base models are not correlated.

The random forest algorithm attempts to overcome this problem by not only bootstrapping the data points in the overall training dataset, but also bootstrapping the features available for each tree to split on. This ensures that when the greedy algorithm is searching for the *best* feature to split on, the overall *best* feature may not always be available in the bootstrapped features for the base estimator, and so would not be chosen – resulting in base trees that have different structures. This simple tweak lets the best estimators be trained in such a way that the predictions from each tree in the forest have a lower probability of being correlated to the predictions from other trees.

Each base estimator in the random forest has a random sample of data points as well as a random sample of features. And since the ensemble is made up of decision trees, the algorithm is called a random forest.

EXERCISE 6.03: BUILDING THE ENSEMBLE MODEL USING RANDOM FOREST

The two primary parameters that random forest takes are the fraction of features and the fraction of data points to bootstrap on, to train each base decision tree.

In this exercise, we will use scikit-learn's random forest classifier to build the ensemble model.

The dataset that we will use in this exercise is the Titanic dataset. This exercise is a continuation of *Exercise 6.02, Using a Bagging Classifier*:

1. Import the ensemble classifier:

```
from sklearn.ensemble import RandomForestClassifier
```

2. Specify the hyperparameters and initialize the model.

   Here, we will use entropy as the splitting criterion for the decision trees in a forest comprising 100 trees. As before, we will not specify any limits regarding the depth of the trees or the size/number of leaves. Unlike the bagging classifier, which took **max_samples** as an input during initialization, the random forest algorithm takes in only **max_features**, indicating the number (or fraction) of features in the bootstrap sample. We will specify the value for this as 0.5, so that only three out of six features are considered for each tree:

```
rf_params = {'n_estimators': 100, 'criterion': 'entropy', \
             'max_features': 0.5, 'min_samples_leaf': 10, \
             'random_state': 11, 'n_jobs': -1}
rf = RandomForestClassifier(**rf_params)
```

3. Fit the random forest classifier model to the training data and calculate the prediction accuracy.

   Let's now fit the random forest model and find the meta predictions for both the training and validation sets. Following this, let's find the prediction accuracy on the training and validation datasets:

```
rf.fit(x_train, y_train)
rf_preds_train = rf.predict(x_train)
rf_preds_val = rf.predict(x_val)
print('Random Forest:\n> Accuracy on training data = {:.4f}'\
      '\n> Accuracy on validation data = {:.4f}'\
      .format(accuracy_score(y_true=y_train, \
                             y_pred=rf_preds_train), \
              accuracy_score(y_true=y_val, y_pred=rf_preds_val)))
```

The output is as follows:

```
Random Forest:
> Accuracy on training data = 0.8385
> Accuracy on validation data = 0.8771
```

If we compare the prediction accuracies of random forest on our dataset to that of the bagging classifier, we can see that the accuracy on the validation set is pretty much the same, although the latter has higher accuracy with regard to the training dataset.

> **NOTE**
>
> To access the source code for this specific section, please refer to
> https://packt.live/3dlvGtd.
>
> You can also run this example online at https://packt.live/2NkSPS5.
> You must execute the entire Notebook in order to get the desired result.

BOOSTING

The second ensemble technique we'll be looking at is boosting, which involves incrementally training new models that focus on the misclassified data points in the previous model and utilizes weighted averages to turn weak models (underfitting models having a high bias) into stronger models. Unlike bagging, where each base estimator could be trained independently of the others, the training of each base estimator in a boosted algorithm depends on the previous one.

Although boosting also uses the concept of bootstrapping, it's done differently from bagging, since each sample of data is weighted, implying that some bootstrapped samples can be used for training more often than other samples. When training each model, the algorithm keeps track of which features are most useful and which data samples have the most prediction error; these are given higher weightage and are considered to require more iterations to properly train the model.

When predicting the output, the boosting ensemble takes a weighted average of the predictions from each base estimator, giving a higher weight to the ones that had lower errors during the training stage. This means that, for the data points that are misclassified by the model in an iteration, the weights for those data points are increased so that the next model is more likely to classify it correctly.

As was the case with bagging, the results from all the boosting base estimators are aggregated to produce a meta prediction. However, unlike bagging, the accuracy of a boosted ensemble increases significantly with the number of base estimators in the boosted ensemble:

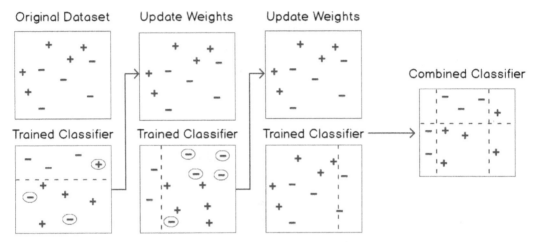

Figure 6.9: A boosted ensemble

In the diagram, we can see that, after each iteration, the misclassified points have increased weights (represented by larger icons) so that the next base estimator that is trained is able to focus on those points. The final predictor has aggregated the decision boundaries from each of its base estimators.

Boosting is used extensively in real-world applications. For example, the commercial web search engines Yahoo and Yandex use variants of boosting in their machine-learned ranking engines. Ranking is the task of finding the most relevant documents given a search query. Particularly, in the case of Yandex, they use a gradient boosting-based approach to build an ensemble tree model that outperforms other models, including Yandex's previously used models, by achieving the lowest discounted cumulative gain of **4.14123**. This shows how useful boosting-based modeling can prove in real-life scenarios.

> **NOTE**
>
> Read more on Yandex at the following link:
> http://webmaster.ya.ru/replies.xml?item_no=5707&ncrnd=5118.

ADAPTIVE BOOSTING

Let's now talk about a boosting technique called **adaptive boosting**, which is best used to boost the performance of decision stumps for binary classification problems. Decision stumps are essentially decision trees with a maximum depth of one (only one split is made on a single feature), and, as such, are weak learners. The primary principle that adaptive boosting works on is the same: to improve the areas where the base estimator fails to turn an ensemble of weak learners into a strong learner.

To start with, the first base estimator takes a bootstrap of data points from the main training set and fits a decision stump to classify the sampled points, after which the trained decision tree stump is fit to the complete training data. For the samples that are misclassified, the weights are increased so that there is a higher probability of these data points being selected in the bootstrap for the next base estimator. A decision stump is again trained on the new bootstrap to classify the data points in the sample. Subsequently, the mini ensemble comprising the two base estimators is used to classify the data points in the entire training set. The misclassified data points from the second round are given a higher weight to improve their probability of selection and so on until the ensemble reaches the limit regarding the number of base estimators it should contain.

One drawback of adaptive boosting is that the algorithm is easily influenced by noisy data points and outliers since it tries to fit every point perfectly. As such, it is prone to overfitting if the number of estimators is very high.

EXERCISE 6.04: IMPLEMENTING ADAPTIVE BOOSTING

In this exercise, we'll use scikit-learn's implementation of adaptive boosting for classification, **AdaBoostClassifier**:

We will again be using the Titanic dataset. This exercise is a continuation of *Exercise 6.03, Building the Ensemble Model Using Random Forest*:

1. Import the classifier:

    ```
    from sklearn.ensemble import AdaBoostClassifier
    ```

2. Specify the hyperparameters and initialize the model.

Here, we will first specify the hyperparameters of the base estimator, for which we are using the decision tree classifier with a maximum depth of one, that is, a decision stump. Following this, we will define the hyperparameters for the AdaBoost classifier and pass the base estimator object to the classifier as a hyperparameter:

```
dt_params = {'max_depth': 1, 'random_state': 11}
dt = DecisionTreeClassifier(**dt_params)

ab_params = {'n_estimators': 100, 'base_estimator': dt, \
             'random_state': 11}
ab = AdaBoostClassifier(**ab_params)
```

3. Fit the model to the training data.

Let's now fit the **AdaBoost** model and find the meta predictions for both the training and validation sets. Following this, let's find the prediction accuracy on the training and validation datasets:

```
ab.fit(x_train, y_train)
ab_preds_train = ab.predict(x_train)
ab_preds_val = ab.predict(x_val)

print('Adaptive Boosting:\n> Accuracy on training data = {:.4f}'\
      '\n> Accuracy on validation data = {:.4f}'\
      .format(accuracy_score(y_true=y_train, \
                             y_pred=ab_preds_train), \
              accuracy_score(y_true=y_val, y_pred=ab_preds_val)
))
```

The output is as follows:

```
Adaptive Boosting:
> Accuracy on training data = 0.8272
> Accuracy on validation data = 0.8547
```

4. Calculate the prediction accuracy of the model on the training and validation data for a varying number of base estimators.

    Earlier, we claimed that the accuracy tends to increase with an increasing number of base estimators, but also that the model has a tendency to overfit if too many base estimators are used. Let's calculate the prediction accuracies so that we can find the point where the model begins to overfit the training data:

```
ab_params = {'base_estimator': dt, 'random_state': 11}


n_estimator_values = list(range(10, 210, 10))
train_accuracies, val_accuracies = [], []


for n_estimators in n_estimator_values:
    ab = AdaBoostClassifier(n_estimators=n_estimators, **ab_params)
    ab.fit(x_train, y_train)
    ab_preds_train = ab.predict(x_train)
    ab_preds_val = ab.predict(x_val)
    train_accuracies.append(accuracy_score(y_true=y_train, \
                            y_pred=ab_preds_train))
    val_accuracies.append(accuracy_score(y_true=y_val, \
                          y_pred=ab_preds_val))
```

5. Plot a line graph to visualize the trend of the prediction accuracies on both the training and validation datasets:

```
plt.figure(figsize=(10,7))
plt.plot(n_estimator_values, train_accuracies, label='Train')
plt.plot(n_estimator_values, val_accuracies, label='Validation')


plt.ylabel('Accuracy score')
plt.xlabel('n_estimators')


plt.legend()
plt.show()
```

The output is as follows:

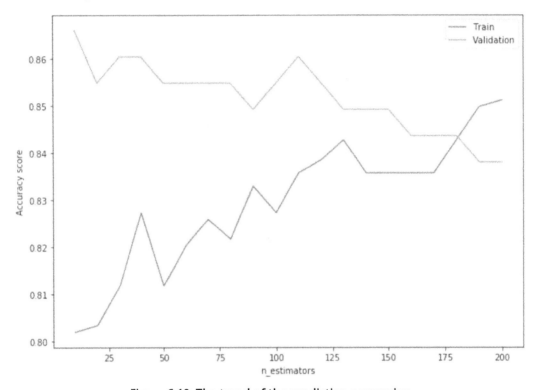

Figure 6.10: The trend of the prediction accuracies

As was mentioned earlier, we can see that the training accuracy almost consistently increases as the number of decision tree stumps increases from 10 to 200. However, the validation accuracy fluctuates between 0.84 and 0.86 and begins to drop as the number of decision stumps goes higher. This happens because the AdaBoost algorithm is trying to fit the noisy data points and outliers as well.

> **NOTE**
>
> To access the source code for this specific section, please refer to https://packt.live/2V4zB7K.
>
> You can also run this example online at https://packt.live/3dhSBpu.
> You must execute the entire Notebook in order to get the desired result.

GRADIENT BOOSTING

Gradient boosting is an extension of the boosting method that visualizes boosting as an optimization problem. A loss function is defined that is representative of the error residuals (the difference between the predicted and true values), and the gradient descent algorithm is used to optimize the loss function.

In the first step, a base estimator (which would be a weak learner) is added and trained on the entire training dataset. The loss associated with the prediction is calculated and, in order to reduce the error residuals, the loss function is updated to add more base estimators for the data points where the existing estimators are performing poorly. Subsequently, the algorithm iteratively adds new base estimators and computes the loss to allow the optimization algorithm to update the model and minimize the residuals themselves.

In the case of adaptive boosting, decision stumps were used as the weak learners for the base estimators. However, for gradient boosting methods, larger trees can be used, but the weak learners should still be constrained by providing a limit to the maximum number of layers, nodes, splits, or leaf nodes. This ensures that the base estimators are still weak learners, but they can be constructed in a greedy manner.

From the previous chapters, we know that the gradient descent algorithm can be used to minimize a set of parameters, such as the coefficients in a regression equation. When building an ensemble, however, we have decision trees instead of parameters that need to be optimized. After calculating the loss at each step, the gradient descent algorithm then has to modify the parameters of the new tree that's to be added to the ensemble in such a way that reduces the loss. This approach is more commonly known as **functional gradient descent**.

EXERCISE 6.05: IMPLEMENTING GRADIENTBOOSTINGCLASSIFIER TO BUILD AN ENSEMBLE MODEL

The two primary parameters that the gradient boosting classifier takes are the fraction of features and the fraction of data points to bootstrap on, to train each base decision tree.

In this exercise, we will use scikit-learn's gradient boosting classifier to build the boosting ensemble model.

This exercise is a continuation of *Exercise 6.04, Implementing Adaptive Boosting*:

1. Import the ensemble classifier:

```
from sklearn.ensemble import GradientBoostingClassifier
```

2. Specify the hyperparameters and initialize the model.

    Here, we will use 100 decision trees as the base estimator, with each tree having a maximum depth of three and a minimum of five samples in each of its leaves. Although we are not using decision stumps, as in the previous example, the tree is still small and would be considered a weak learner:

```
gbc_params = {'n_estimators': 100, 'max_depth': 3, \
              'min_samples_leaf': 5, 'random_state': 11}
gbc = GradientBoostingClassifier(**gbc_params)
```

3. Fit the gradient boosting model to the training data and calculate the prediction accuracy.

    Let's now fit the ensemble model and find the meta predictions for both the training and validation set. Following this, we will find the prediction accuracy on the training and validation datasets:

```
gbc.fit(x_train, y_train)
gbc_preds_train = gbc.predict(x_train)
gbc_preds_val = gbc.predict(x_val)

print('Gradient Boosting Classifier:'\
      '\n> Accuracy on training data = {:.4f}'\
      '\n> Accuracy on validation data = {:.4f}'\
      .format(accuracy_score(y_true=y_train, \
                             y_pred=gbc_preds_train), \
      accuracy_score(y_true=y_val, y_pred=gbc_preds_val)))
```

The output is as follows:

```
Gradient Boosting Classifier:
> Accuracy on training data = 0.8961
> Accuracy on validation data = 0.8771
```

> **NOTE**
>
> To access the source code for this specific section, please refer to
> https://packt.live/37QANjZ.
>
> You can also run this example online at https://packt.live/2YljJ2D.
> You must execute the entire Notebook in order to get the desired result.

We can see that the gradient boosting ensemble has greater accuracy on both the training and validation datasets compared to those for the adaptive boosting ensemble.

STACKING

Stacking, or stacked generalization, is also called **meta ensembling**. It is a model ensembling technique that consists of combining data from multiple models' predictions and using them as features to generate a new model. The stacked model will most likely outperform each of the individual models due to the smoothing effect it adds, as well as due to its ability to "choose" the base model that performs best in certain scenarios. Keeping this in mind, stacking is usually most effective when each of the base models is significantly different from each other.

Stacking is widely used in real-world applications. One popular example comes from the well-known Netflix competition whose two top performers built solutions that were based on stacking models. Netflix is a well-known streaming platform and the competition was about building the best recommendation engine. The winning algorithm was based on feature-weighted-linear-stacking, which basically had meta features derived from individual models/algorithms such as **Singular Value Decomposition (SVD)**, **Restricted Boltzmann Machines (RBMs)**, and **K-Nearest Neighbors (KNN)**. One such meta feature was the standard deviation of the prediction of a 60-factor ordinal SVD. These meta features were found necessary to be able to achieve the winning model, which proves the power of stacking in real-world applications.

Stacking uses the predictions of the base models as additional features when training the final model – these are known as **meta features**. The stacked model essentially acts as a classifier that determines where each model is performing well and where it is performing poorly.

However, you cannot simply train the base models on the full training data, generate predictions on the full validation dataset, and then output these for second-level training. This runs the risk of your base model predictions already having "seen" the test set and therefore overfitting when feeding these predictions.

It is important to note that the value of the meta features for each row cannot be predicted using a model that contained that row in the training data, as we then run the risk of overfitting since the base predictions would have already "seen" the target variable for that row. The common practice is to divide the training data into **k** subsets so that, when finding the meta features for each of those subsets, we only train the model on the remaining data. Doing this also avoids the problem of overfitting the data the model has already "seen":

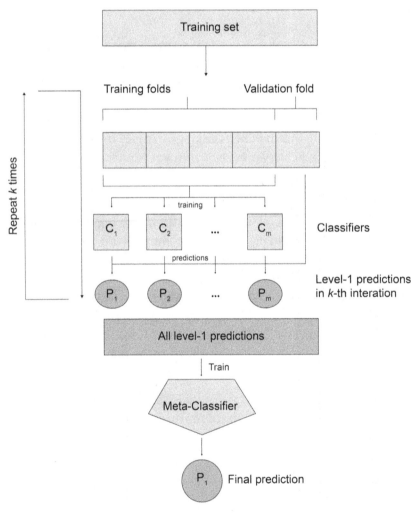

Figure 6.11: A stacking ensemble

The preceding diagram shows how this is done: we divide the training data into **k** folds and find the predictions from the base models on each fold by training the model on the remaining **k−1** folds. So, once we have the meta predictions for each of the folds, we can use those meta predictions along with the original features to train the stacked model.

EXERCISE 6.06: BUILDING A STACKED MODEL

In this exercise, we will use a support vector machine (scikit-learn's **LinearSVC**) and k-nearest neighbors (scikit-learn's **KNeighborsClassifier**) as the base predictors, and the stacked model will be a logistic regression classifier.

This exercise is a continuation of *Exercise 6.05, Implementing GradientBoostingClassifier to Build an Ensemble Model*:

1. Import the base models and the model used for stacking:

```
# Base models
from sklearn.neighbors import KNeighborsClassifier
from sklearn.svm import LinearSVC
# Stacking model
from sklearn.linear_model import LogisticRegression
```

2. Create a new training set with additional columns for predictions from base predictors.

    We need to create two new columns for predicted values from each model to be used as features for the ensemble model in both the test and training set. Since NumPy arrays are immutable, we will create a new array that will have the same number of rows as the training dataset, and two columns more than those in the training dataset. Once the dataset is created, let's print it to see what it looks like:

```
x_train_with_metapreds = np.zeros((x_train.shape[0], \
                                    x_train.shape[1]+2))
x_train_with_metapreds[:, :-2] = x_train
x_train_with_metapreds[:, -2:] = -1
print(x_train_with_metapreds)
```

The output is as follows:

```
[[ 3.   0.  16.  ...   1. -1. -1.]
 [ 1.   0.  47.  ...   1. -1. -1.]
 [ 3.   0.  32.  ...   1. -1. -1.]
 ...
 [ 3.   0.  20.  ...   1. -1. -1.]
 [ 3.   0.  22.  ...   1. -1. -1.]
 [ 3.   0.  25.  ...   0. -1. -1.]]
```

Figure 6.12: The new columns for the predicted values

As we can see, there are two extra columns filled with -1 values at the end of each row.

3. Train base models using the **k-fold** strategy.

    Let's take *k=5*. For each of the five folds, train on the other four folds and predict on the fifth fold. These predictions should then be added to the placeholder columns for base predictions in the new NumPy array.

    First, we initialize the **KFold** object with the value of **k** and a random state to maintain reproducibility. The **kf.split()** function takes the dataset to split as an input and returns an iterator, with each element in the iterator corresponding to the list of indices in the training and validation folds respectively. These index values in each loop over the iterator can be used to subdivide the training data for training and prediction for each row.

    Once the data is adequately divided, we train the two base predictors on four-fifths of the data and predict the values on the remaining one-fifth of the rows. These predictions are then inserted into the two placeholder columns we initialized with **−1** in *Step 2*:

```
kf = KFold(n_splits=5, random_state=11)


for train_indices, val_indices in kf.split(x_train):
    kfold_x_train, kfold_x_val = x_train[train_indices], \
                                 x_train[val_indices]
    kfold_y_train, kfold_y_val = y_train[train_indices], \
                                 y_train[val_indices]
    svm = LinearSVC(random_state=11, max_iter=1000)
    svm.fit(kfold_x_train, kfold_y_train)
    svm_pred = svm.predict(kfold_x_val)
    knn = KNeighborsClassifier(n_neighbors=4)
```

```
    knn.fit(kfold_x_train, kfold_y_train)
    knn_pred = knn.predict(kfold_x_val)
    x_train_with_metapreds[val_indices, -2] = svm_pred
    x_train_with_metapreds[val_indices, -1] = knn_pred
```

4. Create a new validation set with additional columns for predictions from base predictors.

   As we did in *Step 2*, we will add two placeholder columns for the base model predictions in the validation dataset as well:

```
x_val_with_metapreds = np.zeros((x_val.shape[0], \
                                 x_val.shape[1]+2))
x_val_with_metapreds[:, :-2] = x_val
x_val_with_metapreds[:, -2:] = -1
print(x_val_with_metapreds)
```

   The output is as follows:

```
[[ 3.   1.  -1.  ...   1.  -1.  -1.]
 [ 3.   0.  27.  ...   1.  -1.  -1.]
 [ 3.   0.  -1.  ...   0.  -1.  -1.]
 ...
 [ 3.   0.  22.  ...   1.  -1.  -1.]
 [ 1.   0.  -1.  ...   1.  -1.  -1.]
 [ 1.   0.  25.  ...   0.  -1.  -1.]]
```

   Figure 6.13: Additional columns for predictions from base predictors

5. Fit base models on the complete training set to get meta features for the validation set.

   Next, we will train the two base predictors on the complete training dataset to get the meta prediction values for the validation dataset. This is similar to what we did for each fold in *Step 3*:

```
svm = LinearSVC(random_state=11, max_iter=1000)
svm.fit(x_train, y_train)

knn = KNeighborsClassifier(n_neighbors=4)
knn.fit(x_train, y_train)

svm_pred = svm.predict(x_val)
knn_pred = knn.predict(x_val)
```

```
x_val_with_metapreds[:, -2] = svm_pred
x_val_with_metapreds[:, -1] = knn_pred
```

6. Train the stacked model and use the final predictions to calculate accuracy.

The final step is to train the logistic regression model on all the columns of the training dataset plus the meta predictions from the base estimators. We use the model to find the prediction accuracies for both the training and validation datasets:

```
lr = LogisticRegression(random_state=11)
lr.fit(x_train_with_metapreds, y_train)
lr_preds_train = lr.predict(x_train_with_metapreds)
lr_preds_val = lr.predict(x_val_with_metapreds)
print('Stacked Classifier:\n> Accuracy on training data = {:.4f}'\
      '\n> Accuracy on validation data = {:.4f}'\
      .format(accuracy_score(y_true=y_train, \
                             y_pred=lr_preds_train), \
              accuracy_score(y_true=y_val, y_pred=lr_preds_val)))
```

The output is as follows:

```
Stacked Classifier:
> Accuracy on training data = 0.7837
> Accuracy on validation data = 0.8827
```

> **NOTE**
>
> Owing to randomization, you might get an output that varies slightly in comparison to the output presented in the preceding step.

7. Compare the accuracy with that of base models.

To get a sense of the performance boost from stacking, we calculate the accuracies of the base predictors on the training and validation datasets and compare this with that of the stacked model:

```
print('SVM:\n> Accuracy on training data = {:.4f}'\
      '\n> Accuracy on validation data = {:.4f}'\
```

```
           .format(accuracy_score(y_true=y_train, \
                            y_pred=svm.predict(x_train)), \
               accuracy_score(y_true=y_val, y_pred=svm_pred)))
    print('kNN:\n> Accuracy on training data = {:.4f}'\
          '\n> Accuracy on validation data = {:.4f}'\
           .format(accuracy_score(y_true=y_train, \
                            y_pred=knn.predict(x_train)), \
               accuracy_score(y_true=y_val, y_pred=knn_pred)))
```

The output is as follows:

```
SVM
> Accuracy on training data = 0.7205
> Accuracy on validation data = 0.7430
kNN:
> Accuracy on training data = 0.7921
> Accuracy on validation data = 0.6816
```

> **NOTE**
>
> Owing to randomization, you might get an output that varies slightly in comparison to the output presented in the preceding step.

As we can see, not only does the stacked model give us a validation accuracy that is significantly higher than either of the base predictors, but it also has the highest accuracy, nearly 89%, of all the ensemble models discussed in this chapter.

> **NOTE**
>
> To access the source code for this specific section, please refer to https://packt.live/37QANjZ.
>
> You can also run this example online at https://packt.live/2YljJ2D.
> You must execute the entire Notebook in order to get the desired result.

ACTIVITY 6.01: STACKING WITH STANDALONE AND ENSEMBLE ALGORITHMS

In this activity, we'll use the Boston House Prices: Advanced Regression Techniques Database (available at https://archive.ics.uci.edu/ml/machine-learning-databases/housing/ or on GitHub at https://packt.live/2Vk002e).

This dataset is aimed toward solving a regression problem (that is, the target variable takes on a range of continuous values). In this activity, we will use decision trees, k-nearest neighbors, random forest, and gradient boosting algorithms to train individual regressors on the data. Then, we will build a stacked linear regression model that uses all these algorithms and compare the performance of each. We will use the **mean absolute error** (**MAE**) as the evaluation metric for this activity.

> **NOTE**
>
> The MAE function, **mean_absolute_error()**, can be used in a similar way to the **accuracy_score()** measure used previously.

The steps to be performed are as follows:

1. Import the relevant libraries.

2. Read the data.

3. Preprocess the dataset to remove null values and one-hot encoded categorical variables to prepare the data for modeling.

4. Divide the dataset into train and validation DataFrames.

5. Initialize dictionaries in which to store the train and validation MAE values.

6. Train a **DecisionTreeRegressor** model (**dt**) with the following hyperparameters and save the scores:

```
dt_params = {
    'criterion': 'mae',
    'min_samples_leaf': 15,
    'random_state': 11
}
```

7. Train a **KNeighborsRegressor** model (**knn**) with the following hyperparameters and save the scores:

```
knn_params = {
    'n_neighbors': 5
}
```

8. Train a **RandomForestRegressor** model (**rf**) with the following hyperparameters and save the scores:

```
rf_params = {
    'n_estimators': 20,
    'criterion': 'mae',
    'max_features': 'sqrt',
    'min_samples_leaf': 10,
    'random_state': 11,
    'n_jobs': -1
}
```

9. Train a **GradientBoostingRegressor** model (**gbr**) with the following hyperparameters and save the scores:

```
gbr_params = {
    'n_estimators': 20,
    'criterion': 'mae',
    'max_features': 'sqrt',
    'min_samples_leaf': 10,
    'random_state': 11
}
```

10. Prepare the training and validation datasets, with the four meta estimators having the same hyperparameters that were used in the previous steps.

11. Train a **LinearRegression** model (**lr**) as the stacked model.

12. Visualize the train and validation errors for each individual model and the stacked model.

The output will be as follows:

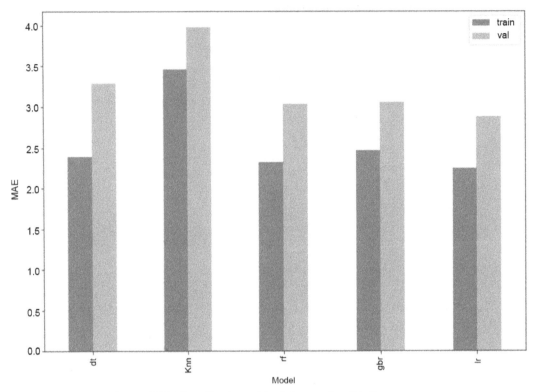

Figure 6.14: Visualization of training and validation errors

> **NOTE**
>
> The solution to this activity can be found on page 486.

Thus, we have successfully demonstrated how stacking as an ensembling technique proves to be superior to any individual machine learning model in terms of the validation set accuracy across different datasets.

SUMMARY

In this chapter, we started off with a discussion on overfitting and underfitting and how they can affect the performance of a model on unseen data. The chapter looked at ensemble modeling as a solution for these models and went on to discuss different ensemble methods that could be used, and how they could decrease the overall bias or variance encountered when making predictions. We first discussed bagging algorithms and introduced the concept of bootstrapping.

Then, we looked at random forest as a classic example of a bagged ensemble and solved exercises that involved building a bagging classifier and random forest classifier on the previously seen Titanic dataset. We then moved on to discussing boosting algorithms, how they successfully reduce bias in the system, and gained an understanding of how to implement adaptive boosting and gradient boosting. The last ensemble method we discussed was stacking, which, as we saw from the exercise, gave us the best accuracy score of all the ensemble methods we implemented. Although building an ensemble model is a great way to decrease bias and variance, and such models generally outperform any single model by itself, they themselves come with their own problems and use cases. While bagging is great when trying to avoid overfitting, boosting can reduce both bias and variance, though it may still have a tendency to overfit. Stacking, on the other hand, is a good choice for when one model performs well on a portion of the data while another model performs better on another portion of the data.

In the next chapter, we will explore more ways to overcome the problems of overfitting and underfitting in detail by looking at validation techniques, that is, ways to judge our model's performance, and how to use different metrics as indicators to build the best possible model for our use case.

7

MODEL EVALUATION

OVERVIEW

This chapter is an introduction to how you can improve a model's performance by using hyperparameters and model evaluation metrics. You will see how to evaluate regression and classification models using a number of metrics and learn how to choose a suitable metric for evaluating and tuning a model.

By the end of this chapter, you will be able to implement various sampling techniques and perform hyperparameter tuning to find the best model. You will also be well equipped to calculate feature importance for model evaluation.

INTRODUCTION

In the previous chapters, we discussed the two types of supervised learning problems, regression and classification, followed by ensemble models, which are built from a combination of base models. We built several models and discussed how and why they work. However, that is not enough to take a model to production. Model development is an iterative process, and the model training step is followed by validation and updating steps, as shown in the following figure:

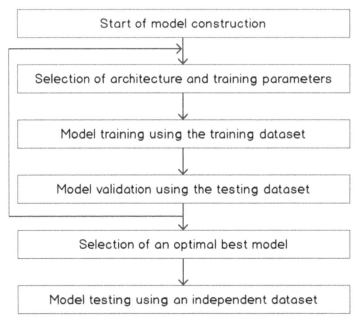

Figure 7.1: Machine learning model development process

This chapter will explain the peripheral steps in the process shown in the preceding flowchart; we will discuss how to select the appropriate hyperparameters and how to perform model validation using the appropriate error metrics. Improving a model's performance happens by iteratively performing these two tasks. But why is it important to evaluate your model? Say you've trained your model and provided some hyperparameters, made predictions, and found its accuracy. That's the gist of it, but how do you make sure that your model is performing to the best of its ability? We need to ensure that the performance measure that you've come up with is actually representative of the model and that it will indeed perform well on an unseen test dataset. The essential part of making sure that the model is the best version of itself comes after the initial training: the process of evaluating and improving the performance of the model. This chapter will take you through the essential techniques required when it comes to this.

In this chapter, we will first discuss why model evaluation is important, and introduce several evaluation metrics for both regression tasks and classification tasks that can be used to quantify the predictive performance of a model. This will be followed by a discussion on hold-out datasets and k-fold cross-validation and why it is imperative to have a test set that is independent of the validation set. After this, we'll look at tactics we can use to boost the performance of the model. In the previous chapter, we talked about how having a model with a high bias or a high variance can result in suboptimal performance, and how building an ensemble of models can help us build a robust system that makes more accurate predictions without increasing the overall variance. We also mentioned the following as techniques to avoid overfitting our model to the training data:

- To get more data: A highly complex model can easily overfit to a small dataset but may not be able to as easily on a larger dataset.

- Dimensionality reduction: Reducing the number of features can help make the model less complex.

- Regularization: A new term is added to the cost function in order to adjust the coefficients (especially the high-degree coefficients in linear regression) toward a small value.

In this chapter, we'll introduce learning curves and validation curves as a way to see how variations in training and validation errors allow us to see whether the model needs more data, and where the appropriate level of complexity is. This will be followed by a section on hyperparameter tuning in an effort to boost performance, and a brief introduction to feature importance.

> **NOTE**
>
> All the relevant code for this chapter can be found here:
> https://packt.live/2T1fCWM.

IMPORTING THE MODULES AND PREPARING OUR DATASET

In the previous exercises and activities, we used terms such as **Mean Absolute Error (MAE)** and accuracy. In machine learning terms, these are called evaluation metrics and, in the next sections, we will discuss some useful evaluation metrics, what they are, and how and when to use them.

> **NOTE**
>
> Although this section is not positioned as an exercise, we encourage you to follow through this section carefully by executing the presented code. We will be using the code presented here in the upcoming exercises.

We will now load the data and models that we trained as part of *Chapter 6, Ensemble Modeling*. We will use the stacked linear regression model from *Activity 6.01, Stacking with Standalone and Ensemble Algorithms*, and the random forest classification model to predict the survival of passengers from *Exercise 6.06, Building the Ensemble Model Using Random Forest*.

First, we need to import the relevant libraries:

```
import pandas as pd
import numpy as np
import pickle

%matplotlib inline
import matplotlib.pyplot as plt
```

Next, load the processed data files from *Chapter 6, Ensemble Modeling*. We will use pandas' **read_csv()** method to read in our prepared datasets, which we will use in the exercises in this chapter. First, we'll read the house price data:

```
house_prices_reg = \
pd.read_csv('../Datasets/boston_house_prices_regression.csv')
house_prices_reg.head()
```

We'll see the following output:

	0	1	2	3	4	5	6	7	8	9	10	11	12	13	14	15	16	y
0	0.04981	21.0	5.64	0.0	0.439	5.998	21.4	6.8147	4.0	243.0	16.8	396.90	8.43	-1.0	22.507577	27.08	19.40	23.4
1	0.20746	0.0	27.74	0.0	0.609	5.093	98.0	1.8226	4.0	711.0	20.1	318.43	29.68	-1.0	16.238796	17.46	16.55	8.1
2	0.11329	30.0	4.93	0.0	0.428	6.897	54.3	6.3361	6.0	300.0	16.6	391.25	11.38	-1.0	27.423950	21.84	28.20	22.0
3	19.60910	0.0	18.10	0.0	0.671	7.313	97.9	1.3163	24.0	666.0	20.2	396.90	13.44	-1.0	20.939772	10.50	28.20	15.0
4	25.94060	0.0	18.10	0.0	0.679	5.304	89.1	1.6475	24.0	666.0	20.2	127.36	26.64	-1.0	11.319594	14.70	10.20	10.4

Figure 7.2: First five rows of house_prices

Next, we'll read in the Titanic data:

```
titanic_clf = pd.read_csv('../Datasets/titanic_classification.csv')
titanic_clf.head()
```

We'll see the following output:

	Pclass	Gender	Age	SibSp	Parch	Fare	Emb_C	Emb_Q	Emb_S	Survived
0	3	0	22.0	1	0	7.2500	0	0	1	0
1	1	0	38.0	1	0	71.2833	1	0	0	1
2	3	0	26.0	0	0	7.9250	0	0	1	1
3	1	0	35.0	1	0	53.1000	0	0	1	1
4	3	0	35.0	0	0	8.0500	0	0	1	0

Figure 7.3: First five rows of Titanic

Next, load the model files that we will use for the exercises in this chapter by using the **pickle** library to load them from a binary file:

```
with open('../../Saved_Models/titanic_regression.pkl', 'rb') as f:
    reg = pickle.load(f)

with open('../../Saved_Models/random_forest_clf.pkl', 'rb') as f:
    rf = pickle.load(f)
with open('../../Saved_Models/stacked_linear_regression.pkl',\
         'rb') as f:
    reg = pickle.load(f)
```

So far, we have successfully loaded the necessary datasets as well as trained machine learning models from our previous exercises and activities in this section. Before starting to use these loaded datasets and models to explore the evaluation metrics, let's first acquire an understanding of different kinds of evaluation metrics.

> **NOTE**
>
> You can find the files for saved models at the following link: https://packt.live/2vjoSwf.

EVALUATION METRICS

Evaluating a machine learning model is an essential part of any project: once we have allowed our model to learn from the training data, the next step is to measure the performance of the model. We need to find a metric that can not only tell us how accurate the predictions made by the model are, but also allow us to compare the performance of a number of models so that we can select the one best suited for our use case.

Defining a metric is usually one of the first things we should do when defining our problem statement and before we begin the exploratory data analysis, since it's a good idea to plan ahead and think about how we intend to evaluate the performance of any model we build and how to judge whether it is performing optimally. Eventually, calculating the performance evaluation metric will fit into the machine learning pipeline.

Needless to say, evaluation metrics will be different for regression tasks and classification tasks, since the output values in the former are continuous, while the outputs in the latter are categorical. In this section, we'll look at the different metrics we can use to quantify the predictive performance of a model.

REGRESSION METRICS

For an input variable, x, a regression model gives us a predicted value that can take on a range of values. The ideal scenario would be to have the model predict values that are as close as possible to the actual value of y. Therefore, the smaller the difference between the two, the better the model performs. Regression metrics mostly involve looking at the numerical difference between the predicted value and actual value (that is, the residual or error value) for each data point, and subsequently aggregating these differences in some way.

Let's look at the following plot, which plots the actual and predicted values for every point **X**:

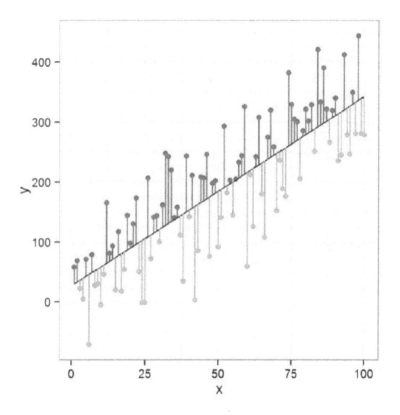

Figure 7.4: Residuals between actual and predicted outputs in a linear regression problem

However, we can't just find the mean value of overall data points, since there could be data points that have a prediction error that is positive or negative, and the aggregate would ultimately end up canceling out a lot of the errors and severely overestimate the performance of the model.

Instead, we can consider the absolute error for each data point and find the MAE, which is given by the following:

$$MAE = \frac{1}{n} \sum_{i=1}^{n} \left| y^i - \widehat{y}^i \right|$$

Figure 7.5: MAE

Here, **y**^{i} and **ŷ**^{i} are the actual and predicted values, respectively, for the **i**th data point.

MAE is a **linear scoring function**, which means that it gives each residual an equal weight when it aggregates the errors. The MAE can take on any value from zero to infinity and is indifferent to the direction (positive or negative) of errors. Since these are error metrics, a lower value (as close to zero as possible) is usually desirable.

In order to not let the direction of the error affect the performance estimate, we can also take the square of the error terms. Taking the mean of the squared errors gives us the **Mean Squared Error** (**MSE**):

$$MSE = \frac{1}{n} \sum_{i=1}^{n} \left(y^i - \widehat{y}^i\right)^2$$

Figure 7.6: MSE

While the MAE has the same units as the target variable, **y**, the units for the MSE will be the squared unit of **y**, which may make the MSE slightly less interpretable while judging the model in real-world terms. However, if we take the square root of the MSE, we get the **Root Mean Squared Error** (**RMSE**):

$$RMSE = \sqrt{MSE} = \sqrt{\frac{1}{n} \sum_{i=1}^{n} \left(y^i - \widehat{y}^i\right)^2}$$

Figure 7.7: Root Mean Squared Error

Since the errors are squared before they are averaged, having even a few error values that are high can cause the RMSE value to significantly increase. This means that the RMSE is more useful than MAE for judging models in which we want to penalize large errors.

Since MAE and RMSE have the same units as the target variable, it can be hard to judge whether a particular value of the MAE or RMSE is good or bad, since there is no scale to refer to. A metric that is commonly used to overcome this problem is the **R²** **Score**, or the **R-Squared Score**:

$$R^2 = 1 - \frac{MSE(\ model)}{MSE(\ base\ model)}$$

Figure 7.8: R-squared score

The **R²** score has a lower limit of **-∞** and an upper limit of **1**. The base model predicts the target variable to be equal to the mean of the target values in the training dataset, **µ**, mathematically written as:

$$\mu = \frac{1}{n} \sum_{i=1}^{n} y^i$$

Figure 7.9: Expression for the mean of the target values in the training dataset

And so, for the base model:

$$\hat{y}^i = \mu \; ; \; \forall i \in \left[1, \; n\right]$$

Figure 7.10: Expression for the base model target variable

Keeping this in mind, a negative value of R^2 would be one where the trained model makes a prediction that is worse than simply predicting the mean value for all the data, and a value close to 1 would be achieved if the MSE of the model is close to 0.

EXERCISE 7.01: CALCULATING REGRESSION METRICS

In this exercise, we will use the same model and processed dataset that we trained in *Activity 6.01, Stacking with Standalone and Ensemble Algorithms*, in *Chapter 6, Ensemble Modeling*, to calculate regression metrics. We will use scikit-learn's implementation of MAE and MSE:

> **NOTE**
>
> Before beginning this exercise, make sure you have imported the relevant libraries and models as listed in the *Importing the Modules and Preparing Our Dataset* section.

The code for this exercise can be found here:

1. Import the metric functions:

```
from sklearn.metrics import mean_absolute_error, \
mean_squared_error, r2_score
from math import sqrt
```

2. Use the loaded model to predict the output on the given data. We will use the same features as we did in *Activity 6.01, Stacking with Standalone and Ensemble Algorithms*, in *Chapter 6, Ensemble Modeling*, and use the model to make a prediction on the loaded dataset. The column we saved as **y** is the target variable, and we will create **X** and **y** accordingly:

```
X = house_prices_reg.drop(columns=['y'])
y = house_prices_reg['y'].values


y_pred = reg.predict(X)
```

3. Calculate the MAE, RMSE, and R^2 scores. Let's print the values of the MAE and the RMSE from the predicted values. Also, print the R^2 score for the model:

```
print('Mean Absolute Error = {}'\
        .format(mean_absolute_error(y, y_pred)))
print('Root Mean Squared Error = {}'\
        .format(sqrt(mean_squared_error(y, y_pred))))
print('R Squared Score = {}'.format(r2_score(y, y_pred)))
```

The output will be as follows:

```
Mean Absolute Error = 2.874084343939712
Root Mean Squared Error = 4.50458397908091
R Squared Score = 0.7634986504091822
```

We can see that the RMSE is higher than the MAE. This shows that there are some data points where the residuals are particularly high, which is being highlighted by the larger RMSE value. But the R^2 score is close to 1, indicating that the model actually has close to ideal performance compared to a base model, which would predict a mean value.

> **NOTE**
>
> To access the source code for this specific section, please refer to https://packt.live/3epdfp3.
>
> You can also run this example online at https://packt.live/3hMLBnY. You must execute the entire Notebook in order to get the desired result.

CLASSIFICATION METRICS

For an input variable, **X**, a classification task gives us a predicted value, which can take on a limited set of values (two in the case of binary classification problems). Since the ideal scenario would be to predict a class for each data point that is the same as the actual class, there is no measure of how *close* or *far* the predicted class is from the actual class. Therefore, to judge the model's performance, it would be as simple as determining whether the model predicted the class correctly.

Judging a classification model's performance can be done in two ways: using numerical metrics, or by plotting a curve and looking at the shape of the curve. Let's explore both of these options in greater detail.

NUMERICAL METRICS

The simplest and most basic way to judge the performance of the model is to calculate the proportion of the correct predictions to the total number of predictions, which gives us the **accuracy**, as shown in the following figure:

$$Accuracy = \frac{Number\ of\ correct\ predictions}{Total\ no.of\ predictions}$$

Figure 7.11: Accuracy

Although the accuracy metric is the same irrespective of the number of classes, the next few metrics are discussed keeping in mind a binary classification problem. Additionally, accuracy may not be the best metric to judge the performance of a classification task in many cases.

Let's look at an example of fraud detection: say the problem statement is to detect whether a particular email is fraudulent. Our dataset, in this case, is highly skewed (or imbalanced, that is, there are many more data points belonging to one class compared to the other class), with 100 out of 10,000 emails (1% of the total) having been classified as fraudulent (having class 1). Say we build two models:

- The first model simply predicts each email as not being fraud, that is, each of the 10,000 emails is classified with class 0. In this case, 9,900 of the 10,000 were classified correctly, which means the model has 99% accuracy.

- The second model predicts the 100 fraud emails as being fraud, but also predicts another 100 emails incorrectly as fraud. In this case as well, 100 data points were misclassified out of 10,000, and the model has an accuracy level of 99%.

How do we compare these two models? The purpose of building a fraud detection model is to allow us to know *how well the fraud was detected*: it matters more that the fraudulent emails were correctly classified than if non-fraudulent emails were classified as fraudulent. Although both the models were equally high in accuracy, the second was actually more effective than the first.

Since this cannot be captured using accuracy, we need the **confusion matrix**, a table with *n* different combinations of predicted and actual values, where *n* is the number of classes. The confusion matrix essentially gives us a summary of the prediction results of a classification problem. *Figure 7.12* shows an example confusion matrix for a binary classification problem:

		Predicted	
		0	1
Actual	0	Correctly Classified	Incorrectly Classified
	1	Incorrectly Classified	Correctly Classified

Figure 7.12: Confusion matrix

Since it is a binary classification problem, the preceding confusion matrix can be viewed directly as a table of confusion, in other words, a matrix of true positives, true negatives, false positives, and false negatives, as shown in *Figure 7.13*. The table of confusion is always **2 x 2** in size, regardless of binary or multiclass classification. In the case of multiclass classification, if we use the one-versus-all classification approach, then there will be as many tables of confusion as the number of classes:

		Predicted	
		0	1
Actual	0	True negatives	False positives
	1	False negatives	True positives

Figure 7.13: Table of confusion

Here is what the terms used in the table of confusion mean:

- **True positives** and **true negatives**: These are the counts of the correctly predicted data points in the positive and negative classes, respectively.

- **False positives**: These are also known as **Type 1** errors and refer to the count of the data points that actually belong to the negative class but were predicted to be positive. Continuing from the previous example, a false positive case would be if a normal email is classified as a fraudulent email.

- **False negatives**: These are also known as **Type 2** errors and refer to the count of the data points that actually belong to the positive class but were predicted to be negative. An example of a false negative case would be if a fraudulent email was classified as not being one.

Two extremely important metrics can be derived from a confusion matrix: **precision** and **recall**:

$$Precision = \frac{True\ positives}{Total\ predicted\ positives} = \frac{True\ positives}{True\ positives\ +\ Fasle\ positives}$$

Figure 7.14: Precision

$$Recall = \frac{True\ positives}{Total\ actual\ positives} = \frac{True\ positives}{True\ positives\ +\ False\ negatives}$$

Figure 7.15: Recall

While precision tells us how many of the predicted positives were actually positive (from the results the model says are relevant, how many are actually relevant?), recall tells us how many of the actual positives were correctly predicted to be positive (from the real relevant results, how many are included in the model's list of relevant results?). These two metrics are especially useful when there is an imbalance between the two classes.

There is usually a trade-off between the precision and recall of a model: if you have to recall all the relevant results, the model will generate more results that are not accurate, thereby lowering the precision. On the other hand, having a higher percentage of relevant results from the generated results would involve including as few results as possible. In most cases, you would give a higher priority to either the precision or the recall, and this entirely depends on the problem statement. For example, since it matters more that all the fraudulent emails are correctly classified, recall would be an important metric that would need to be maximized.

The next question that arises is how we take both precision and recall, evaluating our model using a single number instead of balancing two separate metrics. The **F₁** score combines the two into a single number that can be used for a fair judgment of the model and is equal to the harmonic mean of precision and recall:

$$F_1 \; Score = 2 \times \frac{Precision \; \times \; Recall}{Precision \; + \; Recall}$$

Figure 7.16: F_1 score

The value of the **F₁** score will always lie between 0 (if either precision or recall is 0) and 1 (if both precision and recall are 1). The higher the score, the better the model's performance is said to be. The **F₁** score allows equal weightage to both measures. It is a specific example of the **Fᵦ** metric, where β can be adjusted to give more weight to either of the two parameters (recall or precision score) using the following formula:

$$F_\beta \; Score = \left(1 + \beta^2\right) \times \frac{Precision \; \times \; Recall}{\left(\beta^2 \; \times \; Precision\right) + Recall}$$

Figure 7.17: F beta score

A value of **β < 1** focuses more on precision, while taking **β > 1** focuses more on recall. The F₁ score takes **β = 1** to give both equal weight.

CURVE PLOTS

Sometimes, instead of predicting the class, we have the class probabilities at our disposal. Say, in a binary classification task, the class probabilities of both the positive (class A) and negative (class B) classes will always add up to unity (or 1), which means that if we take the classification probability as equal to the probability of class A and apply a threshold, we can essentially use it as a cut-off value to either round up (to 1) or down (to 0), which will give the output class.

Usually, by varying the threshold, we can get data points that have classification probabilities closer to 0.5 from one class to another. For example, with a threshold of 0.5, a data point having a probability of 0.4 would be assigned class B and a data point having probability 0.6 would be assigned class A. But if we change the threshold to 0.35 or 0.65, both those data points would be classified as the other class.

As it turns out, varying the probability threshold changes the precision and recall values and this can be captured by plotting the **precision-recall** curve. The plot has precision on the **Y** axis and recall on the **X** axis, and for a range of thresholds starting from 0 to 1 plot each (**recall**, **precision**) point. Connecting these points gives us the curve. The following graph provides an example:

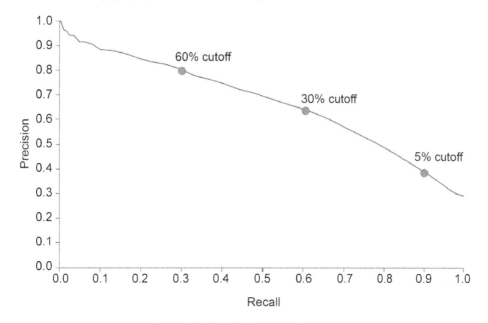

Figure 7.18: Precision-recall curve

We know that in an ideal case, the values of precision and recall will be unity. This means that upon increasing the threshold from 0 to 1, the precision would stay constant at 1, but the recall would increase from 0 to 1 as more and more (relevant) data points would be classified correctly. Thus, in an ideal case, the precision-recall curve would essentially just be a square and the **Area Under the Curve (AUC)** would be equal to one.

Thus, we can see that, as with the F_1 score, the AUC is another metric derived from the precision and recall behavior that uses a combination of their values to evaluate the performance of the model. We want the model to achieve an AUC as high and close to 1 as possible.

The **Receiver Operating Characteristic (ROC)** curve is another technique used for visualizing the performance of a classification model. The ROC curve plots the relationship between the **True Positive Rate (TPR)** on the Y axis and the **False Positive Rate (FPR)** on the X axis across a varying classification probability threshold. TPR is exactly the same as the recall (and is also known as the **sensitivity** of the model), and FPR is an equal complement of the **specificity** (that is, **1 – FPR = Specificity**); both can be derived from the confusion matrix using these formulas:

$$TPR = \frac{True\ positives}{Total\ actual\ positives} = \frac{True\ positives}{True\ positives\ +\ False\ negatives}$$

Figure 7.19: True positive rate

$$FPR = \frac{False\ postives}{Total\ actual\ positives} = \frac{True\ positives}{False\ postives\ +\ True\ negatives}$$

Figure 7.20: False positive rate

The following diagram shows an example of an ROC curve, plotted in the same way as the precision-recall curve, by varying the probability threshold such that each point on the curve represents a **(TPR, FPR)** data point corresponding to a specific probability threshold:

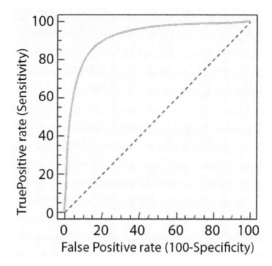

Figure 7.21: ROC curve

ROC curves are more useful when the classes are fairly balanced, since they tend to represent a favorable output of the model on datasets with a class imbalance via their use of true negatives in the false positive rate in the ROC curve (which is not present in the precision-recall curve).

EXERCISE 7.02: CALCULATING CLASSIFICATION METRICS

In this exercise, we will use the random forest model we trained in *Chapter 6, Ensemble Modeling*, and use its predictions to generate the confusion matrix and calculate the precision, recall, and F_1 scores as a way of rating our model. We will use scikit-learn's implementations to calculate these metrics:

> **NOTE**
>
> Before beginning this exercise, make sure you have imported the relevant libraries and models as listed in the *Importing the Modules and Preparing Our Dataset* section.

1. Import the relevant libraries and functions:

```
from sklearn.metrics import (accuracy_score, confusion_matrix, \
precision_score, recall_score, f1_score)
```

2. Use the model to predict classes for all data points. We will use the same features as we did earlier and use the random forest classifier to make a prediction in relation to the loaded dataset. Every classifier in scikit-learn has a `.predict_proba()` function, which we will use here along with the standard `.predict()` function to give us the class probabilities and the classes, respectively:

```
X = titanic_clf.iloc[:, :-1]
y = titanic_clf.iloc[:, -1]

y_pred = rf.predict(X)
y_pred_probs = rf.predict_proba(X)
```

3. Calculate the accuracy:

```
print('Accuracy Score = {}'.format(accuracy_score(y, y_pred)))
```

The output will be as follows:

```
Accuracy Score = 0.6251402918069585
```

An accuracy score of **62.5%** is not that great, especially considering the fact that flipping a coin for guessing each output would result in an accuracy of **50%**. However, the goal of the current exercise is to get an understanding of how metrics work. Hence, after noticing that our classifier doesn't really do well in terms of accuracy, we move on to some other metrics that will help us to analyze the model performance in more detail.

4. Print the confusion matrix:

```
print(confusion_matrix(y_pred=y_pred, y_true=y))
```

The output will be as follows:

$$[[548 \quad 1] \\ [333 \quad 9]]$$

Figure 7.22: Confusion matrix

Here, we can see that the model seems to have a high number of false negatives, which means that we can expect the recall value for this model to be extremely low. Similarly, since the count of the false positives is just one, we can expect the model to have high precision.

5. Calculate the precision and recall:

```
print('Precision Score = {}'.format(precision_score(y, y_pred)))
print('Recall Score = {}'.format(recall_score(y, y_pred)))
```

The output will be as follows:

```
Precision Score = 0.9
Recall Score = 0.02631578947368421
```

6. Calculate the F_1 score:

```
print('F1 Score = {}'.format(f1_score(y, y_pred)))
```

The output will be as follows:

```
F1 Score = 0.05113636363636364
```

We can see that, since the recall is extremely low, this is affecting the F_1 score as well, making it close to zero.

> **NOTE**
>
> To access the source code for this specific section, please refer to
> https://packt.live/2V6mbYQ.
>
> You can also run this example online at https://packt.live/37XirOr.
> You must execute the entire Notebook in order to get the desired result.

Now that we have talked about the metrics that we can use to measure the predictive performance of the model, let's talk about validation strategies, in which we will use a metric to evaluate the performance of the model in different cases and situations.

SPLITTING A DATASET

A common mistake made when determining how well a model is performing is to calculate the prediction error on the data that the model was trained on and conclude that a model performs really well on the basis of a high prediction accuracy on the training dataset.

This means that we are trying to test the model on data that the model has already *seen*, that is, the model has already learned the behavior of the training data because it was exposed to it—if asked to predict the behavior of the training data again, it would undoubtedly perform well. And the better the performance on the training data, the higher the chances that the model knows the data *too well*, so much so that it has even learned the noise and behavior of outliers in the data.

Now, high training accuracy results in a model having high variance, as we saw in the previous chapter. In order to get an unbiased estimate of the model's performance, we need to find its prediction accuracy on data it has not already been exposed to during training. This is where the hold-out dataset comes into the picture.

HOLD-OUT DATA

The **hold-out dataset** refers to a sample of the dataset that has been held back from training the model on and is essentially *unseen* by the model. The hold-out data points will likely contain outliers and noisy data points that behave differently from those in the training dataset, given that noise is random. Thus, calculating the performance on the hold-out dataset would allow us to validate whether the model is overfitting or not, as well as give us an unbiased view of the model's performance.

We began our previous chapter by splitting the Titanic dataset into training and validation sets. What is this validation dataset, and how is it different from a test dataset? We often see the terms **validation set** and **test set** used interchangeably— although they both characterize a hold-out dataset, there are some differences in purpose:

- **Validation data**: After the model learns from the training data, its performance is evaluated on the validation dataset. However, in order to get the model to perform the best it can, we need to fine-tune the model and iteratively evaluate the updated model's performance repeatedly, and this is done on the validation dataset. The fine-tuned version of the model that performs best on the validation dataset is usually chosen to be the final model.

  The model is therefore exposed to the validation dataset multiple times, at each iteration of improvement, although it does not essentially *learn* from the data. It can be said that the validation set does affect the model, although indirectly.

- **Test data**: The final model that was chosen is now evaluated on the test dataset. The performance measured on this dataset will be an unbiased measure that is reported as the final performance metric of the model. This final evaluation is done once the model has been completely trained on the combined training and validation datasets. No training or updating of the model is performed after this metric has been calculated.

This means that the model is exposed to the test dataset only once, when calculating the final performance metric.

It should be kept in mind that the validation dataset should never be used to evaluate the final performance of the model: our estimate of the true performance of a model will be positively biased if the model has seen and been modified subsequently in an effort to specifically improve performance in relation to the validation set.

Having a single hold-out validation dataset does have some limitations, however since the model is only validated once in each iteration of improvement, it might be difficult to capture the uncertainty in prediction using this single evaluation.

Dividing the data into training and validation sets decreases the size of the data upon which the model is trained, and this can lead to the model having a high variance.

The final model may *overfit* to this validation set since it was tuned in order to maximize performance on this dataset.

These challenges can be overcome if we use a validation technique called k-fold cross-validation instead of using a single validation dataset.

K-FOLD CROSS-VALIDATION

K-fold cross-validation is a validation technique that helps us get an unbiased estimate of the model's performance by essentially rotating the validation set in **k** folds. This is how it works:

1. First, we choose the value of **k** and divide the data into **k** subsets.

2. Then, we set aside the first subset as the validation set and use the remaining data to train the model.

3. We measure the performance of the model on the validation subset.

4. Then, we set aside the second subset as the validation subset and repeat the process.

5. Once we have done this **k** times, we aggregate the performance metric values over all the folds and present the final metric.

The following figure explains this visually:

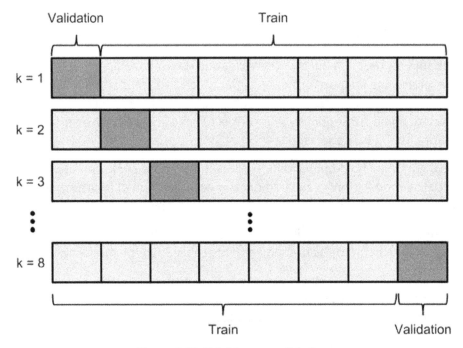

Figure 7.23: K-fold cross-validation

Although this method of validation is more computationally expensive, the benefits outweigh the costs. This approach makes sure that the model is validated on each example in the training dataset exactly once and that the performance estimate we achieve in the end is not biased in favor of a validation dataset, especially in the case of small datasets. A special case is **leave-one-out** cross-validation, where the value of **k** is equal to the number of data points.

SAMPLING

Now that we've looked at the strategies for splitting the dataset for training and validating the model, let's discuss how to allocate data points to these splits. There are two ways we can sample the data in the splits, and these are as follows:

- **Random sampling**: This is as simple as allocating random samples from the overall dataset into training, validation, and/or test datasets. Randomly splitting the data only works when all the data points are independent of each other. For example, random splitting would not be the way to go if the data was in the form of a time series, since the data points are ordered, and each depends on the previous one. Randomly splitting the data would destroy that order and not take into account this dependence. One common real-world example where random sampling could be used to split training and test datasets is for the handwritten digits classification task, because in this case, all data samples (images of handwritten digits) are independent of one another and data is roughly equally distributed among all 10 classes (digits).

- **Stratified sampling**: This is a way to ensure that each subset has the same distribution of values of the target variable as the original dataset. For example, if the original dataset has two classes in the ratio 3:7, stratified sampling ensures that each subset will also contain the two classes in the ratio 3:7.

Stratified sampling is important since testing our model on a dataset with a different distribution of target values from the dataset on which the model was trained can give us a performance estimate that is not representative of the model's actual performance.

A real-life example where this sampling technique is used is fraud detection in financial transactions. Because frauds occur rarely, the imbalance between the *FRAUD* and *NOT_FRAUD* classes is huge. In order to split 1,000 financial transactions, of which 5 are fraudulent, into training and test sets for the fraud detection task, we must use stratified sampling. If we don't, then all 5 fraudulent samples might end up in the training set (or test set), which will prevent us from performing any useful validation.

The size of the train, validation, and test samples also plays an important role in the model evaluation process. Keeping aside a large dataset on which to test the final performance of the model will help us get an unbiased estimate of the model's performance and reduce the variance in prediction, but if the test set is so large that it compromises the model's ability to train due to a lack of training data, this will severely affect the model as well. This is a consideration that is especially relevant for smaller datasets.

EXERCISE 7.03: PERFORMING K-FOLD CROSS-VALIDATION WITH STRATIFIED SAMPLING

In this exercise, we'll implement K-fold cross-validation with stratified sampling on scikit-learn's random forest classifier. The **StratifiedKFold** class in scikit-learn implements a combination of cross-validation and sampling together in one class, and we will use this in our exercise:

> **NOTE**
>
> Before beginning this exercise, make sure you have imported the relevant libraries and models as listed in the *Importing the Modules and Preparing Our Dataset* section.

1. Import the relevant classes. We will import scikit-learn's **StratifiedKFold** class, which is a variation of **KFold** that returns stratified folds, along with **RandomForestClassifier**:

    ```
    from sklearn.metrics import accuracy_score
    from sklearn.model_selection import StratifiedKFold
    from sklearn.ensemble import RandomForestClassifier
    ```

2. Prepare data for training and initialize the k-fold object. Here, we will use five folds to evaluate the model, and hence will give the **n_splits** parameter a value of **5**:

    ```
    X = titanic_clf.iloc[:, :-1].values
    y = titanic_clf.iloc[:, -1].values
    skf = StratifiedKFold(n_splits=5)
    ```

3. Train a classifier for each fold and record the score. The functioning of the **StratifiedKFold** class is similar to the **KFold** class that we used in the previous chapter, *Chapter 6, Ensemble Modeling* in *Exercise 6.06, Building a Stacked Model*. For each of the five folds, we will train on the other four folds and predict on the fifth fold, and find the accuracy score for predictions in relation to the fifth fold. As we saw in the previous chapter, the **skf.split()** function takes the dataset to split as input and returns an iterator comprising the index values used to subdivide the training data for training and validation for each row:

    ```
    scores = []

    for train_index, val_index in skf.split(X, y):
        X_train, X_val = X[train_index], X[val_index]
    ```

```
    y_train, y_val = y[train_index], y[val_index]
    rf_skf = RandomForestClassifier(**rf.get_params())
    rf_skf.fit(X_train, y_train)
    y_pred = rf_skf.predict(X_val)
    scores.append(accuracy_score(y_val, y_pred))
scores
```

The output will be as follows:

```
[0.6145251396648045,
 0.6983240223463687,
 0.74719101112359551,
 0.7808988764044944,
 0.711864406779661]
```

Figure 7.24: Scores using the random forest classifier

4. Print the aggregated accuracy score:

```
print('Mean Accuracy Score = {}'.format(np.mean(scores)))
```

The output will be as follows:

```
Mean Accuracy Score = 0.7105606912862568
```

> **NOTE**
>
> To access the source code for this specific section, please refer to
> https://packt.live/316TUF5.
>
> You can also run this example online at https://packt.live/2V6JilY.
> You must execute the entire Notebook in order to get the desired result.

Thus, we have demonstrated how we can use k-fold cross-validation to have a robust assessment of model performance. And we use stratified sampling in the preceding approach that ensures that the training and validation sets have similar class distribution. Next, we will focus on how to improve model performance.

PERFORMANCE IMPROVEMENT TACTICS

Performance improvement for supervised machine learning models is an iterative process, and a continuous cycle of updating and evaluation is usually required to get the perfect model. While the previous sections in this chapter dealt with the evaluation strategies, this section will talk about model updating: we will discuss some ways we can determine what our model needs to give it that performance boost, and how to effect that change in our model.

VARIATION IN TRAIN AND TEST ERRORS

In the previous chapter, we introduced the concepts of underfitting and overfitting, and mentioned a few ways to overcome them, later introducing ensemble models. But we didn't talk about how to identify whether our model was underfitting or overfitting to the training data.

It's usually useful to look at the learning and validation curves.

LEARNING CURVE

The learning curve shows the variation in the training and validation errors with the training data increasing in size. By looking at the shape of the curves, we can get a good idea of whether more data will benefit the modeling and possibly improve the model's performance.

Let's look at the following figure: the dotted curve represents the validation error, and the solid curve represents the training error. The plot on the left shows the two curves converging to an error value that is quite high. This means that the model has a high bias and adding more data isn't likely to affect the model's performance. So instead of wasting time and money collecting more data, all we need to do is increase model complexity.

On the other hand, the plot on the right shows a significant difference between the training and test errors, even with an increasing number of data points in the training set. The wide gap indicates a high variance in the system, which means the model is overfitting. In this case, adding more data points will probably help the model generalize better, as you can see in the following figure:

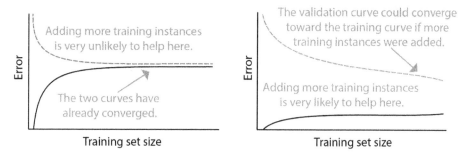

Figure 7.25: Learning curve for increasing data size

But how will we recognize the perfect learning curve? When we have a model with low bias and low variance, we will see a curve like the one shown in the following figure. It shows a low training error (low bias) as well as a low gap between the validation and training curves (low variance) as they converge. In practice, the best possible learning curves we can see are those that converge to the value of an irreducible error value (which exists due to noise and outliers in the dataset), as shown in the following figure:

Figure 7.26: Variation in training and validation error with an increasing training data size for a low bias and variance model

VALIDATION CURVE

As we have discussed previously, the goal of a machine learning model is to be able to generalize to unseen data. Validation curves allow us to find the ideal point between an underfitted and an overfitted model where the model would generalize well. In the previous chapter, we talked a bit about how model complexity affects prediction performance: we said that as we move from an overly simplistic to an overly complex model, we go from having an underfitted model with high bias and low variance to an overfitted model with low bias and high variance.

A validation curve shows the variation in training and validation error with a varying value of a model parameter that has some degree of control over the model's complexity—this could be the degree of the polynomial in linear regression, or the depth of a decision tree classifier:

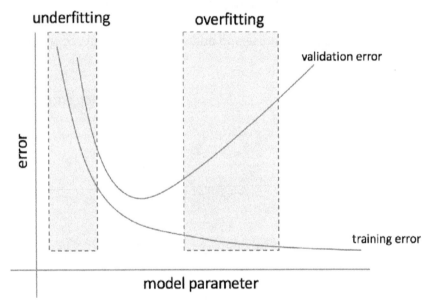

Figure 7.27: Variation in training and validation with increasing model complexity

The preceding figure shows how the validation and training error will vary with model complexity (of which the model parameter is an indicator). We can also see how the point in between the shaded regions is where the total error would be at a minimum, at the sweet spot between underfitting and overfitting. Finding this point will help us find the ideal value of the model's parameters that will help build a model with low bias as well as low variance.

HYPERPARAMETER TUNING

We've talked about hyperparameter tuning several times previously. Now, let's discuss why it's so important. First, it should be noted that model parameters are different from model hyperparameters: while the former are internal to the model and are learned from the data, the latter define the architecture of the model itself.

Examples of hyperparameters include the following:

- The degree of polynomial features to be used for a linear regressor

- The maximum depth allowed for a decision tree classifier

- The number of trees to be included in a random forest classifier

- The learning rate used for the gradient descent algorithm

The design choices that define the architecture of the model can make a huge difference in how well the model performs. Usually, the default values for the hyperparameters work, but getting the perfect combination of values for the hyperparameters can really give the predictive power of the model a boost as the default values may be completely inappropriate for the problem we are trying to model.

In the following diagram, we see how varying the values of two hyperparameters can cause such a difference in the model score:

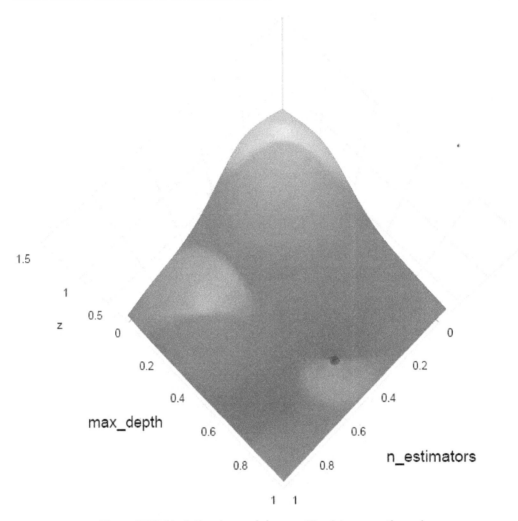

Figure 7.28: Variation in model score (Z axis) across the values
of two model parameters (the X and Y axes)

Finding that perfect combination by exploring a range of possible values is what is referred to as **hyperparameter tuning**. Since there is no loss function that we can use to maximize the model performance, tuning the hyperparameters generally just involves experimenting with different combinations and choosing the one that performs best during validation.

There are a few ways in which we can go about tuning our model's hyperparameters:

- **Hand-tuning**: When we manually choose the values of our hyperparameters, this is known as hand-tuning. It is usually inefficient, since solving a high-dimensional optimization problem by hand can not only be slow, but also would not allow the model to reach its peak performance as we probably wouldn't try out every single combination of hyperparameter values.

- **Grid search**: Grid search involves training and evaluating a model for each combination of the hyperparameter values provided and selecting the combination that produces the best performing model. Since this involves performing an exhaustive sampling of the hyperparameter space, it is quite computationally speaking and, hence, inefficient.

- **Random search**: While the first method was deemed inefficient because too few combinations were tried, the second one was deemed so because too many combinations were tried. Random search aims to solve this problem by selecting a random subset of hyperparameter combinations from the grid (specified previously), and training and evaluating a model just for those. Alternatively, we can also provide a statistical distribution for each hyperparameter from which the values can be randomly sampled.

The logic behind random search was proved by *Bergstra and Bengio*, which states that if at least 5% of the points on the grid yield a close-to-optimal solution, then random search with 60 trials will find that region with a probability of 95%.

> **NOTE:**
>
> You can read the paper by *Bergstra and Bengio* at http://www.jmlr.org/papers/v13/bergstra12a.html.

- **Bayesian optimization**: The previous two methods involved independently experimenting with combinations of hyperparameter values and recording the model performance for each. However, Bayesian optimization iterates over experiments sequentially and allows us to use the results of a previous experiment to improve the sampling method for the next experiment.

EXERCISE 7.04: HYPERPARAMETER TUNING WITH RANDOM SEARCH

In this exercise, we will perform hyperparameter tuning with the random search method. We will define a grid of hyperparameter ranges and randomly sample from the grid using the **RandomizedSearchCV** method. We will also be performing K-fold cross-validation with each combination of values. This exercise is a continuation of *Exercise 7.03, Performing K-Fold Cross-Validation with Stratified Sampling*:

1. Import the class for random search:

```
from sklearn.ensemble import RandomForestClassifier
from sklearn.model_selection import RandomizedSearchCV
```

2. Prepare data for training and initialize the classifier. Here, we will initialize our random forest classifier without passing any arguments, since this is just a base object that will be instantiated for each grid point on which to perform the random search:

```
X = titanic_clf.iloc[:, :-1].values
y = titanic_clf.iloc[:, -1].values

rf_rand = RandomForestClassifier()
def report(results, max_rank=3):
    for rank in range(1, max_rank+1):
        results_at_rank = np.flatnonzero\
                          (results['rank_test_score'] == i)
def report(results, n_top=3):
    for i in range(1, n_top + 1):
        candidates = np.flatnonzero\
                     (results['rank_test_score'] == i)
```

```
      for candidate in candidates:
          print("Model with rank: {0}".format(i))
          print("Mean validation score: {0:.3f} (std: {1:.3f})"\
              .format(results['mean_test_score'][candidate], \
              results['std_test_score'][candidate]))
          print("Parameters: {0}".format(results['params']\
                                               [candidate]))
          print("")
```

3. Specify the parameters to sample from. Here, we will list the different values for each hyperparameter that we would like to have in the grid:

```
param_dist = {"n_estimators": list(range(10,210,10)), \
              "max_depth": list(range(3,20)), \
              "max_features": list(range(1, 10)), \
              "min_samples_split": list(range(2, 11)), \
              "bootstrap": [True, False], \
              "criterion": ["gini", "entropy"]}
```

4. Run a randomized search. We initialize the random search object with the total number of trials we want to run, the parameter values dictionary, the scoring function, and the number of folds in the K-fold cross-validation. Then, we call the **.fit()** function to perform the search:

```
n_iter_search = 60
random_search = RandomizedSearchCV(rf_rand, \
                                   param_distributions=param_dist, \
                                   scoring='accuracy', \
                                   n_iter=n_iter_search, cv=5)
random_search.fit(X, y)
```

The output will be as follows:

```
RandomizedSearchCV(cv=5, error_score='raise-deprecating',
                estimator=RandomForestClassifier(bootstrap=True,
                                            class_weight=None,
                                            criterion='gini',
                                            max_depth=None,
                                            max_features='auto',
                                            max_leaf_nodes=None,
                                            min_impurity_decrease=0.0,
                                            min_impurity_split=None,
                                            min_samples_leaf=1,
                                            min_samples_split=2,
                                            min_weight_fraction_leaf=0.0,
                                            n_estimators='warn',
                                            n_jobs=None,
                                            oob_sc...
                        'criterion': ['gini', 'entropy'],
                        'max_depth': [3, 4, 5, 6, 7, 8, 9, 10,
                                        11, 12, 13, 14, 15, 16,
                                        17, 18, 19],
                        'max_features': [1, 2, 3, 4, 5, 6, 7, 8,
                                            9],
                        'min_samples_split': [2, 3, 4, 5, 6, 7,
                                                8, 9, 10],
                        'n_estimators': [10, 20, 30, 40, 50, 60,
                                            70, 80, 90, 100, 110,
                                            120, 130, 140, 150,
                                            160, 170, 180, 190,
                                            200]},
                pre_dispatch='2*n_jobs', random_state=None, refit=True,
                return_train_score=False, scoring='accuracy', verbose=0)
```

Figure 7.29: Output for RandomizedSearchCV

5. Print the scores and hyperparameters for the top five models. Convert the **results** dictionary into a pandas DataFrame and sort the values by **rank_test_score**. Then, for the first five rows, print the rank, mean validation score, and the hyperparameters:

```
results = pd.DataFrame(random_search.cv_results_)\
            .sort_values('rank_test_score')
for i, row in results.head().iterrows():
    print("Model rank: {}".format(row.rank_test_score))
    print("Mean validation score: {:.3f} (std: {:.3f})"\
            .format(row.mean_test_score, row.std_test_score))
    print("Model Hyperparameters: {}\n".format(row.params))
```

The output will be as follows:

```
Model rank: 1
Mean validation score: 0.722 (std: 0.055)
Model Hyperparameters: {'n_estimators': 120, 'min_samples_split': 3, 'max_features': 5, 'max_depth': 6, 'criterion': 'entropy',
'bootstrap': True}

Model rank: 2
Mean validation score: 0.721 (std: 0.049)
Model Hyperparameters: {'n_estimators': 50, 'min_samples_split': 7, 'max_features': 5, 'max_depth': 7, 'criterion': 'entropy',
'bootstrap': True}

Model rank: 2
Mean validation score: 0.721 (std: 0.048)
Model Hyperparameters: {'n_estimators': 110, 'min_samples_split': 9, 'max_features': 7, 'max_depth': 8, 'criterion': 'entropy',
'bootstrap': True}

Model rank: 4
Mean validation score: 0.719 (std: 0.037)
Model Hyperparameters: {'n_estimators': 60, 'min_samples_split': 6, 'max_features': 5, 'max_depth': 10, 'criterion': 'entropy',
'bootstrap': True}

Model rank: 4
Mean validation score: 0.719 (std: 0.052)
Model Hyperparameters: {'n_estimators': 120, 'min_samples_split': 9, 'max_features': 4, 'max_depth': 7, 'criterion': 'gini', 'b
ootstrap': False}
```

Figure 7.30: Top five models' scores and hyperparameters

6. Generate the report for random search cv results

```
report(random_search.cv_results_)
```

The output will be as follows:

```
Model with rank: 1
Mean validation score: 0.722 (std: 0.055)
Parameters: {'n_estimators': 120, 'min_samples_split': 3, 'max_features': 5, 'max_depth': 6, 'criterion':
'entropy', 'bootstrap': True}

Model with rank: 2
Mean validation score: 0.721 (std: 0.049)
Parameters: {'n_estimators': 50, 'min_samples_split': 7, 'max_features': 5, 'max_depth': 7, 'criterion':
'entropy', 'bootstrap': True}

Model with rank: 2
Mean validation score: 0.721 (std: 0.048)
Parameters: {'n_estimators': 110, 'min_samples_split': 9, 'max_features': 7, 'max_depth': 8, 'criterion':
'entropy', 'bootstrap': True}
```

Figure 7.31: Report for random search cv results

> **NOTE**
>
> To access the source code for this specific section, please refer to
> https://packt.live/314tqUX.
>
> You can also run this example online at https://packt.live/2V3YC2z.
> You must execute the entire Notebook in order to get the desired result.

We can see that the model that performs best has only 70 trees, compared to the 160+ trees in the models ranked 2 to 7. Also, the model ranked 5 only has 10 trees and still has a performance comparable to that of the more complex models. This demonstrates that the number of trees in a random forest model is not solely indicative of how well the model performs.

A model's performance is impacted by other factors, including the following:

- How many maximum features are used for a tree (**max_features**)

- How descriptive are the features selected for each tree

- How distinct are those feature sets across trees

- How many data samples are used to train each tree

- How many decisions a data instance goes through in a decision tree (**max_depth**)

- How many minimum samples are allowed in a tree leaf (**min_samples_split**) and so on.

FEATURE IMPORTANCE

While it is essential to focus on model performance, it is also important to understand how the features in our model contribute to the prediction:

- We need to be able to explain the model and how different variables affect the prediction to the relevant stakeholders who might demand insight into why our model is successful.

- The data might be biased and training a model on this data could hurt the model's performance and result in a biased model evaluation, in which case the ability to interpret the model by finding the important features and analyzing them will help debug the performance of the model.

- In addition to the previous point, it must be noted that some model biases might just be socially or legally unacceptable. For example, if a model works well because it implicitly places high importance on a feature based on ethnicity, this might cause issues.

Besides these points, finding feature importance can also help in feature selection. If the data has high dimensionality and the trained model has high variance, removing features that have low importance is one way to achieve lowered variance through dimensionality reduction.

EXERCISE 7.05: FEATURE IMPORTANCE USING RANDOM FOREST

In this exercise, we will find the feature importance from the random forest model we loaded earlier. This exercise is a continuation of *Exercise 7.04, Hyperparameter Tuning with Random Search.*

1. Find feature importance. Let's find the feature importance and save it in a pandas DataFrame with an index equal to the column names, and sort this DataFrame in descending order:

```
feat_imps = pd.DataFrame({'importance': rf.feature_importances_}, \
                         index=titanic_clf.columns[:-1])
feat_imps.sort_values(by='importance', ascending=False, \
                      inplace=True)
```

2. Plot the feature importance as a bar plot:

```
feat_imps.plot(kind='bar', figsize=(10,7))
plt.legend()
plt.show()
```

The output will be as follows:

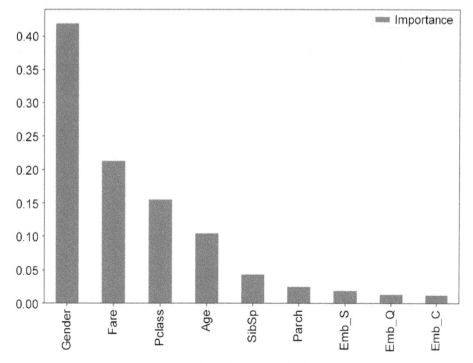

Figure 7.32: Histogram of features

Here, we can see that the **Gender**, **Fare**, and **Pclass** features seem to have the highest importance; that is, they have the greatest impact on the target variable.

> **NOTE**
>
> To access the source code for this specific section, please refer to https://packt.live/2YYnxWz.
>
> You can also run this example online at https://packt.live/2Yo896Y. You must execute the entire Notebook in order to get the desired result.

ACTIVITY 7.01: FINAL TEST PROJECT

In this activity, we'll use the *Breast Cancer Diagnosis* dataset that we used in *Chapter 5, Classification Techniques* (refer to *Activity 5.04, Breast Cancer Diagnosis Classification Using Artificial Neural Networks* for dataset details), to solve a binary classification problem wherein we have to predict whether the breast cell is benign or malignant given the features. In this problem, we want to maximize our recall; that is, we want to be able to identify all malignant cells, because if we miss any of those, we could detect no cancer, when there actually is cancer. And, we do not want to end up in that scenario.

We will use a gradient boosting classifier from scikit-learn to train the model. This activity is intended as a final project that will help consolidate the practical aspects of the concepts learned in this book, and particularly in this chapter.

We will find the most optimal set of hyperparameters for the model by using random search with cross-validation. Then, we will build the final classifier using the gradient boosting algorithm on a portion of the dataset and evaluate its performance using the classification metrics we have learned about on the remaining portion of the dataset. We will use precision and recall as the evaluation metric for this activity.

The steps to be performed are as follows:

1. Import the relevant libraries.

2. Read the **breast-cancer-data.csv** dataset.

3. Split the dataset into training and test sets.

4. Choose a base model and define the range of hyperparameter values corresponding to the model to be searched for hyperparameter tuning.

5. Define the parameters with which to initialize the **RandomizedSearchCV** object and use K-fold cross-validation to find the best model hyperparameters.

6. Split the training dataset further into training and validation sets and train a new model using the final hyperparameters on the subdivided training dataset.

7. Calculate the accuracy, precision, and recall for predictions in relation to the validation set, and print the confusion matrix.

8. Experiment with varying thresholds to find the optimal point with high recall. Plot the precision-recall curve.

The output will be as follows:

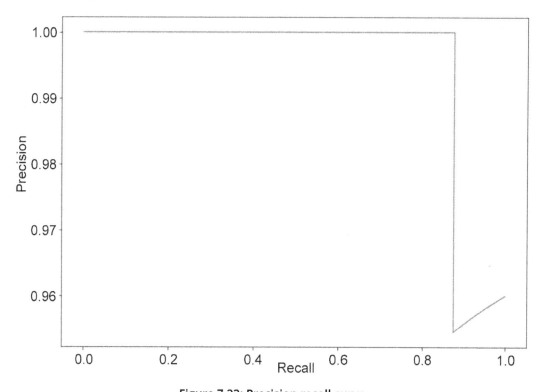

Figure 7.33: Precision recall curve

9. Finalize a threshold that will be used for predictions in relation to the test dataset.

The output will be as follows:

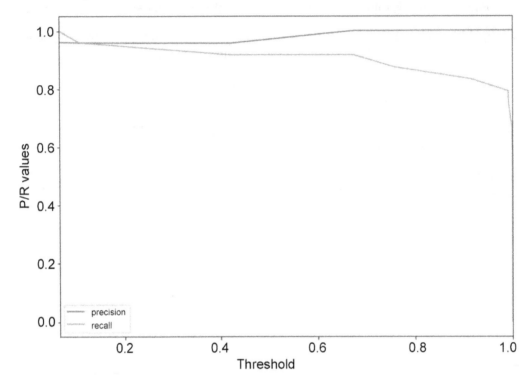

Figure 7.34: Variation in precision and recall with increasing threshold values

10. Predict the final values on the test dataset.

The output will be as follows:

```
array([1, 1, 1, 1, 1, 0, 1, 0, 0, 0, 0, 1, 0, 0, 0, 0, 1, 0, 0, 1, 1, 0,
       0, 0, 0, 0, 0, 0, 0, 0, 0, 0, 0, 0, 0, 0, 0, 0, 0, 0, 1, 0, 0,
       0, 0, 1, 0, 1, 1, 0, 0, 1, 0, 0, 0, 1, 0, 0, 0, 1, 1, 0, 0, 1, 0,
       0, 1, 0, 0, 1, 0, 0, 1, 0, 1, 1, 0, 0, 0, 0, 0, 1, 0, 1, 0, 1, 1,
       0, 0, 1, 1, 0, 0, 1, 0, 0, 0, 0, 1, 1, 0, 1, 0, 1, 1, 1, 0, 0, 0,
       0, 1, 0, 1])
```

Figure 7.35: Predictions for the cancer dataset

NOTE:

The solution to this activity can be found on page 494.

SUMMARY

This chapter discussed why model evaluation is important in supervised machine learning and looked at several important metrics that are used to evaluate regression and classification tasks. We saw that while regression models were fairly straightforward to evaluate, the performance of classification models could be measured in a number of ways, depending on what we want the model to prioritize. Besides numerical metrics, we also looked at how to plot precision-recall and ROC curves to better interpret and evaluate model performance. After this, we talked about why evaluating a model by calculating the prediction error in relation to the data that the model was trained on was a bad idea, and how testing a model on data that it has already seen would lead to the model having a high variance. With this, we introduced the concept of having a hold-out dataset and demonstrated why k-fold cross-validation is a useful strategy to have, along with sampling techniques that ensure that the model training and evaluation processes remain unbiased. The final section on performance improvement tactics started with a discussion on learning and validation curves, and how they can be interpreted to drive the model development process toward finding a better-performing model. This was followed by a section on hyperparameter tuning by way of an effort to boost performance, and a brief introduction to feature importance.

Right from the fundamentals of supervised learning and regression and classification models to the concepts of ensembling and model performance evaluation, we have now added all the necessary tools to our supervised learning toolkit. This means that we are all set to start working on real-life supervised learning projects and apply all the knowledge and skills that we have gained with this Workshop.

APPENDIX

CHAPTER 01: FUNDAMENTALS

ACTIVITY 1.01: IMPLEMENTING PANDAS FUNCTIONS

1. Open a new Jupyter notebook.

2. Use **pandas** to load the Titanic dataset:

```
import pandas as pd
df = pd.read_csv(r'../Datasets/titanic.csv')
```

3. Use the **head** function on the dataset as follows:

```
# Have a look at the first 5 sample of the data
df.head()
```

The output will be as follows:

	Unnamed: 0	Cabin	Embarked	Fare	Pclass	Ticket	Age	Name	Parch	Sex	SibSp	Survived
0	0	NaN	S	7.2500	3	A/5 21171	22.0	Braund, Mr. Owen Harris	0	male	1	0.0
1	1	C85	C	71.2833	1	PC 17599	38.0	Cumings, Mrs. John Bradley (Florence Briggs Th...	0	female	1	1.0
2	2	NaN	S	7.9250	3	STON/O2. 3101282	26.0	Heikkinen, Miss. Laina	0	female	0	1.0
3	3	C123	S	53.1000	1	113803	35.0	Futrelle, Mrs. Jacques Heath (Lily May Peel)	0	female	1	1.0
4	4	NaN	S	8.0500	3	373450	35.0	Allen, Mr. William Henry	0	male	0	0.0

Figure 1.26: First five rows

4. Use the **describe** function as follows:

```
df.describe(include='all')
```

The output will be as follows:

	Unnamed: 0	Cabin	Embarked	Fare	Pclass	Ticket	Age	Name	Parch	Sex
count	1309.000000	295	1307	1308.000000	1309.000000	1309	1046.000000	1309	1309.000000	1309
unique	NaN	186	3	NaN	NaN	929	NaN	1307	NaN	2
top	NaN	C23 C25 C27	S	NaN	NaN	CA. 2343	NaN	Connolly, Miss. Kate	NaN	male
freq	NaN	6	914	NaN	NaN	11	NaN	2	NaN	843
mean	654.000000	NaN	NaN	33.295479	2.294882	NaN	29.881138	NaN	0.385027	NaN
std	378.020061	NaN	NaN	51.758668	0.837836	NaN	14.413493	NaN	0.865560	NaN
min	0.000000	NaN	NaN	0.000000	1.000000	NaN	0.170000	NaN	0.000000	NaN
25%	327.000000	NaN	NaN	7.895800	2.000000	NaN	21.000000	NaN	0.000000	NaN
50%	654.000000	NaN	NaN	14.454200	3.000000	NaN	28.000000	NaN	0.000000	NaN
75%	981.000000	NaN	NaN	31.275000	3.000000	NaN	39.000000	NaN	0.000000	NaN
max	1308.000000	NaN	NaN	512.329200	3.000000	NaN	80.000000	NaN	9.000000	NaN

Figure 1.27: Output of describe()

5. We do not need the **Unnamed: 0** column. We can remove the column without using the **del** command, as follows:

```
del df['Unnamed: 0']
df = df[df.columns[1:]] # Use the columns
df.head()
```

The output will be as follows:

	Embarked	Fare	Pclass	Ticket	Age	Name	Parch	Sex	SibSp	Survived
0	S	7.2500	3	A/5 21171	22.0	Braund, Mr. Owen Harris	0	male	1	0.0
1	C	71.2833	1	PC 17599	38.0	Cumings, Mrs. John Bradley (Florence Briggs Th...	0	female	1	1.0
2	S	7.9250	3	STON/O2. 3101282	26.0	Heikkinen, Miss. Laina	0	female	0	1.0
3	S	53.1000	1	113803	35.0	Futrelle, Mrs. Jacques Heath (Lily May Peel)	0	female	1	1.0
4	S	8.0500	3	373450	35.0	Allen, Mr. William Henry	0	male	0	0.0

Figure 1.28: First five rows after deleting the Unnamed: 0 column

6. Compute the mean, standard deviation, minimum, and maximum values for the columns of the DataFrame without using **describe**:

```
df.mean()
```

The output will be as follows:

```
Fare            33.295479
Pclass           2.294882
Age             29.881138
Parch            0.385027
SibSp            0.498854
Survived         0.383838
dtype: float64
```

Figure 1.29: Output for mean()

Now, calculate the standard deviation:

```
df.std()
```

The output will be as follows:

```
Fare            51.758668
Pclass           0.837836
Age             14.413493
Parch            0.865560
SibSp            1.041658
Survived         0.486592
dtype: float64
```

Figure 1.30: Output for std()

7. Calculate the minimum value of the columns:

```
df.min()
```

The output will be as follows:

```
Fare          0.00
Pclass        1.00
Age           0.17
Parch         0.00
SibSp         0.00
Survived      0.00
dtype: float64
```

Figure 1.31: Output for min()

Next, calculate the maximum value of the column of the dataframe.

```
df.max()
```

The output will be as follows:

```
Fare        512.3292
Pclass        3.0000
Age          80.0000
Parch         9.0000
SibSp         8.0000
Survived      1.0000
dtype: float64
```

Figure 1.32: Output for max()

8. Use the quantile method for the 33, 66, and 99% quantiles, as shown in the following code snippet:

```
df.quantile(0.33)
```

The output will be as follows:

```
Fare          8.559325
Pclass        2.000000
Age          23.000000
Parch         0.000000
SibSp         0.000000
Survived      0.000000
Name: 0.33, dtype: float64
```

Figure 1.33: Output for the 33% quantile

Similarly, use the quantile method for 66%:

```
df.quantile(0.66)
```

The output will be as follows:

```
Fare          26.0
Pclass         3.0
Age           34.0
Parch          0.0
SibSp          0.0
Survived       1.0
Name: 0.66, dtype: float64
```

Figure 1.34: Output for the 66% quantile

Use the same method for 99%:

```
df.quantile(0.99)
```

The output will be as follows:

```
Fare          262.375
Pclass          3.000
Age            65.000
Parch           4.000
SibSp           5.000
Survived        1.000
Name: 0.99, dtype: float64
```

Figure 1.35: Output for the 99% quantile

9. Find out how many passengers were from each class using the **groupby** method:

```
class_groups = df.groupby('Pclass')
for name, index in class_groups:
    print(f'Class: {name}: {len(index)}')
```

The output will be as follows:

```
Class: 1: 323
Class: 2: 277
Class: 3: 709
```

10. Find out how many passengers were from each class by using selecting/indexing methods to count the members of each class:

```
for clsGrp in df.Pclass.unique():
    num_class = len(df[df.Pclass == clsGrp])
    print(f'Class {clsGrp}: {num_class}')
```

The result will be as follows:

```
Class 3: 709
Class 1: 323
Class 2: 277
```

The answers to *Step 6* and *Step 7* do match.

11. Determine who the eldest passenger in third class was:

```
third_class = df.loc[(df.Pclass == 3)]
third_class.loc[(third_class.Age == third_class.Age.max())]
```

The output will be as follows:

	Embarked	Fare	Pclass	Ticket	Age	Name	Parch	Sex	SibSp	Survived
851	S	7.775	3	347060	74.0	Svensson, Mr. Johan	0	male	0	0.0

Figure 1.36: Eldest passenger in third class

12. For a number of machine learning problems, it is very common to scale the numerical values between **0** and **1**. Use the **agg** method with Lambda functions to scale the **Fare** and **Age** columns between 0 and 1:

```
fare_max = df.Fare.max()
age_max = df.Age.max()
df.agg({'Fare': lambda x: x / fare_max, \
        'Age': lambda x: x / age_max,}).head()
```

The output will be as follows:

	Fare	Age
0	0.014151	0.2750
1	0.139136	0.4750
2	0.015469	0.3250
3	0.103644	0.4375
4	0.015713	0.4375

Figure 1.37: Scaling numerical values between 0 and 1

13. Identify the one individual entry in the dataset without a listed **Fare** value:

```
df_nan_fare = df.loc[(df.Fare.isna())]
df_nan_fare
```

The output will be as follows:

	Embarked	Fare	Pclass	Ticket	Age	Name	Parch	Sex	SibSp	Survived
1043	S	NaN	3	3701	60.5	Storey, Mr. Thomas	0	male	0	NaN

Figure 1.38: Individual without a listed fare value

14. Replace the NaN values of this row in the main DataFrame with the mean **Fare** value for those corresponding to the same class and **Embarked** location using the **groupby** method:

```
embarked_class_groups = df.groupby(['Embarked', 'Pclass'])
indices = embarked_class_groups\
        .groups[(df_nan_fare.Embarked.values[0], \
            df_nan_fare.Pclass.values[0])]
mean_fare = df.iloc[indices].Fare.mean()
df.loc[(df.index == 1043), 'Fare'] = mean_fare
df.iloc[1043]
```

The output will be as follows:

```
Embarked                          S
Fare                        14.4354
Pclass                            3
Ticket                         3701
Age                            60.5
Name          Storey, Mr. Thomas
Parch                             0
Sex                            male
SibSp                             0
Survived                        NaN
Name: 1043, dtype: object
```

Figure 1.39: Output for the individual without listed fare details

> **NOTE**
>
> To access the source code for this specific section, please refer to https://packt.live/2AWHbu0.
>
> You can also run this example online at https://packt.live/2NmAnse. You must execute the entire Notebook in order to get the desired result.

CHAPTER 02: EXPLORATORY DATA ANALYSIS AND VISUALIZATION

ACTIVITY 2.01: SUMMARY STATISTICS AND MISSING VALUES

The steps to complete this activity are as follows:

1. Import the required libraries:

```
import json
import pandas as pd
import numpy as np
import missingno as msno
from sklearn.impute import SimpleImputer
import matplotlib.pyplot as plt
import seaborn as sns
```

2. Read the data. Use pandas' **.read_csv** method to read the CSV file into a pandas **DataFrame**:

```
data = pd.read_csv('../Datasets/house_prices.csv')
```

3. Use pandas' **.info()** and **.describe()** methods to view the summary statistics of the dataset:

```
data.info()
data.describe().T
```

The output of **info()** will be as follows:

```
<class 'pandas.core.frame.DataFrame'>
RangeIndex: 1460 entries, 0 to 1459
Data columns (total 81 columns):
Id               1460 non-null int64
MSSubClass       1460 non-null int64
MSZoning         1460 non-null object
LotFrontage      1201 non-null float64
LotArea          1460 non-null int64
Street           1460 non-null object
Alley            91 non-null object
LotShape         1460 non-null object
LandContour      1460 non-null object
Utilities        1460 non-null object
LotConfig        1460 non-null object
LandSlope        1460 non-null object
Neighborhood     1460 non-null object
Condition1       1460 non-null object
Condition2       1460 non-null object
BldgType         1460 non-null object
```

Figure 2.50: The output of the info() method (abbreviated)

The output of **describe()** will be as follows:

	count	mean	std	min	25%	50%	75%	max
Id	1460.0	730.500000	421.610009	1.0	365.75	730.5	1095.25	1460.0
MSSubClass	1460.0	56.897260	42.300571	20.0	20.00	50.0	70.00	190.0
LotFrontage	1201.0	70.049958	24.284752	21.0	59.00	69.0	80.00	313.0
LotArea	1460.0	10516.828082	9981.264932	1300.0	7553.50	9478.5	11601.50	215245.0
OverallQual	1460.0	6.099315	1.382997	1.0	5.00	6.0	7.00	10.0
OverallCond	1460.0	5.575342	1.112799	1.0	5.00	5.0	6.00	9.0
YearBuilt	1460.0	1971.267808	30.202904	1872.0	1954.00	1973.0	2000.00	2010.0
YearRemodAdd	1460.0	1984.865753	20.645407	1950.0	1967.00	1994.0	2004.00	2010.0
MasVnrArea	1452.0	103.685262	181.066207	0.0	0.00	0.0	166.00	1600.0
BsmtFinSF1	1460.0	443.639726	456.098091	0.0	0.00	383.5	712.25	5644.0
BsmtFinSF2	1460.0	46.549315	161.319273	0.0	0.00	0.0	0.00	1474.0
BsmtUnfSF	1460.0	567.240411	441.866955	0.0	223.00	477.5	808.00	2336.0
TotalBsmtSF	1460.0	1057.429452	438.705324	0.0	795.75	991.5	1298.25	6110.0
1stFlrSF	1460.0	1162.626712	386.587738	334.0	882.00	1087.0	1391.25	4692.0

Figure 2.51: The output of the describe() method (abbreviated)

4. Find the total count and total percentage of missing values in each column of the DataFrame and display them for columns having at least one null value, in descending order of missing percentages.

As we did in *Exercise 2.02: Visualizing Missing Values*, we will use the `.isnull()` function on the **DataFrame** to get a mask, find the count of null values in each column by using the `.sum()` function over the **DataFrame** mask and the fraction of null values by using `.mean()` over the **DataFrame** mask, and multiply by 100 to convert it to a percentage. Then, we'll use `pd.concat()` to combine the total and percentage of null values into a single DataFrame and sort the rows according to the percentage of missing values:

```
mask = data.isnull()
total = mask.sum()
percent = 100*mask.mean()
#
missing_data = pd.concat([total, percent], axis=1,join='outer', \
                    keys=['count_missing', 'perc_missing'])
missing_data.sort_values(by='perc_missing', ascending=False, \
                    inplace=True)
#
missing_data[missing_data.count_missing > 0]
```

The output will be as follows:

	count_missing	perc_missing
PoolQC	1453	99.520548
MiscFeature	1406	96.301370
Alley	1369	93.767123
Fence	1179	80.753425
FireplaceQu	690	47.260274
LotFrontage	259	17.739726
GarageYrBlt	81	5.547945
GarageCond	81	5.547945
GarageType	81	5.547945
GarageFinish	81	5.547945
GarageQual	81	5.547945
BsmtFinType2	38	2.602740
BsmtExposure	38	2.602740

Figure 2.52: Total count and percentage of missing values in each column

5. Plot the nullity matrix and nullity correlation heatmap. First, we find the
    list of column names for those having at least one null value. Then, we use
    the **missingno** library to plot the nullity matrix (as we did in *Exercise 2.02:
    Visualizing Missing Values*) for a sample of 500 points, and the nullity correlation
    heatmap for the data in those columns:

```
nullable_columns = data.columns[mask.any()].tolist()
msno.matrix(data[nullable_columns].sample(500))
plt.show()

msno.heatmap(data[nullable_columns], vmin = -0.1, \
             figsize=(18,18))
plt.show()
```

The nullity matrix will look like this:

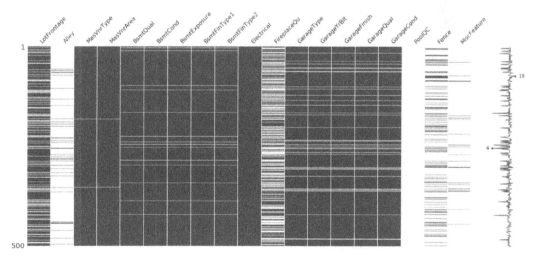

Figure 2.53: Nullity matrix

The nullity correlation heatmap will look like this:

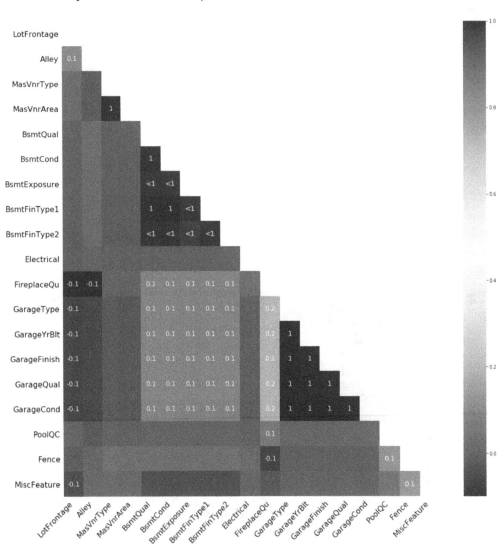

Figure 2.54: Nullity correlation heatmap

6. Delete the columns having more than 80% of values missing. Use the `.loc` operator on the **DataFrame** we created in *Step 2* to select only those columns that had fewer than 80% of their values missing:

```
data = data.loc[:,missing_data[missing_data.perc_missing < 80].index]
```

7. Replace null values in the **FireplaceQu** column with **NA** values. Use the **.fillna()** method to replace null values with the **NA** string:

```
data['FireplaceQu'] = data['FireplaceQu'].fillna('NA')
data['FireplaceQu']
```

The output should appear as follows:

```
0          NA
1          TA
2          TA
3          Gd
4          TA
         ..
1455       TA
1456       TA
1457       Gd
1458       NA
1459       NA
Name: FireplaceQu, Length: 1460, d
type: object
```

Figure 2.55: Replacing null values

NOTE

To access the source code for this specific section, please refer to https://packt.live/316c4a0.

You can also run this example online at https://packt.live/2Z21v5c. You must execute the entire Notebook in order to get the desired result.

ACTIVITY 2.02: REPRESENTING THE DISTRIBUTION OF VALUES VISUALLY

1. Plot a histogram using Matplotlib for the target variable, **SalePrice**. First, we
    initialize the figure using the **plt.figure** command and set the figure size.
    Then, we use matplotlib's **.hist()** function as our primary plotting function, to
    which we pass the **SalePrice** series object for plotting the histogram. Lastly,
    we specify the axes' labels and show the plot:

```
plt.figure(figsize=(8,6))
plt.hist(data.SalePrice, bins=range(0,800000,50000))
plt.ylabel('Number of Houses')
plt.xlabel('Sale Price')
plt.show()
```

The output will be as follows:

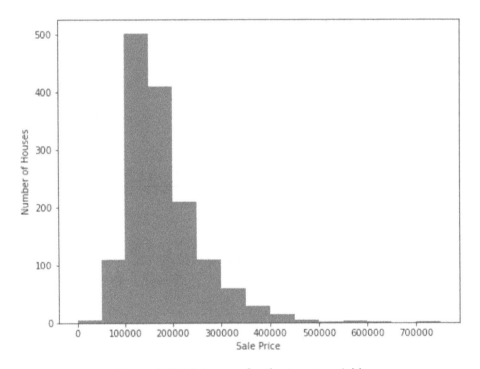

Figure 2.56: Histogram for the target variable

2. Find the number of unique values within each column having the object type. Create a new DataFrame called **object_variables** by using the **.select_ dtypes** function on the original DataFrame to select those columns with the **numpy.object** data type. Then, find the number of unique values for each column in this DataFrame by using the **.nunique()** function, and sort the resultant series:

```
object_variables = data.select_dtypes(include=[np.object])
object_variables.nunique().sort_values()
```

The output will be as follows:

Street	2
Alley	2
CentralAir	2
Utilities	2
LandSlope	3
PoolQC	3
PavedDrive	3
GarageFinish	3
BsmtQual	4
ExterQual	4
MasVnrType	4
KitchenQual	4
BsmtCond	4
BsmtExposure	4

Figure 2.57: Number of unique values within each column having the object type (truncated)

3. Create a DataFrame representing the number of occurrences for each categorical value in the **HouseStyle** column. Use the **.value_counts()** function to calculate the frequencies of each value in decreasing order in the form of a pandas series, and then reset the index to give us a **DataFrame** and sort the values according to the index:

```
counts = data.HouseStyle.value_counts(dropna=False)
counts.reset_index().sort_values(by='index')
```

The output will be as follows:

	index	HouseStyle
2	1.5Fin	154
5	1.5Unf	14
0	1Story	726
7	2.5Fin	8
6	2.5Unf	11
1	2Story	445
4	SFoyer	37
3	SLvl	65

Figure 2.58: Number of occurrences of each categorical value in the HouseStyle column

4. Plot a pie chart representing these counts. As in *Step 1*, we initialize the plot using **plt.figure()** and use the **plt.title()** and **plt.show()** methods to set the figure title and display it, respectively. The primary plotting function used is **plt.pie()**, to which we pass the series we created in the previous step:

```
fig, ax = plt.subplots(figsize=(10,10))
slices = ax.pie(counts, labels = counts.index, \
                colors = ['white'], \
                wedgeprops = {'edgecolor': 'black'})
patches = slices[0]
hatches =  ['/', '\\', '|', '-', '+', 'x', 'o', 'O', '\.', '*']
colors = ['white', 'white', 'lightgrey', 'white', \
          'lightgrey', 'white', 'lightgrey', 'white']
for patch in range(len(patches)):
    patches[patch].set_hatch(hatches[patch])
    patches[patch].set_facecolor(colors[patch])
plt.title('Pie chart showing counts for\nvarious house styles')
plt.show()
```

The output will be as follows:

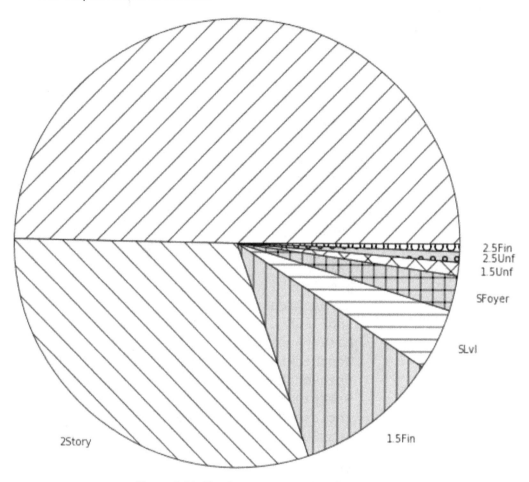

Figure 2.59: Pie chart representing the counts

5. Find the number of unique values within each column having the number type. As was executed in *Step 2*, now select columns having the **numpy.number** data type and find the number of unique values in each column using **.nunique()**. Sort the resultant series in descending order:

```
numeric_variables = data.select_dtypes(include=[np.number])
numeric_variables.nunique().sort_values(ascending=False)
```

The output will be as follows:

Id	1460
LotArea	1073
GrLivArea	861
BsmtUnfSF	780
1stFlrSF	753
TotalBsmtSF	721
SalePrice	663
BsmtFinSF1	637
GarageArea	441
2ndFlrSF	417
MasVnrArea	327
WoodDeckSF	274
OpenPorchSF	202
BsmtFinSF2	144
EnclosedPorch	120
YearBuilt	112

Figure 2.60: Number of unique values within each numeric column (truncated)

6. Plot a histogram using seaborn for the **LotArea** variable. Use seaborn's **.distplot()** function as the primary plotting function, to which the **LotArea** series in the DataFrame needs to be passed (without any null values, use **.dropna()** on the series to remove them). To improve the plot view, also set the **bins** parameter and specify the *X*-axis limits using **plt.xlim()**:

```
plt.figure(figsize=(10,7))
sns.distplot(data.LotArea.dropna(), bins=range(0,100000,1000))
plt.xlim(0,100000)
plt.show()
```

The output will be as follows:

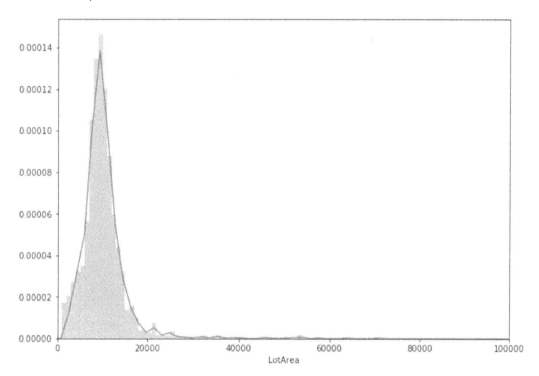

Figure 2.61: Histogram for the LotArea variable

7. Calculate the skew and kurtosis values for the values in each column:

```
data.skew().sort_values()
data.kurt()
```

The output for skew values will be:

```
GarageYrBlt       -0.649415
YearBuilt         -0.613461
YearRemodAdd      -0.503562
GarageCars        -0.342549
Id                 0.000000
FullBath           0.036562
YrSold             0.096269
GarageArea         0.179981
BedroomAbvGr       0.211790
MoSold             0.212053
OverallQual        0.216944
BsmtFullBath       0.596067
Fireplaces         0.649565
HalfBath           0.675897
TotRmsAbvGrd       0.676341
```

Figure 2.62: Skew values for each column (truncated)

The output for kurtosis values will be:

```
Id                -1.200000
MSSubClass         1.580188
LotFrontage       17.452867
LotArea          203.243271
OverallQual        0.096293
OverallCond        1.106413
YearBuilt         -0.439552
YearRemodAdd      -1.272245
MasVnrArea        10.082417
BsmtFinSF1        11.118236
BsmtFinSF2        20.113338
BsmtUnfSF          0.474994
TotalBsmtSF       13.250483
1stFlrSF           5.745841
2ndFlrSF          -0.553464
LowQualFinSF      83.234817
GrLivArea          4.895121
```

Figure 2.63: Kurtosis values for each column (truncated)

> **NOTE**
>
> To access the source code for this specific section, please refer to
> https://packt.live/3fR91qj.
>
> You can also run this example online at https://packt.live/37PYOI4.
> You must execute the entire Notebook in order to get the desired result.

ACTIVITY 2.03: RELATIONSHIPS WITHIN THE DATA

1. Plot the correlation heatmap for the dataset. As we did in *Exercise 2.13: Plotting a Correlation Heatmap*, plot the heatmap using seaborn's **.heatmap()** function and pass the feature correlation matrix (as determined by using pandas' **.corr()** function on the DataFrame). Additionally, set the color map to **RdBu** using the **cmap** parameter, and the minimum and maximum values on the color scale to **-1** and **1** using the **vmin** and **vmax** parameters, respectively:

```
plt.figure(figsize = (12,10))
sns.heatmap(data.corr(), square=True, cmap="RdBu", \
            vmin=-1, vmax=1)
plt.show()
```

The output will be as follows:

Figure 2.64: Correlation heatmap for the dataset

2. Plot a more compact heatmap having annotations for correlation values using the following subset of features:

```
feature_subset = ['GarageArea','GarageCars','GarageCond', \
                  'GarageFinish', 'GarageQual','GarageType', \
                  'GarageYrBlt','GrLivArea','LotArea', \
                  'MasVnrArea','SalePrice']
```

Now do the same as in the previous step, this time selecting only the above columns in the dataset and adding a parameter, **annot**, with a **True** value to the primary plotting function, with everything else remaining the same:

```
plt.figure(figsize = (12,10))
sns.heatmap(data[feature_subset].corr(), square=True, \
           annot=True, cmap="RdBu", vmin=-1, vmax=1)
plt.show()
```

The output will be as follows:

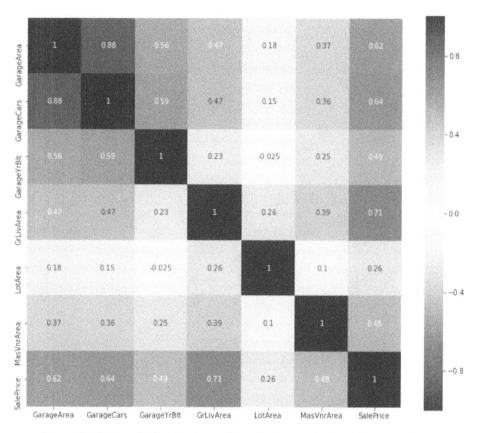

Figure 2.65: Correlation heatmap for a feature subset with annotations
for correlation values

3. Display the pairplot for the same subset of features, with the KDE plot on
    the diagonals and the scatter plot elsewhere. Use seaborn's **.pairplot()**
    function to plot the pairplot for the non-null values in the selected columns of
    the DataFrame. To render the diagonal KDE plots, pass **kde** to the **diag_kind**
    parameter and, to set all other plots as scatter plots, pass **scatter** to the
    kind parameter:

```
sns.pairplot(data[feature_subset].dropna(), \
            kind ='scatter', diag_kind='kde')
plt.show()
```

The output will be as follows:

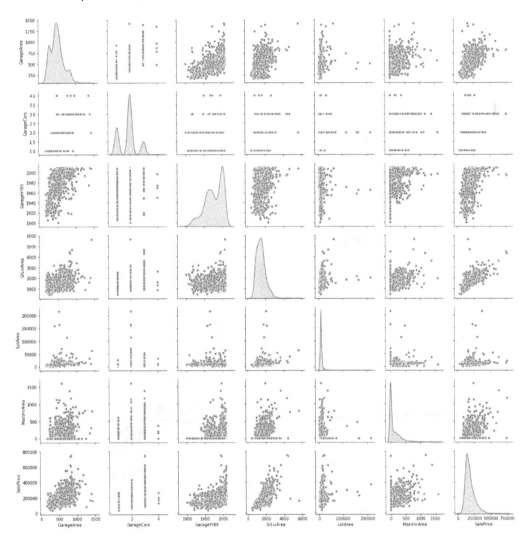

Figure 2.66: Pairplot for the same subset of features

4. Create a boxplot to show the variation in **SalePrice** for each category of **GarageCars**. The primary plotting function used here will be seaborn's **.boxplot()** function, to which we pass the DataFrame along with the parameters **x** and **y**, the former being the categorical variable and the latter the continuous variable over which we want to see the variation within each category, that is, **GarageCars** and **SalePrice**, respectively:

```
plt.figure(figsize=(10, 10))
sns.boxplot(x='GarageCars', y="SalePrice", data=data)
plt.show()
```

The output will be as follows:

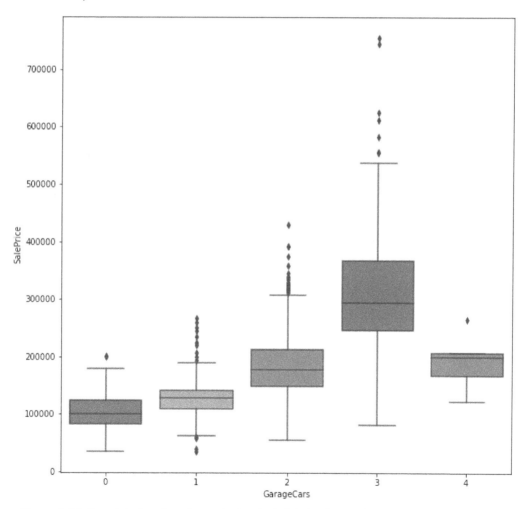

Figure 2.67: Boxplot showing the variation in SalePrice for each category of GarageCars

5. Plot a line graph using seaborn to show the variation in **SalePrice** for older to more recently built flats. Here, we will plot a line graph using seaborn's **.lineplot()** function. Since we want to see the variation in **SalePrice**, we take this as the **y** variable and, since the variation is across a period of time, we take **YearBuilt** as the **x** variable. Keeping this in mind, we pass the respective series as values to the **y** and **x** parameters for the primary plotting function. We also pass a **ci=None** parameter to hide the standard deviation indicator around the line in the plot:

```
plt.figure(figsize=(10,7))
sns.lineplot(x=data.YearBuilt, y=data.SalePrice, ci=None)
plt.show()
```

The output will be as follows:

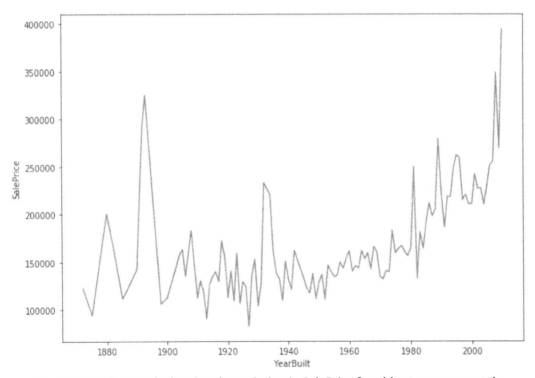

Figure 2.68: Line graph showing the variation in SalePrice for older to more recently built flats

Figure 2.68 illustrates how to use a line chart to emphasize both overall trends and the ups and downs on shorter time cycles. You may want to compare this chart to a scatter chart of the same data and consider what sort of information each conveys.

> **NOTE**
>
> To access the source code for this specific section, please refer to https://packt.live/2Z4bqHM.
>
> You can also run this example online at https://packt.live/2NI5ggl. You must execute the entire Notebook in order to get the desired result.

CHAPTER 03: LINEAR REGRESSION

ACTIVITY 3.01: PLOTTING DATA WITH A MOVING AVERAGE

1. Load the two required packages:

```
import pandas as pd
import matplotlib.pyplot as plt
```

2. Load the dataset into a pandas DataFrame from the CSV file:

```
df = pd.read_csv('../Datasets/austin_weather.csv')
df.head()
```

The output will show the initial five rows of the **austin_weather.csv** file:

	Date	TempHighF	TempAvgF	TempLowF	DewPointHighF	DewPointAvgF	DewPointLowF	HumidityHighPercent
0	2013-12-21	74	60	45	67	49	43	93
1	2013-12-22	56	48	39	43	36	28	93
2	2013-12-23	58	45	32	31	27	23	76
3	2013-12-24	61	46	31	36	28	21	89
4	2013-12-25	58	50	41	44	40	36	86

Figure 3.61: The first five rows of the Austin weather data (note that additional columns to the right are not shown)

3. Since we only need the **Date** and **TempAvgF** columns, we'll remove all the other columns from the dataset:

```
df = df.loc[:, ['Date', 'TempAvgF']]
df.head()
```

The output will be as follows:

	Date	TempAvgF
0	2013-12-21	60
1	2013-12-22	48
2	2013-12-23	45
3	2013-12-24	46
4	2013-12-25	50

Figure 3.62: Date and TempAvgF columns of the Austin weather data

4. Initially, we are only interested in the first year's data, so we need to extract that information only. Create a column in the DataFrame for the year value, extract the year value as an integer from the strings in the **Date** column, and assign these values to the **Year** column (note that temperatures are recorded daily). Repeat the process to create the **Month** and **Day** columns, and then extract the first year's worth of data:

```
df.loc[:, 'Year'] = df.loc[:, 'Date'].str.slice(0, 4).astype('int')
df.loc[:, 'Month'] = df.loc[:, 'Date'].str.slice(5, 7).astype('int')
df.loc[:, 'Day'] = df.loc[:, 'Date'].str.slice(8, 10).astype('int')
df = df.loc[df.index < 365]
print(df.head())
print(df.tail())
```

The output will be as follows:

```
          Date  TempAvgF  Year  Month  Day
0   2013-12-21        60  2013     12   21
1   2013-12-22        48  2013     12   22
2   2013-12-23        45  2013     12   23
3   2013-12-24        46  2013     12   24
4   2013-12-25        50  2013     12   25
            Date  TempAvgF  Year  Month  Day
360   2014-12-16        55  2014     12   16
361   2014-12-17        51  2014     12   17
362   2014-12-18        55  2014     12   18
363   2014-12-19        53  2014     12   19
364   2014-12-20        52  2014     12   20
```

Figure 3.63: New DataFrame with one year's worth of data

5. Compute a 20-day moving average using the **rolling()** method:

```
window = 20
rolling = df.TempAvgF.rolling(window).mean()
print(rolling.head())
print(rolling.tail())
```

The output will be as follows:

```
0       NaN
1       NaN
2       NaN
3       NaN
4       NaN
Name: TempAvgF, dtype: float64
360     59.8
361     59.7
362     59.6
363     59.0
364     58.0
Name: TempAvgF, dtype: float64
```

Figure 3.64: DataFrame with moving average data

6. Plot the raw data and the moving averages, with the *x* axis as the day number in the year:

```
fig = plt.figure(figsize=(10, 7))
ax = fig.add_axes([1, 1, 1, 1]);
# Raw data
ax.scatter(df.index, df.TempAvgF, \
           label = 'Raw Data', c = 'k')
# Moving averages
ax.plot(rolling.index, rolling, c = 'r', \
        linestyle = '--', label = f'{window} day moving average')
ax.set_title('Air Temperature Measurements', fontsize = 16)
ax.set_xlabel('Day', fontsize = 14)
ax.set_ylabel('Temperature ($^\circ$F)', fontsize = 14)
ax.set_xticks(range(df.index.min(), df.index.max(), 30))
ax.tick_params(labelsize = 12)
ax.legend(fontsize = 12)
plt.show()
```

The output will be as follows:

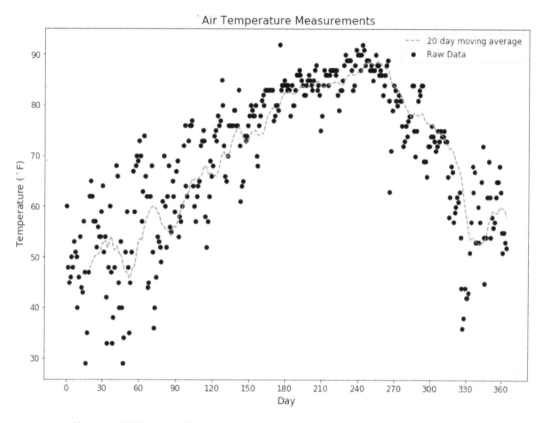

Figure 3.65: Temperature data with the 20-day moving average overlaid

> **NOTE**
>
> To access the source code for this specific section, please refer to
> https://packt.live/2NI5m85.
>
> You can also run this example online at https://packt.live/3epJvs6.
> You must execute the entire Notebook in order to get the desired result.

ACTIVITY 3.02: LINEAR REGRESSION USING THE LEAST SQUARES METHOD

1. Import the required packages and classes:

```
import pandas as pd
import matplotlib.pyplot as plt
from sklearn.linear_model import LinearRegression
```

2. Load the data from the CSV (**austin_weather.csv**) and inspect the data (using the **head()** and **tail()** methods):

```
# load data and inspect
df = pd.read_csv('../Datasets/austin_weather.csv')
print(df.head())
print(df.tail())
```

The output for **df.head()** will be as follows:

```
        Date  TempHighF  TempAvgF  TempLowF  DewPointHighF  DewPointAvgF  \
0  2013-12-21         74        60        45             67            49
1  2013-12-22         56        48        39             43            36
2  2013-12-23         58        45        32             31            27
3  2013-12-24         61        46        31             36            28
4  2013-12-25         58        50        41             44            40

   DewPointLowF  HumidityHighPercent  HumidityAvgPercent  HumidityLowPercent  ... \
0            43                   93                  75                  57  ...
1            28                   93                  68                  43  ...
2            23                   76                  52                  27  ...
3            21                   89                  56                  22  ...
4            36                   86                  71                  56  ...

   SeaLevelPressureAvgInches  SeaLevelPressureLowInches  VisibilityHighMiles  \
0                      29.68                      29.59                   10
1                      30.13                      29.87                   10
2                      30.49                      30.41                   10
3                      30.45                       30.3                   10
4                      30.33                      30.27                   10

   VisibilityAvgMiles  VisibilityLowMiles  WindHighMPH  WindAvgMPH  WindGustMPH  \
0                   7                   2           20           4           31
1                  10                   5           16           6           25
2                  10                  10            8           3           12
3                  10                   7           12           4           20
4                  10                   7           10           2           16

   PrecipitationSumInches                Events
0                    0.46  Rain , Thunderstorm
1                       0
2                       0
3                       0
4                       T

[5 rows x 21 columns]
```

Figure 3.66: Output for df.head()

The output for **df.tail()** will be as follows:

```
          Date  TempHighF  TempAvgF  TempLowF  DewPointHighF  DewPointAvgF  \
1314  2017-07-27        103        89        75             71            67
1315  2017-07-28        105        91        76             71            64
1316  2017-07-29        107        92        77             72            64
1317  2017-07-30        106        93        79             70            68
1318  2017-07-31         99        88        77             66            61

      DewPointLowF  HumidityHighPercent  HumidityAvgPercent  HumidityLowPercent  \
1314            61                   82                  54                  25
1315            55                   87                  54                  20
1316            55                   82                  51                  19
1317            63                   69                  48                  27
1318            54                   64                  43                  22

      ...  SeaLevelPressureAvgInches  SeaLevelPressureLowInches  \
1314  ...                      29.97                      29.88
1315  ...                       29.9                      29.81
1316  ...                      29.86                      29.79
1317  ...                      29.91                      29.87
1318  ...                      29.97                      29.91

      VisibilityHighMiles  VisibilityAvgMiles  VisibilityLowMiles  WindHighMPH  \
1314                   10                  10                  10           12
1315                   10                  10                  10           14
1316                   10                  10                  10           12
1317                   10                  10                  10           13
1318                   10                  10                  10           12

      WindAvgMPH  WindGustMPH  PrecipitationSumInches  Events
1314           5           21                       0
1315           5           20                       0
1316           4           17                       0
1317           4           20                       0
1318           4           20                       0

[5 rows x 21 columns]
```

Figure 3.67: Output for df.tail()

3. Drop everything except the **Date** and **TempAvgF** columns:

```
df = df.loc[:, ['Date', 'TempAvgF']]
df.head()
```

The output will be as follows:

	Date	TempAvgF
0	2013-12-21	60
1	2013-12-22	48
2	2013-12-23	45
3	2013-12-24	46
4	2013-12-25	50

Figure 3.68: Two columns used for Activity 3.02

4. Create new **Year**, **Month**, and **Day** columns and populate them by parsing the **Date** column:

```
# add some useful columns
df.loc[:, 'Year'] = df.loc[:, 'Date']\
                    .str.slice(0, 4).astype('int')
df.loc[:, 'Month'] = df.loc[:, 'Date']\
                    .str.slice(5, 7).astype('int')
df.loc[:, 'Day'] = df.loc[:, 'Date']\
                    .str.slice(8, 10).astype('int')
print(df.head())
print(df.tail())
```

The output will be as follows:

```
        Date  TempAvgF  Year  Month  Day
0  2013-12-21        60  2013     12   21
1  2013-12-22        48  2013     12   22
2  2013-12-23        45  2013     12   23
3  2013-12-24        46  2013     12   24
4  2013-12-25        50  2013     12   25
           Date  TempAvgF  Year  Month  Day
1314  2017-07-27        89  2017      7   27
1315  2017-07-28        91  2017      7   28
1316  2017-07-29        92  2017      7   29
1317  2017-07-30        93  2017      7   30
1318  2017-07-31        88  2017      7   31
```

Figure 3.69: Augmented data

5. Create a new column for a moving average and populate it with a 20-day moving average of the **TempAvgF** column:

```
"""
set a 20 day window then use that to smooth temperature in a new
column
"""
window = 20
df['20_d_mov_avg'] = df.TempAvgF.rolling(window).mean()
print(df.head())
print(df.tail())
```

The output will be as follows:

```
          Date  TempAvgF  Year  Month  Day  20_d_mov_avg
0   2013-12-21        60  2013     12   21           NaN
1   2013-12-22        48  2013     12   22           NaN
2   2013-12-23        45  2013     12   23           NaN
3   2013-12-24        46  2013     12   24           NaN
4   2013-12-25        50  2013     12   25           NaN
            Date  TempAvgF   Year  Month   Day   20_d_mov_avg
1314  2017-07-27        89   2017      7    27          88.95
1315  2017-07-28        91   2017      7    28          89.10
1316  2017-07-29        92   2017      7    29          89.25
1317  2017-07-30        93   2017      7    30          89.50
1318  2017-07-31        88   2017      7    31          89.45
```

Figure 3.70: Addition of the 20-day moving average

6. Slice one complete year of data to use in a model. Ensure the year doesn't have missing data due to the moving average. Also create a column for **Day_of_Year** (it should start at 1):

```
"""
now let's slice exactly one year on the
calendar start and end dates
we see from the previous output that
2014 is the first year with complete data,
however it will still have NaN values for
the moving average, so we'll use 2015
"""
df_one_year = df.loc[df.Year == 2015, :].reset_index()
df_one_year['Day_of_Year'] = df_one_year.index + 1
print(df_one_year.head())
print(df_one_year.tail())
```

The output will be as follows:

```
     index          Date  TempAvgF  Year  Month  Day  20_d_mov_avg  Day_of_Year
0      376   2015-01-01        37   2015      1    1         52.70            1
1      377   2015-01-02        41   2015      1    2         51.50            2
2      378   2015-01-03        51   2015      1    3         50.65            3
3      379   2015-01-04        43   2015      1    4         49.65            4
4      380   2015-01-05        41   2015      1    5         48.95            5
     index          Date  TempAvgF  Year  Month  Day  20_d_mov_avg  Day_of_Year
360    736   2015-12-27        55   2015     12   27         61.10          361
361    737   2015-12-28        41   2015     12   28         60.20          362
362    738   2015-12-29        43   2015     12   29         59.25          363
363    739   2015-12-30        49   2015     12   30         58.45          364
364    740   2015-12-31        46   2015     12   31         57.45          365
```

Figure 3.71: One year's worth of data

7. Create a scatterplot of the raw data (the original **TempAvgF** column) and overlay it with a line for the 20-day moving average:

```
fig = plt.figure(figsize=(10, 7))
ax = fig.add_axes([1, 1, 1, 1]);
# Raw data
ax.scatter(df_one_year.Day_of_Year, df_one_year.TempAvgF, \
           label = 'Raw Data', c = 'k')
# Moving averages
ax.plot(df_one_year.Day_of_Year, df_one_year['20_d_mov_avg'], \
        c = 'r', linestyle = '--', \
        label = f'{window} day moving average')
ax.set_title('Air Temperature Measurements', fontsize = 16)
ax.set_xlabel('Day', fontsize = 14)
ax.set_ylabel('Temperature ($^\circ$F)', fontsize = 14)
ax.set_xticks(range(df_one_year.Day_of_Year.min(), \
                    df_one_year.Day_of_Year.max(), 30))
ax.tick_params(labelsize = 12)
ax.legend(fontsize = 12)
plt.show()
```

The output will be as follows:

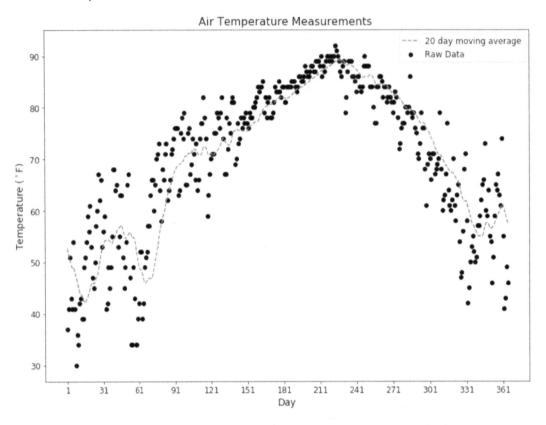

Figure 3.72: Raw data with the 20-day moving average overlaid

8. Create a linear regression model using the default parameters, that is, calculate a *y* intercept for the model and do not normalize the data. The day numbers for the year (1 to 365) constitute the input data and the average temperatures constitute the output data. Print the parameters of the model and the r^2 value:

```
# fit a linear model
linear_model = LinearRegression(fit_intercept = True)
linear_model.fit(df_one_year['Day_of_Year']\
                 .values.reshape((-1, 1)), \
                 df_one_year.TempAvgF)
print('model slope: ', linear_model.coef_)
print('model intercept: ', linear_model.intercept_)
print('model r squared: ', \
```

```
linear_model.score(df_one_year['Day_of_Year']\
                    .values.reshape((-1, 1)), \
                    df_one_year.TempAvgF))
```

The results should be as follows:

```
model slope: [0.04304568]
model intercept: 62.23496914044859
model r squared: 0.09549593659736466
```

Note that the r^2 value is very low, which is not surprising given that the data has a significant variation in the slope over time, and we are fitting a single linear model with a constant slope.

9. Generate predictions from the model using the same *x* data:

```
# make predictions using the training data
y_pred = linear_model.predict(df_one_year['Day_of_Year']\
                    .values.reshape((-1, 1)))
x_pred = df_one_year.Day_of_Year
```

10. Create a new scatterplot, as before, adding an overlay of the predictions of the model:

```
fig = plt.figure(figsize=(10, 7))
ax = fig.add_axes([1, 1, 1, 1]);
# Raw data
ax.scatter(df_one_year.Day_of_Year, df_one_year.TempAvgF, \
           label = 'Raw Data', c = 'k')
# Moving averages
ax.plot(df_one_year.Day_of_Year, df_one_year['20_d_mov_avg'], \
        c = 'r', linestyle = '--', \
        label = f'{window} day moving average')
# linear model
ax.plot(x_pred, y_pred, c = "blue", linestyle = '-.', \
        label = 'linear model')
ax.set_title('Air Temperature Measurements', fontsize = 16)
ax.set_xlabel('Day', fontsize = 14)
ax.set_ylabel('Temperature ($^\circ$F)', fontsize = 14)
ax.set_xticks(range(df_one_year.Day_of_Year.min(), \
                    df_one_year.Day_of_Year.max(), 30))
ax.tick_params(labelsize = 12)
ax.legend(fontsize = 12)
plt.show()
```

The output will be as follows:

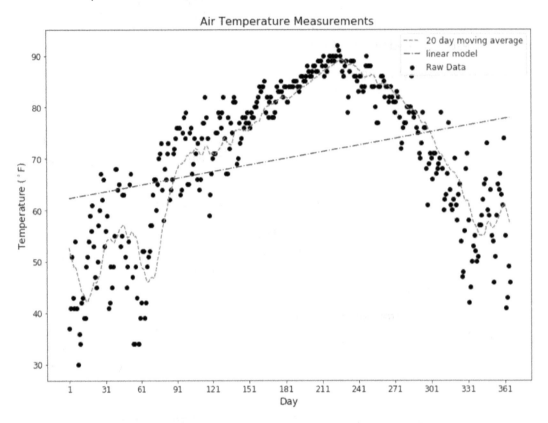

Figure 3.73: Raw data, 20-day moving average, and linear fit

> **NOTE**
>
> To access the source code for this specific section, please refer to
> https://packt.live/2CwEKyT.
>
> You can also run this example online at https://packt.live/3hKJSzD.
> You must execute the entire Notebook in order to get the desired result.

ACTIVITY 3.03: DUMMY VARIABLES

1. Import the required packages and classes:

```
import pandas as pd
import matplotlib.pyplot as plt
from sklearn.linear_model import LinearRegression
```

2. Load and inspect the data:

```
# load data and inspect
df = pd.read_csv('../Datasets/austin_weather.csv')
print(df.head())
print(df.tail())
```

The output for **df.head()** should appear as follows:

```
        Date  TempHighF  TempAvgF  TempLowF  DewPointHighF  DewPointAvgF  \
0  2013-12-21         74        60        45             67            49
1  2013-12-22         56        48        39             43            36
2  2013-12-23         58        45        32             31            27
3  2013-12-24         61        46        31             36            28
4  2013-12-25         58        50        41             44            40

   DewPointLowF  HumidityHighPercent  HumidityAvgPercent  HumidityLowPercent   ...
\
0            43                   93                  75                  57  ...
1            28                   93                  68                  43  ...
2            23                   76                  52                  27  ...
3            21                   89                  56                  22  ...
4            36                   86                  71                  56  ...

   SeaLevelPressureAvgInches  SeaLevelPressureLowInches  VisibilityHighMiles  \
0                      29.68                      29.59                   10
1                      30.13                      29.87                   10
2                      30.49                      30.41                   10
3                      30.45                       30.3                   10
4                      30.33                      30.27                   10

   VisibilityAvgMiles  VisibilityLowMiles  WindHighMPH  WindAvgMPH  WindGustMPH  \
0                   7                   2           20           4           31
1                  10                   5           16           6           25
2                  10                  10            8           3           12
3                  10                   7           12           4           20
4                  10                   7           10           2           16

   PrecipitationSumInches                Events
0                    0.46  Rain , Thunderstorm
1                       0
2                       0
3                       0
4                       T

[5 rows x 21 columns]
```

Figure 3.74: Output for the df.head() function

The output for `df.tail()` should appear as follows:

	Date	TempHighF	TempAvgF	TempLowF	DewPointHighF	DewPointAvgF	\
1314	2017-07-27	103	89	75	71	67	
1315	2017-07-28	105	91	76	71	64	
1316	2017-07-29	107	92	77	72	64	
1317	2017-07-30	106	93	79	70	68	
1318	2017-07-31	99	88	77	66	61	

	DewPointLowF	HumidityHighPercent	HumidityAvgPercent	HumidityLowPercent	\
1314	61	82	54	25	
1315	55	87	54	20	
1316	55	82	51	19	
1317	63	69	48	27	
1318	54	64	43	22	

	...	SeaLevelPressureAvgInches	SeaLevelPressureLowInches	\
1314	...	29.97	29.88	
1315	...	29.9	29.81	
1316	...	29.86	29.79	
1317	...	29.91	29.87	
1318	...	29.97	29.91	

	VisibilityHighMiles	VisibilityAvgMiles	VisibilityLowMiles	WindHighMPH	\
1314	10	10	10	12	
1315	10	10	10	14	
1316	10	10	10	12	
1317	10	10	10	13	
1318	10	10	10	12	

	WindAvgMPH	WindGustMPH	PrecipitationSumInches	Events
1314	5	21	0	
1315	5	20	0	
1316	4	17	0	
1317	4	20	0	
1318	4	20	0	

[5 rows x 21 columns]

Figure 3.75: Output for the df.tail() function

3. Carry out the preprocessing as before. Drop all but the **Date** and **TempAvgF** columns. Add columns for **Year**, **Month**, and **Day**. Create a new column with a 20-day moving average. Slice out the first complete year (**2015**):

```
df = df.loc[:, ['Date', 'TempAvgF']]
# add some useful columns
df.loc[:, 'Year'] = df.loc[:, 'Date'].str.slice(0, 4).astype('int')
df.loc[:, 'Month'] = df.loc[:, 'Date'].str.slice(5, 7).astype('int')
df.loc[:, 'Day'] = df.loc[:, 'Date'].str.slice(8, 10).astype('int')
"""
set a 20 day window then use that to smooth
temperature in a new column
"""
window = 20
df['20_d_mov_avg'] = df.TempAvgF.rolling(window).mean()
"""
now let's slice exactly one year on the
calendar start and end dates
we see from the previous output that
2014 is the first year with complete data,
however it will still have NaN values for
the moving average, so we'll use 2015
"""
df_one_year = df.loc[df.Year == 2015, :].reset_index()
df_one_year['Day_of_Year'] = df_one_year.index + 1
print(df_one_year.head())
print(df_one_year.tail())
```

The data should appear as follows:

```
     index          Date  TempAvgF  Year  Month  Day  20_d_mov_avg  Day_of_Year
0      376    2015-01-01        37  2015      1    1         52.70            1
1      377    2015-01-02        41  2015      1    2         51.50            2
2      378    2015-01-03        51  2015      1    3         50.65            3
3      379    2015-01-04        43  2015      1    4         49.65            4
4      380    2015-01-05        41  2015      1    5         48.95            5
     index          Date  TempAvgF  Year  Month  Day  20_d_mov_avg  Day_of_Year
360    736    2015-12-27        55  2015     12   27         61.10          361
361    737    2015-12-28        41  2015     12   28         60.20          362
362    738    2015-12-29        43  2015     12   29         59.25          363
363    739    2015-12-30        49  2015     12   30         58.45          364
364    740    2015-12-31        46  2015     12   31         57.45          365
```

Figure 3.76: Preprocessed data

4. Visualize the results:

```
fig = plt.figure(figsize=(10, 7))
ax = fig.add_axes([1, 1, 1, 1]);
# Raw data
ax.scatter(df_one_year.Day_of_Year, df_one_year.TempAvgF, \
        label = 'Raw Data', c = 'k')
# Moving averages
ax.plot(df_one_year.Day_of_Year, df_one_year['20_d_mov_avg'], \
        c = 'r', linestyle = '--', \
        label = f'{window} day moving average')
ax.set_title('Air Temperature Measurements', fontsize = 16)
ax.set_xlabel('Day', fontsize = 14)
ax.set_ylabel('Temperature ($^\circ$F)', fontsize = 14)
ax.set_xticks(range(df_one_year.Day_of_Year.min(), \
                    df_one_year.Day_of_Year.max(), 30))
ax.tick_params(labelsize = 12)
ax.legend(fontsize = 12)
plt.show()
```

The plot should appear as follows:

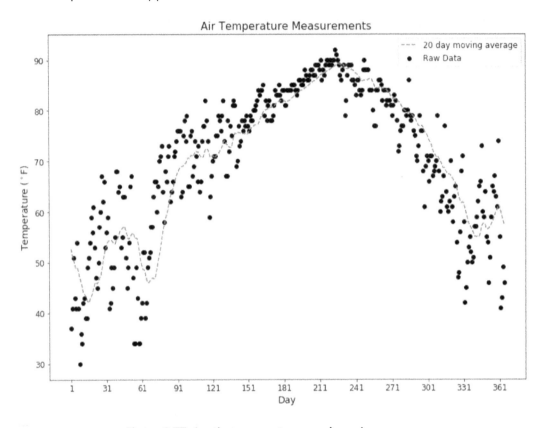

Figure 3.77: Austin temperatures and moving average

5. We can see that the temperature rises from January to around September, and then falls again. This is a clear seasonal cycle. As a first improvement, we can include the month in the model. As described in the introduction to dummy variables, if we just encoded the months as integers **1** to **12**, the model might interpret that December (12) was more important than January (1). So, we encode the month as dummy variables to avoid this:

```
# use the month as a dummy variable
dummy_vars = pd.get_dummies(df_one_year['Month'], drop_first = True)
dummy_vars.columns = ['Feb', 'Mar', 'Apr', 'May', 'Jun', \
                      'Jul', 'Aug', 'Sep', 'Oct', 'Nov', 'Dec']
df_one_year = pd.concat([df_one_year, dummy_vars], \
                        axis = 1).drop('Month', axis = 1)

df_one_year
```

The data should appear as follows:

	index	Date	TempAvgF	Year	Day	20_d_mov_avg	Day_of_Year	Feb	Mar	Apr	May	Jun	Jul	Aug	Sep	Oct	Nov	Dec
0	376	2015-01-01	37	2015	1	52.70	1	0	0	0	0	0	0	0	0	0	0	0
1	377	2015-01-02	41	2015	2	51.50	2	0	0	0	0	0	0	0	0	0	0	0
2	378	2015-01-03	51	2015	3	50.65	3	0	0	0	0	0	0	0	0	0	0	0
3	379	2015-01-04	43	2015	4	49.65	4	0	0	0	0	0	0	0	0	0	0	0
4	380	2015-01-05	41	2015	5	48.95	5	0	0	0	0	0	0	0	0	0	0	0
...	...	...	...	...	...	...	...	...	...	...	...	...	...	...	...	...	...	...
360	736	2015-12-27	55	2015	27	61.10	361	0	0	0	0	0	0	0	0	0	0	1
361	737	2015-12-28	41	2015	28	60.20	362	0	0	0	0	0	0	0	0	0	0	1
362	738	2015-12-29	43	2015	29	59.25	363	0	0	0	0	0	0	0	0	0	0	1
363	739	2015-12-30	49	2015	30	58.45	364	0	0	0	0	0	0	0	0	0	0	1
364	740	2015-12-31	46	2015	31	57.45	365	0	0	0	0	0	0	0	0	0	0	1

365 rows × 18 columns

Figure 3.78: Data augmented with dummy variables for the month

6. Now, fit a linear model using **Day_of_Year** and the dummy variables, and print the model coefficients and the r^2 value:

```
# fit model using the month dummy vars
linear_model = LinearRegression(fit_intercept = True)
linear_model.fit(pd.concat([df_one_year.Day_of_Year, \
                        df_one_year.loc[:, 'Feb':'Dec']], \
                                axis = 1),
                        df_one_year['TempAvgF'])
print('model coefficients: ', linear_model.coef_)
print('model intercept: ', linear_model.intercept_)
print('model r squared: ', \
        linear_model.score(pd.concat([df_one_year.Day_of_Year, \
                                df_one_year.loc[:, 'Feb':'Dec']], \
\
                                        axis = 1),
                        df_one_year['TempAvgF']))
```

The results should be as follows:

```
model coefficients:  [ 0.03719346 1.57445204 9.35397321 19.16903518
22.02065629 26.80023439
 30.17121033 30.82466482 25.6117698 15.71715435 1.542969
-4.06777548]
model intercept: 48.34038858048261
model r squared: 0.7834805472165678
```

Note the signs on the coefficients—the first value associated with **Day_of_Year**, and then the values for January through December follow. The coefficients for January, February, March, November, and December are negative, while those for June through September are positive. This makes sense for the seasons in Texas.

7. Now, make predictions using the single-year data, and visualize the results:

```
# make predictions using the data
y_pred = \
linear_model.predict(pd.concat([df_one_year.Day_of_Year, \
                                df_one_year.loc[:, 'Feb':'Dec']], \
                                axis = 1))

x_pred = df_one_year.Day_of_Year

fig = plt.figure(figsize=(10, 7))
ax = fig.add_axes([1, 1, 1, 1]);
# Raw data
ax.scatter(df_one_year.Day_of_Year, df_one_year.TempAvgF, \
           label = 'Raw Data', c = 'k')
# Moving averages
ax.plot(df_one_year.Day_of_Year, df_one_year['20_d_mov_avg'], \
        c = 'r', linestyle = '--', \
        label = f'{window} day moving average')
# regression predictions
ax.plot(x_pred, y_pred, c = "blue", linestyle = '-.', \
        label = 'linear model w/dummy vars')
ax.set_title('Air Temperature Measurements', fontsize = 16)
ax.set_xlabel('Day', fontsize = 14)
ax.set_ylabel('Temperature ($^\circ$F)', fontsize = 14)
ax.set_xticks(range(df_one_year.Day_of_Year.min(), \
                    df_one_year.Day_of_Year.max(), 30))
ax.tick_params(labelsize = 12)
ax.legend(fontsize = 12, loc = 'upper left')
plt.show()
```

The output should appear as follows:

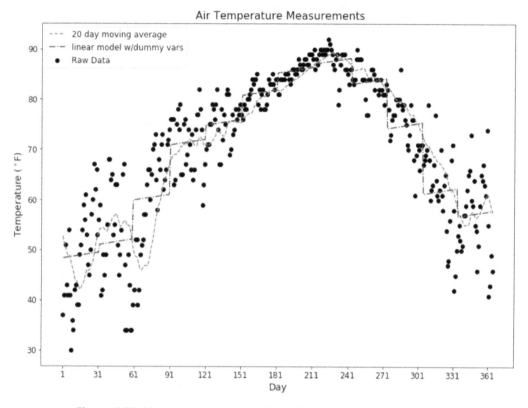

Figure 3.79: Linear regression results with month dummy variables

> **NOTE**
>
> To access the source code for this specific section, please refer to
> https://packt.live/3enegOg.
>
> You can also run this example online at https://packt.live/2V4VgMM.
> You must execute the entire Notebook in order to get the desired result.

ACTIVITY 3.04: FEATURE ENGINEERING WITH LINEAR REGRESSION

1. Load the required packages and classes:

```
import pandas as pd
import numpy as np
import matplotlib.pyplot as plt
from sklearn.linear_model import LinearRegression
```

2. Load the data and carry out preprocessing through to the point where **Day_of_Year** is added:

```
# load data
df = pd.read_csv('../Datasets/austin_weather.csv')
df = df.loc[:, ['Date', 'TempAvgF']]
# add some useful columns
df.loc[:, 'Year'] = df.loc[:, 'Date'].str.slice(0, 4).astype('int')
df.loc[:, 'Month'] = df.loc[:, 'Date'].str.slice(5, 7).astype('int')
df.loc[:, 'Day'] = df.loc[:, 'Date'].str.slice(8, 10).astype('int')
"""
set a 20 day window then use that to smooth
temperature in a new column
"""
window = 20
df['20_d_mov_avg'] = df.TempAvgF.rolling(window).mean()
"""
now let's slice exactly one year on the
calendar start and end dates
we see from the previous output that
2014 is the first year with complete data,
however it will still have NaN values for
the moving average, so we'll use 2015
"""
df_one_year = df.loc[df.Year == 2015, :].reset_index()
df_one_year['Day_of_Year'] = df_one_year.index + 1
```

3. Now, for the feature engineering, we construct the sine and cosine of **Day_of_Year** with a period of 365 days:

```
# add two columns for sine and cosine of the Day_of_Year
df_one_year['sine_Day'] = np.sin(2 * np.pi \
                            * df_one_year['Day_of_Year'] / 365)
df_one_year['cosine_Day'] = np.cos(2 * np.pi \
                            * df_one_year['Day_of_Year'] / 365)
df_one_year
```

The data should appear as follows:

	index	Date	TempAvgF	Year	Month	Day	20_d_mov_avg	Day_of_Year	sine_Day	cosine_Day
0	376	2015-01-01	37	2015	1	1	52.70	1	1.721336e-02	0.999852
1	377	2015-01-02	41	2015	1	2	51.50	2	3.442161e-02	0.999407
2	378	2015-01-03	51	2015	1	3	50.65	3	5.161967e-02	0.998667
3	379	2015-01-04	43	2015	1	4	49.65	4	6.880243e-02	0.997630
4	380	2015-01-05	41	2015	1	5	48.95	5	8.596480e-02	0.996298
...	...	...	...	...	...	...	...	...	...	...
360	736	2015-12-27	55	2015	12	27	61.10	361	-6.880243e-02	0.997630
361	737	2015-12-28	41	2015	12	28	60.20	362	-5.161967e-02	0.998667
362	738	2015-12-29	43	2015	12	29	59.25	363	-3.442161e-02	0.999407
363	739	2015-12-30	49	2015	12	30	58.45	364	-1.721336e-02	0.999852
364	740	2015-12-31	46	2015	12	31	57.45	365	6.432491e-16	1.000000

365 rows × 10 columns

Figure 3.80: Austin weather data with the new features, sine_Day and cosine_Day

4. We can now fit the model using the **LinearRegression** class from scikit-learn, and print the coefficients and the r^2 score:

```
# fit model using the Day_of_Year and sin/cos
linear_model = LinearRegression(fit_intercept = True)
linear_model.fit(df_one_year[['Day_of_Year', 'sine_Day', \
                            'cosine_Day']], \
                    df_one_year['TempAvgF'])
print('model coefficients: ', linear_model.coef_)
print('model intercept: ', linear_model.intercept_)
print('model r squared: ', \
linear_model.score(df_one_year[['Day_of_Year', 'sine_Day', \
                            'cosine_Day']], \
                    df_one_year['TempAvgF']))
```

The output should be as follows:

```
model coefficients: [ 1.46396364e-02 -5.57332499e+00 -1.67824174e+01]
model intercept: 67.43327530313064
model r squared: 0.779745650129063
```

Note that the r^2 value is about the same as we achieved with the dummy variables. However, let's look at the predictions and see whether this model might be more or less suitable than before.

5. Generate predictions using the augmented data:

```
# make predictions using the data
y_pred = \
linear_model.predict(df_one_year[['Day_of_Year', 'sine_Day', \
                                  'cosine_Day']])
x_pred = df_one_year.Day_of_Year
```

6. Now, visualize the results:

```
fig = plt.figure(figsize=(10, 7))
ax = fig.add_axes([1, 1, 1, 1])
# Raw data
ax.scatter(df_one_year.Day_of_Year, df_one_year.TempAvgF, \
           label = 'Raw Data', c = 'k')
# Moving averages
ax.plot(df_one_year.Day_of_Year, df_one_year['20_d_mov_avg'], \
        c = 'r', linestyle = '--', \
        label = f'{window} day moving average')
# regression predictions
ax.plot(x_pred, y_pred, c = "blue", linestyle = '-.', \
        label = 'linear model w/sin-cos fit')
ax.set_title('Air Temperature Measurements', fontsize = 16)
ax.set_xlabel('Day', fontsize = 14)
ax.set_ylabel('Temperature ($^\circ$F)', fontsize = 14)
ax.set_xticks(range(df_one_year.Day_of_Year.min(), \
                    df_one_year.Day_of_Year.max(), 30))
ax.tick_params(labelsize = 12)
ax.legend(fontsize = 12, loc = 'upper left')
```

The output will be as follows:

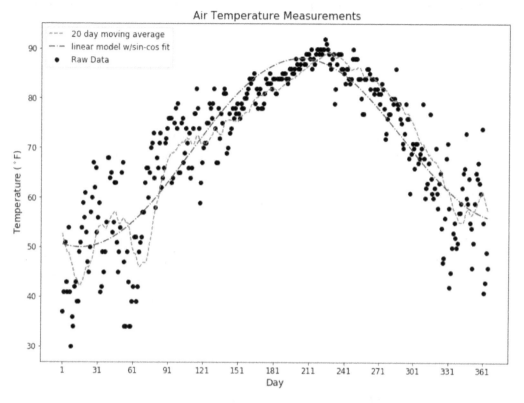

Figure 3.81: Austin temperature data with moving average overlay
and periodic feature fit overlay

NOTE

To access the source code for this specific section, please refer to
https://packt.live/3dvkmet.

You can also run this example online at https://packt.live/3epnOlJ.
You must execute the entire Notebook in order to get the desired result.

ACTIVITY 3.05: GRADIENT DESCENT

1. Import the modules and classes:

```
import pandas as pd
import numpy as np
import matplotlib.pyplot as plt
from sklearn.metrics import r2_score
from sklearn.linear_model import SGDRegressor
```

2. Load the data (**austin_weather.csv**) and preprocess it up to the point of creating the **Day_of_Year** column and slicing one full year (2015):

```
# load data and inspect
df = pd.read_csv('../Datasets/austin_weather.csv')
df = df.loc[:, ['Date', 'TempAvgF']]
# add time-based columns
df.loc[:, 'Year'] = df.loc[:, 'Date'].str.slice(0, 4).astype('int')
df.loc[:, 'Month'] = df.loc[:, 'Date'].str.slice(5, 7).astype('int')
df.loc[:, 'Day'] = df.loc[:, 'Date'].str.slice(8, 10).astype('int')
"""
set a 20 day window then use that to smooth
temperature in a new column
"""
window = 20
df['20_d_mov_avg'] = df.TempAvgF.rolling(window).mean()
"""
now let's slice exactly one year on the
calendar start and end dates
we see from the previous output that
2014 is the first year with complete data,
however it will still have NaN values for
the moving average, so we'll use 2015
"""
df_one_year = df.loc[df.Year == 2015, :].reset_index()
df_one_year['Day_of_Year'] = df_one_year.index + 1
print(df_one_year.head())
print(df_one_year.tail())
```

The output will be as follows:

```
     index      Date  TempAvgF  Year  Month  Day  20_d_mov_avg  Day_of_Year
0      376  2015-01-01       37  2015      1    1         52.70            1
1      377  2015-01-02       41  2015      1    2         51.50            2
2      378  2015-01-03       51  2015      1    3         50.65            3
3      379  2015-01-04       43  2015      1    4         49.65            4
4      380  2015-01-05       41  2015      1    5         48.95            5
     index      Date  TempAvgF  Year  Month  Day  20_d_mov_avg  Day_of_Year
360    736  2015-12-27       55  2015     12   27         61.10          361
361    737  2015-12-28       41  2015     12   28         60.20          362
362    738  2015-12-29       43  2015     12   29         59.25          363
363    739  2015-12-30       49  2015     12   30         58.45          364
364    740  2015-12-31       46  2015     12   31         57.45          365
```

Figure 3.82: Preprocessed data before scaling

3. Scale the data for training:

```
# scale the data
X_min = df_one_year.Day_of_Year.min()
X_range = df_one_year.Day_of_Year.max() \
          - df_one_year.Day_of_Year.min()
Y_min = df_one_year.TempAvgF.min()
Y_range = df_one_year.TempAvgF.max() \
          - df_one_year.TempAvgF.min()
scale_X = (df_one_year.Day_of_Year - X_min) / X_range
train_X = scale_X.ravel()
train_Y = ((df_one_year.TempAvgF - Y_min) / Y_range).ravel()
```

4. Set **random.seed**, instantiate the model object with **SGDRegressor**, and fit the model to the training data:

```
# create the model object
np.random.seed(42)
model = SGDRegressor(loss = 'squared_loss', max_iter = 100, \
                     learning_rate = 'constant', eta0 = 0.0005, \
                     tol = 0.00009, penalty = 'none')
# fit the model
model.fit(train_X.reshape((-1, 1)), train_Y)
```

The output should be as follows:

```
SGDRegressor(alpha=0.0001, average=False, early_stopping=False, epsilon=0.1,
             eta0=0.0005, fit_intercept=True, l1_ratio=0.15,
             learning_rate='constant', loss='squared_loss', max_iter=100,
             n_iter_no_change=5, penalty='none', power_t=0.25,
             random_state=None, shuffle=True, tol=9e-05,
             validation_fraction=0.1, verbose=0, warm_start=False)
```

Figure 3.83: Model object using SGDRegressor

5. Extract the model coefficients and rescale:

```
Beta0 = (Y_min + Y_range * model.intercept_[0] \
        - Y_range * model.coef_[0] * X_min / X_range)
Beta1 = Y_range * model.coef_[0] / X_range
print(Beta0)
print(Beta1)
```

The output should be similar to the following:

```
61.45512325422412
0.04533603293003107
```

6. Generate predictions using the scaled data, and then get the r^2 value:

```
# generate predictions
pred_X = df_one_year['Day_of_Year']
pred_Y = model.predict(train_X.reshape((-1, 1)))
# calculate the r squared value
r2 = r2_score(train_Y, pred_Y)
print('r squared = ', r2)
```

The result should be similar to the following:

```
r squared = 0.09462157379706759
```

7. Scale the predictions back to real values and then visualize the results:

```
# scale predictions back to real values
pred_Y = (pred_Y * Y_range) + Y_min
fig = plt.figure(figsize = (10, 7))
ax = fig.add_axes([1, 1, 1, 1])
# Raw data
ax.scatter(df_one_year.Day_of_Year, df_one_year.TempAvgF, \
           label = 'Raw Data', c = 'k')
# Moving averages
ax.plot(df_one_year.Day_of_Year, df_one_year['20_d_mov_avg'], \
        c = 'r', linestyle = '--', \
        label = f'{window} day moving average')
# Regression predictions
ax.plot(pred_X, pred_Y, c = "blue", linestyle = '-.', \
        linewidth = 4, label = 'linear fit (from SGD)')
# put the model on the plot
ax.text(1, 85, 'Temp = ' + str(round(Beta0, 2)) + ' + ' \
            + str(round(Beta1, 4)) + ' * Day', fontsize = 16)#
ax.set_title('Air Temperature Measurements', fontsize = 16)
ax.set_xlabel('Day', fontsize = 16)
ax.set_ylabel('Temperature ($^\circ$F)', fontsize = 14)
ax.set_xticks(range(df_one_year.Day_of_Year.min(), \
                    df_one_year.Day_of_Year.max(), 30))
ax.tick_params(labelsize = 12)
ax.legend(fontsize = 12)
plt.show()
```

The output will be as follows:

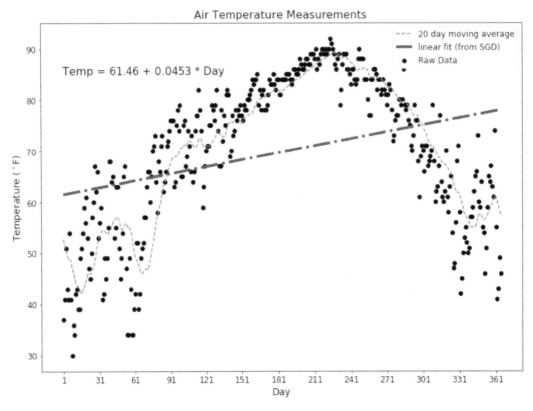

Figure 3.84: Results of linear regression using SGDRegressor

CHAPTER 04: AUTOREGRESSION

ACTIVITY 4.01: AUTOREGRESSION MODEL BASED ON PERIODIC DATA

1. Import the necessary packages, classes, and libraries.

> **NOTE**
>
> This activity will work on an earlier version of pandas, ensure that you downgrade the version of pandas using the command:
>
> **pip install pandas==0.24.2**

The code is as follows:

```
import pandas as pd
import numpy as np
from statsmodels.tsa.ar_model import AR
from statsmodels.graphics.tsaplots import plot_acf
import matplotlib.pyplot as plt
```

2. Load the data and convert the **Date** column to **datetime**:

```
df = pd.read_csv('../Datasets/austin_weather.csv')
df.Date = pd.to_datetime(df.Date)
print(df.head())
print(df.tail())
```

The output for **df.head()** should look as follows:

```
         Date  TempHighF  TempAvgF  TempLowF  DewPointHighF  DewPointAvgF  \
0  2013-12-21         74        60        45             67            49
1  2013-12-22         56        48        39             43            36
2  2013-12-23         58        45        32             31            27
3  2013-12-24         61        46        31             36            28
4  2013-12-25         58        50        41             44            40

   DewPointLowF  HumidityHighPercent  HumidityAvgPercent  HumidityLowPercent  ...  \
0            43                   93                  75                  57  ...
1            28                   93                  68                  43  ...
2            23                   76                  52                  27  ...
3            21                   89                  56                  22  ...
4            36                   86                  71                  56  ...

   SeaLevelPressureAvgInches  SeaLevelPressureLowInches  VisibilityHighMiles  \
0                      29.68                      29.59                   10
1                      30.13                      29.87                   10
2                      30.49                      30.41                   10
3                      30.45                       30.3                   10
4                      30.33                      30.27                   10

   VisibilityAvgMiles  VisibilityLowMiles  WindHighMPH  WindAvgMPH  WindGustMPH  \
0                   7                   2           20           4           31
1                  10                   5           16           6           25
2                  10                  10            8           3           12
3                  10                   7           12           4           20
4                  10                   7           10           2           16

   PrecipitationSumInches                Events
0                    0.46  Rain , Thunderstorm
1                       0
2                       0
3                       0
4                       T

[5 rows x 21 columns]
```

Figure 4.22: Output for df.head()

The output for **df.tail()** should look as follows:

```
            Date  TempHighF  TempAvgF  TempLowF  DewPointHighF  DewPointAvgF  \
1314  2017-07-27        103        89        75             71            67
1315  2017-07-28        105        91        76             71            64
1316  2017-07-29        107        92        77             72            64
1317  2017-07-30        106        93        79             70            68
1318  2017-07-31         99        88        77             66            61

      DewPointLowF  HumidityHighPercent  HumidityAvgPercent  HumidityLowPercent  \
1314            61                   82                  54                  25
1315            55                   87                  54                  20
1316            55                   82                  51                  19
1317            63                   69                  48                  27
1318            54                   64                  43                  22

      ...  SeaLevelPressureAvgInches  SeaLevelPressureLowInches  \
1314  ...                      29.97                      29.88
1315  ...                      29.9                       29.81
1316  ...                      29.86                      29.79
1317  ...                      29.91                      29.87
1318  ...                      29.97                      29.91

      VisibilityHighMiles  VisibilityAvgMiles  VisibilityLowMiles  WindHighMPH  \
1314                   10                  10                  10           12
1315                   10                  10                  10           14
1316                   10                  10                  10           12
1317                   10                  10                  10           13
1318                   10                  10                  10           12

      WindAvgMPH  WindGustMPH  PrecipitationSumInches  Events
1314           5           21                       0
1315           5           20                       0
1316           4           17                       0
1317           4           20                       0
1318           4           20                       0

[5 rows x 21 columns]
```

Figure 4.23: Output for df.tail()

3. Plot the complete set of average temperature values (**df.TempAvgF**) with **Date** on the *x* axis:

```
fig, ax = plt.subplots(figsize = (10, 7))
ax.scatter(df.Date, df.TempAvgF)
plt.show()
```

The output will be as follows:

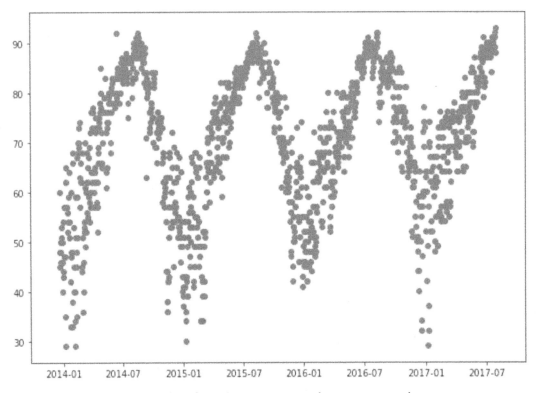

Figure 4.24: Plot of Austin temperature data over several years

Note the periodic behavior of the data. It's sensible given that temperature varies over an annual weather cycle.

4. Construct an autocorrelation plot (using **statsmodels**) to see whether the average temperature can be used with an autoregression model. Where is the lag acceptable and where is it not for an autoregression model? Check the following code:

```
max_lag = 730
fig, ax = plt.subplots(figsize = (10, 7))
acf_plot = plot_acf(x = df.TempAvgF, ax = ax, lags = max_lag, \
                     use_vlines = False, alpha = 0.9, \
                     title = 'Autocorrelation of Austin Temperature '\
                     'vs. lag')
ax.grid(True)
ax.text(280, -0.01, '90% confidence interval', fontsize = 9)
ax.set_xlabel('Lag', fontsize = 14)
ax.tick_params(axis = 'both', labelsize = 12)
```

The plot should look as follows:

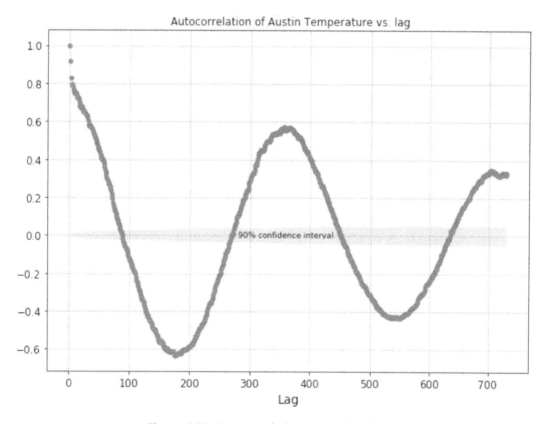

Figure 4.25: Autocorrelation versus lag (days)

The lag is acceptable only when the autocorrelation line lies outside the 90% confidence bounds, as represented by the shaded area. Note that, in this case, instead of a steadily decreasing ACF value, we see peaks and valleys. This should match your intuition because the original data shows a periodic pattern. Also, note that there are very strong positive and negative correlations. It is possible to leverage the strong negative correlation at around 180 days (half a year), but that is a more advanced time series topic beyond our scope here. The main takeaway from *Figure 4.25* is that there is a very steep drop in the ACF after short lag times. Now, use the same methods as before to look at the lag plots versus the ACF.

5. Get the actual ACF values:

```
corr0 = np.correlate(df.TempAvgF[0: ] - df.TempAvgF.mean(), \
        df.TempAvgF[0: ] - df.TempAvgF.mean(), mode = 'valid')
corrs = [np.correlate(df.TempAvgF[:(df.TempAvgF.shape[0] - i)] \
         - df.TempAvgF.mean(), df.TempAvgF[i: ] \
         - df.TempAvgF.mean(), mode = 'valid')
        for i in range(max_lag)] / corr0
```

6. We need the same utility grid plotting function we developed in *Exercise 4.01, Creating an Autoregression Model*:

```
"""
utility function to plot out a range of
plots depicting self-correlation
"""
def plot_lag_grid(series, corrs, axis_min, axis_max, \
                  num_plots, total_lag, n_rows, n_cols):
    lag_step = int(total_lag / num_plots)
    fig = plt.figure(figsize = (18, 16))
    for i, var_name in enumerate(range(num_plots)):
        corr = corrs[lag_step * i]
        ax = fig.add_subplot(n_rows, n_cols, i + 1)
        ax.scatter(series, series.shift(lag_step * i))
        ax.set_xlim(axis_min, axis_max)
        ax.set_ylim(axis_min, axis_max)
        ax.set_title('lag = ' + str(lag_step * i))
        ax.text(axis_min + 0.05 * (axis_max - axis_min), \
                axis_max - 0.05 * (axis_max - axis_min), \
                'correlation = ' + str(round(corr[0], 3)))
    fig.tight_layout()
    plt.show()
```

7. Now, given that we have an indication that we are interested in short lags, but also that there are strong correlations around a half year and a full year, let's look at two timescales:

```
plot_lag_grid(df.TempAvgF, corrs, df.TempAvgF.min(), \
              df.TempAvgF.max(), 9, 45, 3, 3)
plot_lag_grid(df.TempAvgF, corrs, df.TempAvgF.min(), \
              df.TempAvgF.max(), 9, 405, 3, 3)
```

The output for short lags will be as follows:

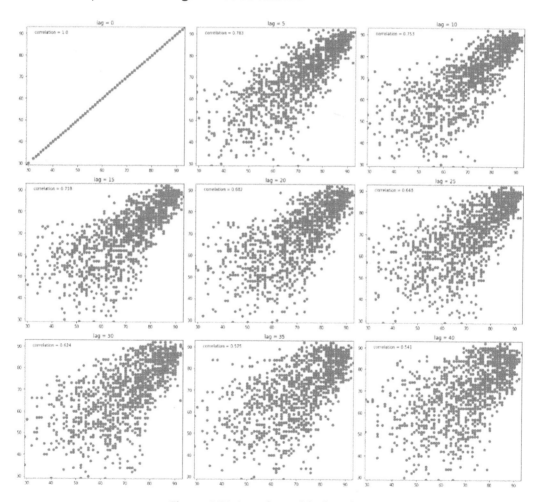

Figure 4.26: Lag plots with short lags

The output for longer lags will be as follows:

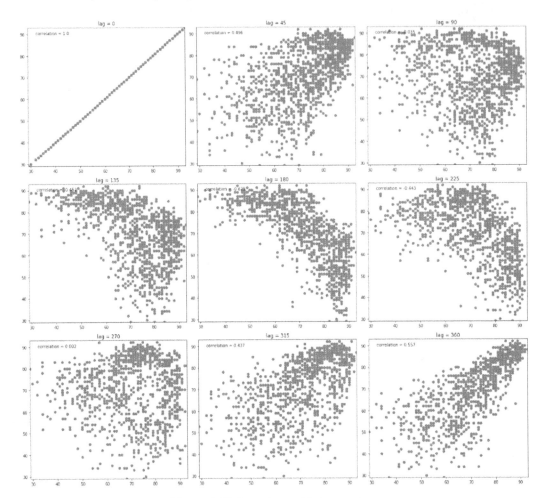

Figure 4.27: Lag plots with longer lags

We can see from *Figure 4.26* that the correlation degrades consistently from lag 5 to 40. Over a longer timescale, *Figure 4.27* shows that the correlation degrades rapidly and then improves as we near a lag of one year. This matches the intuition from the plot of the raw data (side note—this should reinforce the importance of EDA).

8. We would expect from our initial analysis that the autoregression model would focus on fairly short lags. Let's use the **statsmodels AR** function to build a model and see the results:

```
"""
statsmodels AR function builds an autoregression model
using all the defaults, it will determine the max lag
and provide all the model coefficients
"""
model = AR(df.TempAvgF)
model_fit = model.fit()
# model fit now contains all the model information
max_lag = model_fit.k_ar
"""
note that by using defaults, the maximum lag is
computed as round(12*(nobs/100.)**(1/4.))
see https://www.statsmodels.org/devel/generated/statsmodels.tsa.ar_model.AR.fit.
html#statsmodels.tsa.ar_model.AR.fit
"""
print('Max Lag: ' + str(max_lag))
print('Coefficients: \n' + str(model_fit.params))
# how far into the future we want to predict
max_forecast = 365
# generate predictions from the model
pred_temp = pd.DataFrame({'pred_temp': \
                    model_fit.predict(start = max_lag, \
                                      end = df.shape[0] \
                                      + max_forecast - 1)})
# attach the dates for visualization
pred_temp['Date'] = df.loc[pred_temp.index, 'Date'].reindex()
pred_temp.loc[(max(df.index) + 1):, 'Date'] = \
    pd.to_datetime([max(df.Date) \
                   + pd.Timedelta(days = i)
                   for i in range(1, max_forecast + 1)])
```

The result is a model with lags of up to 23 days:

```
Max Lag: 23
Coefficients:
const            1.909395
L1.TempAvgF      0.912076
L2.TempAvgF     -0.334043
L3.TempAvgF      0.157353
L4.TempAvgF      0.025721
L5.TempAvgF      0.041342
L6.TempAvgF      0.030831
L7.TempAvgF     -0.021230
L8.TempAvgF      0.020324
L9.TempAvgF      0.025147
L10.TempAvgF     0.059739
L11.TempAvgF    -0.017337
L12.TempAvgF     0.043553
L13.TempAvgF    -0.027795
L14.TempAvgF     0.053547
L15.TempAvgF     0.013070
L16.TempAvgF    -0.033157
L17.TempAvgF    -0.000072
L18.TempAvgF    -0.026307
L19.TempAvgF     0.025258
L20.TempAvgF     0.038341
L21.TempAvgF     0.007885
L22.TempAvgF    -0.008889
L23.TempAvgF    -0.011080
dtype: float64
```

Figure 4.28: AR model of Austin temperature data

9. Plot the predictions, forecast, and raw data on the same plot:

```
"""
visualize the predictions overlaid on the real data
as well as the extrapolation to the future
"""
fig, ax = plt.subplots(figsize = (10, 7))
ax.plot(df.Date, df.TempAvgF, c = "blue", \
        linewidth = 4, label = 'Actual Average Temperature')
```

```
ax.plot(pred_temp.loc[0 : len(df.TempAvgF), 'Date'], \
        pred_temp.loc[0 : len(df.TempAvgF), 'pred_temp'], \
        c = "yellow", linewidth = 0.5, \
        label = 'Predicted Temperature')
ax.plot(pred_temp.loc[len(df.TempAvgF):, 'Date'], \
        pred_temp.loc[len(df.TempAvgF):, 'pred_temp'], \
        c = "red", linewidth = 2, \
        label = 'Forecast Temperature')
ax.set_xlabel('Date', fontsize = 14)
ax.tick_params(axis = 'both', labelsize = 12)
ax.set_title('Austin Texas Average Daily Temperature')
ax.tick_params(axis = 'both', labelsize = 12)
ax.legend()
plt.show()
```

The output will be as follows:

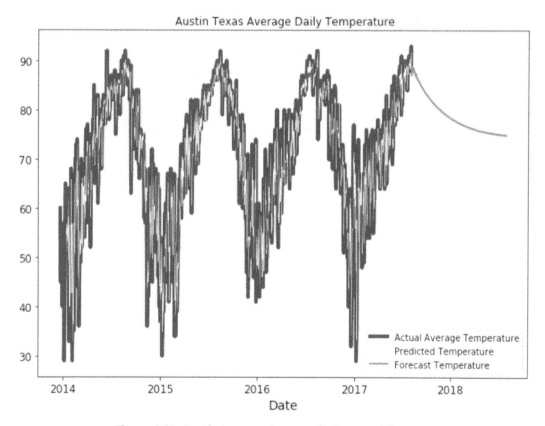

Figure 4.29: Austin temperature predictions and forecast

10. Let's zoom in on the end of the data, on the last 30 days of the data and on the first 30 forecast values:

```
# zoom in on a window near the end of the raw data
window = 30
fig, ax = plt.subplots(figsize = (10, 7))
ax.plot(df.Date[(len(df.TempAvgF) - window) : len(df.TempAvgF)], \
        df.TempAvgF[(len(df.TempAvgF) - window) : \
                    len(df.TempAvgF)], \
        c = "blue", linewidth = 4, \
        label = 'Actual Average Temperature')

ax.plot(pred_temp.Date.iloc[(-max_forecast \
                             - window):(-max_forecast)], \
        pred_temp.pred_temp.iloc[(-max_forecast \
                                  - window):(-max_forecast)], \
        c = "red", linewidth = 2, label = 'Predicted Temperature')

ax.plot(pred_temp.loc[len(df.TempAvgF):\
                      (len(df.TempAvgF) + window), 'Date'], \
        pred_temp.loc[len(df.TempAvgF):\
                      (len(df.TempAvgF) + window), 'pred_temp'], \
        c = "green", linewidth = 2, label = 'Forecast Temperature')
ax.set_xlabel('Date', fontsize = 14)
ax.tick_params(axis = 'both', labelsize = 12)
ax.set_title('Austin Texas Average Daily Temperature')
ax.tick_params(axis = 'both', labelsize = 12)
ax.set_xticks(pd.date_range(df.Date[len(df.TempAvgF) - window], \
                            df.Date[len(df.TempAvgF) - 1] \
                            + pd.Timedelta(days = window), 5))
ax.legend()
plt.show()
```

We will get the following output:

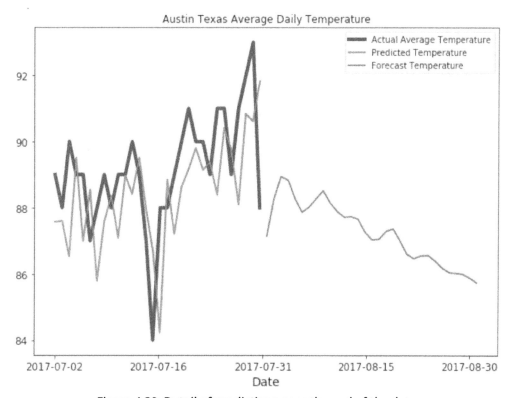

Figure 4.30: Detail of predictions near the end of the data

> **NOTE**
>
> To access the source code for this specific section, please refer to https://packt.live/3hOXUQL.
>
> You can also run this example online at https://packt.live/313Vmbl.
> You must execute the entire Notebook in order to get the desired result.
>
> Now that the activity is successfully completed, upgrade the version of pandas to continue to smoothly run the exercises and activities present in the rest of the book. To upgrade pandas, run:
>
> ```
> pip install pandas==1.0.3
> ```

CHAPTER 05: CLASSIFICATION TECHNIQUES

ACTIVITY 5.01: ORDINARY LEAST SQUARES CLASSIFIER – BINARY CLASSIFIER

Solution:

1. Import the required dependencies:

```
import struct
import numpy as np
import gzip
import urllib.request
import matplotlib.pyplot as plt
from array import array
from sklearn.linear_model import LinearRegression
```

2. Load the MNIST data into memory:

```
with gzip.open('../Datasets/train-images-idx3-ubyte.gz', 'rb') as f:
    magic, size, rows, cols = struct.unpack(">IIII", f.read(16))

    img = np.array(array("B", f.read())).reshape((size, rows, cols))

with gzip.open('../Datasets/train-labels-idx1-ubyte.gz', 'rb') as f:
    magic, size = struct.unpack(">II", f.read(8))
    labels = np.array(array("B", f.read()))

with gzip.open('../Datasets/t10k-images-idx3-ubyte.gz', 'rb') as f:
    magic, size, rows, cols = struct.unpack(">IIII", f.read(16))

    img_test = np.array(array("B", f.read()))\
                .reshape((size, rows, cols))

with gzip.open('../Datasets/t10k-labels-idx1-ubyte.gz', 'rb') as f:
    magic, size = struct.unpack(">II", f.read(8))
    labels_test = np.array(array("B", f.read()))
```

3. Visualize a sample of the data:

```
for i in range(10):
    plt.subplot(2, 5, i + 1)
    plt.imshow(img[i], cmap='gray');
    plt.title(f'{labels[i]}');
    plt.axis('off')
```

The output will be as follows:

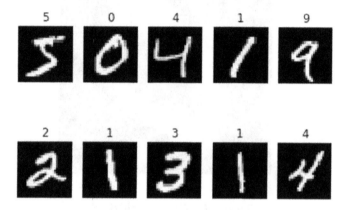

Figure 5.63: Sample data

4. Construct a linear classifier model to classify the digits 0 and 1. The model we are going to create is to determine whether the samples are either the digits 0 or 1. To do this, we first need to select only those samples:

```
samples_0_1 = np.where((labels == 0) | (labels == 1))[0]
images_0_1 = img[samples_0_1]
labels_0_1 = labels[samples_0_1]

samples_0_1_test = np.where((labels_test == 0) | (labels_test == 1))
images_0_1_test = img_test[samples_0_1_test]\
                    .reshape((-1, rows * cols))
labels_0_1_test = labels_test[samples_0_1_test]
```

5. Visualize the selected information. Here's the code for 0:

```
sample_0 = np.where((labels == 0))[0][0]
plt.imshow(img[sample_0], cmap='gray');
```

The output will be as follows:

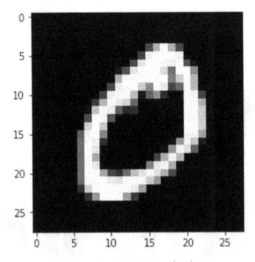

Figure 5.64: First sample data

Here's the code for 1:

```
sample_1 = np.where((labels == 1))[0][0]
plt.imshow(img[sample_1], cmap='gray');
```

The output will be as follows:

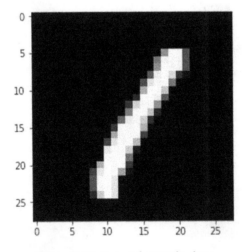

Figure 5.65: Second sample data

6. In order to provide the image information to the model, we must first flatten the data out so that each image is 1 x 784 pixels in shape:

```
images_0_1 = images_0_1.reshape((-1, rows * cols))
images_0_1.shape
```

The output will be as follows:

```
(12665, 784)
```

7. Let's construct the model; use the **LinearRegression** API and call the **fit** function:

```
model = LinearRegression()
model.fit(X=images_0_1, y=labels_0_1)
```

The output will be as follows:

```
LinearRegression(copy_X=True, fit_intercept=True, n_jobs=None,
                 normalize=False)
```

8. Determine the training set accuracy:

```
model.score(X=images_0_1, y=labels_0_1)
```

The output will be as follows:

```
0.9705320567708795
```

9. Determine the label predictions for each of the training samples, using a threshold of 0.5. Values greater than 0.5 classify as 1, while values less than, or equal to, 0.5 classify as 0:

```
y_pred = model.predict(images_0_1) > 0.5
y_pred = y_pred.astype(int)
y_pred
```

The output will be as follows:

```
array([0, 1, 1, ..., 1, 0, 1])
```

10. Compute the classification accuracy of the predicted training values versus the ground truth:

```
np.sum(y_pred == labels_0_1) / len(labels_0_1)
```

The output will be as follows:

```
0.9947887879984209
```

11. 10. Compare the performance against the test set:

```
y_pred = model.predict(images_0_1_test) > 0.5
y_pred = y_pred.astype(int)
np.sum(y_pred == labels_0_1_test) / len(labels_0_1_test)
```

The output will be as follows:

```
0.9938534278959811
```

> **NOTE**
>
> To access the source code for this specific section, please refer to
> https://packt.live/3emRZAk.
>
> You can also run this example online at https://packt.live/37T4bGh.
> You must execute the entire Notebook in order to get the desired result.

ACTIVITY 5.02: KNN MULTICLASS CLASSIFIER

1. Import the following packages:

```
import struct
import numpy as np
import gzip
import urllib.request
import matplotlib.pyplot as plt
from array import array
from sklearn.neighbors import KNeighborsClassifier as KNN
```

2. Load the MNIST data into memory.

Training images:

```
with gzip.open('../Datasets/train-images-idx3-ubyte.gz', 'rb') as f:
    magic, size, rows, cols = struct.unpack(">IIII", f.read(16))

    img = np.array(array("B", f.read())).reshape((size, rows, cols))
```

Training labels:

```
with gzip.open('../Datasets/train-labels-idx1-ubyte.gz', 'rb') as f:
    magic, size = struct.unpack(">II", f.read(8))
    labels = np.array(array("B", f.read()))
```

Test images:

```
with gzip.open('../Datasets/t10k-images-idx3-ubyte.gz', 'rb') as f:
    magic, size, rows, cols = struct.unpack(">IIII", f.read(16))

    img_test = np.array(array("B", f.read()))\
                .reshape((size, rows, cols))
```

Test labels:

```
with gzip.open('../Datasets/t10k-labels-idx1-ubyte.gz', 'rb') as f:
    magic, size = struct.unpack(">II", f.read(8))
    labels_test = np.array(array("B", f.read()))
```

3. Visualize a sample of the data:

```
for i in range(10):
    plt.subplot(2, 5, i + 1)
    plt.imshow(img[i], cmap='gray');
    plt.title(f'{labels[i]}');
    plt.axis('off')
```

The output will be as follows:

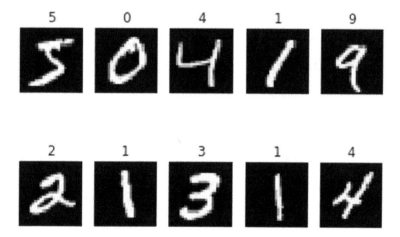

Figure 5.66: Sample images

4. Construct a KNN classifier with **k=3** to classify the MNIST dataset. Again, to save processing power, randomly sample 5,000 images for use in training:

```
np.random.seed(0)
selection = np.random.choice(len(img), 5000)
selected_images = img[selection]
selected_labels = labels[selection]
```

5. In order to provide the image information to the model, we must first flatten the data out so that each image is 1 x 784 pixels in shape:

```
selected_images = selected_images.reshape((-1, rows * cols))
selected_images.shape
```

The output will be as follows:

```
(5000, 784)
```

6. Build the three-neighbor KNN model and fit the data to the model. Note that, in this activity, we are providing 784 features or dimensions to the model, not just 2:

```
model = KNN(n_neighbors=3)
model.fit(X=selected_images, y=selected_labels)
```

The output will be as follows:

```
KNeighborsClassifier(algorithm='auto', leaf_size=30,
metric='minkowski',
                     metric_params=None, n_jobs=None, n_neighbors=3,
p=2,
                     weights='uniform')
```

7. Determine the score against the training set:

```
model.score(X=selected_images, y=selected_labels)
```

The output will be as follows:

```
0.9692
```

8. Display the first two predictions for the model against the training data:

```
model.predict(selected_images)[:2]


plt.subplot(1, 2, 1)
plt.imshow(selected_images[0].reshape((28, 28)), cmap='gray');
plt.axis('off');
plt.subplot(1, 2, 2)
plt.imshow(selected_images[1].reshape((28, 28)), cmap='gray');
plt.axis('off');
```

The output will be as follows:

Figure 5.67: First two values of the test set

9. Compare the performance against the test set:

```
model.score(X=img_test.reshape((-1, rows * cols)), y=labels_test)
```

The output will be as follows:

```
0.9376
```

> **NOTE**
>
> To access the source code for this specific section, please refer to https://packt.live/313xdlc.
>
> You can also run this example online at https://packt.live/2NI6DMo.
> You must execute the entire Notebook in order to get the desired result.

ACTIVITY 5.03: BINARY CLASSIFICATION USING A CART DECISION TREE

Solution:

1. Import the required dependencies:

```
import struct
import numpy as np
import pandas as pd
import gzip
import urllib.request
import matplotlib.pyplot as plt
from array import array
from sklearn.model_selection import train_test_split
from sklearn.tree import DecisionTreeClassifier
```

2. Load the MNIST data into memory:

```
with gzip.open('../Datasets/train-images-idx3-ubyte.gz', 'rb') as f:
    magic, size, rows, cols = struct.unpack(">IIII", f.read(16))

    img = np.array(array("B", f.read())).reshape((size, rows, cols))


with gzip.open('../Datasets/train-labels-idx1-ubyte.gz', 'rb') as f:
    magic, size = struct.unpack(">II", f.read(8))
    labels = np.array(array("B", f.read()))


with gzip.open('../Datasets/t10k-images-idx3-ubyte.gz', 'rb') as f:
    magic, size, rows, cols = struct.unpack(">IIII", f.read(16))

    img_test = np.array(array("B", f.read()))\
               .reshape((size, rows, cols))


with gzip.open('../Datasets/t10k-labels-idx1-ubyte.gz', 'rb') as f:
    magic, size = struct.unpack(">II", f.read(8))
    labels_test = np.array(array("B", f.read()))
```

3. Visualize a sample of the data:

```
for i in range(10):
    plt.subplot(2, 5, i + 1)
    plt.imshow(img[i], cmap='gray');
    plt.title(f'{labels[i]}');
    plt.axis('off')
```

The output will be as follows:

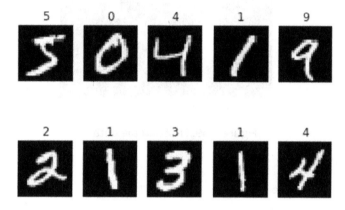

Figure 5.68: Sample data

4. Construct a linear classifier model to classify the digits 0 and 1. The model we are going to create is to determine whether the samples are either the digits 0 or 1. To do this, we first need to select only those samples:

```
samples_0_1 = np.where((labels == 0) | (labels == 1))[0]
images_0_1 = img[samples_0_1]
labels_0_1 = labels[samples_0_1]

samples_0_1_test = np.where((labels_test == 0) | (labels_test == 1))
images_0_1_test = img_test[samples_0_1_test]\
                    .reshape((-1, rows * cols))
labels_0_1_test = labels_test[samples_0_1_test]
```

5. Visualize the selected information. Here's the code for 0:

```
sample_0 = np.where((labels == 0))[0][0]
plt.imshow(img[sample_0], cmap='gray');
```

The output will be as follows:

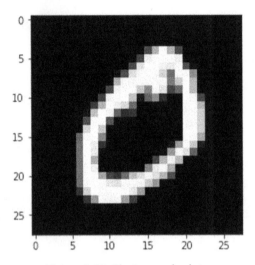

Figure 5.69: First sample data

Here's the code for 1:

```
sample_1 = np.where((labels == 1))[0][0]
plt.imshow(img[sample_1], cmap='gray');
```

The output will be as follows:

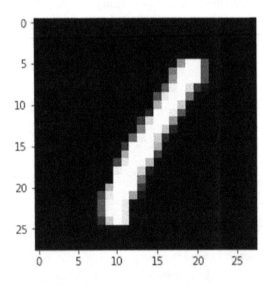

Figure 5.70: Second sample data

6. In order to provide the image information to the model, we must first flatten the data out so that each image is 1 x 784 pixels in shape:

```
images_0_1 = images_0_1.reshape((-1, rows * cols))
images_0_1.shape
```

The output will be as follows:

```
(12665, 784)
```

7. Let's construct the model; use the **DecisionTreeClassifier** API and call the **fit** function:

```
model = DecisionTreeClassifier(random_state=123)
model = model.fit(X=images_0_1, y=labels_0_1)
model
```

The output will be as follows:

```
DecisionTreeClassifier(class_weight=None, criterion='gini', max_
depth=None,
                        max_features=None, max_leaf_nodes=None,
                        min_impurity_decrease=0.0, min_impurity_
split=None,
                        min_samples_leaf=1, min_samples_split=2,
                        min_weight_fraction_leaf=0.0, presort=False,
                        random_state=None, splitter='best')
```

8. Determine the training set accuracy:

```
model.score(X=images_0_1, y=labels_0_1)
```

The output will be as follows:

```
1.0
```

9. Determine the label predictions for each of the training samples, using a threshold of 0.5. Values greater than 0.5 classify as 1, values less than or equal to 0.5, classify as 0:

```
y_pred = model.predict(images_0_1) > 0.5
y_pred = y_pred.astype(int)
y_pred
```

10. Compute the classification accuracy of the predicted training values versus the ground truth:

```
np.sum(y_pred == labels_0_1) / len(labels_0_1)
```

11. Compare the performance against the test set:

```
y_pred = model.predict(images_0_1_test) > 0.5
y_pred = y_pred.astype(int)
np.sum(y_pred == labels_0_1_test) / len(labels_0_1_test)
```

The output will be as follows:

```
0.9962174940898345
```

> **NOTE**
>
> To access the source code for this specific section, please refer to https://packt.live/3hNUJbT.
>
> You can also run this example online at https://packt.live/2Cq5W25.
> You must execute the entire Notebook in order to get the desired result.

ACTIVITY 5.04: BREAST CANCER DIAGNOSIS CLASSIFICATION USING ARTIFICIAL NEURAL NETWORKS

1. Import the required packages. For this activity, we will require the **pandas** package for loading the data, the **matplotlib** package for plotting, and scikit-learn for creating the neural network model, as well as to split the dataset into training and test sets. Import all the required packages and relevant modules for these tasks:

```
import pandas as pd
import matplotlib.pyplot as plt
from sklearn.neural_network import MLPClassifier
from sklearn.model_selection import train_test_split
from sklearn import preprocessing
```

2. Load the Breast Cancer Diagnosis dataset using pandas and examine the first five rows:

```
df = pd.read_csv('../Datasets/breast-cancer-data.csv')
df.head()
```

The output will be as follows:

	mean radius	mean texture	mean perimeter	mean area	mean smoothness	mean compactness	mean concavity	mean concave points	mean symmetry	mean fractal dimension	...	worst texture	worst perimeter	worst area	worst smoothness
0	17.99	10.38	122.80	1001.0	0.11840	0.27760	0.3001	0.14710	0.2419	0.07871	...	17.33	184.60	2019.0	0.1622
1	20.57	17.77	132.90	1326.0	0.08474	0.07864	0.0869	0.07017	0.1812	0.05667	...	23.41	158.80	1956.0	0.1238
2	19.69	21.25	130.00	1203.0	0.10960	0.15990	0.1974	0.12790	0.2069	0.05999	...	25.53	152.50	1709.0	0.1444
3	11.42	20.38	77.58	386.1	0.14250	0.28390	0.2414	0.10520	0.2597	0.09744	...	26.50	98.87	567.7	0.2098
4	20.29	14.34	135.10	1297.0	0.10030	0.13280	0.1980	0.10430	0.1809	0.05883	...	16.67	152.20	1575.0	0.1374

5 rows × 31 columns

Figure 5.71: First five rows of the breast cancer dataset

Additionally, dissect the dataset into input (X) and output (y) variables:

```
X, y = df[[c for c in df.columns if c != 'diagnosis']], df.diagnosis
```

3. The next step is feature engineering. Different columns of this dataset have different scales of magnitude; hence, before constructing and training a neural network model, we normalize the dataset. For this, we use the **MinMaxScaler** API from **sklearn**, which normalizes each column's values between 0 and 1, as discussed in the *Logistic Regression* section of this chapter (see *Exercise 5.03, Logistic Regression – Multiclass Classifier*): https://scikit-learn.org/stable/modules/generated/sklearn.preprocessing.MinMaxScaler.html:

```
X_array = X.values #returns a numpy array
min_max_scaler = preprocessing.MinMaxScaler()
X_array_scaled = min_max_scaler.fit_transform(X_array)
X = pd.DataFrame(X_array_scaled, columns=X.columns)
```

Examine the first five rows of the normalized dataset:

```
X = pd.DataFrame(X_array_scaled, columns=X.columns)
X.head()
```

The output will be as follows:

	mean radius	mean texture	mean perimeter	mean area	mean smoothness	mean compactness	mean concavity	mean concave points	mean symmetry	mean fractal dimension
0	0.521037	0.022658	0.545989	0.363733	0.593753	0.792037	0.703140	0.731113	0.686364	0.605518
1	0.643144	0.272574	0.615783	0.501591	0.289880	0.181768	0.203608	0.348757	0.379798	0.141323
2	0.601496	0.390260	0.595743	0.449417	0.514309	0.431017	0.462512	0.635686	0.509596	0.211247
3	0.210090	0.360839	0.233501	0.102906	0.811321	0.811361	0.565604	0.522863	0.776263	1.000000
4	0.629893	0.156578	0.630986	0.489290	0.430351	0.347893	0.463918	0.518390	0.378283	0.186816

5 rows × 30 columns

Figure 5.72: First five rows of the normalized dataset

4. Before we can construct the model, we must first convert the **diagnosis** values into labels that can be used within the model. Replace the **benign** diagnosis string with the value **0**, and the **malignant** diagnosis string with the value **1**:

```
diagnoses = ['benign', 'malignant',]
output = [diagnoses.index(diag) for diag in y]
```

5. Also, in order to impartially evaluate the model, we should split the training dataset into a training and a validation set:

```
train_X, valid_X, \
train_y, valid_y = train_test_split(X, output, \
                                     test_size=0.2, random_state=123)
```

6. Create the model using the normalized dataset and the assigned **diagnosis** labels:

```
model = MLPClassifier(solver='sgd', hidden_layer_sizes=(100,), \
                      max_iter=1000, random_state=1, \
                      learning_rate_init=.01)
model.fit(X=train_X, y=train_y)
```

The output will be as follows:

```
MLPClassifier(activation='relu', alpha=0.0001, batch_size='auto',
              beta_1=0.9, beta_2=0.999, early_stopping=False,
              epsilon=1e-08, hidden_layer_sizes=(100,),
              learning_rate='constant',
              learning_rate_init=0.01, max_iter=1000, momentum=0.9,
              n_iter_no_change=10, nesterovs_momentum=True, power_
t=0.5,
              random_state=1, shuffle=True, solver='sgd', tol=0.0001,
              validation_fraction=0.1, verbose=False, warm_
start=False)
```

7. Compute the accuracy of the model against the validation set:

```
model.score(valid_X, valid_y)
```

The output will be as follows:

```
0.9824561403508771
```

> **NOTE**
>
> To access the source code for this specific section, please refer to https://packt.live/3dpNt2G.
>
> You can also run this example online at https://packt.live/37OpdWM. You must execute the entire Notebook in order to get the desired result.

CHAPTER 06: ENSEMBLE MODELING

ACTIVITY 6.01: STACKING WITH STANDALONE AND ENSEMBLE ALGORITHMS

Solution

1. Import the relevant libraries:

```
import pandas as pd
import numpy as np
import seaborn as sns

%matplotlib inline
import matplotlib.pyplot as plt

from sklearn.model_selection import train_test_split
from sklearn.metrics import mean_absolute_error
from sklearn.model_selection import KFold
from sklearn.linear_model import LinearRegression
from sklearn.tree import DecisionTreeRegressor
from sklearn.neighbors import KNeighborsRegressor
from sklearn.ensemble import GradientBoostingRegressor, \
RandomForestRegressor
```

2. Read the data:

```
data = pd.read_csv('boston_house_prices.csv')
data.head()
```

> **NOTE**
>
> The preceding code snippet assumes that the dataset is presented in the same folder as that of the exercise notebook. However, if your dataset is present in the **Datasets** folder, you need to use the following code: **data = pd.read_csv('../Datasets/boston_house_prices.csv')**

You will get the following output:

	CRIM	ZN	INDUS	CHAS	NOX	RM	AGE	DIS	RAD	TAX	PTRATIO	B	LSTAT	PRICE
0	0.00632	18.0	2.31	0.0	0.538	6.575	65.2	4.0900	1.0	296.0	15.3	396.90	4.98	24.0
1	0.02731	0.0	7.07	0.0	0.469	6.421	78.9	4.9671	2.0	242.0	17.8	396.90	9.14	21.6
2	0.02729	0.0	7.07	0.0	0.469	7.185	61.1	4.9671	2.0	242.0	17.8	392.83	4.03	34.7
3	0.03237	0.0	2.18	0.0	0.458	6.998	45.8	6.0622	3.0	222.0	18.7	394.63	2.94	33.4
4	0.06905	0.0	2.18	0.0	0.458	7.147	54.2	6.0622	3.0	222.0	18.7	396.90	5.33	36.2

Figure 6.15: Top rows of the Boston housing dataset

3. Preprocess the dataset to remove null values to prepare the data for modeling:

```
# check how many columns have less than 10 % null data
perc_missing = data.isnull().mean()*100
cols = perc_missing[perc_missing < 10].index.tolist()
cols
```

You will get the following output:

```
['CRIM',
 'ZN',
 'INDUS',
 'CHAS',
 'NOX',
 'RM',
 'AGE',
 'DIS',
 'RAD',
 'TAX',
 'PTRATIO',
 'B',
 'LSTAT',
 'PRICE']
```

Figure 6.16: Number of columns

And then fill in the missing values, if any:

```
data_final = data.fillna(-1)
```

4. Divide the dataset into train and validation DataFrames:

```
train, val = train, val = train_test_split(data_final, \
                                            test_size=0.2, \
                                            random_state=11)

x_train = train.drop(columns=['PRICE'])
y_train = train['PRICE'].values

x_val = val.drop(columns=['PRICE'])
y_val = val['PRICE'].values
```

5. Initialize dictionaries in which to store the train and validation MAE values:

```
train_mae_values, val_mae_values = {}, {}
```

6. Train a decision tree (**dt**) model with the following hyperparameters and save the scores:

```
dt_params = {'criterion': 'mae', 'min_samples_leaf': 15, \
             'random_state': 11}
dt = DecisionTreeRegressor(**dt_params)

dt.fit(x_train, y_train)
dt_preds_train = dt.predict(x_train)
dt_preds_val = dt.predict(x_val)

train_mae_values['dt'] = mean_absolute_error(y_true=y_train, \
                                             y_pred=dt_preds_train)
val_mae_values['dt'] = mean_absolute_error(y_true=y_val, \
                                           y_pred=dt_preds_val)
```

7. Train a k-nearest neighbours (**knn**) model with the following hyperparameters and save the scores:

```
knn_params = {'n_neighbors': 5}
knn = KNeighborsRegressor(**knn_params)
knn.fit(x_train, y_train)
knn_preds_train = knn.predict(x_train)
```

```
knn_preds_val = knn.predict(x_val)


train_mae_values['knn'] = mean_absolute_error(y_true=y_train, \
                                              y_pred=knn_preds_train)
val_mae_values['knn'] = mean_absolute_error(y_true=y_val, \
                                            y_pred=knn_preds_val)
```

8. Train a random forest (**rf**) model with the following hyperparameters and save the scores:

```
rf_params = {'n_estimators': 20, 'criterion': 'mae', \
             'max_features': 'sqrt', 'min_samples_leaf': 10, \
             'random_state': 11, 'n_jobs': -1}
rf = RandomForestRegressor(**rf_params)

rf.fit(x_train, y_train)
rf_preds_train = rf.predict(x_train)
rf_preds_val = rf.predict(x_val)


train_mae_values['rf'] = mean_absolute_error(y_true=y_train, \
                                             y_pred=rf_preds_train)
val_mae_values['rf'] = mean_absolute_error(y_true=y_val, \
                                           y_pred=rf_preds_val)
```

9. Train a gradient boosting regression (**gbr**) model with the following hyperparameters and save the scores:

```
gbr_params = {'n_estimators': 20, 'criterion': 'mae', \
              'max_features': 'sqrt', 'min_samples_leaf': 10, \
              'random_state': 11}
gbr = GradientBoostingRegressor(**gbr_params)

gbr.fit(x_train, y_train)
gbr_preds_train = gbr.predict(x_train)
gbr_preds_val = gbr.predict(x_val)


train_mae_values['gbr'] = mean_absolute_error(y_true=y_train, \
                                              y_pred=gbr_preds_train)
val_mae_values['gbr'] = mean_absolute_error(y_true=y_val, \
                                            y_pred=gbr_preds_val)
```

10. Prepare the training and validation datasets, with the four meta estimators having the same hyperparameters that were used in the previous steps. First, we build the training set:

```
num_base_predictors = len(train_mae_values) # 4

x_train_with_metapreds = np.zeros((x_train.shape[0], \
                              x_train.shape[1]+num_base_predictors))
x_train_with_metapreds[:, :-num_base_predictors] = x_train
x_train_with_metapreds[:, -num_base_predictors:] = -1

kf = KFold(n_splits=5, random_state=11)

for train_indices, val_indices in kf.split(x_train):
    kfold_x_train, kfold_x_val = x_train.iloc[train_indices], \
                                 x_train.iloc[val_indices]
    kfold_y_train, kfold_y_val = y_train[train_indices], \
                                 y_train[val_indices]

    predictions = []

    dt = DecisionTreeRegressor(**dt_params)
    dt.fit(kfold_x_train, kfold_y_train)
    predictions.append(dt.predict(kfold_x_val))

    knn = KNeighborsRegressor(**knn_params)
    knn.fit(kfold_x_train, kfold_y_train)
    predictions.append(knn.predict(kfold_x_val))

    gbr = GradientBoostingRegressor(**gbr_params)
    rf.fit(kfold_x_train, kfold_y_train)
    predictions.append(rf.predict(kfold_x_val))

    gbr = GradientBoostingRegressor(**gbr_params)
    gbr.fit(kfold_x_train, kfold_y_train)
    predictions.append(gbr.predict(kfold_x_val))

    for i, preds in enumerate(predictions):
        x_train_with_metapreds[val_indices, -(i+1)] = preds
```

11. Prepare the validation set:

```
x_val_with_metapreds = np.zeros((x_val.shape[0], \
                                 x_val.shape[1]+num_base_predictors))
x_val_with_metapreds[:, :-num_base_predictors] = x_val
x_val_with_metapreds[:, -num_base_predictors:] = -1

predictions = []

dt = DecisionTreeRegressor(**dt_params)
dt.fit(x_train, y_train)
predictions.append(dt.predict(x_val))

knn = KNeighborsRegressor(**knn_params)
knn.fit(x_train, y_train)
predictions.append(knn.predict(x_val))

gbr = GradientBoostingRegressor(**gbr_params)
rf.fit(x_train, y_train)
predictions.append(rf.predict(x_val))

gbr = GradientBoostingRegressor(**gbr_params)
gbr.fit(x_train, y_train)
predictions.append(gbr.predict(x_val))

for i, preds in enumerate(predictions):
    x_val_with_metapreds[:, -(i+1)] = preds
```

12. Train a linear regression (**lr**) model as the stacked model:

```
lr = LinearRegression(normalize=True)
lr.fit(x_train_with_metapreds, y_train)
lr_preds_train = lr.predict(x_train_with_metapreds)
lr_preds_val = lr.predict(x_val_with_metapreds)

train_mae_values['lr'] = mean_absolute_error(y_true=y_train, \
                                              y_pred=lr_preds_train)
val_mae_values['lr'] = mean_absolute_error(y_true=y_val, \
                                           y_pred=lr_preds_val)
```

13. Visualize the train and validation errors for each individual model and the stacked model:

```
mae_scores = pd.concat([pd.Series(train_mae_values, name='train'), \
                        pd.Series(val_mae_values, name='val')], \
                        axis=1)
mae_scores
```

First, you get the following output:

	train	val
dt	2.384406	3.282353
knn	3.455545	3.978039
rf	2.316120	3.029828
gbr	2.463436	3.058634
lr	2.248086	2.850166

Figure 6.17: Values of training and validation errors

Now, plot the MAE scores on a bar plot using the following code:

```
mae_scores.plot(kind='bar', figsize=(10,7))
plt.ylabel('MAE')
plt.xlabel('Model')
plt.show()
```

The final output will be as follows:

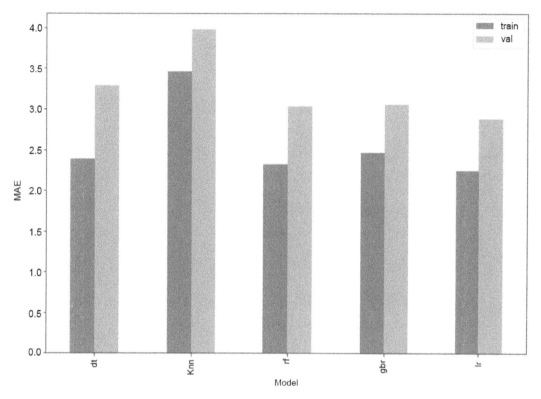

Figure 6.18: Visualization of training and validation errors

> **NOTE**
>
> To access the source code for this specific section, please refer to
> https://packt.live/3fNqtMG.
>
> You can also run this example online at https://packt.live/2Yn2VlI.
> You must execute the entire Notebook in order to get the desired result.

CHAPTER 07: MODEL EVALUATION

ACTIVITY 7.01: FINAL TEST PROJECT

1. Import the relevant libraries:

```
import pandas as pd
import numpy as np
import json

%matplotlib inline
import matplotlib.pyplot as plt

from sklearn.preprocessing import OneHotEncoder
from sklearn.model_selection import RandomizedSearchCV, train_test_
split
from sklearn.ensemble import GradientBoostingClassifier
from sklearn.metrics import (accuracy_score, precision_score, \
recall_score, confusion_matrix, precision_recall_curve)
```

2. Read the **breast-cancer-data.csv** dataset:

```
data = pd.read_csv('../Datasets/breast-cancer-data.csv')
data.info()
```

3. Let's separate the input data (**X**) and the target (**y**):

```
X = data.drop(columns=['diagnosis'])
y = data['diagnosis'].map({'malignant': 1, 'benign': 0}.get).values
```

4. Split the dataset into training and test sets:

```
X_train, X_test, \
y_train, y_test = train_test_split(X, y, \
                                   test_size=0.2, random_state=11)

print(X_train.shape)
print(y_train.shape)
print(X_test.shape)
print(y_test.shape)
```

You should get the following output:

```
(455, 30)
(455,)
(114, 30)
(114,)
```

5. Choose a base model and define the range of hyperparameter values corresponding to the model to be searched for hyperparameter tuning. Let's use a gradient-boosted classifier as our model. We then define ranges of values for all hyperparameters we want to tune in the form of a dictionary:

```
meta_gbc = GradientBoostingClassifier()

param_dist = {'n_estimators': list(range(10, 210, 10)), \
              'criterion': ['mae', 'mse'],\
              'max_features': ['sqrt', 'log2', 0.25, 0.3, \
                               0.5, 0.8, None], \
              'max_depth': list(range(1, 10)), \
              'min_samples_leaf': list(range(1, 10))}
```

6. Define the parameters with which to initialize the **RandomizedSearchCV** object and use K-fold cross-validation to identify the best model hyperparameters. Define the parameters required for random search, including **cv** as **5**, indicating that the hyperparameters should be chosen by evaluating the performance using 5-fold cross-validation. Then, initialize the **RandomizedSearchCV** object and use the `.fit()` method to initiate optimization:

```
rand_search_params = {'param_distributions': param_dist, \
                      'scoring': 'accuracy', 'n_iter': 100, \
                      'cv': 5, 'return_train_score': True, \
                      'n_jobs': -1, 'random_state': 11 }
random_search = RandomizedSearchCV(meta_gbc, **rand_search_params)
random_search.fit(X_train, y_train)
```

You should get the following output:

```
RandomizedSearchCV(cv=5, error_score='raise-deprecating',
                   estimator=GradientBoostingClassifier(criterion='friedman_mse',
                                                        init=None,
                                                        learning_rate=0.1,
                                                        loss='deviance',
                                                        max_depth=3,
                                                        max_features=None,
                                                        max_leaf_nodes=None,
                                                        min_impurity_decrease=0.0,
                                                        min_impurity_split=None,
                                                        min_samples_leaf=1,
                                                        min_samples_split=2,
                                                        min_weight_fraction_leaf=0.0,
                                                        n_estimators=100,
                                                        n_i...
                   param_distributions={'criterion': ['mae', 'mse'],
                                        'max_depth': [1, 2, 3, 4, 5, 6, 7, 8,
                                                      9],
                                        'max_features': ['sqrt', 'log2', 0.25,
                                                         0.3, 0.5, 0.8, None],
                                        'min_samples_leaf': [1, 2, 3, 4, 5, 6,
                                                             7, 8, 9],
                                        'n_estimators': [10, 20, 30, 40, 50, 60,
                                                         70, 80, 90, 100, 110,
                                                         120, 130, 140, 150,
                                                         160, 170, 180, 190,
                                                         200]},
                   pre_dispatch='2*n_jobs', random_state=11, refit=True,
                   return_train_score=True, scoring='accuracy', verbose=0)
```

Figure 7.36: The RandomizedSearchCSV object

Once the tuning is complete, find the position (iteration number) at which the highest mean test score was obtained. Find the corresponding hyperparameters and save them to a dictionary:

```
idx = np.argmax(random_search.cv_results_['mean_test_score'])
final_params = random_search.cv_results_['params'][idx]
final_params
```

You should get the following output:

```
{'n_estimators': 190,
 'min_samples_leaf': 8,
 'max_features': 0.3,
 'max_depth': 7,
 'criterion': 'mse'}
```

Figure 7.37: Hyperparameters

7. Split the training dataset further into training and validation sets and train a new model using the final hyperparameters on the training dataset. Use scikit-learn's **`train_test_split()`** method to split **X** and **y** into train and validation components, with the validation set comprising 15% of the dataset:

```
train_X, val_X, \
train_y, val_y = train_test_split(X_train, y_train, \
                                    test_size=0.15, random_state=11)
train_X.shape, train_y.shape, val_X.shape, val_y.shape
```

You should get the following output:

```
((386, 30), (386,), (69, 30), (69,))
```

8. Train the gradient-boosted classification model using the final hyperparameters and make predictions in relation to the training and validation sets. Also, calculate the probability regarding the validation set:

```
gbc = GradientBoostingClassifier(**final_params)
gbc.fit(train_X, train_y)

preds_train = gbc.predict(train_X)
preds_val = gbc.predict(val_X)
pred_probs_val = np.array([each[1] \
                for each in gbc.predict_proba(val_X)])
```

9. Calculate **accuracy, precision**, and **recall** for predictions in relation to the validation set, and print the confusion matrix:

```
print('train accuracy_score = {}'\
.format(accuracy_score(y_true=train_y, y_pred=preds_train)))

print('validation accuracy_score = {}'\
.format(accuracy_score(y_true=val_y, y_pred=preds_val)))

print('confusion_matrix: \n{}'\
.format(confusion_matrix(y_true=val_y, y_pred=preds_val)))

print('precision_score = {}'\
.format(precision_score(y_true=val_y, y_pred=preds_val)))

print('recall_score = {}'\
.format(recall_score(y_true=val_y, y_pred=preds_val)))
```

You should get the following output:

```
train accuracy_score = 1.0
validation accuracy_score = 0.9565217391304348
confusion_matrix:
[[45  0]
 [ 3 21]]
precision_score = 1.0
recall_score = 0.875
```

Figure 7.38: Evaluation scores and the confusion matrix

10. Experiment with varying thresholds to find the optimal point having a high recall.

   Plot the precision-recall curve:

```
plt.figure(figsize=(10,7))
precision, recall, \
thresholds = precision_recall_curve(val_y, \
                         pred_probs_val)
plt.plot(recall, precision)
plt.xlabel('Recall')
plt.ylabel('Precision')
plt.show()
```

The output will be as follows:

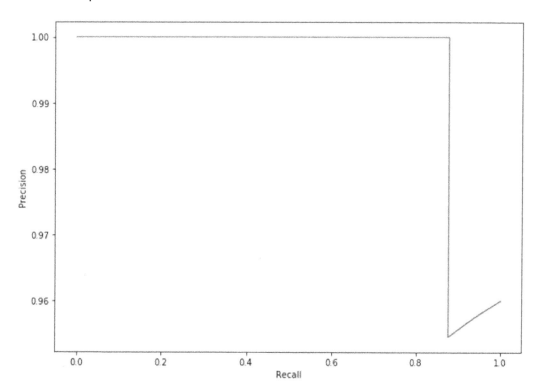

Figure 7.39: Precision recall curve

```
"""
Plot the variation in precision and recall with increasing threshold
values.
"""
PR_variation_df = pd.DataFrame({'precision': precision, \
                                'recall': recall}, \
                                index=list(thresholds)+[1])

PR_variation_df.plot(figsize=(10,7))
plt.xlabel('Threshold')
plt.ylabel('P/R values')
plt.show()
```

You should get the following output:

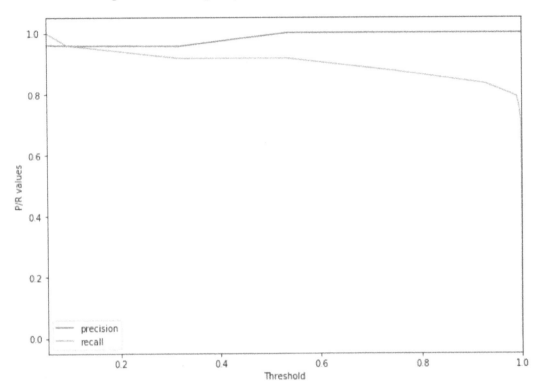

Figure 7.40: Variation in precision and recall with increasing threshold values

11. Finalize a threshold that will be used for predictions in relation to the test dataset. Let's finalize a value, say, 0.05. This value is entirely dependent on what you feel would be optimal based on your exploration in the previous step:

```
final_threshold = 0.05
```

12. Predict the final values in relation to the test dataset and save them to a file. Use the final threshold value determined in *Step 10* to find the classes for each value in the training set. Then, write the final predictions to the *final_predictions.csv* file:

```
pred_probs_test = np.array([each[1] \
                    for each in gbc.predict_proba(X_test)])
preds_test = (pred_probs_test > final_threshold).astype(int)
preds_test
```

The output will be as follows:

```
array([1, 1, 1, 1, 1, 0, 1, 0, 0, 0, 0, 1, 0, 0, 0, 0, 1, 0, 0, 1, 1, 0,
       0, 0, 0, 0, 0, 0, 0, 0, 0, 0, 0, 0, 0, 0, 0, 0, 0, 0, 0, 1, 0, 0,
       0, 0, 1, 0, 1, 1, 0, 0, 1, 0, 0, 0, 1, 0, 0, 0, 1, 1, 0, 0, 1, 0,
       0, 1, 0, 0, 1, 0, 0, 1, 0, 1, 1, 0, 0, 0, 0, 0, 1, 0, 1, 0, 1, 1,
       0, 0, 1, 1, 0, 0, 1, 0, 0, 0, 0, 1, 1, 0, 1, 0, 1, 1, 1, 0, 0, 0,
       0, 1, 0, 1])
```

Figure 7.41: Prediction for final values for the test dataset

Alternatively, you can also get the output in CSV format:

```
with open('final_predictions.csv', 'w') as f:
    f.writelines([str(val)+'\n' for val in preds_test])
```

The output will be a CSV file as follows:

final_predictions
1
1
1
1
1
0
1
0
0
0
0
1
0
0
0
0
1
0
0

Figure 7.42: Output for the final values

NOTE

To access the source code for this specific section, please refer to https://packt.live/2Ynw6Lt.

You can also run this example online at https://packt.live/3erAajt.
You must execute the entire Notebook in order to get the desired result.

INDEX